GRANTA BOOKS

IMAGINARY HOMELANDS

Salman Rushdie was born in Bombay in 1947. He is the author of five novels, *Grimus, Midnight's Children, Shame, The Satanic Verses* and *Haroun and the Sea of Stories*. He is also the author of *The Jaguar Smile: A Nicaraguan Journey* and two documentary films, *The Riddle of Midnight* and *The Painter and the Pest*. He has won a number of literary prizes, including the Booker Prize in 1981 and the Whitbread Prize for the best novel of 1988.

To my mother
Negin Rushdie
with my love

SALMAN RUSHDIE

IMAGINARY HOMELANDS

ESSAYS AND CRITICISM 1981-1991

GRANTA BOOKS

LONDON

in association with

PENGUIN BOOKS

GRANTA BOOKS
2/3 Hanover Yard, Noel Road, Islington, London N1 8BE

Published in association with the Penguin Group
Penguin Books Ltd, 27 Wrights Lane, London W8 5TZ, England
Viking Penguin, a division of Penguin Books USA Inc.,
375 Hudson Street, New York 10014, USA
Penguin Books Australia Ltd, Ringwood, Victoria, Australia
Penguin Books Canada Ltd, 2801 John Street, Markham,
Ontario, Canada L3R 1B4
Penguin Books (NZ) Ltd, 182-190 Wairau Road,
Auckland 10, New Zealand

Penguin Books Ltd, Registered Offices: Harmondsworth,
Middlesex, England

First published in Great Britain by Granta Books 1991
This edition published 1992

11 13 15 17 19 20 18 16 14 12

Printed in England

CONTENTS

INTRODUCTION

The essay from which this collection takes its title was my contribution to a seminar about Indian writing in English held in London during the Festival of India in 1982. In those days Indira Gandhi was back as India's premier. In Pakistan, the Zia regime was consolidating its power in the aftermath of the execution of Zulfiqar Ali Bhutto. Britain was in the early throes of the Thatcher revolution, and in the United States, Ronald Reagan was still an unregenerate Cold Warrior. The structures of the world retained their uninspiringly familiar form.

The upheavals of 1989 and 1990 changed all that. Now that we're contemplating a transformed international scene, with its new possibilities, uncertainties, intransigences and dangers, it seems not inappropriate to pull together our thoughts on the rapidly receding decade in which, as Gramsci would have said, the old was dying, and yet the new could not be born. 'In this interregnum there arises a great diversity of morbid symptoms,' Gramsci suggested. This book is an incomplete, personal view of the interregnum of the 1980s, not all of whose symptoms, it has to be said, were morbid.

In 1981 I had just published my second novel, and was enjoying the unique pleasure of having written, for the first time, a book that people liked. Before *Midnight's Children*, I had had one novel rejected, abandoned two others, and published one, *Grimus*, which, to put it mildly, bombed. Now, after ten years of blunders, incompetence and commercials for cream cakes, hair colourants and the *Daily Mirror*, I could begin to live by my pen. It felt good.

Almost all the important 'Indo-Anglian' writers were at the London seminar: Nirad C. Chaudhuri, Anita Desai, Raja Rao, Mulk Raj Anand among them. Of the big names, only R. K. Narayan was absent, though I'd been told earlier that he'd accepted the invitation. 'Narayan is so courteous that he always accepts,' somebody told me, 'but he never shows up.'

It was exhilarating for me to meet and listen to these writers. But there were worrying moments, too; indications of some participants' desire to describe Indian culture—which I had always thought of as a rich mixture of traditions—in exclusive, and excluding, Hindu terms.

One distinguished novelist began his contribution by reciting a Sanskrit *sloka*. Then, instead of translating the verse, he declared: 'Every educated Indian will understand what I've just said.' This was not simply a form of intellectual grandeur. In the room were Indian writers and scholars of every conceivable background—Christian, Parsi, Muslim, Sikh. None of us had been raised in a Sanskritic tradition. We were all reasonably 'educated', however; so what were we being told? Perhaps that we weren't really 'Indian'?

Later in the day, an eminent Indian academic delivered a paper on Indian culture that utterly ignored all minority communities. When questioned about this from the floor, the professor smiled benignly and allowed that of course India contained many diverse traditions—including Buddhists, Christians and 'Mughals'. This characterization of Muslim culture was more than merely peculiar. It was a technique of alienation. For if Muslims were 'Mughals', then they were foreign invaders, and Indian Muslim culture was both imperialist and inauthentic. At the time we made light of the gibe, but it stayed with me, pricking at me like a thorn.

A decade later, India has arrived at a full-blown crisis of descriptions. Religious militancy threatens the foundations of the secular state. Many Indian intellectuals now appear to accept the Hindu nationalist definitions of the state; minority groups respond with growing extremisms of their own. It is perhaps significant that there is no commonly used Hindustani word for 'secularism'; the importance of the secular ideal in India has simply been assumed, in a rather unexamined way. Now that communalist forces would appear to have all the momentum, secularism's defenders are in alarming disarray. And yet, if the secularist principle were abandoned, India could simply explode. It is a paradoxical fact that secularism, which has been much under attack of late, outside India as well as inside it, is the only way of safeguarding the constitutional, civil, human and, yes, religious rights of minority groups. Does India still have the political will to insist on this safeguard? I hope so. We must all hope so. And we shall see.

The first three sections of this volume deal with subcontinental themes. Section one contains work roughly grouped around *Midnight's Children*; section two is about the politics of India and Pakistan; section three is about literature. Indo-Anglian literature is presently in excellent shape. Many new writers made their reputations in the 1980s — Vikram Seth, Allan Sealy, Amitav Ghosh, Rohinton Mistry, Upamanyu Chatterjee, Shashi Tharoor, and more — and are producing work of growing confidence and originality. If only the political scene were as healthy! But, alas, the damage done to Indian life by 'the Emergency', Mrs Gandhi's period of authoritarian rule between 1974 and 1977, is now all too plain. The reason why so many of us were outraged by the Emergency went beyond the dictatorial atmosphere of those days, beyond the jailing of opponents and the forcible sterilizations. The reason was (as I first suggested six years ago in the essay here entitled 'Dynasty') that it was during the Emergency that the lid flew off the Pandora's box of communal discord. The box may be shut now, but the goblins of sectarianism are still on the loose. Indian painters like Vivan Sundaram rose nobly to the challenge of the Emergency. No doubt Indian writers and artists will respond with equal skill to the new crisis. Bad times, after all, traditionally produce good books.

The fourth section deals primarily with movies and television. I have tinkered only a little with the original form of these pieces, but I should say that, seven years on, I find 'Outside the Whale' a little unfair to George Orwell and to Henry Miller, too. I have not changed my mind about Richard Attenborough's film *Gandhi*, but it must be accepted that the film's influence outside India was often very positive; radical and progressive groups and movements in South America, Eastern Europe and southern Africa, too, found it uplifting.

The piece about *Handsworth Songs* stimulated a lively debate among black British film-makers, some of it supportive of my views, some of it critical, all of it fascinating and, I think, helpful. And one footnote to the piece about Satyajit Ray. When I met him, he was shooting scenes for *The Home and the World* in an old zamindar's mansion in the depths of rural Bengal. He rightly thought it the perfect setting for his movie. I found that I needed it, too, and it became the model for the dream-mansion, 'Perownistan', occupied by Mirza Saeed Akhtar and his wife in the 'Titlipur' sections of *The Satanic Verses*. (The giant banyan infested by butterflies wasn't there, however. I saw that in southern India, not far from Mysore.)

Section five contains five pieces about the experience of migrants, primarily Indian migrants to Britain. Of these, 'The New Empire Within Britain' requires a few words of comment, because of its rather strange afterlife. It was originally written for the *Opinions* slot in the very early days of Channel 4. (It was the second programme in the series, following E. P. Thompson.) The many British blacks and Asians who phoned in or wrote agreed, virtually unanimously, that the lecture had done no more than tell the simple truth. To them, I had gone no further than the ABC of racial prejudice in Britain. There was also, unsurprisingly, a hostile response from some members of the white community, though they were outnumbered by other white Britons who had found the piece informative and useful. My purpose had been simple: to tell the white majority how life in Britain all too often felt to members of racial minority groups. (I've been in a minority group all my life—a member of an Indian Muslim family in Bombay, then of a 'mohajir'—migrant—family in Pakistan, and now as a British Asian.) By articulating a grievance, I could help, or so I hoped, to build bridges of understanding.

I had thought of television programmes as evanescent, here-today-gone-tomorrow things. But we were at the beginning of the video boom, and to my surprise the tape of the broadcast circulated widely, through the Commission for Racial Equality and other organizations. This was satisfying, of course, but also a little worrying. I had written and spoken at a particular moment in the history of British race relations. Those relationships moved on, developed, changed. Some things (more black faces in television programmes and in the commercial breaks) got a bit better, others (racial harassment) got rather worse. The tape remained the same.

What I had, perhaps naïvely, failed to anticipate was that the text of the lecture would be distorted, falsified and used against me by people of a different political disposition than myself. I was accused both by Geoffrey Howe and by Norman Tebbit of having equated Britain with Nazi Germany, and so of having 'betrayed and insulted' my adopted country. Now it's true that the text of this essay is deliberately polemical, and no doubt that upset the Howes and Tebbits. I make no apology for being angry about racial prejudice. But it is also true that the piece repeatedly insists that the situation in Britain is *not* comparable to life under Nazism or apartheid. I draw attention to this now, because distortions and falsehoods have a way of becoming true by virtue of being repeated frequently. The 'Nazi Britain' smear has been around for long enough. The republication of 'The New Empire Within Britain' in this volume enables readers to decide for themselves whether it was justified or not.

I am, of course, by no means the only British writer to have come under fire in these past years. The regular scoldings meted out in the newspapers to all of us who wrote against the grain of Thatcherism were a notable feature of the past decade. Ian McEwan was scolded by a *Sunday Times* leader for his novel *The Child in Time*. Harold Pinter was scolded for his views about American policy in Nicaragua. Margaret Drabble was scolded for being worthy, Hampsteadish and boring. In between scoldings, such writers were dismissed as 'champagne socialists'. This is because their books and plays and films were popular. If the work had been unpopular, no doubt they would have been attacked as failures. It was a good decade for double binds.

Section six contains three pieces—reflections on the Thatcher/Foot election, on Charter 88 and on the question of Palestine—of, I suppose, the scolding-provoking variety.

The next five sections—on writers from Africa, Britain, Europe, South America and the United States—need no footnotes. The last section deals with a subject—the crisis that engulfed my novel *The Satanic Verses*—to which far too many notes have already been appended. I have little to add.

Finally, some necessary acknowledgements. To the original publishers of these pieces, who include the *London Review of Books, Guardian, Index on Censorship, Observer, Granta, The Times, American Film, New Society, New York Times, Washington Post, New Republic, Times Literary Supplement* and *Independent on Sunday*, my thanks; most particularly to Bill Webb and Blake Morrison, the best of two generations of British literary editors. Thanks, too, to Bill Buford, Bob Tashman and everyone at Granta Books who helped to pull this book together. Edward Said kindly allowed me to reproduce the text of our public conversation at the Institute of Contemporary Arts. And to Susannah Clapp, for plucking out of the text of an essay the phrase that became first its title and then the title of this book, a big hug of gratitude.

1991

1

IMAGINARY HOMELANDS

'ERRATA'

THE RIDDLE OF MIDNIGHT

IMAGINARY HOMELANDS

An old photograph in a cheap frame hangs on a wall of the room where I work. It's a picture dating from 1946 of a house into which, at the time of its taking, I had not yet been born. The house is rather peculiar—a three-storeyed gabled affair with tiled roofs and round towers in two corners, each wearing a pointy tiled hat. 'The past is a foreign country,' goes the famous opening sentence of L. P. Hartley's novel *The Go-Between*, 'they do things differently there.' But the photograph tells me to invert this idea; it reminds me that it's my present that is foreign, and that the past is home. albeit a lost home in a lost city in the mists of lost time.

A few years ago I revisited Bombay, which is my lost city, after an absence of something like half my life. Shortly after arriving, acting on an impulse, I opened the telephone directory and looked for my father's name. And, amazingly, there it was; his name, our old address, the unchanged telephone number, as if we had never gone away to the unmentionable country across the border. It was an eerie discovery. I felt as if I were being claimed, or informed that the facts of my faraway life were illusions, and that this continuity was the reality. Then I went to visit the house in the photograph and stood outside it, neither daring nor wishing to announce myself to its new owners. (I didn't want to see how they'd ruined the interior.) I was overwhelmed. The photograph had naturally been taken in black and white; and my memory, feeding on such images as this, had begun to see my childhood in the same way, monochromatically. The colours of my history had seeped out of my mind's eye; now my other two eyes were assaulted by colours, by the vividness of the red tiles, the yellow-edged green of cactus-leaves, the brilliance of bougainvillaea creeper. It is probably not too romantic to say that that was when my novel *Midnight's Children* was really born; when I realized how much I wanted

to restore the past to myself, not in the faded greys of old
family-album snapshots, but whole, in CinemaScope and
glorious Technicolor.

Bombay is a city built by foreigners upon reclaimed land;
I, who had been away so long that I almost qualified for the
title, was gripped by the conviction that I, too, had a city and
a history to reclaim.

It may be that writers in my position, exiles or emigrants
or expatriates, are haunted by some sense of loss, some urge
to reclaim, to look back, even at the risk of being mutated into
pillars of salt. But if we do look back, we must also do so in
the knowledge—which gives rise to profound uncertainties—
that our physical alienation from India almost inevitably
means that we will not be capable of reclaiming precisely
the thing that was lost; that we will, in short, create fictions,
not actual cities or villages, but invisible ones, imaginary
homelands, Indias of the mind.

Writing my book in North London, looking out through
my window on to a city scene totally unlike the ones I was
imagining on to paper, I was constantly plagued by this
problem, until I felt obliged to face it in the text, to make
clear that (in spite of my original and I suppose somewhat
Proustian ambition to unlock the gates of lost time so that the
past reappeared as it actually had been, unaffected by the
distortions of memory) what I was actually doing was a novel
of memory and about memory, so that my India was just that:
'my' India, a version and no more than one version of all the
hundreds of millions of possible versions. I tried to make it
as imaginatively true as I could, but imaginative truth is
simultaneously honourable and suspect, and I knew that my
India may only have been one to which I (who am no longer
what I was, and who by quitting Bombay never became what
perhaps I was meant to be) was, let us say, willing to admit I
belonged.

This is why I made my narrator, Saleem, suspect in his
narration; his mistakes are the mistakes of a fallible memory
compounded by quirks of character and of circumstance, and
his vision is fragmentary. It may be that when the Indian writer

10

who writes from outside India tries to reflect that world, he is obliged to deal in broken mirrors, some of whose fragments have been irretrievably lost.

But there is a paradox here. The broken mirror may actually be as valuable as the one which is supposedly unflawed. Let me again try and explain this from my own experience. Before beginning *Midnight's Children*, I spent many months trying simply to recall as much of the Bombay of the 1950s and 1960s as I could; and not only Bombay—Kashmir, too, and Delhi and Aligarh, which, in my book, I've moved to Agra to heighten a certain joke about the Taj Mahal. I was genuinely amazed by how much came back to me. I found myself remembering what clothes people had worn on certain days, and school scenes, and whole passages of Bombay dialogue verbatim, or so it seemed; I even remembered advertisements, film-posters, the neon Jeep sign on Marine Drive, toothpaste ads for Binaca and for Kolynos, and a footbridge over the local railway line which bore, on one side, the legend 'Esso puts a tiger in your tank' and, on the other, the curiously contradictory admonition: 'Drive like Hell and you will get there.' Old songs came back to me from nowhere: a street entertainer's version of 'Good Night, Ladies', and, from the film *Mr 420* (a very appropriate source for my narrator to have used), the hit number 'Mera Joota Hai Japani',* which could almost be Saleem's theme song.

I knew that I had tapped a rich seam; but the point I want to make is that of course I'm not gifted with total recall, and

---

Mera joota hai Japani
Yé patloon Inglistani
Sar pé lal topi Rusi—
Phir bhi dil hai Hindustani
—which translates roughly as:
O, my shoes are Japanese
These trousers English, if you please
On my head, red Russian hat—
My heart's Indian for all that.
[This is also the song sung by Gibreel Farishta as he tumbles from the heavens at the beginning of *The Satanic Verses*.]

it was precisely the partial nature of these memories, their fragmentation, that made them so evocative for me. The shards of memory acquired greater status, greater resonance, because they were *remains*; fragmentation made trivial things seem like symbols, and the mundane acquired numinous qualities. There is an obvious parallel here with archaeology. The broken pots of antiquity, from which the past can sometimes, but always provisionally, be reconstructed, are exciting to discover, even if they are pieces of the most quotidian objects.

It may be argued that the past is a country from which we have all emigrated, that its loss is part of our common humanity. Which seems to me self-evidently true; but I suggest that the writer who is out-of-country and even out-of-language may experience this loss in an intensified form. It is made more concrete for him by the physical fact of discontinuity, of his present being in a different place from his past, of his being 'elsewhere'. This may enable him to speak properly and concretely on a subject of universal significance and appeal.

But let me go further. The broken glass is not merely a mirror of nostalgia. It is also, I believe, a useful tool with which to work in the present.

John Fowles begins *Daniel Martin* with the words: 'Whole sight: or all the rest is desolation.' But human beings do not perceive things whole; we are not gods but wounded creatures, cracked lenses, capable only of fractured perceptions. Partial beings, in all the senses of that phrase. Meaning is a shaky edifice we build out of scraps, dogmas, childhood injuries, newspaper articles, chance remarks, old films, small victories, people hated, people loved; perhaps it is because our sense of what is the case is constructed from such inadequate materials that we defend it so fiercely, even to the death. The Fowles position seems to me a way of succumbing to the guru-illusion. Writers are no longer sages, dispensing the wisdom of the centuries. And those of us who have been forced by cultural displacement to accept the provisional nature of all truths, all certainties, have perhaps had modernism forced upon us. We can't lay claim to Olympus, and are thus released to describe our worlds in the way in which all of us, whether writers or not, perceive it from day to day.

In *Midnight's Children*, my narrator Saleem uses, at one point, the metaphor of a cinema screen to discuss this business of perception: 'Suppose yourself in a large cinema, sitting at first in the back row, and gradually moving up, . . . until your nose is almost pressed against the screen. Gradually the stars' faces dissolve into dancing grain; tiny details assume grotesque proportions; . . . it becomes clear that the illusion itself is reality.' The movement towards the cinema screen is a metaphor for the narrative's movement through time towards the present, and the book itself, as it nears contemporary events, quite deliberately loses deep perspective, becomes more 'partial'. I wasn't trying to write about (for instance) the Emergency in the same way as I wrote about events half a century earlier. I felt it would be dishonest to pretend, when writing about the day before yesterday, that it was possible to see the whole picture. I showed certain blobs and slabs of the scene.

I once took part in a conference on modern writing at New College, Oxford. Various novelists, myself included, were talking earnestly of such matters as the need for new ways of describing the world. Then the playwright Howard Brenton suggested that this might be a somewhat limited aim: does literature seek to do no more than to describe? Flustered, all the novelists at once began talking about politics.

Let me apply Brenton's question to the specific case of Indian writers, in England, writing about India. Can they do no more than describe, from a distance, the world that they have left? Or does the distance open any other doors?

These are of course political questions, and must be answered at least partly in political terms. I must say first of all that description is itself a political act. The black American writer Richard Wright once wrote that black and white Americans were engaged in a war over the nature of reality. Their descriptions were incompatible. So it is clear that redescribing a world is the necessary first step towards changing it. And particularly at times when the State takes reality into its own hands, and sets about distorting it, altering the past to fit its present needs, then the making of the alternative realities of art, including the novel of memory, becomes politicized. 'The struggle of man against power,' Milan Kundera has written, 'is the struggle of memory against forgetting.' Writers and politicians are natural rivals. Both groups try to make the world in their own images; they fight for the same territory. And the novel is one way of denying the official, politicians' version of truth.

The 'State truth' about the war in Bangladesh, for instance, is that no atrocities were committed by the Pakistani army in what was then the East Wing. This version is sanctified by many persons who would describe themselves as intellectuals. And the official version of the Emergency in India was well expressed by Mrs Gandhi in a recent BBC interview. She said that there were some people around who claimed that bad things had happened during the Emergency, forced sterilizations, things like that; but, she stated, this was all false. Nothing of this type had ever occurred. The interviewer, Mr Robert Kee, did not probe this statement at all. Instead he told Mrs Gandhi and the *Panorama* audience that she had proved, many times over, her right to be called a democrat.

So literature can, and perhaps must, give the lie to official facts. But is this a proper function of those of us who write from outside India? Or are we just dilettantes in such affairs, because we are not involved in their day-to-day unfolding, because by speaking out we take no risks, because our personal safety is not threatened? What right do we have to speak at all?

My answer is very simple. Literature is self-validating. That is to say, a book is not justified by its author's worthiness to write it, but by the quality of what has been written. There are terrible books that arise directly out of experience, and extraordinary imaginative feats dealing with themes which the author has been obliged to approach from the outside.

Literature is not in the business of copyrighting certain themes for certain groups. And as for risk: the real risks of any artist are taken in the work, in pushing the work to the limits of what is possible, in the attempt to increase the sum of what it is possible to think. Books become good when they go to this edge and risk falling over it—when they endanger the artist by reason of what he has, or has not, *artistically* dared.

So if I am to speak for Indian writers in England I would say this, paraphrasing G. V. Desani's H. Hatterr: The migrations of the fifties and sixties happened. 'We are. We are here.' And we are not willing to be excluded from any part of our heritage; which heritage includes both a Bradford-born Indian kid's right to be treated as a full member of British society, and also the right of any member of this post-diaspora community to draw on its roots for its art, just as all the world's community of displaced writers has always done. (I'm thinking, for instance, of Grass's Danzig-become-Gdansk, of Joyce's abandoned Dublin, of Isaac Bashevis Singer and Maxine Hong Kingston and Milan Kundera and many others. It's a long list.)

Let me override at once the faintly defensive note that has crept into these last few remarks. The Indian writer, looking back at India, does so through guilt-tinted spectacles. (I am of course, once more, talking about myself.) I am speaking now of those of us who emigrated . . . and I suspect that there are times when the move seems wrong to us all, when we seem, to ourselves, post-lapsarian men and women. We are Hindus who have crossed the black water; we are Muslims who eat pork. And as a result—as my use of the Christian notion of the Fall indicates—we are now partly of the West. Our identity is at once plural and partial. Sometimes we feel that we straddle two cultures; at other times, that we fall between two stools. But however ambiguous and shifting this ground may be, it is not an infertile territory for a writer to occupy. If literature is in part the business of finding new angles at which to enter reality, then once again our distance, our long geographical perspective, may provide us with such angles.

Or it may be that that is simply what we must think in order to do our work.

Midnight's Children enters its subject from the point of view of a secular man. I am a member of that generation of Indians who were sold the secular ideal. One of the things I liked, and still like, about India is that it is based on a non-sectarian philosophy. I was not raised in a narrowly Muslim environment; I do not consider Hindu culture to be either alien from me or more important than the Islamic heritage. I believe this has something to do with the nature of Bombay, a metropolis in which the multiplicity of commingled faiths and cultures curiously creates a remarkably secular ambience. Saleem Sinai makes use, eclectically, of whatever elements from whatever sources he chooses. It may have been easier for his author to do this from outside modern India than inside it.

I want to make one last point about the description of India that *Midnight's Children* attempts. It is a point about pessimism. The book has been criticised in India for its allegedly despairing tone. And the despair of the writer-from-outside may indeed look a little easy, a little pat. But I do not see the book as despairing or nihilistic. The point of view of the narrator is not entirely that of the author. What I tried to do was to set up a tension in the text, a paradoxical opposition between the form and content of the narrative. The story of Saleem does indeed lead him to despair. But the story is told in a manner designed to echo, as closely as my abilities allowed, the Indian talent for non-stop self-regeneration. This is why the narrative constantly throws up new stories, why it 'teems'. The form—multitudinous, hinting at the infinite possibilities of the country—is the optimistic counterweight to Saleem's personal tragedy. I do not think that a book written in such a manner can really be called a despairing work.

England's Indian writers are by no means all the same type of animal. Some of us, for instance, are Pakistani. Others Bangladeshi. Others West, or East, or even South African.

And V. S. Naipaul, by now, is something else entirely. This word 'Indian' is getting to be a pretty scattered concept. Indian writers in England include political exiles, first-generation migrants, affluent expatriates whose residence here is frequently temporary, naturalized Britons, and people born here who may never have laid eyes on the subcontinent. Clearly, nothing that I say can apply across all these categories. But one of the interesting things about this diverse community is that, as far as Indo-British fiction is concerned, its existence changes the ball game, because that fiction is in future going to come as much from addresses in London, Birmingham and Yorkshire as from Delhi or Bombay.

One of the changes has to do with attitudes towards the use of English. Many have referred to the argument about the appropriateness of this language to Indian themes. And I hope all of us share the view that we can't simply use the language in the way the British did; that it needs remaking for our own purposes. Those of us who do use English do so in spite of our ambiguity towards it, or perhaps because of that, perhaps because we can find in that linguistic struggle a reflection of other struggles taking place in the real world, struggles between the cultures within ourselves and the influences at work upon our societies. To conquer English may be to complete the process of making ourselves free.

But the British Indian writer simply does not have the option of rejecting English, anyway. His children, her children, will grow up speaking it, probably as a first language; and in the forging of a British Indian identity the English language is of central importance. It must, in spite of everything, be embraced. (The word 'translation' comes, etymologically, from the Latin for 'bearing across'. Having been borne across the world, we are translated men. It is normally supposed that something always gets lost in translation; I cling, obstinately, to the notion that something can also be gained.)

To be an Indian writer in this society is to face, every day, problems of definition. What does it mean to be 'Indian' outside India? How can culture be preserved without becoming ossified? How should we discuss the need for

change within ourselves and our community without seeming
to play into the hands of our racial enemies? What are the
consequences, both spiritual and practical, of refusing to make
any concessions to Western ideas and practices? What are the
consequences of embracing those ideas and practices and
turning away from the ones that came here with us? These
questions are all a single, existential question: How are we to
live in the world?

I do not propose to offer, prescriptively, any answers to
these questions; only to state that these are some of the issues
with which each of us will have to come to terms.

To turn my eyes outwards now, and to say a little about the
relationship between the Indian writer and the majority
white culture in whose midst he lives, and with which his
work will sooner or later have to deal:

In common with many Bombay-raised middle-class
children of my generation, I grew up with an intimate
knowledge of, and even sense of friendship with, a certain
kind of England: a dream-England composed of Test Matches
at Lord's presided over by the voice of John Arlott, at which
Freddie Trueman bowled unceasingly and without success at
Polly Umrigar; of Enid Blyton and Billy Bunter, in which we
were even prepared to smile indulgently at portraits such as
'Hurree Jamset Ram Singh', 'the dusky nabob of Bhanipur'. I
wanted to come to England. I couldn't wait. And to be fair,
England has done all right by me; but I find it a little difficult
to be properly grateful. I can't escape the view that my
relatively easy ride is not the result of the dream-England's
famous sense of tolerance and fair play, but of my social class,
my freak fair skin and my 'English' English accent. Take away
any of these, and the story would have been very different.
Because of course the dream-England is no more than a
dream.

Sadly, it's a dream from which too many white Britons
refuse to awake. Recently, on a live radio programme, a
professional humorist asked me, in all seriousness, why I
objected to being called a wog. He said he had always thought

it a rather charming word, a term of endearment. 'I was at the zoo the other day,' he revealed, 'and a zoo keeper told me that the wogs were best with the animals; they stuck their fingers in their ears and wiggled them about and the animals felt at home.' The ghost of Hurree Jamset Ram Singh walks among us still.

As Richard Wright found long ago in America, black and white descriptions of society are no longer compatible. Fantasy, or the mingling of fantasy and naturalism, is one way of dealing with these problems. It offers a way of echoing in the form of our work the issues faced by all of us: how to build a new, 'modern' world out of an old, legend-haunted civilization, an old culture which we have brought into the heart of a newer one. But whatever technical solutions we may find, Indian writers in these islands, like others who have migrated into the north from the south, are capable of writing from a kind of double perspective: because they, we, are at one and the same time insiders and outsiders in this society. This stereoscopic vision is perhaps what we can offer in place of 'whole sight'.

There is one last idea that I should like to explore, even though it may, on first hearing, seem to contradict much of what I've so far said. It is this: of all the many elephant traps lying ahead of us, the largest and most dangerous pitfall would be the adoption of a ghetto mentality. To forget that there is a world beyond the community to which we belong, to confine ourselves within narrowly defined cultural frontiers, would be, I believe, to go voluntarily into that form of internal exile which in South Africa is called the 'homeland'. We must guard against creating, for the most virtuous of reasons, British–Indian literary equivalents of Bophuthatswana or the Transkei.

This raises immediately the question of whom one is writing 'for'. My own, short, answer is that I have never had a reader in mind. I have ideas, people, events, shapes, and I write 'for' those things, and hope that the completed work will be of interest to others. But which others? In the case of

Midnight's Children I certainly felt that if its subcontinental readers had rejected the work, I should have thought it a failure, no matter what the reaction in the West. So I would say that I write 'for' people who feel part of the things I write 'about', but also for everyone else whom I can reach. In this I am of the same opinion as the black American writer Ralph Ellison, who, in his collection of essays *Shadow and Act*, says that he finds something precious in being black in America at this time; but that he is also reaching for more than that. 'I was taken very early,' he writes, 'with a passion to link together all I loved within the Negro community and all those things I felt in the world which lay beyond.'

Art is a passion of the mind. And the imagination works best when it is most free. Western writers have always felt free to be eclectic in their selection of theme, setting, form; Western visual artists have, in this century, been happily raiding the visual storehouses of Africa, Asia, the Philippines. I am sure that we must grant ourselves an equal freedom.

Let me suggest that Indian writers in England have access to a second tradition, quite apart from their own racial history. It is the culture and political history of the phenomenon of migration, displacement, life in a minority group. We can quite legitimately claim as our ancestors the Huguenots, the Irish, the Jews; the past to which we belong is an English past, the history of immigrant Britain. Swift, Conrad, Marx are as much our literary forebears as Tagore or Ram Mohan Roy. America, a nation of immigrants, has created great literature out of the phenomenon of cultural transplantation, out of examining the ways in which people cope with a new world; it may be that by discovering what we have in common with those who preceded us into this country, we can begin to do the same.

I stress this is only one of many possible strategies. But we are inescapably international writers at a time when the novel has never been a more international form (a writer like Borges speaks of the influence of Robert Louis Stevenson on his work; Heinrich Böll acknowledges the influence of Irish literature; cross-pollination is everywhere); and it is perhaps one of the more pleasant freedoms of the literary migrant to be able to choose his parents. My own—selected half consciously, half not—include Gogol, Cervantes, Kafka, Melville, Machado de Assis; a polyglot family tree, against which I measure myself, and to which I would be honoured to belong.

There's a beautiful image in Saul Bellow's latest novel, *The Dean's December*. The central character, the Dean, Corde, hears a dog barking wildly somewhere. He imagines that the barking is the dog's protest against the limit of dog experience. 'For God's sake,' the dog is saying, 'open the universe a little more!' And because Bellow is, of course, not really talking about dogs, or not only about dogs, I have the feeling that the dog's rage, and its desire, is also mine, ours, everyone's. 'For God's sake, open the universe a little more!'

1982

'ERRATA': OR, UNRELIABLE
NARRATION IN *MIDNIGHT'S CHILDREN*

According to Hindu tradition, the elephant-headed god Ganesha is very fond of literature; so fond that he agrees to sit at the feet of the bard Vyasa and take down the entire text of the *Mahabharata*, from start to finish, in an unparalleled act of stenographic love.

In *Midnight's Children*, Saleem Sinai makes a reference, at one point, to this old tradition. But his version is a little different. According to Saleem, Ganesha sat at the feet of the poet Valmiki and took down the *Ramayana*. Saleem is wrong.

It is not his only mistake. During his account of the evolution of the city of Bombay, he tells us that the city's patron-goddess Mumbadevi has fallen out of favour with contemporary Bombayites: 'The calendar of festivals reveals her decline . . . Where is Mumbadevi's day?' As a matter of fact, the calendar of festivals includes a perfectly good Mumbadevi Day, or at least it does in all versions of India except Saleem's.

And how could Lata Mangeshkar have been heard singing on All-India Radio as early as 1946? And does Saleem not know that it was not General Sam Manekshaw who accepted the surrender of the Pakistan Army at the end of the Bangladesh War—the Indian officer who was Tiger Niazi's old chum being, of course, Jagjit Singh Arora? And why does Saleem allege that the brand of cigarettes, State Express 555, is manufactured by W. D. & H. O. Wills?

I could continue. Concrete tetrapods have never been used in Bombay as part of any land reclamation scheme, but only to shore up and protect the sea wall along the Marine Drive promenade. Nor could the train that brings Picture Singh and Saleem from Delhi to Bombay possibly have passed through Kurla, which is on a different line.

Etcetera. It is by now obvious, I hope, that Saleem Sinai is an unreliable narrator, and that *Midnight's Children* is far from being an authoritative guide to the history of post-independence India.

But this isn't quite how unreliable narration usually works in novels. Conventionally unreliable narrators are often a little stupid, less able to work out what's going on around them than the reader. In such narratives, one deciphers the true meaning of events by 'seeing through' the narrator's faulty vision. However, the narrator of *Midnight's Children* is neither particularly stupid, nor particularly unaware of what's happening.

Why, then, all the errata? One answer could be that the author has been sloppy in his research. 'If you're going to use Hindu traditions in your story, Mr Rushdie,' I was asked by an irate and shiny-headed gentleman in Bangalore—he had spotted the Valmiki/Vyasa confusion—'don't you think you could take the trouble to look it up?' I have also received letters arguing about Bombay bus routes, and informing me that certain ranks used by the Pakistan Army in the text are not in fact used by the Pakistan Army in Pakistan. In these letters there is always an undertone of pleasure: the reader's delight at having 'caught the writer out'.

So let me confess that the novel does contain a few mistakes that are mine as well as Saleem's. One is to be found in the description of the Amritsar massacre, during which I have Saleem say that Dyer entered the Jallianwala Bagh compound followed by 'fifty white troops'. The truth is that there were fifty troops, but they weren't white. When I first found out my error I was upset and tried to have it corrected. Now I'm not so sure. The mistake feels more and more like Saleem's; its wrongness feels *right*.

Elsewhere, though, I went to some trouble to get things wrong. Originally error-free passages had the taint of inaccuracy introduced. Unintentional mistakes were, on being discovered, not expunged from the text but, rather, emphasized, given more prominence in the story. This odd behaviour requires an explanation.

When I began the novel (as I've written elsewhere) my purpose was somewhat Proustian. Time and migration had placed a double filter between me and my subject, and I hoped that if I could only imagine vividly enough it might be possible to see beyond those filters, to write as if the years had not passed, as if I had never left India for the West. But as I worked I found that what interested me was the process of filtration itself. So my subject changed, was no longer a search for lost time, had become the way in which we remake the past to suit our present purposes, using memory as our tool. Saleem's greatest desire is for what he calls meaning, and near the end of his broken life he sets out to *write himself*, in the hope that by doing so he may achieve the significance that the events of his adulthood have drained from him. He is no dispassionate, disinterested chronicler. He wants so to shape his material that the reader will be forced to concede his central role. He is cutting up history to suit himself, just as he did when he cut up newspapers to compose his earlier text, the anonymous note to Commander Sabarmati. The small errors in the text can be read as clues, as indications that Saleem is capable of distortions both great and small. He is an interested party in the events he narrates.

He is also *remembering*, of course, and one of the simplest truths about any set of memories is that many of them will be false. I myself have a clear memory of having been in India during the China War. I 'remember' how frightened we all were, I 'recall' people making nervy little jokes about needing to buy themselves a Chinese phrase book or two, because the Chinese Army was not expected to stop until it reached Delhi. I also know that I could not possibly have been in India at that time. I was interested to find that *even after I found out that my memory was playing tricks* my brain simply refused to unscramble itself. It clung to the false memory, preferring it to mere literal happenstance. I thought that was an important lesson to learn.

Thereafter, as I wrote the novel, and whenever a conflict arose between literal and remembered truth, I would favour the remembered version. This is why, even though Saleem admits that no tidal wave passed through the Sundarbans in the year of the Bangladesh War, he continues to be borne out

24

of the jungle on the crest of that fictional wave. His truth is too important to him to allow it to be unseated by a mere weather report. It is memory's truth, he insists, and only a madman would prefer someone else's version to his own.

Saleem Sinai is not an oracle; he's only adopting a kind of oracular language. His story is not history, but it plays with historical shapes. Ironically, the book's success—its Booker Prize, etc—initially distorted the way in which it was read. Many readers wanted it to be the history, even the guide-book, which it was never meant to be; others resented it for its incompleteness, pointing out, among other things, that I had failed to mention the glories of Urdu poetry, or the plight of the Harijans, or untouchables, or what some people think of as the new imperialism of the Hindi language in South India. These variously disappointed readers were judging the book not as a novel, but as some sort of inadequate reference book or encyclopaedia.

The passage of time has smoothed out such wrinkles. I'd just like to clear up that mistake of Saleem's about the god Ganesha. It happens just after Saleem has been boasting about his own erudition. In spite of coming from a Muslim background, he tells us, he's well up on the Hindu stories. That he should instantly perpetrate a howler about the myth which is, after all, most central to himself (Ganesha's elephantine nose, and dubious parentage, prefigure his own) was, I thought, a way of deflating that narratorial pomposity; but it was also—along with Saleem's other blunder about the date of Mahatma Gandhi's assassination—a way of telling the reader to maintain a healthy distrust.

History is always ambiguous. Facts are hard to establish, and capable of being given many meanings. Reality is built on our prejudices, misconceptions and ignorance as well as on our perceptiveness and knowledge. The reading of Saleem's unreliable narration might be, I believed, a useful analogy for the way in which we all, every day, attempt to 'read' the world.

1983

THE RIDDLE OF MIDNIGHT:
INDIA, AUGUST 1987

Forty years ago, the independent nation of India and I were born within eight weeks of one another. I came first. This gave rise to a family joke—that the departure of the British was occasioned by my arrival on the scene—and the joke, in turn, became the germ of a novel, *Midnight's Children*, in which not just one child, but one thousand and one children born in the midnight hour of freedom, the first hour of 15 August 1947, were comically and tragically connected to the birth of a nation.

(I worked out, by the way, that the Indian birth rate in August 1947 was approximately two babies per second, so my fictional figure of 1,001 per hour was, if anything, a little on the low side.)

The chain reaction continued. The novel's title became, for many Indians, a familiar catch-phrase defining that generation which was too young to remember the Empire or the liberation struggle; and when Rajiv Gandhi became Prime Minister, I found his administration being welcomed in the newspapers by such headlines as: 'Enter midnight's children.'

So when forty came around, it occurred to me to take a look at the state of the Indian nation that was, like me, entering its fifth decade; and to look, in particular, through the eyes of the class of '47, the country's citizen-twins, my generation. I flew to the subcontinent in search of the real-life counterparts of the imaginary beings I once made up. Midnight's real children: to meet them would be like closing a circle.

There was a riddle I wanted to try and answer, with their help: *Does India exist?* A strange, redundant sort of inquiry, on the face of it. After all, there the gigantic place manifestly is, a rough diamond two thousand miles long and more or less as wide, as large as Europe though you'd never guess it from the Mercator projection, populated by around a sixth of the human race, home of the largest film industry on earth, spawning Festivals the world over, famous as the 'world's biggest democracy'. Does India exist? If it doesn't, what's keeping Pakistan and Bangladesh apart?

It's when you start thinking about the political entity, the nation of India, the thing whose fortieth anniversary it is, that the question starts making sense. After all, in all the thousands of years of Indian history, there never was such a creature as a united India. Nobody ever managed to rule the whole place, not the Mughals, not the British. And then, that midnight, the thing that had never existed was suddenly 'free'. But what on earth was it? On what common ground (if any) did it, does it, stand?

Some countries are united by a common language; India has around fifteen major languages and numberless minor ones. Nor are its people united by race, religion or culture. These days, you can even hear some voices suggesting that the preservation of the union is not in the common interest. J. K. Galbraith's description of India as 'functioning anarchy' still fits, but the stresses on the country have never been so great. Does India exist? If it doesn't, the explanation is to be found in a single word: communalism. The politics of religious hatred.

There is a medium-sized town called Ayodhya in the state of Uttar Pradesh, and in this town there is a fairly commonplace mosque named Babri Masjid. According to the *Ramayana*, however, Ayodhya was the home town of Rama himself, and according to a local legend the spot where he was born—the *Ramjanmabhoomi*—is the one on which the Muslim place of worship stands today. The site has been disputed territory ever since independence, but for most of the forty years the lid has been kept on the problem by the very Indian method of shelving the case, locking the mosque's gates, and allowing neither Hindus nor Muslims to enter.

Last year, however, the case finally came to court, and the judgement seemed to favour the Hindus. Babri Masjid became the target of the extremist Hindu fundamentalist organization,

27

the Vishwa Hindu Parishad. Since then, Hindus and Muslims all over North India have been clashing, and in every outbreak of communal violence the Babri Masjid affair is cited as a primary cause.

When I arrived in Delhi the old Walled City was under heavy curfew because of just such an outbreak of communal violence. In the little alleys of Chandni Chowk I met a Hindu tailor, Harbans Lal, born in 1947 and as mild and gentle a man as you could wish to find. The violence terrified him. 'When it started,' he said, 'I shut up the shop and ran away.' But in spite of all his mildness, Harbans Lal was a firm supporter of the Hindu nationalist party that used to be called the Jan Sangh and is now the BJP. 'I voted for Rajiv Gandhi in the election after Mrs Gandhi died,' he said. 'It was a big mistake. I won't do it again.' I asked him what should be done about the Babri Masjid issue. Should it be locked up again as it had been for so many years? Should it be a place where both Hindus and Muslims could go to worship? 'It's a Hindu shrine,' he said, 'It should be for the Hindus.' There was no possibility, in his mind, of a compromise.

A couple of days later the Walled City was still bubbling with tension. The curfew was lifted for an hour or two every day to enable people to go out and buy food. The rest of the time, security was very tight. It was Eid, the great Muslim festival celebrating the end of the month of fasting, but the city's leading imams had said that Eid should not be celebrated. In Meerut, the mutilated corpses of Muslims floated in the river. The city's predominantly Hindu police force, the PAC, had run amok. Once again, Babri Masjid was one of the bones of contention.

I met Abdul Ghani, a Delhi Muslim who worked in a sari shop, and who, like Harbans Lal, India and me, was 1947-born. I was struck by how much like Harbans Lal he was. They were both slightly built, mild-mannered men with low, courteous voices and attractive smiles. They each earned about 1,000 rupees (100 dollars) a month, and dreamed of owning their own shops, knowing they never would. And when it came to the Hindu–Muslim communal divide,

Abdul Ghani was just as unyielding as Harbans Lal had been. 'What belongs to the Muslims,' he said when I asked about Babri Masjid, 'should be given back to the Muslims. There is nothing else to be done.'

The gentleness of Harbans Lal and Abdul Ghani made their religious divisions especially telling. Nor was Babri Masjid the only issue between the faiths. At Ahmedabad, in the state of Gujarat, Hindu–Muslim violence was again centred in the old walled-city area of Manek Chowk, and had long ago acquired its own internal logic: so many families had lost members in the fighting that the cycle of revenge was unstoppable. Political forces were at work, too. At Ahmedabad hospital the doctors found that many of the knife wounds they treated were professionally inflicted. Somebody was sending trained killers into town.

All over India—Meerut, Delhi, Ahmedabad, Bombay— tension between Hindus and Muslims was rising. In Bombay, a (1947-born) journalist told me that many communal incidents took place in areas where Muslims had begun to prosper and move up the economic scale. Behind the flash- points like Ayodhya, she suggested, was Hindus' resentment of Muslim prosperity.

The Vishwa Hindu Parishad has a list of over a hundred disputed sites of the Babri Masjid type. Two are especially important. In Mathura, a Muslim shrine stands on the supposed birthplace of the god Krishna; and in Benares, a site allegedly sacred to Shiva is also in Muslim hands . . .

In Bombay, I found a 'midnight child', a clerical worker in the docks, a Muslim named Mukadam who was such a super- citizen that he was almost too good to be true. Mukadam was absolutely dedicated to the unity of India. He believed in small families. He thought all Indians had a duty to educate themselves, and he had put himself through many evening courses. He had been named Best Worker at his dock. In his village, he claimed proudly, people of all faiths lived together in complete harmony. 'That is how it should be,' he said. 'After all, these religions are only words. What is behind them is the same, whichever faith it is.'

But when communal violence came to the Bombay docks in 1985, Mukadam's super-citizenship wasn't of much use. On the day the mob came to his dock, he was saved because he happened to be away. He didn't dare to return to work for weeks. And now, he says, he worries that it may come again at any time.

Like Mukadam, many members of Indian minority groups started out as devotees of the old, secular definition of India, and there were no Indians as patriotic as the Sikhs. Until 1984, you could say that the Sikhs were *the* Indian nationalists. Then came the storming of the Golden Temple, and the assassination of Mrs Gandhi; and everything changed.

The group of Sikh radicals led by Sant Jarnail Singh Bhindranwale, the religious leader who died in the Golden Temple storming, could not be said to represent more than a small minority of all Sikhs. The campaign for a separate Sikh state, Khalistan, had similarly found few takers among India's Sikhs—until November 1984, when Indira Gandhi died, and it became known that her assassins were Sikhs.

In Delhi, angry Hindu mobs—among whom party workers of Mrs Gandhi's Congress-I were everywhere observed—decided to hold all Sikhs responsible for the deeds of the assassins. Thus an entirely new form of communal violence — Hindu–Sikh riots — came into being, and in the next ten days the Sikh community suffered a series of traumatizing attacks from which it has not recovered, and perhaps never will.

In Block 32 of the Delhi suburb called Trilokpuri, perhaps 350 Sikhs were burned alive. I walked past streets of charred, gutted houses in some of which you could still see the bones of the dead. It was the worst place I have ever seen, not least because, in the surrounding streets, children played normally, the neighbours went on with their lives. Yet some of these neighbours were the very people who perpetrated the crime of 32 Trilokpuri, which was only one of the many massacres of Sikhs that took place that November. Many Sikh 'midnight children' never reached forty at all.

I heard about many of these deaths, and will let one story stand for all. When the mob came for Hari Singh, a taxi-driver like so many Delhi Sikhs, his son fled into a nearby patch of overgrown waste land. His wife was obliged to watch as the mob literally ripped her husband's beard off his face. (This beard-ripping ritual was a feature of many of the November killings.) She managed to get hold of the beard, thinking that it was, at least, a part of him that she could keep for herself, and she ran into their house to hide it. Some members of the mob followed her in, found the beard and removed it. Then they poured kerosene over Hari Singh and set fire to him. They also chased his teenage son, found him, beat him unconscious, and burned him, too. They knew he was a Sikh even though he had cut his hair, because when they found his father's beard they found his cut hair as well. His mother had preserved the sacred locks that identified her son.

Another taxi-driver, Pal Singh (born November 1947), told me that he had never had time for the Khalistan movement, but after 1984 he had changed his mind. 'Now it will come,' he said, 'maybe within ten years.' Sikhs were selling up their property in Delhi and buying land in the Punjab, so that if the time came when they had to flee back to the Sikh heartland they wouldn't have to leave their assets behind. 'I'm doing it, too,' Pal Singh said.

Almost three years after the 1984 massacres, not one person has been charged with murdering a Sikh in those fearsome days. The Congress-I, Rajiv Gandhi's party, increasingly relies on the Hindu vote, and is reluctant to alienate it.

The new element in Indian communalism is the emergence of a collective Hindu consciousness that transcends caste, and that believes Hinduism to be under threat from other Indian minorities. There is evidence that Rajiv's Congress-I is trying to ride that tiger. In Bombay, the tiger is actually in power. The ruling Shiv Sena Party, whose symbol is the tiger, is the most overtly Hindu-fundamentalist grouping ever to achieve office anywhere in India.

Its leader, Bal Thackeray, a former cartoonist, speaks openly of his belief that democracy has failed in India. He makes no secret of his open hostility towards Muslims. In the

31

Bhiwandi riots of 1985, a few months before the Shiv Sena won the Bombay municipal elections, Shiv Sena activists were deeply involved in the anti-Muslim violence. And today, as the Sena seeks to spread its influence into the rural areas of Maharashtra (the state of which Bombay is the capital), incidents of communal violence are being reported from villages in which nothing of the sort has ever happened before.

I come from Bombay, and from a Muslim family, too. 'My' India has always been based on ideas of multiplicity, pluralism, hybridity: ideas to which the ideologies of the communalists are diametrically opposed. To my mind, the defining image of India is the crowd, and a crowd is by its very nature superabundant, heterogeneous, many things at once. But the India of the communalists is none of these things.

I spent one long evening in the company of a ('47-born) Bengali intellectual, Robi Chatterjee, for whom the inadequacies of society are a cause for deep, permanent, operatic anguish. 'Does India exist?' I asked him.

'What do you mean?' he cried. 'Where the hell do you think this is?' I told him that I meant the idea of the nation. Forty years after a nationalist revolution, where could it be said to reside?

He said, 'To the devil with all that nationalism. I am an Indian because I am born here and I live here. So is everyone else of whom that is true. What's the need for any more definitions?'

I asked, 'If you do without the idea of nationalism, then what's the glue holding the country together?'

'We don't need glue,' he said. 'India isn't going to fall apart. All that Balkanization stuff. I reject it completely. We are simply here and we will remain here. It's this nationalism business that is the danger.'

According to Robi, the idea of nationalism in India had grown more and more chauvinistic, had become narrower and narrower. The ideas of Hindu nationalism had infected it. I was struck by a remarkable paradox: that, in a country created by the Congress's nationalist campaign, the well-being of the people might now require that all nationalist rhetoric be abandoned.

Unfortunately for India, the linkage between Hindu fundamentalism and the idea of the nation shows no signs of weakening. India is increasingly defined as Hindu India, and Sikh and Muslim fundamentalism grows ever fiercer and entrenched in response. 'These days,' a young Hindu woman said to me, 'one's religion is worn on one's sleeve.' She was corrected by a Sikh friend. 'It is worn,' he said, 'in a scabbard at the hip.'

I remember that when *Midnight's Children* was first published in 1981, the most common Indian criticism of it was that it was too pessimistic about the future. It's a sad truth that nobody finds the novel's ending pessimistic any more, because what has happened in India since 1981 is so much darker than I had imagined. If anything, the book's last pages, with their suggestion of a new, more pragmatic generation rising up to take over from the midnight children, now seem absurdly, romantically optimistic.

But India regularly confounds its critics by its resilience, its survival in spite of everything. I don't believe in the Balkanization of India any more than Robi Chatterjee does. It's my guess that the old functioning anarchy will, somehow or other, keep on functioning, for another forty years, and no doubt another forty after that. But don't ask me how.

1987

2

Censorship

The Assassination of Indira Gandhi

Dynasty

Zia ul-Haq. 17 August 1988

Daughter of the East

CENSORSHIP

My first memories of censorship are cinematic: screen kisses brutalized by prudish scissors which chopped out the moments of actual contact. (Briefly, before comprehension dawned, I wondered if that were all there was to kissing, the languorous approach and then the sudden turkey-jerk away.) The effect was usually somewhat comic, and censorship still retains, in contemporary Pakistan, a strong element of comedy. When the Pakistani censors found that the movie *El Cid* ended with a dead Charlton Heston leading the Christians to victory over live Muslims, they nearly banned it, until they had the idea óf simply cutting out the entire climax, so that the film as screened showed El Cid mortally wounded, El Cid dying nobly, and then ended. Muslims 1, Christians 0.

The comedy is sometimes black. The burning of the film *Kissa Kursi Ka* (*Tale of a Chair*) during Mrs Gandhi's Emergency rule in India is notorious; and, in Pakistan, a reader's letter to the *Pakistan Times*, in support of the decision to ban the film *Gandhi* because of its unflattering portrayal of M. A. Jinnah, criticized certain 'liberal elements' for having dared to suggest that the film should be released so that Pakistanis could make up their own minds about it. If they were less broad-minded, the letter-writer suggested, these persons would be better citizens of Pakistan.

My first direct encounter with censorship took place in 1968, when I was twenty-one, fresh out of Cambridge and full of the radical fervour of that famous year. I returned to Karachi, where a small magazine commissioned me to write a piece about my impressions on returning home. I remember very little about this piece (mercifully, memory is a censor, too), except that it was not at all political. It tended, I think, to linger melodramatically, on images of dying horses with flies settling on their eyeballs. You can imagine the sort of thing.

Anyway, I submitted my piece, and a couple of weeks later was told by the magazine's editor that the Press Council, the national censors, had banned it completely. Now it so happened that I had an uncle on the Press Council, and in a very unradical, string-pulling mood I thought I'd just go and see him and everything would be sorted out. He looked tired when I confronted him. 'Publication,' he said immovably, 'would not be in your best interest.' I never found out why.

Next I persuaded Karachi TV to let me produce and act in Edward Albee's *The Zoo Story*, which they liked because it was forty-five minutes long, had a cast of two and required only a park bench for a set. I then had to go through a series of astonishing censorship conferences. The character I played had a long monologue in which he described his landlady's dog's repeated attacks on him. In an attempt to befriend the dog, he bought it half a dozen hamburgers. The dog refused the hamburgers and attacked him again. 'I was offended,' I was supposed to say. 'It was six perfectly good hamburgers with not enough pork in them to make it disgusting.' 'Pork,' a TV executive told me solemnly, 'is a four-letter word.' He had said the same thing about 'sex', and 'homosexual', but this time I argued back. The text, I pleaded, was saying the right thing about pork. Pork, in Albee's view, made hamburgers so disgusting that even dogs refused them. This was superb anti-pork propaganda. It must stay. 'You don't see,' the executive told me, wearing the same tired expression as my uncle had, 'the word pork may not be spoken on Pakistan television.' And that was that. I also had to cut the line about God being a coloured queen who wears a kimono and plucks his eyebrows.

The point I'm making is not that censorship is a source of amusement, which it usually isn't, but that—in Pakistan, at any rate—it is everywhere, inescapable, permitting no appeal. In India the authorities control the media that matter—radio and television—and allow some leeway to the press, comforted by their knowledge of the country's low literacy level. In Pakistan they go further. Not only do they control the press, but the journalists, too. At the recent conference of the Non-Aligned Movement in New Delhi, the Pakistan press corps was notable for its fearfulness. Each member was worried one of the other guys might inform on him when they returned—for drinking, or consorting too closely with Hindus, or performing other unpatriotic acts. Indian journalists were deeply depressed by the sight of their opposite numbers behaving like scared rabbits one moment and quislings the next.

What are the effects of total censorship? Obviously, the absence of information and the presence of lies. During Mr Bhutto's campaign of genocide in Baluchistan, the news media remained silent. Officially, Baluchistan was at peace. Those who died, died unofficial deaths. It must have comforted them to know that the State's truth declared them all to be alive. Another example: you will not find the involvement of Pakistan's military rulers with the booming heroin industry much discussed in the country's news media. Yet this is what underlies General Zia's concern for the lot of the Afghan refugees. Afghan entrepreneurs help to run the Pakistan heroin business, and they have had the good sense to make sure that they make the army rich as well as themselves. How fortunate that the Qur'an does not mention anything about the ethics of heroin pushing.

But the worst, most insidious effect of censorship is that, in the end, it can deaden the imagination of the people. Where there is no debate, it is hard to go on remembering, every day, that there is a suppressed side to every argument. It becomes almost impossible to conceive of what the suppressed things might be. It becomes easy to think that what has been suppressed was valueless, anyway, or so dangerous that it needed to be suppressed. And then the victory of the censor is total. The anti-*Gandhi* letter-writer who recommended narrow-mindedness as a national virtue is one such casualty of censorship; he loves Big Brother—or *Burra Bhai*, perhaps.

It seems, now, that General Zia's days are numbered. I do not believe that the present disturbances are the end, but they are the beginning of the end, because they show that the people have lost their fear of his brutal regime, and if the people cease to be afraid, he is done for. But Pakistan's big test will come after the end of dictatorship, after the restoration of civilian rule and free elections, whenever that is, in one year or two or five; because if leaders do not then emerge who are willing to lift censorship, to permit dissent, to believe and to demonstrate that opposition is the bedrock of democracy, then, I am afraid, the last chance will have been lost. For the moment, however, one can hope.

1983

THE ASSASSINATION OF
INDIRA GANDHI

All of us who love India are in mourning today. It is of no importance whether we numbered ourselves amongst Indira Gandhi's most fervent supporters or her most implacable opponents; her murder diminishes us all, and leaves a deep and alarming scar upon the very idea of India, very like that left on Pakistani society by General Zia's execution of the leader who was in so many ways *son semblable, son frère*, Prime Minister Bhutto. During the time of Mrs Gandhi's father Jawaharlal Nehru, the India news media's favourite catch-phrase was the rather nervous 'After Nehru, who?' Today, we ask ourselves a more fearful question: 'After Indira, what?' And it is clear that what is most to be feared is an outbreak of reprisal killings, of Hindu–Sikh communal violence, both inside and outside the Punjab. The wind was sown in Amritsar; now, perhaps (and it would be good to be wrong), the whirlwind ripens.

Where, in all this, can we find any scrap of hope for India's future? Where is the way forward that leads away from destruction, disintegration and blood? I believe that if it is to be found anywhere then it must begin, at this most difficult of times, with the clearest possible analysis of the mistakes of recent years. Those who forget the past are condemned to repeat it.

At the heart of the idea of India there lies a paradox: that its component parts, the States which coalesced into the union, are ancient historical entities, with cultures and independent existences going back many centuries; whereas India itself is a mere thirty-seven years old. And yet it is the 'new-born' India, the baby, so to speak, the Central government, that holds sway over the greybeards. Centre–State relations have always, inevitably, been somewhat delicate, fragile affairs.

In recent years, however, that delicate relationship has

developed severe imbalances, and much of the responsibility must lie at Mrs Gandhi's door. During her time in office, power has systematically been removed from the States to the Centre; and the resentments created by this process have been building up for years. The troubles in the Punjab began when the Congress-I leadership persistently refused to discuss the then very moderate demands of the Akali Dal Party for the restitution to the State government of powers which the Centre had seized. There can be no doubt that this intransigence was a major contributing factor to the growth in support for Sant Jarnail Singh Bhindranwale's terrorists, and to the whole sorry process which resulted in the attack on the Golden Temple.

Elsewhere in India, too, the Centre's power hunger has been very unpopular, and the Congress-I has suffered a string of defeats in State elections. Mrs Gandhi's reaction to these defeats was sadly all too predictable, and very far from democratic. She embarked on covert programmes of destabilization, one of which succeeded, at least temporarily, in toppling the popular and elected Chief Minister of Kashmir, Farooq Abdullah, and another of which backfired when N. T. Rama Rao was dismissed, in Andhra, and then had to be reinstated when it turned out that he still commanded a majority.

It is clear to any student of Indian affairs, and I hope it will be crystal clear to whoever succeeds Mrs Gandhi as India's Prime Minister, that all this nonsense has got to stop. There is no denying that the Central government must govern; but it is time that the States' legitimate grievances received the kind of sympathetic hearing which they have been denied for years. If this happens, then there is a glimmer of hope for the future. If it does not, then one must fear for the union.

The dangers of communalism, of the kind of religious sectarianism which motivated the assassins' bullets, are even more to be feared. Here is another of the paradoxes at the heart of the India-idea: that the ethic of the independence movement, and of the independent State, has always been secular; yet there can be few nations on earth in which religion plays a more direct or central role in the citizens' daily lives. In this area, too, there have always been tensions; but in recent years these tensions have been getting more and more extreme. The growth of Hindu fanaticism, as evidenced by the increasing strength of the RSS, the organization which was behind the assassination of Mahatma Gandhi, has been very worrying; and it has had its parallel in the Bhindranwale group and, recently, in the increased support for the Muslim extremist Jamaat Party in Kashmir—this support being, itself, the result of the toppling of Farooq Abdullah by the Centre, which seemed to legitimize the Jamaat's view that Muslims have no place in present-day India.

One of the saddest aspects of the growth of communalism has been that, at times, Mrs Gandhi's Congress Party has seemed to be going out to get the Hindu vote. That she was willing to sacrifice the Sikh vote by her attack on the Golden Temple, and the Muslim vote by her deposing of Farooq Abdullah, may be seen as evidence of this; and it comes all the more depressingly from the leader of a party whose electoral success has always been based on its reputation as the guardian of minority groups' rights and safety. In recent times, the minorities—the Harijans, or untouchables, as well as Sikhs and Muslims—have been deserting the Congress fold. I very much hope that the new Congress leadership will give up, once and for all, the idea that the party can win elections by playing the communalist card, and remember the secular ethic on which the future of the country depends.

It is also necessary to say—and it is hard to say this on such a day—that, in my opinion, one of the threats to democracy in India has come, in recent years, from the dynastic aspirations of the Nehru family itself, and from the peculiarly monarchic style of government which Mrs Gandhi developed. Let us remember about the Nehrus—Motilal, his son Jawaharlal, his daughter Indira, her sons Rajiv and Sanjay—that when it comes to power they make the Kennedys look like amateurs. After all, for no less than thirty-one of the thirty-seven years of independent Indian history, there has been a Nehru in control. And latterly New Delhi has not felt like the capital of an elective democracy at all, but rather like an old-fashioned *durbar*, a court. The powerful figures in this court have not been, in many cases, members of the government or even of the Indian Parliament. They have, rather, been a motley assortment of old school chums of Sanjay or Rajiv, billionaire businessmen, even, at times, one or two manifestations of that group now known in India as 'Godmen'. This cloud of courtiers has enveloped the Indian Prime Minister, and it would be a great advance if it were now to lose power. For this reason, it would seem to me quite wrong for the Congress-I to choose, as its new leader, a man as untried, and as unsuited for high office, as Rajiv Gandhi; it is time for India to assert, and for its ruling party to demonstrate, that the nation is not owned by any one family, no matter how illustrious. The Queen is dead; *vive la République*.

No, I am not trying to lay all of modern India's many ills at the door of the butchered Prime Minister. Political corruption is one of India's besetting ills, and there has been plenty of it in the Congress Party, but of course it is not all Mrs Gandhi's responsibility. Nor will the task of cleaning the stables be easy. But it is up to the new leadership to show the way. To reject the idea of getting votes by appealing to religious sectarianism. To give up using the Congress party machine as an instrument of patronage. To stop the process of undermining the authority of the civil service. To desist from bribing and corrupting the supporters of one's political opponents in order to achieve in back-rooms what has not been achieved by the ballot-box. To show that India is not in the grip of any new *imperium*. And to restore our faith in the India-idea.

What, centrally, is that idea? It is based on the most obvious and apparent fact about the great subcontinent: multitude. For a nation of seven hundred millions to make any kind of sense, it must base itself firmly on the concept of multiplicity, of plurality and tolerance, of devolution and decentralization wherever possible. There can be no one way—religious, cultural, or linguistic—of being an Indian; let difference reign.

On the face of it, Mrs Gandhi's legacy in the field of

external relations presents her son's administration with fewer problems. Ever since she left her husband, Feroze Gandhi, in 1949, and moved back into her father's house to become Jawaharlal Nehru's 'official hostess', Mrs Gandhi has moved with considerable assurance and no little skill in the world of international affairs; the speed with which she managed to persuade the world to forget the atrocities committed during her years of Emergency rule is evidence of her gifts. She managed, for the most part, to keep the balance between America and the Soviet Union (the long-standing Russian alliance never led to any ideological shift towards Soviet-style communism; quite the reverse, in fact, because in recent years Mrs Gandhi openly abandoned her earlier socialist rhetoric in favour of a nakedly capitalist programme). And as leader of the Non-Aligned Movement she gave India great stature in the eyes of the people of the Third World, for many of whom the relative stability and liberty of the Indian system have been things to take pride in and admire.

There are, however, deep uncertainties in this area as well. It's easy to say that the new administration should, and in all likelihood will, attempt simply to continue the foreign policies of the last; things will be much trickier in practice. Our knowledge of Mrs Gandhi's great experience in diplomacy only underlines the complete inexperience of Rajiv and his group. Add to this the possibility of a period of prolonged political instability in India, and you have a recipe for a rapid increase in superpower meddling. India may be about to become the world's biggest political football.

And then there is Pakistan. It's only a matter of weeks since rumours of Mrs Gandhi's willingness to find a pretext for a war with Pakistan were rife in the Indian capital. There are some grounds for giving credence to these rumours. Mrs Gandhi was, with good reason, extremely nervous about the outcome of the approaching general election, and she well remembered the electoral landslide which she achieved after the Bangladesh War (to say nothing of Mrs Thatcher and the Falklands). And a couple of months ago Rajiv Gandhi made some very odd, sabre-rattling noises, accusing Pakistan of trying to start a war. This was, to many observers, a manifest absurdity. Even a general is unlikely to fail to notice that it would be foolish to go to war with India when India's biggest ally, Russia, is sitting on your other frontier . . . At any rate, the question remains: if the situation in India continues to deteriorate, will Rajiv's thoughts turn once again to war? One can only hope they do not.

Two clichés about India must, before I conclude, be dismissed, especially as both of them have, in these first hours since the news of the assassination broke, reared their wizened old heads. Firstly, the probability of a military coup in India to establish a parallel dictatorship to that of Zia is, I believe, so slight that it can be discounted, if only because the entire history of India demonstrates the impossibility of conquering the place by military force. Secondly, the bullets that killed Mrs Gandhi did not 'prove' the unsuitability of democracy for India, any more than the killing of two Kennedys, or the Brighton bombing, proved the same about America or Britain. The idea of a united, democratic, secular India can survive this terrible day.

For the moment, however, all of us who are Indian by citizenship, or birth, or race, must accept that the assassination of Indira Priyadarshini Gandhi shames us all; and in that shame, we must hope, the people and leaders of India will find the strength to act with honour in the days to come.

1984

DYNASTY

Rajiv Gandhi was sworn in as India's Prime Minister within forty minutes of the announcement, on All-India Radio and the television network Doordarshan, of his mother's assassination; and on that day when nothing in the world seemed certain, the one fact upon which everybody agreed was that he, Rajiv, had been *the only possible choice*. He was repeatedly referred to as the 'heir-apparent'. We were told that he was 'coming into his inheritance'. The 'succession' was smooth, the 'dynastic changeover' had been 'inevitable'.

This sounds more like the language of courtiers than of political commentators. But, side by side with it, there was another kind of rhetoric in use: the already tired description of India as 'the world's largest democracy' grew a good deal more exhausted in the hours and days after Indira Gandhi's murder. And nobody seemed to hear the loud dissonance between the two forms of discourse. This national deafness was an indication of how great the power of the descendants of Motilal Nehru had become. On 31 October 1984, Rajiv Gandhi was indeed the only possible choice, endorsed by his party's power-brokers and by the few men who might have challenged him for the job. It was as if something utterly natural, some organic process of the body politic, had taken place. And, in one of the most ironic twists of all, this imperial accession to India's 'throne' was presented to the world as proof of the resilience of India's democratic system.

In fact, what happened was anything but natural: a forty-year-old man, a political novice who had previously been thought of as a vote-loser, weak, even uninterested in politics, had been transformed into the automatic selection for the most important job in the country, in the space of a few, chaotic moments. Was this the same Rajiv Gandhi who had been nervously thinking of standing in more than one constituency in the general election, lest he lose his brother's old seat of Amethi to his alienated sister-in-law, Sanjay's widow, Menaka? What magic had been worked to turn this grounded airline pilot into the potential saviour of the nation?

It seems to me that the answers to such questions must go beyond politics and history and enter the zone of myth. The Nehru–Gandhi family has, by now, been thoroughly mythologized; its story has been, to borrow a term from Lévi-Strauss, 'cooked'. And in that cooking we may discover the source of the magic.

Matter, as we now know, is nothing but compressed energy: your little finger contains many Nagasakis. By analogy, we may describe myths as being composed out of compressed meanings. Any mythological tale can bear a thousand and one interpretations, because the peoples who have lived with and used the story have, over time, poured all those meanings into it. This wealth of meaning is the secret of the power of any myth.

The continuing saga of the Nehru family, of the vicissitudes of Jawaharlal, Indira, Sanjay and Rajiv, has been, for hundreds of millions of us, an obsession spanning more than three decades. We have poured ourselves into this story, inventing its characters, then ripping them up and reinventing them. In our inexhaustible speculations lies one source of their power over us. We became addicted to these speculations, and they, unsurprisingly, took advantage of our addiction. Or: we dreamed them, so intensely that they came to life. And now, as the dream decays, we cannot quite bring ourselves to leave it, to awake.

In this version—the dynasty as collective dream—Jawaharlal Nehru represents the dream's noblest part, its most idealistic phase. Indira Gandhi, always the pragmatist, often unscrupulously so, becomes a figure of decline, and brutal Sanjay is a further debasement of the currency. It's hard to say, as yet, what Rajiv Gandhi stands for in this analysis. Perhaps he is the moment before the awakening, after all. In the decaying moments of a dream, the sounds of the real world begin to penetrate the dreamer's consciousness; and certainly, in India today, the sounds of reality are insistent and harsh. Rajiv may not be enough of a sandman to keep the people asleep. We shall see.

Jawaharlal Nehru was flatly opposed to Mahatma Gandhi's bizarre attempt to marginalize human sexuality by saying that 'the natural affinity between man and woman is the attraction between brother and sister, mother and son, father and daughter.' And yet, in Jawaharlal's own family, such affinities of blood have indeed proved more durable than marriages. Those who have married Nehrus—Jawaharlal's Kamala, Indira's Feroze, Sanjay's Menaka—have rarely been happy spouses. The crucial relationships have been those between father and daughter (Jawaharlal and Indira) and Indira and Sanjay, that is, mother and son. This ingrown, closed-ranks atmosphere has been, I suggest, the rock upon which the appeal of the dynasty-as-myth has been built. A myth requires a closed system; and here, once again, is evidence that Rajiv, whose family life gives every appearance of being happy, and who never seemed particularly close to Indira, is simply not a mythic figure. (It can be argued, of course, that this is no bad thing.)

Public speculation in India has feasted on these relationships, taking the raw material and cooking up all manner of notions, one of which may be quoted to demonstrate the extremes to which gossip about the 'royal family' could go. During the Emergency, at the height of Sanjay Gandhi's power, an absurd and entirely unfounded rumour had it that the intimacy between Sanjay and his mother might be incestuous. Here is a case of Oedipal ambiguities being wildly exaggerated by the overheated imaginations of some scrutineers. In this and many other instances the story of the Nehrus and Gandhis became a figment of their subjects' fancies. But there were also enough 'real life' scandals to keep the speculation-factories working—because myths, like soap-operas, which contain the mythic in its most debased form, require a high level of spice. So we have had public quarrels between Jawaharlal Nehru and Feroze Gandhi; we have seen Indira in post-Emergency disgrace, and witnessed the death—in what some called an act of divine retribution—of Sanjay Gandhi in a plane crash; we have had the extraordinary, virulent quarrel between Indira and Menaka Gandhi. Already, speculation is beginning to focus on the next generation. Who will be the dynasty's next candidate? Sanjay and Menaka's son Feroze Varun, or Rajiv and Sonia's Rahul? What do the two princelings think of each other? And so on. It has often seemed that the story of the Nehrus and Gandhis has provided more engrossing material than anything in the cinemas or on television: a real dynasty better than *Dynasty*, a Delhi to rival *Dallas*.

Let us remember, however, that the Indian public has been by no means the only mythologizing force at work. The family itself has set about self-mythification with a will. But here we must exempt Jawaharlal Nehru, who, as Tariq Ali reminds us, once told an Indian crowd that *they*, the people, and not mother earth or anything else, were India. What a contrast is to be found in the notorious election slogan adopted by his daughter: *India is Indira and Indira is India*. Unlike her father, Mrs Gandhi was clearly suffering badly from the grandiloquent, *l'état c'est moi* delusions of a Louis XIV. Her use of the cult of the mother—of Hindu mother-goddess symbols and allusions—and the idea of *shakti*, of the fact that the dynamic element of the Hindu pantheon is represented as female—was calculated and shrewd, but one feels that this, too, would have disturbed her father, who had never been in favour of Mahatma Gandhi's use of Hindu mysticism. Jawaharlal saw the divisiveness implicit in the elevating of any one Indian ethic over the others; Indira, less squeamish, became, by the end, too much a Hindu, and too little a national leader. And, because it helped her mystique, she exploited the accident of her marriage to a quite different Gandhi, as well: the surname and its attendant confusions were not without uses. (On the night of her death, *The Times*'s first edition carried a photograph of the Mahatma and the young Indira over the caption, *The grand-daughter*; by the second edition, this howler had been amended to read *The disciple*, which wasn't much more accurate.)

Sanjay Gandhi, too, developed around himself a cult of

personality; and now, Rajiv, as ever the least flamboyant, the most prosaic of the clan, has installed a new icon in his quarters: a computer. Already, the image of 'computer kid' Rajiv, leader of the technological revolution, is being polished up. Jawaharlal Nehru once said that India had just entered the age of the bicycle; Rajiv—or, rather, the myth of Rajiv—clearly has other ideas.

The third element in the process of myth-making has been the West. In the coverage of India by the news media of the West, the concentration on the Family has been so great that I doubt if many Europeans or Americans could name a single Indian politician who was called neither Nehru nor Gandhi. This kind of reportage has created the impression that there have been no other possible leaders; and, for all of Jawaharlal's time in office and most of Indira's, this has simply not been true. Even today, when the Indian political scene looks a little impoverished, there are signs of a new generation emerging; there are a number of political figures—Farooq Abdullah, Ramakrishna Hegde, even Chandra Shekhar—with whom Rajiv and his people will have to reckon in the near future. Yet we hear little about them in the Western press.

The leaders of the West, too, have played their part. This has been particularly noticeable in the period since 1979, when the Janata Party's disintegration let Mrs Gandhi back into power. Her major aim in the following years was to achieve a personal rehabilitation, to obliterate the memory of the Emergency and its atrocities, to be cleansed of its taint, absolved of history. With the help of numerous prime ministers and presidents, that aim was all but achieved by the time of her death. She told the world that the horror stories about the Emergency were all fictions; and the world allowed her to get away with the lie. It was a triumph of image over substance. It's difficult to resist the conclusion that the West—in particular, Western capital—saw that a rehabilitated Mrs Gandhi would be of great use, and set about inventing her.

It would, obviously, be possible to offer counter-myths to set against the mythologized Family. One such myth might usefully be that of Pandora and her box. It has seemed to me, ever since it happened, that the imposition of the Emergency was an act of folly comparable to the opening of that legendary box; and that many of the evils besetting India today—notably the resurgence of religious extremism—can be traced back to those days of dictatorship and State violence. The Emergency represented the triumph of cynicism in Indian public life; and it would be difficult to say that that triumph has since been reversed. Mrs Gandhi was much praised internationally for acting democratically by giving up power when she lost the 1977 elections; which seems rather like congratulating Pandora for shutting her box, long after the evils of the world had escaped into the air.

But it's better to counter myths with facts. And the facts indicate that Family rule has not left Indian democracy in particularly good shape. The drawing of all the power to the Centre has created deep, and sometimes violently expressed, resentments in the States; the replacement of Nehru's more idealistic vision by his descendants' politics of power-at-any-cost has resulted in a sharp lowering of the standards of public life; and the creation, in Delhi, of a sort of royal court, a ruling élite of intimates of the Family, unelected and unanswerable to anyone but the Prime Minister, has further damaged the structure of Indian democracy. It is beginning to look just possible—is it not?—that the interests of 'the world's largest democracy' and those of its ruling family might not be quite the same.

1985

ZIA UL-HAQ. 17 AUGUST 1988

When a tyrant falls, the world's shadows lighten, and only hypocrites grieve; and General Mohammad Zia ul-Haq was one of the cruellest of modern tyrants, whatever his 'great friend' George Bush and his staunch supporter Margaret Thatcher would have us think. Eleven years ago, he burst out of his bottle like an *Arabian Nights* goblin, and although he seemed, at first, a small, puny sort of demon, he instantly commenced to grow, until he was gigantic enough to be able to grab the whole of Pakistan by the throat. Now, after an eternity of repression (even the clocks ran slowly under the pressure of Zia's thumb), that sad, strangulated nation may, for a few moments, breathe a little more freely.

Deferential, unassuming, humbly religious Zia, the plain soldier's plain soldier: it was easy for a man as brilliant, patrician and autocratic as Zulfikar Ali Bhutto—no stranger to despotism himself—to see such a fellow as a useful, controllable fool, a corked and bottled genie with a comical Groucho moustache. Zia became Bhutto's Chief of Staff in 1976 largely because Bhutto felt he had him safely in his pocket. But Pakistani generals have a way of leaping out of such pockets and sealing up their former masters instead. The protégé deposed the patron in July 1977, and became his executioner two years later, initiating a blood feud with the Bhutto dynasty which could probably have ended only with his death. One of the more optimistic aspects of the new situation is that Pakistan's remaining generals have no reason to fear the Bhuttos' revenge if power should return to Pakistan's long-denied democratic process.

Pakistan under Zia has become a nightmarish, surreal land, in which battlefield armaments meant for the Afghan rebels are traded more or less openly on the country's black markets; in which the citizens of Karachi speak, with a shrug, of the daily collusion between the police force and large-scale gangs of thieves; in which private armies of heavily armed men defend and service one of the world's biggest narcotics industries; in which 'elections' take place without the participation of any political parties. That such a situation should be described, around the world, as 'stability' would be funny if it were not vile; that it has been concealed beneath a cloak of religious faith is more terrible still.

It needs to be said repeatedly in the West that Islam is no more monolithically cruel, no more an 'evil empire', than Christianity, capitalism or communism. The medieval, misogynistic, stultifying ideology which Zia imposed on Pakistan in his 'Islamization' programme was the ugliest possible face of the faith, and one by which most Pakistani Muslims were, I believe, disturbed and frightened. To be a believer is not by any means to be a zealot. Islam in the Indo-Pakistani subcontinent has developed historically along moderate lines, with a strong strain of pluralistic Sufi philosophy; Zia was this Islam's enemy. Now that he has gone, much of the Islamization programme may quickly follow him. Pakistan neither wants nor needs a legal system which makes the evidence of women worth less than that of men; nor one which bans the showing on Pakistani TV of the women's events from the Seoul Olympic Games.

This is how Pakistan's greatest poet, Faiz Ahmed Faiz, wrote of these matters in his poem *Zalim* (*The Tyrant*, translated by Naomi Lazard):

> *This is the festival; we will inter hope*
> *with appropriate mourning. Come, my people.*
> *We will celebrate the massacre of the multitudes . . .*
> *Mine is the new religion, the new morality.*
> *Mine are the new laws, and a new dogma.*
> *From now on the priests in God's temple*
> *will touch their lips to the hands of idols . . .*
> *Every gate of prayer throughout heaven*
> *is slammed shut today.*

Well, the tyrant has had his day, and has gone. How did it happen? The possibility of accidental death can, I think, safely be discounted. Nor am I convinced by suggestions of an internal army coup, or a 'hit' from across the Indian frontier. An assassination by members of the Afghan secret service is a real possibility; and there are many other more speculative options. The truth, if it ever emerges, will no doubt surprise us all.

The death of the US ambassador is, of course, a sadness; but his proximity to General Zia illustrates how much the late President depended on American good will and support. It is Pakistan's tragedy that the United States, in its role as freedom's global policeman, should have chosen to defend freedom in Afghanistan by sacrificing the human, civil and political rights of General Zia's subjects.

What happens now? Seasoned observers of the Pakistani scene will not be throwing too many hats in the air. It seems unlikely that the army will be prepared to relinquish real power while the Afghan situation remains volatile. And although several leading generals died with Zia in the C-130 explosion, two of the toughest are still very much alive: Fazle Haq, for a long time Zia's closest associate, his reputation tarnished by persistent allegations of his involvement with drugs traffickers, and Aslam Beg, who is perhaps the man most likely to succeed. It's always easiest, when surveying the bleak Pakistani political scene, to foresee the worst. But this time there is another option: a long shot, but worth a mention.

If the US administration could bring itself to see that General Zia's brand of 'stability' has left behind a legacy of profound instability; and if America were then to decide to back the democratic forces in Pakistan rather than the military ones, then a new stability centred on that quaint old idea, representative government, might become possible. I am talking, of course, about Benazir Bhutto and the coalition of political parties she leads, and which she must now work hard to preserve. This ought to be Benazir's moment; it remains to be seen whether the obduracy of the Pakistan Army, the fissiparous nature of the coalition (now that its great uniting foe has gone), and the contortions of geopolitics conspire to deprive her of it.

1988

DAUGHTER OF THE EAST

'*Cogito, ergo sum*,' Benazir Bhutto muses, translating helpfully: 'I think, therefore I am. I always had difficulty with this philosophical premise at Oxford and I am having much more difficulty with it now.' It's not that she doesn't think, you understand—actually, she thinks *even when she doesn't want to*—but that the thinking doesn't seem to help her *be*. 'I feel that I have nothing on which to leave my imprint,' she laments. One might think an autobiography the very place for such imprint-leaving, but alas, Benazir is curiously absent from her own book, *Daughter of the East*. The voice that speaks, the marks that are made here, belong to an American ghost.

It is a staccato ghost-voice that hates verbs and is much enamoured of sound effects. Here it is, describing what the Pakistan Army did in Bangladesh in 1971: 'Looting. Rape. Kidnappings. Murder.' Here it tells us of Benazir's solitary confinement: 'Time, relentless, monotonous . . . Flaking cement. Iron bars. And silence. Utter silence.' And here is the funeral of her brother Shah Nawaz: 'Black. Black armbands. Black *shalwar kameez* and *dupattas* . . . Black. More black.' And what were the people doing, 'in the fever of their grief'?—'Crying. Wailing.'

But even this is lyrical by comparison with the evocation of Benazir's ear infection: 'Click. Click. Click. Click.' (Eleven times in all on page 61.) Or of the sounds of prison as heard from a lonely cell: 'Tinkle, Tinkle. Clank, Clank.' Or of Benazir's choice of a husband: 'Asif Zardari. Asif Zardari. Asif Zardari.' Perhaps it is as well that Ms Bhutto's phantom doesn't attempt too much in the way of drama. When it does, this happens: '"No!" I screamed. "No!"' (On hearing of her brother's death.) And: '"No!" I cried in Eliot Hall, throwing down the newspaper.' (On hearing of the Indian Army's invasion of Bangladesh.) And, most tragically of all, when she dreams her father's execution: '"No!" the scream burst through the knots in my throat. "No!"'

If the worst smell emanating from this book had been that of rotten writing, however, it would have been possible—even proper—to be reasonably forgiving. After all, Ms Bhutto has had one hell of a life, and it ought to be an absorbing tale, even decked out in Joan Collins prose. Unfortunately, the politics stink, too. Daughter of the East, she calls herself, but in truth she's still Zulfikar Ali Bhutto's little girl, still unwilling to admit that the martyred parent even committed the tiniest of sins.

The resulting omissions from the story are as revealing as the bits she puts in. She manages, for example, to get through her entire account of her father's government without once mentioning the little matter of genocide in Baluchistan. She speaks quite correctly of the Zia regime's torture camps, both in Baluchistan and elsewhere—'Chains. Blocks of ice. Chilis inserted into the prisoners' rectums'—but draws a daughterly veil over the Bhutto people's very similar misdeeds. She fails entirely to mention Bhutto's strenuous efforts at election-rigging in 1977, efforts which, by giving him a victory of ludicrously implausible proportions, gave Zia his opening, allowing him to take over on the pretext of holding new, non-controversial polls. Worst of all, she falsifies Bhutto's role in the events leading to the secession of Bangladesh to a quite scandalous degree.

In Benazir's version, the blame is placed firmly on the shoulders of Sheikh Mujib, leader of the then East Pakistani Awami League. After the 1970 elections, Benazir says, 'instead of working with my father, . . . Mujib instigated an independence movement . . . Mujib showed an obstinacy the logic of which to this day defies me.' You feel like using words of one syllable to explain. Listen, dear child, the man had *won*, and it was your father who dug in his heels . . . in the elections of 1970, the Awami League won an absolute majority of all seats in Pakistan's two 'Wings' combined. Mujib had every right to insist, 'obstinately', on being Prime Minister, and it was Bhutto and General Yahya Khan who conspired to prevent this from happening. *That* was how the war of secession began, but you wouldn't know it from reading this book.

It is depressing to find Benazir still being so daughterly. She is a brave woman, has had a hard life and has come a long way as a politician from the inexperienced days when she would issue Zia with ultimatums she could not enforce. In Pakistan's forthcoming elections Benazir Bhutto and the People's Party represent Pakistan's best hope, and if I had a vote in those elections, I would probably cast it in her favour. But this book's naïvety, and its willingness to turn a blind eye to unpalatable facts, are indications of the faintness, the hollowness of that hope. If Benazir is the best, you can guess what the rest are like.

Her book does, inevitably, have its moments, when, for example, she tells us how she mistook Hubert Humphrey for Bob Hope, or when she gives us the behind-the-scenes dope on the post-Bangladesh peace negotiations at Simla between Mrs Gandhi and Mr Bhutto. And by far the most powerful chapter is the one about the farcical trial and subsequent execution of Bhutto by that fearsome 'cartoon', Zia ul-Haq. But by the end it's Benazir's difficulty with cogitation that strikes one most forcefully.

On my beloved's forehead, his hair is shining, Benazir's ghost sings at the henna ceremony preceding the marriage to Asif Asif Asif. On his forehead, eh? Well, no highbrow he, by all accounts, and on this evidence, his arranged marriage looks like a perfect match.

1988

3

'COMMONWEALTH LITERATURE' DOES NOT EXIST

ANITA DESAI

KIPLING

HOBSON-JOBSON

'COMMONWEALTH LITERATURE'
DOES NOT EXIST

When I was invited to speak at the 1983 English Studies Seminar in Cambridge, the lady from the British Council offered me a few words of reassurance. 'It's all right,' I was told, 'for the purposes of our seminar, English studies are taken to include Commonwealth literature.' At all other times, one was forced to conclude, these two would be kept strictly apart, like squabbling children, or sexually incompatible pandas, or, perhaps, like unstable, fissile materials whose union might cause explosions.

A few weeks later I was talking to a literature don—a specialist, I ought to say, in *English* literature—a friendly and perceptive man. 'As a Commonwealth writer,' he suggested, 'you probably find, don't you, that there's a kind of liberty, certain advantages, in occupying, as you do, a position on the periphery?'

And then a British magazine published, in the same issue, interviews with Shiva Naipaul, Buchi Emecheta and myself. In my interview, I admitted that I had begun to find this strange term, 'Commonwealth literature', unhelpful and even a little distasteful; and I was interested to read that in *their* interviews, both Shiva Naipaul and Buchi Emecheta, in their own ways, said much the same thing. The three interviews appeared, therefore, under the headline: 'Commonwealth writers . . . but don't call them that!'

By this point, the Commonwealth was becoming unpopular with me.

Isn't this the very oddest of beasts, I thought—a school of literature whose supposed members deny vehemently that they belong to it. Worse, these denials are simply disregarded! It seems the creature has taken on a life of its own. So when I was invited to a conference about the animal in—of all places—Sweden, I thought I'd better go along to take a closer look at it.

The conference was beautifully organized, packed with erudite and sophisticated persons capable of discoursing at length about the new spirit of experiment in English-language writing in the Philippines. Also, I was able to meet writers from all over the world—or, rather, the Commonwealth. It was such a seductive environment that it almost persuaded me that the subject under discussion actually existed, and was not simply a fiction, and a fiction of a unique type, at that, in that it has been created solely by critics and academics, who have then proceeded to believe in it wholeheartedly . . . but the doubts did, in spite of all temptations to succumb, persist.

Many of the delegates, I found, were willing freely to admit that the term 'Commonwealth literature' was a bad one. South Africa and Pakistan, for instance, are not members of the Commonwealth, but their authors apparently belong to its literature. On the other hand, England, which, as far as I'm aware, has not been expelled from the Commonwealth quite yet, has been excluded from its literary manifestation. For obvious reasons. It would never do to include English literature, the great sacred thing itself, with this bunch of upstarts, huddling together under this new and badly made umbrella.

At the Commonwealth literature conference I talked with and listened to the Australian poet Randolph Stow; the West Indian, Wilson Harris; Ngugi wa Thiong'o from Kenya; Anita Desai from India and the Canadian novelist Aritha van Herk. I became quite sure that our differences were so much more significant than our similarities, that it was impossible to say what 'Commonwealth literature'—the idea which had, after all, made possible our assembly—might conceivably mean. Van Herk spoke eloquently about the problem of drawing imaginative maps of the great emptinesses of Canada; Wilson Harris soared into great flights of metaphysical lyricism and high abstraction; Anita Desai spoke in whispers, her novel the novel of sensibility, and I wondered what on earth she could be held to have in common with the committed Marxist Ngugi, an overtly political writer, who expressed his rejection of the English language by reading his own work in

Swahili, with a Swedish version read by his translator, leaving the rest of us completely bemused. Now obviously this great diversity would be entirely natural in a general literature conference—but this was a particular school of literature, and I was trying to work out what that school was supposed to be.

The nearest I could get to a definition sounded distinctly patronizing: 'Commonwealth literature', it appears, is that body of writing created, I think, in the English language, by persons who are not themselves white Britons, or Irish, or citizens of the United States of America. I don't know whether black Americans are citizens of this bizarre Commonwealth or not. Probably not. It is also uncertain whether citizens of Commonwealth countries writing in languages other than English—Hindi, for example—or who switch out of English, like Ngugi, are permitted into the club or asked to keep out.

By now 'Commonwealth literature' was sounding very unlikeable indeed. Not only was it a ghetto, but it was actually an exclusive ghetto. And the effect of creating such a ghetto was, is, to change the meaning of the far broader term 'English literature'—which I'd always taken to mean simply the literature of the English language—into something far narrower, something topographical, nationalistic, possibly even racially segregationist.

It occurred to me, as I surveyed this muddle, that the category is a chimera, and in very precise terms. The word has of course come to mean an unreal, monstrous creature of the imagination; but you will recall that the classical chimera was a monster of a rather special type. It had the head of a lion, the body of a goat and a serpent's tail. This is to say, it could exist only in dreams, being composed of elements which could not possibly be joined together in the real world.

The dangers of unleashing such a phantom into the groves of literature are, it seems to me, manifold. As I mentioned, there is the effect of creating a ghetto, and that, in turn, does lead to a ghetto mentality amongst some of its occupants. Also, the creation of a false category can and does lead to excessively narrow, and sometimes misleading readings of some of the artists it is held to include; and again, the existence—or putative existence—of the beast distracts attention from what is actually worth looking at, what is actually going on. I thought it might be worth spending a few minutes reflecting further on these dangers.

I'll begin from an obvious starting place. English is by now the world language. It achieved this status partly as a result of the physical colonization of a quarter of the globe by the British, and it remains ambiguous but central to the affairs of just about all the countries to whom it was given, along with mission schools, trunk roads and the rules of cricket, as a gift of the British colonizers.

But its present-day pre-eminence is not solely—perhaps not even primarily—the result of the British legacy. It is also the effect of the primacy of the United States of America in the affairs of the world. This second impetus towards English could be termed a kind of linguistic neo-colonialism, or just plain pragmatism on the part of many of the world's governments and educationists, according to your point of view.

As for myself, I don't think it is always necessary to take up the anti-colonial—or is it post-colonial?—cudgels against English. What seems to me to be happening is that those peoples who were once colonized by the language are now rapidly remaking it, domesticating it, becoming more and more relaxed about the way they use it—assisted by the English language's enormous flexibility and size, they are carving out large territories for themselves within its frontiers.

To take the case of India, only because it's the one with which I'm most familiar. The debate about the appropriateness of English in post-British India has been raging ever since 1947; but today, I find, it is a debate which has meaning only for the older generation. The children of independent India seem not to think of English as being irredeemably tainted by its colonial provenance. They use it as an Indian language, as one of the tools they have to hand.

(I am simplifying, of course, but the point is broadly true.) There is also an interesting North–South divide in Indian attitudes to English. In the North, in the so-called 'Hindi belt', where the capital, Delhi, is located, it is possible to think of Hindi as a future national language; but in South India, which is at present suffering from the attempts of central government to *impose* this national language on it, the resentment of Hindi is far greater than of English. After spending quite some time in South India, I've become convinced that English is an essential language in India, not only because of its technical vocabularies and the international communication which it makes possible, but also simply to permit two Indians to talk to each other in a tongue which neither party hates.

Incidentally, in West Bengal, where there is a State-led move against English, the following graffito, a sharp dig at the State's Marxist chief minister, Jyoti Basu, appeared on a wall, in English: it said, 'My son won't learn English; your son won't learn English; but Jyoti Basu will send his son abroad to learn English.'

One of the points I want to make is that what I've said indicates, I hope, that Indian society and Indian literature have a complex and developing relationship with the English language. This kind of post-colonial dialectic is propounded as one of the unifying factors in 'Commonwealth literature'; but it clearly does not exist, or at least is far more peripheral to the problems of literatures in Canada, Australia, even South Africa. Every time you examine the general theories of 'Commonwealth literature' they come apart in your hands.

English literature has its Indian branch. By this I mean the literature of the English language. This literature is also Indian literature. There is no incompatibility here. If history creates complexities, let us not try to simplify them.

So: English is an Indian literary language, and by now, thanks to writers like Tagore, Desani, Chaudhuri, Mulk Raj Anand, Raja Rao, Anita Desai and others, it has quite a pedigree. Now it is certainly true that the English-language literatures of England, Ireland and the USA are older than, for example, the Indian; so it's possible that 'Commonwealth literature' is no more than an ungainly name for the world's younger English literatures. If that were true or, rather, if that were all, it would be a relatively unimportant misnomer. But it isn't all. Because the term is not used simply to describe, or even misdescribe, but also to *divide*. It permits academic institutions, publishers, critics and even readers to dump a large segment of English literature into a box and then more or less ignore it. At best, what is called 'Commonwealth literature' is positioned *below* English literature 'proper'—or, to come back to my friend the don, it places Eng. Lit. at the centre and the rest of the world at the periphery. How depressing that such a view should persist in the study of literature long after it has been discarded in the study of everything else English.

What is life like inside the ghetto of 'Commonwealth literature'? Well, every ghetto has its own rules, and this one is no exception.

One of the rules, one of the ideas on which the edifice rests, is that literature is an expression of nationality. What Commonwealth literature finds interesting in Patrick White is his Australianness; in Doris Lessing, her Africanness; in V. S. Naipaul, his West Indianness, although I doubt that anyone would have the nerve to say so to his face. Books are almost always praised for using motifs and symbols out of the author's own national tradition, or when their form echoes some traditional form, obviously pre-English, and when the influences at work upon the writer can be seen to be wholly internal to the culture from which he 'springs'. Books which mix traditions, or which seek consciously to break with tradition, are often treated as highly suspect. To give one example. A few years ago the Indian poet, Arun Kolatkar, who works with equal facility in English and Marathi, wrote, in English, an award-winning series of poems called *Jejuri*, the account of his visit to a Hindu temple town. (Ironically, I should say, it won the Commonwealth Poetry Prize.) The poems are marvellous, contemporary, witty, and in spite of their subject they are the work of a non-religious man. They aroused the wrath of one of the doyens of Commonwealth literary studies in India, Professor C. D. Narasimhaiah, who, while admitting the brilliance of the poems, accused Kolatkar of making his work irrelevant by seeking to defy tradition.

What we are facing here is the bogy of Authenticity. This is something which the Indian art critic Geeta Kapur has explored in connection with modern Indian painting, but it applies equally well to literature. 'Authenticity' is the respectable child of old-fashioned exoticism. It demands that sources, forms, style, language and symbol all derive from a supposedly homogeneous and unbroken tradition. Or else. What is revealing is that the term, so much in use inside the little world of 'Commonwealth literature', and always as a term of praise, would seem ridiculous outside this world. Imagine a novel being eulogized for being 'authentically English', or 'authentically German'. It would seem absurd. Yet such absurdities persist in the ghetto.

In my own case, I have constantly been asked whether I am British, or Indian. The formulation 'Indian-born British writer' has been invented to explain me. But, as I said last night, my new book deals with Pakistan. So what now? 'British-resident Indo-Pakistani writer'? You see the folly of trying to contain writers inside passports.

One of the most absurd aspects of this quest for national authenticity is that—as far as India is concerned, anyway—it is completely fallacious to suppose that there is such a thing as a pure, unalloyed tradition from which to draw. The only people who seriously believe this are religious extremists. The rest of us understand that the very essence of Indian culture is that we possess a mixed tradition, a *mélange* of elements as disparate as ancient Mughal and contemporary Coca-Cola American. To say nothing of Muslim, Buddhist, Jain, Christian, Jewish, British, French, Portuguese, Marxist, Maoist, Trotskyist, Vietnamese, capitalist, and of course Hindu elements. Eclecticism, the ability to take from the world what seems fitting and to leave the rest, has always been a hallmark of the Indian tradition, and today it is at the centre of the best work being done both in the visual arts and in literature. Yet eclecticism is not really a nice word in the lexicon of 'Commonwealth literature'. So the reality of the mixed tradition is replaced by the fantasy of purity.

You will perhaps have noticed that the purpose of this literary ghetto—like that of all ghettos, perhaps—is to confine, to restrain. Its rules are basically conservative. Tradition is all; radical breaches with the past are frowned upon. No wonder so many of the writers claimed by 'Commonwealth literature' deny that they have anything to do with it.

I said that the concept of 'Commonwealth literature' did disservice to some writers, leading to false readings of their work; in India, I think this is true of the work of Ruth Jhabvala and, to a lesser extent, Anita Desai. You see, looked at from the point of view that literature must be nationally connected and even committed, it becomes simply impossible to understand the cast of mind and vision of a rootless intellect like Jhabvala's. In Europe, of course, there are enough instances of uprooted, wandering writers and even peoples to make Ruth Jhabvala's work readily comprehensible; but by the rules of the Commonwealth ghetto, she is beyond the pale. As a result, her reputation in India is much lower than it is in the West. Anita Desai, too, gets into trouble when she states with complete honesty that her work has no Indian models. The novel is a Western form, she says, so the influences on her are Western. Yet her delicate but tough fictions are magnificent studies of Indian life. This confuses the cohorts of the Commonwealth. But then, where 'Commonwealth literature' is concerned, confusion is the norm.

I also said that the creation of this phantom category served to obscure what was really going on, and worth talking about. To expand on this, let me say that if we were to forget about 'Commonwealth literature', we might see that there is a kind of commonality about much literature, in many languages, emerging from those parts of the world which one could loosely term the less powerful, or the powerless. The magical realism of the Latin Americans influences Indian-language writers in India today. The rich, folk-tale quality of a novel like *Sandro of Chegem*, by the Muslim Russian Fazil Iskander, finds its parallels in the work—for instance—of the Nigerian, Amos Tutuola, or even Cervantes. It is possible, I think, to begin to theorize common factors between writers from these societies—poor countries, or deprived minorities in powerful countries—and to say that much of what is new in world literature comes from this group. This seems to me to be a 'real' theory, bounded by frontiers which are neither political nor linguistic but imaginative. And it is developments of this kind which the chimera of 'Commonwealth literature' obscures.

This transnational, cross-lingual process of pollination is not new. The works of Rabindranath Tagore, for example, have long been widely available in Spanish-speaking America, thanks to his close friendship with the Argentinian intellectual Victoria Ocampo. Thus an entire generation, or even two, of South American writers have read *Gitanjali*, *The Home and the World* and other works, and some, like Mario Vargas Llosa, say that they found them very exciting and stimulating.

If this 'Third World literature' is one development obscured by the ghost of 'Commonwealth literature', then 'Commonwealth literature's' emphasis on writing in English distracts attention from much else that is worth our attention. I tried to show how in India the whole issue of language was a subject of deep contention. It is also worth saying that major work is being done in India in many languages other than English; yet outside India there is just about no interest in any of this work. The Indo-Anglians seize all the limelight. Very little is translated; very few of the best writers—Premchand, Anantha Moorthy—or the best novels are known, even by name.

To go on in this vein: it strikes me that, at the moment, the greatest area of friction in Indian literature has nothing to do with English literature, but with the effects of the hegemony of Hindi on the literatures of other Indian languages, particularly other North Indian languages. I recently met the distinguished Gujarati novelist, Suresh Joshi. He told me that he could write in Hindi but felt obliged to write in Gujarati because it was a language under threat. Not from English, or the West: from Hindi. In two or three generations, he said,

Gujarati could easily die. And he compared it, interestingly, to the state of the Czech language under the yoke of Russian, as described by Milan Kundera.

This is clearly a matter of central importance for Indian literature. 'Commonwealth literature' is not interested in such matters.

It strikes me that my title may not really be accurate. There is clearly such a thing as 'Commonwealth literature', because even ghosts can be made to exist if you set up enough faculties, if you write enough books and appoint enough research students. It does not exist in the sense that writers do not write it, but that is of minor importance. So perhaps I should rephrase myself: 'Commonwealth literature' should not exist. If it did not, we could appreciate writers for what they are, whether in English or not; we could discuss literature in terms of its real groupings, which may well be national, which may well be linguistic, but which may also be international, and based on imaginative affinities; and as far as Eng. Lit. itself is concerned, I think that if *all* English literatures could be studied together, a shape would emerge which would truly reflect the new shape of the language in the world, and we could see that Eng. Lit. has never been in better shape, because the world language now also possesses a world literature, which is proliferating in every conceivable direction.

The English language ceased to be the sole possession of the English some time ago. Perhaps 'Commonwealth literature' was invented to delay the day when we rough beasts actually slouch into Bethlehem. In which case, it's time to admit that the centre cannot hold.

1983

ANITA DESAI

The subject of Anita Desai's fiction has, thus far, been solitude. Her most memorable creations—the old woman, Nanda Kaul, in *Fire on the Mountain*, or Bim in *Clear Light of Day*—have been isolated, singular figures. And the books themselves have been private universes, illuminated by the author's perceptiveness, delicacy of language and sharp wit, but remaining, in a sense, as solitary, as separate, as their characters.

Her novel *In Custody* is, therefore, a doubly remarkable piece of work; because in this magnificent book Anita Desai has chosen to write not of solitude but of friendship, of the perils and responsibilities of joining oneself to others rather than holding oneself apart. And at the same time she has written a very public fiction, shedding the reserve of her earlier work to take on such sensitive themes as the unease of minority communities in modern India, the new imperialism of the Hindi language and the decay that is, tragically, all too evident throughout the fissuring body of Indian society. The courage of the novel is considerable.

The story contrasts the slow death of a false friendship and the painful birth of a true one. Deven, a lover of Urdu poetry who has been obliged to teach Hindi in a small-town college for financial reasons, is bullied by his boyhood chum Murad to go to Delhi and interview the great, ageing Urdu poet Nur Shahjehanabadi for Murad's rather ridiculous magazine. The relationship between the weak, unworldly Deven and the posturing bully Murad seems at first like something out of R. K. Narayan. But Narayan's meek characters usually stand for traditional India and his bullies for some aspect of the modern world. *In Custody* has no such allegorical intentions. Murad's appalling behaviour—he all but ruins Deven while appearing to help, wasting money on a poor tape recorder for the interview, then arranging for an incompetent 'assistant' who completely fouls up the recording, and finally refusing to settle the bills arising from the event—makes the fine, unsentimental point that our friends are as likely to destroy us as our enemies.

But the novel's emotional heart lies in the relationship between Deven and his hero Nur. At first the young teacher's dream of the literary giant appears to have become true. Then, superbly, we are shown the feet of clay: Nur beset by pigeons and other, human, hangers-on; Nur gluttonous, Nur drunk, Nur vomiting on the floor. Here allegory perhaps is intended. 'How can there be Urdu poetry,' the poet asks rhetorically, 'when there is no Urdu language left?' And his decrepitude—like the derelict condition of the once-grand ancestral home of Deven's fellow-lecturer, the Muslim Siddiqui—is a figure of the decline of the language and the culture for which he stands. The poet's very name, Nur, is ironic: the word means *light*, but it is a light grown very dim indeed.

Once again, however, the central point being made is not allegorical. The beauty of *In Custody* is that what seems to be a story of inevitable tragedies—the tragicomedy of Deven's attempts to get his interview being the counterpoint to the more sombre tragedy of Nur—turns out to be a tale of triumph over these tragedies. At the very end, Deven, beset by crises, hounded by Nur's demands for money (for a cataract operation, for a pilgrimage to Mecca), understands that he has become the 'custodian' both of Nur's friendship and of his poetry,

> and that meant he was the custodian of Nur's very
> soul and spirit. It was a great distinction. He could
> not deny or abandon that under any pressure.

Once Deven has understood this, the calamities of his life seem suddenly unimportant. 'He would run to meet them,' and he does.

The high exaltation of such a conclusion is saved from lushness by Anita Desai's wholly admirable lack of sentimentality. Her vision is unsparing: Urdu may be dying, but in the character of Siddiqui she shows us the worst side of Urdu/Muslim culture—its snobbishness, its eternal nostalgia for the lost glory of an early Empire. And, most significantly, we see that while Deven may be willing to embrace his responsibilities to Nur, he utterly fails to do likewise with Nur's wife or his own. He feels too threatened by the former even to read her poetry, and too careless of his own poor Sarla with her faded dreams of 'fan, phone, frigidaire' to build any sort of real relationship with her at all. That Anita Desai has so brilliantly portrayed the world of male friendship in order to demonstrate how this, too, is a part of the process by which women are excluded from power over their own lives is a bitter irony behind what is an anguished, but not at all a bitter book.

1984

KIPLING

In Luis Buñuel's last film, *Cet obscur objet de désir*, the heroine was played by two actresses, one cool and poised, the other fiery and sensual. The two women looked utterly dissimilar, yet it was not uncommon for people to watch the entire movie without noticing the device. Their need to believe in the homogeneity of personality was so deeply rooted as to make them discount the evidence of their own eyes.

I once thought of borrowing Buñuel's idea for a TV programme about Rudyard Kipling. I wanted him to be played by an Indian actor as well as an English one, to speak Hindi in some scenes and English in others. After all, when the child Rudyard was admitted to his parents' presence, the servants would have to remind him to 'speak English now to Mama and Papa.' The influence of India on Kipling—on his picture of the world as well as his language—resulted in what has always struck me as a personality in conflict with itself, part bazaar-boy, part sahib. In the early Indian stories (this essay confines itself to the two collections, *Soldiers Three* and *In Black and White*), that conflict is to be found everywhere, and Kipling does not always seem fully conscious of it. (By the time he wrote *Kim*, twelve years later, his control had grown. But Kim's torn loyalties have never seemed as interesting to me as the ambiguous, shifting relationships between the Indians and the English in, for example, 'On the City Wall'.)

The early Kipling is a writer with a storm inside him, and he creates a mirror-storm of contradictory responses in the reader, particularly, I think, if the reader is Indian. I have never been able to read Kipling calmly. Anger and delight are incompatible emotions, yet these early stories do indeed have the power simultaneously to infuriate and to entrance.

Kipling's racial bigotry is often excused on the grounds that he merely reflected in his writing the attitudes of his age. It's hard for members of the allegedly inferior race to accept such an excuse. Ought we to exculpate anti-Semites in Nazi

Germany on the same grounds? If Kipling had maintained any sort of distance between himself and the attitudes he recorded, it would be a different matter. But, as story after story makes plain, the author's attitudes—the attitudes, that is, of Kipling as played by the English actor—are identical with those of his white characters. The Indians he portrays are wife-killers ('Dray Wara Yow Dee'), scamps ('At Howli Thana'), betrayers of their own brothers ('Gemini'), unfaithful wives ('At Twenty-Two') and the like. Even the Eurasian Mrs DeSussa in 'Private Learoyd's Story' is a fat figure of fun. Indians bribe witnesses, desert their political leaders, and are gullible, too: 'Overmuch tenderness . . . has bred a strong belief among many natives that the native is capable of administering the country.' Mr Kipling knows better. 'It [India] will never stand alone.'

But there is the Indian actor, too; Ruddy Baba as well as Kipling Sahib. And it is on account of this fellow that Kipling remains so popular in India. This popularity looks like, and indeed is, an extraordinary piece of cultural generosity. But it is real. No other Western writer has ever known India as Kipling knew it, and it is this knowledge of place, and procedure, and detail that gives his stories their undeniable authority. The plot of 'Black Jack' turns on the operational differences between two different kinds of rifle; while the story 'In Flood Time' owes its quality to Kipling's precise and magnificent description of a swollen river in the monsoon rains. Nor could he have created the salon of the courtesan Lalun in 'On the City Wall' had he not been a regular visitor to such establishments himself.

Not all the stories have stood the test of time—'The Sending of Dana Da' seems particularly flimsy—but all of them are packed with information about a lost world. It used to be said that one read in order to learn something, and nobody can teach you British India better than Rudyard Kipling.

These stories are, above all, experiments in voice. In *Soldiers Three*, Kipling has sought to give voice to the ordinary British soldier whom he admired so much. (The original version of the first story, 'The God from the Machine', was published in the Railway Library edition with a dedication to 'that very strong man, T. ATKINS, . . . in all admiration and good fellowship'.) How well he has succeeded is open to dispute.

There can be no doubt that he knew his characters inside out, and, by abandoning the world of the officer classes in favour of the view from the ranks, opened up a unique subculture that would otherwise have been very largely lost to literature; or that many of these are very good indeed. 'The Big Drunk Draf' ', in which a company of men on its way to board the ship for England nearly turns upon its young officer, but is thwarted by the wiles of Terence Mulvaney and the courage of the officer himself, is one such splendid tale; while 'Black Jack', which tells of a murder plot, and owes something—as Kipling admitted in the Railway Library edition—to Robert Louis Stevenson's story 'The Suicide Club', is my own favourite yarn.

But the surface of the text is made strangely impenetrable by Kipling's determination to render the speech of his three musketeers in thick Oirish (Mulvaney), broad Cockney (Ortheris) and ee-ba-goom Northern (Learoyd). Mulvaney's 'menowdherin', an' minandherin', an' blandandherin'' soon grows tiresome, and Ortheris drops so many initial H's and final G's and D's that the apostrophes begin to swim before our eyes. George Orwell suggested, of Kipling's verse, that such mimicry of lower-class speech actually made the poems worse than they would be in standard English, and 'restored' some of the lines to prove his point. I must confess to feeling something similar about these stories. There is something condescending about Kipling's mimicry:

> 'Ah doan't care. Ah would not care, but ma heart is plaayin' tivvy-tivvy on ma ribs. Let ma die! Oh, leave ma die!'

Learoyd's suffering is curiously diminished by the music-hall orthography. Kipling's affection for the Soldiers Three can often seem *de haut en bas*.

The other main point of linguistic interest in the *Soldiers*

Three stories is the incorporation of a number of Hindi words and phrases. This is kept at a pidgin, *Hobson-Jobson* level: 'Take him away, an' av you iver say wan wurrud about fwhat you've *dekkoed*, I'll *marrow* you till your own wife won't *sumjao* who you are!' The Indian critic S. S. Azfar Hussain has pointed out that, of the eleven Hindi sentences which appear in *Soldiers Three* (and these are the only complete Hindi sentences to be found in the whole of Kipling's *œuvre*), ten are imperative sentences; and nine of these are orders from English masters to their servants. It is important, then, not to overstate the extent to which Kipling's Indian childhood influenced his work. It seems certain that Kipling did not remain literate in Hindi or Urdu. Dr Hussain reports that 'Kipling's manuscripts in the British Museum . . . show that he tried several times to write his name in Urdu, but oddly enough did not succeed once. It reads "Kinling", "Kiplig" and "Kipenling".'

In the *Soldiers Three* stories the Hindi/Urdu words are simply sprinkled over the text, like curry powder. The *In Black and White* stories attempt something altogether more ambitious. Here it is the Indians who have been given voice, and since, in many cases, they would not actually be speaking English, a whole idiolect has had to be invented.

Much of this invented Indiaspeak is so exclamatory, so full of 'Ahoo! Ahoo!' and 'Ahi! Ahi!' and even 'Auggrh!' as to suggest that Indians are a people incapable of anything but outbursts. Some of it sounds very like the salaaming exoticism of the pantomime: 'The mind of an old man is like the *numah*-tree. Fruit, bud, blossom, and the dead leaves of all the years of the past flourish together.' Sometimes Kipling's own convictions place impossible sentences in Indian mouths: 'Great is the mercy of these fools of English' is one such contorted utterance. But much of it is brilliantly *right*. The device of literal translations of metaphors is certainly exotic, but it does also lend a kind of authenticity to the dialogue: '. . . it is the Sahib himself! My heart is made fat and my eye glad.' And the Indian *banias*, policemen, miners and whores sound Indian in a way that—for example—

Forster's never do. This is because they think like Indians, or at least they do when Kipling lets them. For the problem of condescension remains. Kipling could never have dedicated a story to the 'natives' as he did to 'T. Atkins', after all. And if the tone of *Soldiers Three* seems patronizing at times, in *In Black and White* it can sound far, far worse.

Kipling's Indian women, in particular, are (at best) the cause of trouble and danger for men—the Hindu heroine of 'In Flood Time' is the cause of a deadly rivalry between a Muslim and a Sikh—while, at worst, they cheat on their old, blind husbands as Unda does in 'At Twenty-Two', or on their ferocious Pathan husbands, as the 'woman of the Abazai' does, with unhappy results, in 'Dray Wara Yow Dee':

> And she bowed her head, and I smote it off at the neck-bone so that it leaped between my feet. Thereafter the rage of our people came upon me, and I hacked off the breasts, that the men of Little Malikand might know the crime . . .

And yet, and yet. It is impossible not to admire Kipling's skill at creating convincing portraits of horse-thieves, or rural policemen, or Punjabi money-lenders. The story of how the blind miner Janki Meah finds the way out of a collapsed mine may feature a flighty female, but the world, and the psychology, and the language of the men are superlatively created.

The most remarkable story in this collection is unquestionably 'On the City Wall'. In it, the two Kiplings are openly at war with one another; and, in the end, it seems to me, the Indian Kipling manages to subvert what the English Kipling takes to be the meaning of the tale.

'On the City Wall' is not narrated by an Indian voice, but by an English journalist who, in common with 'all the City', is fond of visiting Lalun's brothel on the Lahore city wall to smoke and to talk. The brothel is presented as an oasis of peace in the turbulence of India; here Muslims, Hindus, Sikhs and Europeans mingle without conflict. Only one group is excluded: 'Lalun admits no Jews here.' One of the most vocal figures at Lalun's is Wali Dad, the Westernized young man who calls himself 'a Product—a Demnition Product. *That* also I owe to you and yours: that I cannot make an end to my sentence without quoting from your authors.' The deracinated—or seemingly deracinated—Wali Dad is one of the story's main actors. Another is the imprisoned revolutionary Khem Singh, who is kept locked in Fort Amara. The third major 'character' is the crowd of Shia Muslims thronging the city streets, for it is the time of the Muharram processions, and violence is in the air.

Kipling's treatment of Wali Dad is, by any standards, pretty appalling. He builds him up purely in order to knock him down, and when the young man, seeing the frenzy of the Muharram processions, is transformed into a sort of savage— 'His nostrils were distended, his eyes were fixed, and he was smiting himself softly on the breast,' Kipling tells us, and makes Wali Dad say things like 'These swine of Hindus! We shall be killing kine in their temples tonight!'—the meaning is clear: Western civilization has been no more than a veneer; a native remains a native beneath his European jackets and ties. Blood will out. Wali Dad's regression is not only unbelievable; it also shows us that Kipling has failed to appreciate that it was among these very people, these Wali Dads, Jawaharlal Nehrus and M. K. Gandhis, that the Indian revolution would be made; that they would assimilate Western culture without being deracinated by it, and then turn their knowledge against the British, and gain the victory.

In the story's other main narrative strand, Lalun tricks the narrator into assisting in the escape of the revolutionary, Khem Singh. Kipling suggests that the old leader's followers have lost their appetite for revolution, so that Khem Singh has no option but to return voluntarily into captivity. But his narrator understands the meaning of the story rather better than that: 'I was thinking,' he concludes, 'how I had become Lalun's Vizier, after all.' Louis Cornell, in his study of this story, suggests rather oddly that 'the ostensible climax . . . where the reporter discovers that he has unwittingly helped a revolutionary to escape from the police, is too minor an

incident, placed too close to the end of the tale, to seem in
proportion with the rest of the story.' It seems to me not at all
unusual for a climax to be placed near a story's end; and, far
from being a minor incident, Khem Singh's escape seems
central to the story's significance. India, Lalun-India, bewitches
and tricks the English, in the character of the reporter; the
master is made the servant, the Vizier. So that the conclusion
of the very text in which Kipling states most emphatically
his belief that India can never stand alone, without British
leadership, and in which he ridicules Indian attempts to
acquire the superior culture of England, leaves us with an
image of the inability of the sahibs to comprehend what they
pretend to rule. Lalun deceived the narrator; Wali Dad
deceived the author. 'On the City Wall' is Ruddy Baba's
victory over Kipling Sahib. And now that the 'great idol
called *Pax Britannica* which, as the newspapers say, lives
between Peshawar and Cape Comorin,' has been broken, the
story stands, along with the others in this volume, as a
testament to the old quarrel between colonizer and colonized.
There will always be plenty in Kipling that I will find difficult
to forgive; but there is also enough truth in these stories to
make them impossible to ignore.

1990

HOBSON-JOBSON

The British Empire, many *pundits* now agree, descended like a *juggernaut* upon the *barbicans* of the East, in search of *loot*. The *moguls* of the *raj* went in *palanquins*, smoking *cheroots*, to sip *toddy* or *sherbet* on the *verandahs* of the *gymkhana* club, while the *memsahibs* fretted about the *thugs* in *bandannas* and *dungarees* who roamed the night like *pariahs*, plotting *ghoul*ish deeds.

All the italicized words in the above paragraph can be found, with their Eastern family trees, in *Hobson-Jobson*, the legendary dictionary of British India, on whose reissue Routledge are to be congratulated. These thousand-odd pages bear eloquent testimony to the unparalleled intermingling that took place between English and the languages of India, and while some of the Indian loan-words will be familiar—*pukka, curry, cummerbund*—others should surprise many modern readers.

Did you know, for example, that the word *tank* has Gujarati and Marathi origins? Or that *cash* was originally the Sanskrit *karsha*, 'a weight of silver or gold equal to 1/400th of a *Tula*'? Or that a *shampoo* was a massage, nothing to do with the hair at all, deriving from the imperative form—*champo!*—of the Hindi verb *champna*, 'to knead and press the muscles with the view of relieving fatigue, etc.'? Every column of this book contains revelations like these, written up in a pleasingly idiosyncratic, not to say cranky, style. The authors, Henry Yule and A. C. Burnell, are not averse to ticking off an untrustworthy source, witness their entry under *muddle*, meaning a double, or secretary, or interpreter: 'This word is only known to us from the clever—perhaps too clever—little book quoted below . . . probably a misapprehension of *budlee*.'

The chief interest of *Hobson-Jobson*, though, lies not so much in its etymologies for words still in use, but in the richnesses of what one must call the Anglo-Indian language whose memorial it is, that language which was in regular use just forty years ago and which is now as dead as a dodo. In Anglo-Indian a *jam* was a Gujarati chief, a *sneaker* was 'a large cup (or small basin) with a saucer and cover', a *guinea-pig* was a midshipman on an India-bound boat, an *owl* was a disease, *Macheen* was not a spelling mistake but a name, abbreviated from 'Maha-Cheen', for 'great China'. Even a commonplace word like *cheese* was transformed. The Hindi *chiz*, meaning a thing, gave the English word a new, slangy sense of 'anything good, first-rate in quality, genuine, pleasant or advantageous' as, we are told, in the phrase, 'these cheroots are the real cheese.'

Some of the distortions of Indian words—'perhaps by vulgar lips'—have moved a long way from their sources. It takes an effort of the will to see, in the Anglo-Indian *snow-rupee*, meaning 'authority', the Telugu word *tsanauvu*. The dictionary's own title, chosen, we are told, to help it sell, is of this type. It originates in the cries of *Ya Hasan! Ya Hussain!* uttered by Shia Muslims during the Muharram processions. I don't quite see how the colonial British managed to hear this as *Hobson! Jobson!*, but this is clearly a failure of imagination on my part.

It's just about a century since this volume's first publication, and in 1886 it was actually possible for Yule and Burnell (whom it's tempting to rename Hobson and Jobson) to make puns which conflated Hindi with, of all things, Latin. The Anglo-Indian word *poggle*, a madman, comes from the Hindi *pagal*, and so we're offered the following 'macaronic adage which we fear the non-Indian will fail to appreciate: *pagal et pecunia jaldé separantur.*' (A fool and his money are soon parted.)

British India had absorbed enough of Indian ways to call their Masonic lodges 'jadoogurs' after the Hindi for a place of sorcery, to cry 'kubberdaur' (*khabardaar*) when they meant 'look out', and to 'puckerow' an Indian (catch him) before they started to 'samjao' him—literally, to make him understand something, but, idiomatically, to beat him up.

Strange, then, to find certain well-known words missing. No *kaffir*, no *gully*, not even a *wog*, although there is a *wug*, a

Baloch or Sindhi word meaning either loot or a herd of camels. (*Hobson-Jobson* can be wonderfully imprecise at times.) I thought, too, that a modern appendix might usefully be commissioned, to include the many English words which have taken on, in independent India, new 'Hinglish' meanings. In India today, the prisoner in the dock is the *undertrial*; a boss is often an *incharge*; and, in a sinister euphemism, those who perish at the hands of law enforcement officers are held to have died in a 'police *encounter*'.

To spend a few days with *Hobson-Jobson* is, almost, to regret the passing of the intimate connection that made this linguistic *kedgeree* possible. But then one remembers what sort of connection it was, and is moved to remark—as Rhett Butler once said to Scarlett O'Hara—'Frankly, my dear, I don't give a small copper coin weighing one tolah, eight mashas and seven surkhs, being the fortieth part of a rupee.' Or, to put it more concisely, a *dam*.

1985

4

OUTSIDE THE WHALE

ATTENBOROUGH'S GANDHI

SATYAJIT RAY

HANDSWORTH SONGS

THE LOCATION OF *BRAZIL*

OUTSIDE THE WHALE

Anyone who has switched on the television set, been to the cinema or entered a bookshop in the last few months will be aware that the British Raj, after three and a half decades in retirement, has been making a sort of comeback. After the big-budget fantasy double-bill of *Gandhi* and *Octopussy* we have had the blackface minstrel-show of *The Far Pavilions* in its TV serial incarnation, and immediately afterwards the overpraised *Jewel in the Crown*. I should also include the alleged 'documentary' about Subhas Chandra Bose, Granada Television's *War of the Springing Tiger*, which, in the finest traditions of journalistic impartiality, described India's second-most-revered independence leader as a 'clown'. And lest we begin to console ourselves that the painful experiences are coming to an end, we are reminded that David Lean's film of *A Passage to India* is in the offing. I remember seeing an interview with Mr Lean in *The Times*, in which he explained his reasons for wishing to make a film of Forster's novel. 'I haven't seen Dickie Attenborough's *Gandhi* yet,' he said, 'but as far as I'm aware, nobody has yet succeeded in putting India on the screen.' The Indian film industry, from Satyajit Ray to Mr N. T. Rama Rao, will no doubt feel suitably humbled by the great man's opinion.

These are dark days. Having expressed my reservations about the *Gandhi* film elsewhere, I have no wish to renew my quarrel with Mahatma Dickie. As for *Octopussy*, one can only say that its portrait of modern India was as grittily and uncompromisingly realistic as its depiction of the skill, integrity and sophistication of the British secret services.

In defence of the Mahattenborough, he did allow a few Indians to be played by Indians. (One is becoming grateful for the smallest of mercies.) Those responsible for transferring *The Far Pavilions* to the screen would have no truck with such tomfoolery. True, Indian actors were allowed to play the villains (Saeed Jaffrey, who has turned the Raj revival into a personal cottage industry, with parts in *Gandhi* and *Jewel in the Crown* as well, did his hissing and hand-rubbing party piece; and Sneh Gupta played the selfish princess but, unluckily for her, her entire part consisted of the interminably repeated line, 'Ram Ram'). Meanwhile, the good-guy roles were firmly commandeered by Ben Cross, Christopher Lee, Omar Sharif, and, most memorably, Amy Irving as the good princess, whose make-up person obviously believed that Indian princesses dip their eyes in black ink and get sun-tans on their lips.

Now of course *The Far Pavilions* is the purest bilge. The great processing machines of TV soap-opera have taken the somewhat more fibrous garbage of the M. M. Kaye book and puréed it into easy-swallow, no-chewing-necessary drivel. Thus, the two central characters, both supposedly raised as Indians, have been lobotomized to the point of being incapable of pronouncing their own names. The man calls himself 'A Shock', and the woman 'An Jooly'. Around and about them there is branding of human flesh and snakery and widow-burning by the natives. There are Pathans who cannot speak Pushto. And, to avoid offending the Christian market, we are asked to believe that the child 'A Shock', while being raised by Hindus and Muslims, somehow knew that neither 'way' was for him, and instinctively, when he wished to raise his voice in prayer, 'prayed to the mountains'. It would be easy to conclude that such material could not possibly be taken seriously by anyone, and that it is therefore unnecessary to get worked up about it. Should we not simply rise above the twaddle, switch off our sets and not care?

I should be happier about this, the quietist option—and I shall have more to say about quietism later on—if I did not believe that it matters, it always matters, to name rubbish as rubbish; that to do otherwise is to legitimize it. I should also mind less, were it not for the fact that *The Far Pavilions*, book as well as TV serial, is only the latest in a very long line of fake portraits inflicted by the West on the East. The creation of a false Orient of cruel-lipped princes and dusky slim-hipped maidens, of ungodliness, fire and the sword, has been brilliantly described by Edward Said in his classic study *Orientalism*, in which he makes clear that the purpose of such false portraits was to provide moral, cultural and artistic justification for imperialism and for its underpinning ideology, that of the racial superiority of the Caucasian over the Asiatic. Let me add only that stereotypes are easier to shrug off if yours is not the culture being stereotyped; or, at the very least, if your culture has the power to counterpunch against the stereotype. If the TV screens of the West were regularly filled by equally hyped, big-budget productions depicting the realities of India, one could stomach the odd M. M. Kaye. When praying to the mountains is the norm, the stomach begins to heave.

Paul Scott was M. M. Kaye's agent, and it has always seemed to me a damning indictment of his literary judgement that he believed *The Far Pavilions* to be a good book. Even stranger is the fact that *The Raj Quartet* and the Kaye novel are founded on identical strategies of what, to be polite, one must call borrowing. In both cases, the central plot motifs are lifted from earlier, and much finer novels. In *The Far Pavilions*, the hero Ash ('A Shock'), raised an Indian, discovered to be a sahib, and ever afterwards torn between his two selves, will be instantly recognizable as the cardboard cut-out version of Kipling's Kim. And the rape of Daphne Manners in the Bibighar Gardens derives just as plainly from Forster's *A Passage to India*. But because Kaye and Scott are vastly inferior to the writers they follow, they turn what they touch to pure lead. Where Forster's scene in the Marabar caves retains its ambiguity and mystery, Scott gives us not one rape but a gang assault, and one perpetrated, what is more, by peasants. Smelly persons of the worst sort. So class as well as sex is violated; Daphne gets the works. It is useless, I'm sure, to suggest that if rape must be used as the metaphor of the Indo-British connection, then surely, in the interests of accuracy, it should be the rape of an Indian woman by one or more Englishmen of whatever class. But not even Forster dared to write about such a crime. So much more evocative to conjure up white society's fear of the darkie, of big brown cocks.

You will say I am being unfair; Scott is a writer of a different calibre to M. M. Kaye. What's more, very few of the British characters come at all well out of the *Quartet*—Barbie, Sarah, Daphne, none of the men. (Kaye, reviewing the TV adaptation, found it excessively rude about the British.)

In point of fact, I am not so sure that Scott is so much finer an artist. Like Kaye, he has an instinct for the cliché. Sadistic, bottom-flogging policeman Merrick turns out to be (surprise!) a closet homosexual. His grammar school origins give him (what else?) a chip on the shoulder. And all around him is a galaxy of chinless wonders, regimental *grandes dames*, lushes, empty-headed blondes, silly-asses, plucky young things, good sorts, bad eggs and Russian counts with eyepatches. The overall effect is rather like a literary version of Mulligatawny soup. It tries to taste Indian, but ends up being ultra-parochially British, only with too much pepper.

And yes, Scott is harsh in his portraits of many British characters; but I want to try and make a rather more difficult point, a point about *form*. The *Quartet*'s form tells us, in effect, that the history of the end of the Raj was largely composed of the doings of the officer class and its wife. Indians get walk-ons, but remain, for the most part, bit-players in their own history. Once this form has been set, it scarcely matters that individual fictional Brits get unsympathetic treatment from their author. The form insists that *they are the ones whose stories matter*, and that is so much less than the whole truth that it must be called a falsehood. It will not do to argue that Scott was attempting to portray the British in India, and that such was the nature of imperialist society that the Indians *would* only have had bit-parts. It is no defence to say that a work adopts, in its structure, the very ethic which, in its content and tone, it pretends to dislike. It is, in fact, the case for the prosecution.

I cannot end this brief account of the Raj revival without returning to David Lean, a film director whose mere interviews merit reviews. I have already quoted his masterpiece in *The Times*; here now are three passages from his conversation with Derek Malcolm in the *Guardian* of

23 January, 1984:

(1) Forster was a bit anti-English, anti-Raj and so on. I suppose it's a tricky thing to say, but I'm not so much. I intend to keep the balance more. I don't believe all the English were a lot of idiots. Forster rather made them so. He came down hard against them. I've cut out that bit at the trial where they try to take over the court. Richard [Goodwin, the producer] wanted me to leave it in. But I said no, it just wasn't right. They wouldn't have done that.

(2) As for Aziz, there's a hell of a lot of Indian in him. They're marvellous people but maddening sometimes, you know . . . He's a goose. But he's warm and you like him awfully. I don't mean that in a derogatory way—things just happen. He can't help it. And Miss Quested . . . well, she's a bit of a prig and a bore in the book, you know. I've changed her, made her more sympathetic. Forster wasn't always very good with women.

(3) One other thing. I've got rid of that 'Not yet, not yet' bit. You know, when the Quit India stuff comes up, and we have the passage about driving us into the sea? Forster experts have always said it was important, but the Fielding–Aziz friendship was not sustained by those sort of things. At least I don't think so. The book came out at the time of the trial of General Dyer and had a tremendous success in America for that reason. But I thought that bit rather tacked on. Anyway I see it as a personal not a political story.

Forster's lifelong refusal to permit his novel to be filmed begins to look rather sensible. But once a revisionist enterprise gets under way, the mere wishes of a dead novelist provide no obstacle. And there can be little doubt that in Britain today the refurbishment of the Empire's tarnished image is under way. The continuing decline, the growing poverty and the meanness of spirit of much of Thatcherite Britain encourages many Britons to turn their eyes nostalgically to the lost hour of their precedence. The recrudescence of imperialist ideology and the popularity of Raj fictions put one in mind of the phantom twitchings of an amputated limb. Britain is in danger of entering a condition of cultural psychosis, in which it begins once again to strut and to posture like a great power while, in fact, its power diminishes every year. The jewel in the crown is made, these days, of paste.

Anthony Barnett has cogently argued, in his television essay *Let's Take the 'Great' Out of Britain*, that the idea of a *great* Britain (originally just a collective term for the countries of the British Isles, but repeatedly used to bolster the myth of national grandeur) has bedevilled the actions of all post-war governments. But it was Margaret Thatcher who, in the euphoria of the Falklands victory, most plainly nailed her colours to the old colonial mast, claiming that the success in the South Atlantic proved that the British were still the people 'who had ruled a quarter of the world.' Shortly afterwards she called for a return to Victorian values, thus demonstrating that she had embarked upon a heroic battle against the linear passage of Time.

I am trying to say something which is not easily heard above the clamour of praise for the present spate of British–Indian fictions: that works of art, even works of entertainment, do not come into being in a social and political vacuum; and that the way they operate in a society cannot be separated from politics, from history. For every text, a context; and the rise of Raj revisionism, exemplified by the huge success of these fictions, is the artistic counterpart of the rise of conservative ideologies in modern Britain. And no matter how innocently the writers and film-makers work, no matter how skilfully the actors act (and nobody would deny the brilliance of, for example, the performances of Susan Wooldridge as Daphne and Peggy Ashcroft as Barbie in the TV *Jewel*), they run the grave risk of helping to shore up the conservatism, by offering it the fictional glamour which its reality so grievously lacks.

The title of this essay derives, obviously, from that of an earlier piece (1940) by 1984's other literary phenomenon, Mr Orwell. And as I'm going to dispute its assertions about the relationship between politics and literature, I must of necessity begin by offering a summary of that essay, 'Inside the Whale'.

It opens with a largely admiring analysis of the writing of Henry Miller:

> On the face of it no material could be less promising. When *Tropic of Cancer* was published the Italians were marching into Abyssinia and Hitler's concentration camps were already bulging . . . It did not seem to be a moment at which a novel of outstanding value was likely to be written about American dead-beats cadging drinks in the Latin Quarter. Of course a novelist is not obliged to write directly about contemporary history, but a novelist who simply disregards the major public events of the moment is generally either a footler or a plain idiot. From a mere account of the subject matter of *Tropic of Cancer*, most people would probably assume it to be no more than a bit of naughty-naughty left over from the twenties. Actually, nearly everyone who read it saw at once that it was . . . a very remarkable book. How or why remarkable?

His attempt to answer that question takes Orwell down more and more tortuous roads. He ascribes to Miller the gift of opening up a new world 'not by revealing what is strange, but by revealing what is familiar.' He praises him for using English 'as a spoken language, but spoken *without fear*, i.e., without fear of rhetoric or of the unusual or poetic word. It is a flowing, swelling prose, a prose with rhythms in it.' And most crucially, he likens Miller to Whitman, 'for what he is saying, after all, is "I accept".'

Around here things begin to get a little bizarre. Orwell quite fairly points out that to say 'I accept' in life in the thirties 'is to say that you accept concentration camps, rubber truncheons, Hitler, Stalin, bombs, aeroplanes, tinned food, machine-guns, *putsches*, purges, slogans, Bedaux belts, gas masks, submarines, spies, provocateurs, press censorship, secret prisons, aspirins, Hollywood films and political murders.' (No, I don't know what a Bedaux belt is, either.) But in the very next paragraph he tells us that 'precisely because, in one sense, he is passive to experience, Miller is able to get nearer to the ordinary man than is possible to more purposive writers. For the ordinary man is also passive.' Characterizing the ordinary man as a victim, he then claims that only the Miller type of victim-books, 'non-political, . . . non-ethical, . . . non-literary, . . . non-contemporary', can speak with the people's voice. So to accept concentration camps and Bedaux belts turns out to be pretty worthwhile, after all.

There follows an attack on literary fashion. Orwell, a thirty-seven-year-old patriarch, tells us that 'when one says that a writer is fashionable one practically always means that he is admired by people under thirty.' At first he picks easy targets—A. E. Housman's 'roselipt maidens' and Rupert Brooke's 'Grantchester' ('a sort of accumulated vomit from a stomach stuffed with place-names'). But then the polemic is widened to include 'the movement', the politically committed generation of Auden and Spender and MacNeice. 'On the whole,' Orwell says, 'the literary history of the thirties seems to justify the opinion that a writer does well to keep out of politics.' It is true he scores some points, as when he indicates the bourgeois, boarding-school origins of just about all these literary radicals, or when he connects the popularity of Communism among British intellectuals to the general middle-class disillusion with all traditional values: 'Patriotism, religion, the Empire, the family, the sanctity of marriage, the Old School Tie, birth, breeding, honour, discipline—anyone of ordinary education could turn the whole lot of them inside out in three minutes.' In this vacuum of ideology, he suggests, there was still 'the need for something to believe in', and Stalinist Communism filled the void.

Returning to Henry Miller, Orwell takes up and extends

Miller's comparison of Anaïs Nin to Jonah in the whale's belly.

> The whale's belly is simply a womb big enough for an adult . . . a storm that would sink all the battleships in the world would hardly reach you as an echo . . . Miller himself is inside the whale, . . . a willing Jonah . . . He feels no impulse to alter or control the process that he is undergoing. He has performed the essential Jonah act of allowing himself to be swallowed, remaining passive, *accepting*. It will be seen what this amounts to. It is a species of quietism.

And at the end of this curious essay, Orwell—who began by describing writers who ignored contemporary reality as 'usually footlers or plain idiots'—*embraces* and *espouses* this quietist philosophy, this cetacean version of Pangloss's exhortation to *'cultiver notre jardin'*. 'Progress and reaction,' Orwell concludes, 'have both turned out to be swindles. Seemingly there is nothing left but quietism—robbing reality of its terrors by simply submitting to it. Get inside the whale—or rather, admit you are inside the whale (for you *are*, of course). Give yourself over to the world-process . . . simply accept it, endure it, record it. That seems to be the formula that any sensitive novelist is now likely to adopt.'

The sensitive novelist's reasons are to be found in the essay's last sentence, in which Orwell speaks of 'the *impossibility* of any major literature until the world has shaken itself into its new shape.'

And we are told that fatalism is a quality of Indian thought.

It is impossible not to include in any response to 'Inside the Whale' the suggestion that Orwell's argument is much impaired by his choice, for a quietist model, of Henry Miller. In the forty-four years since the essay was first published, Miller's reputation has more or less completely evaporated, and he now looks to be very little more than the happy pornographer beneath whose scatological surface Orwell saw such improbable depths. If we, in 1984, are asked to choose between, on the one hand, the Miller of *Tropic of Cancer* and 'the first hundred pages of *Black Spring*' and, on the other hand, the collected works of Auden, MacNeice and Spender, I doubt that many of us would go for old Henry. So it would appear that politically committed art can actually prove more durable than messages from the stomach of the fish.

It would also be wrong to go any further without discussing the senses in which Orwell uses the term 'politics'. Six years after 'Inside the Whale', in the essay 'Politics and the English Language' (1946), he wrote: 'In our age there is no such thing as "keeping out of politics". All issues are political issues, and politics itself is a mass of lies, evasions, folly, hatred and schizophrenia.'

For a man as truthful, direct, intelligent, passionate and sane as Orwell, 'politics' had come to represent the antithesis of his own world-view. It was an underworld-become-overworld, Hell on earth. 'Politics' was a portmanteau term which included everything he hated; no wonder he wanted to keep it out of literature.

I cannot resist the idea that Orwell's intellect, and finally his spirit, too, were broken by the horrors of the age in which he lived, the age of Hitler and Stalin (and, to be fair, by the ill health of his later years). Faced with the overwhelming evils of exterminations and purges and fire-bombings, and all the appalling manifestations of politics-gone-wild, he turned his talents to the business of constructing and also of justifying an escape-route. Hence his notion of the ordinary man as victim, and therefore of passivity as the literary stance closest to that of the ordinary man. He is using this type of logic as a means of building a path back to the womb, into the whale and away from the thunder of war. This looks very like the plan of a man who has given up the struggle. Even though he knows that 'there is no such thing as "keeping out of politics"', he attempts the construction of a mechanism with just that purpose. Sit it out, he recommends; we writers will be safe inside the whale, until the storm dies down. I do not presume

to blame him for adopting this position. He lived in the worst
of times. But it is important to dispute his conclusions, because
a philosophy built on an intellectual defeat must always be
rebuilt at a later point. And undoubtedly Orwell did give way
to a kind of defeatism and despair. By the time he wrote
Nineteen Eighty-Four, sick and cloistered on Jura, he had plainly
come to think that resistance was useless. Winston Smith
considers himself a dead man from the moment he rebels. The
secret book of the dissidents turns out to have been written by
the Thought Police. All protest must end in Room 101. In an
age when it often appears that we have all agreed to believe
in entropy, in the proposition that things fall apart, that
history is the irreversible process by which everything
gradually gets worse, the unrelieved pessimism of *Nineteen
Eighty-Four* goes some way towards explaining its status as a
true myth of our times.

What is more (and this connects the year's parallel
phenomena of Empire-revivalism and Orwellmania), the
quietist option, the exhortation to submit to events, is an
intrinsically conservative one. When intellectuals and artists
withdraw from the fray, politicians feel safer. Once, the right
and left in Britain used to argue about which of them
'owned' Orwell. In those days both sides wanted him; and, as
Raymond Williams has said, the tug-of-war did his memory
little honour. I have no wish to reopen these old hostilities;
but the truth cannot be avoided, and the truth is that passivity
always serves the interests of the status quo, of the people
already at the top of the heap, and the Orwell of 'Inside the
Whale' and *Nineteen Eighty-Four* is advocating ideas that can
only be of service to our masters. If resistance is useless, those
whom one might otherwise resist become omnipotent.

It is much easier to find common ground with Orwell
when he comes to discuss the relationship between politics
and language. The discoverer of Newspeak was aware that
'when the general [political] atmosphere is bad, language
must suffer.' In 'Politics and the English Language' he gives
us a series of telling examples of the perversion of meaning
for political purposes. 'Statements like "Marshal Pétain was a

true patriot", "The Soviet Press is the freest in the world", "The Catholic Church is opposed to persecution" are almost always made with intent to deceive,' he writes. He also provides beautiful parodies of politicians' metaphor-mixing: 'The Fascist octopus has sung its swan song, the jackboot is thrown into the melting pot.' Recently, I came across a worthy descendant of these grand old howlers: *The Times*, reporting the smuggling of classified documents out of Civil Service departments, referred to the increased frequency of 'leaks' from 'a high-level mole'.

It's odd, though, that the author of *Animal Farm*, the creator of so much of the vocabulary through which we now comprehend these distortions—doublethink, thoughtcrime, and the rest—should have been unwilling to concede that literature was best able to defend language, to do battle with the twisters, *precisely by entering the political arena*. The writers of the Group 47 in post-war Germany, Grass, Böll and the rest, with their 'rubble literature' whose purpose and great achievement it was to rebuild the German language from the rubble of Nazism, are prime instances of this power. So, in quite another way, is a writer like Joseph Heller. In *Good as Gold* the character of the presidential aide Ralph provides Heller with some superb satire at the expense of Washingtonspeak. Ralph speaks in sentences that usually conclude by contradicting their beginnings: 'This administration will back you all the way until it has to'; 'This President doesn't want yes-men. What we want are independent men of integrity who will agree with all our decisions after we make them.' Every time Ralph opens his oxymoronic mouth he reveals the limitations of Orwell's view of the interaction between literature and politics. It is a view which excludes comedy, satire, deflation; because of course the writer need not always be the servant of some beetle-browed ideology. He can also be its critic, its antagonist, its scourge. From Swift to Solzhenitsyn, writers have discharged this role with honour. And remember Napoleon the Pig.

Just as it is untrue that politics ruins literature (even among 'ideological' political writers, Orwell's case would founder on the great rock of Pablo Neruda), so it is by no means axiomatic that the 'ordinary man', *l'homme moyen sensuel*, is politically passive. We have seen that the myth of this inert commoner was a part of Orwell's logic of retreat; but it is nevertheless worth reminding ourselves of just a few instances in which the 'ordinary man'—not to mention the 'ordinary woman'—has been anything but inactive. We may not approve of Khomeini's Iran, but the revolution there was a genuine mass movement. So is the revolution in Nicaragua. And so, let us not forget, was the Indian revolution. I wonder if independence would have arrived in 1947 if the masses, ignoring Congress and the Muslim League, had remained seated inside what would have had to be a very large whale indeed.

The truth is that there is no whale. We live in a world without hiding places; the missiles have made sure of that. However much we may wish to return to the womb, we cannot be unborn. So we are left with a fairly straightforward choice. Either we agree to delude ourselves, to lose ourselves in the fantasy of the great fish, for which a second metaphor is that of Pangloss's garden; or we can do what all human beings do instinctively when they realize that the womb has been lost for ever—that is, we can make the very devil of a racket. Certainly, when we cry, we cry partly for the safety we have lost; but we also cry to affirm ourselves, to say, here I am, I matter, too, you're going to have to reckon with me. So, in place of Jonah's womb, I am recommending the ancient tradition of making as big a fuss, as noisy a complaint about the world as is humanly possible. Where Orwell wished quietism, let there be rowdyism; in place of the whale, the protesting wail. If we can cease envisaging ourselves as metaphorical foetuses, and substitute the image of a new-born child, then that will be at least a small intellectual advance. In time, perhaps, we may even learn to toddle.

I must make one thing plain: I am not saying that all literature must now be of this protesting, noisy type. Perish the thought; now that we are babies fresh from the womb, we must find it possible to laugh and wonder as well as rage and weep. I have no wish to nail myself, let alone anyone else, to the tree of political literature for the rest of my writing life. Lewis Carroll and Laurence Sterne are as important to literature as Swift or Brecht. What I am saying is that politics and literature, like sport and politics, do mix, are inextricably mixed, and that that mixture has consequences.

The modern world lacks not only hiding places, but certainties. There is no consensus about reality between, for example, the nations of the North and of the South. What President Reagan says is happening in Central America differs so radically from, say, the Sandinista version, that there is almost no common ground. It becomes necessary to take sides, to say whether or not one thinks of Nicaragua as the United States's 'front yard'. (Vietnam, you will recall, was the 'back yard'.) It seems to me imperative that literature enter such arguments, because what is being disputed is nothing less than *what is the case*, what is truth and what untruth. If writers leave the business of making pictures of the world to politicians, it will be one of history's great and most abject abdications.

Outside the whale is the unceasing storm, the continual quarrel, the dialectic of history. Outside the whale there is a genuine need for political fiction, for books that draw new and better maps of reality, and make new languages with which we can understand the world. Outside the whale we see that we are all irradiated by history, we are radioactive with history and politics; we see that it can be as false to create a politics-free fictional universe as to create one in which nobody needs to work or eat or hate or love or sleep. Outside the whale it becomes necessary, and even exhilarating, to grapple with the special problems created by the incorporation of political material, because politics is by turns farce and tragedy, and sometimes (e.g., Zia's Pakistan) both at once. Outside the whale the writer is obliged to accept that he (or she) is part of the crowd, part of the ocean, part of the storm, so that objectivity becomes a great dream, like perfection, an unattainable goal for which one must struggle in spite of the impossibility of success. Outside the whale is the world of Samuel Beckett's famous formula: *I can't go on, I'll go on.*

This is why (to end where I began) it really is necessary to make a fuss about Raj fiction and the zombie-like revival of the defunct Empire. The various films and TV shows and books I discussed earlier propagate a number of notions about history which must be quarrelled with, as loudly and as embarrassingly as possible.

These include: The idea that non-violence makes successful revolutions; the peculiar notion that Kasturba Gandhi could have confided the secrets of her sex-life to Margaret Bourke-White; the bizarre implication that any Indians could look like or speak like Amy Irving or Christopher Lee; the view (which underlies many of these works) that the British and Indians actually understood each other jolly well, and that the end of the Empire was a sort of gentleman's agreement between old pals at the club; the revisionist theory—see David Lean's interviews—that *we, the British, weren't as bad as people make out*; the calumny, to which the use of rape-plots lends credence, that frail English roses were in constant sexual danger from lust-crazed wogs (just such a fear lay behind General Dyer's Amritsar massacre); and, above all, the fantasy that the British Empire represented something 'noble' or 'great' about Britain; that it was, in spite of all its flaws and meannesses and bigotries, fundamentally glamorous.

If books and films could be made and consumed in the belly of the whale, it might be possible to consider them merely as entertainment, or even, on occasion, as art. But in our whaleless world, in this world without quiet corners, there can be no easy escapes from history, from hullabaloo, from terrible, unquiet fuss.

1984

ATTENBOROUGH'S GANDHI

D eification is an Indian disease, and in India, Mohandas Karamchand Gandhi, great soul, little father, has been raised higher than anyone in the pantheon of latter-day gods. 'But,' I was asked more than once in India recently, 'why should an *Englishman* want to deify Gandhi?' And why, one might add, should the American Academy wish to help him, by presenting, like votive offerings in a temple, eight glittering statuettes to a film that is inadequate as biography, appalling as history, and often laughably crude as a film?

The answer may be that *Gandhi* (the film, not the man, who irritated the British immensely, but who is now safely dead) satisfies certain longings in the Western psyche, which can be categorized under three broad headings. First, the exotic impulse, the wish to see India as the fountainhead of spiritual–mystical wisdom. Gandhi, the celluloid guru, follows in the footsteps of other pop holy men. The Maharishi blazed this trail. Second, there is what might be termed the Christian longing, for a 'leader' dedicated to ideals of poverty and simplicity, a man who is too good for this world and is therefore sacrificed on the altars of history. And third, there is the liberal–conservative political desire to hear it said that revolutions can, and should, be made purely by submission, and self-sacrifice, and non-violence *alone*. To make *Gandhi* appeal to the Western market, he had to be sanctified and turned into Christ—an odd fate for a crafty Gujarati lawyer—and the history of one of the century's greatest revolutions had to be mangled. This is nothing new. The British have been mangling Indian history for centuries.

Much of the debate about the film has concerned omissions: why no Subhas Bose? Why no Tagore? The film's makers answer that it would have been impossible to include everything and everyone, and of course selection is central to any work of art. But artistic selection creates meanings, and in *Gandhi* these are frequently dubious and in some cases frighteningly naïve.

Take the Amritsar massacre. This is perhaps the most powerful sequence in the film. Both the massacre and the subsequent court-martial, at which outraged Englishmen question the unrepentant Dyer with barely suppressed horror, are staged accurately and with passion. But what these two scenes mean is that Dyer's actions at Jallianwala Bagh were those of a cruel, over-zealous individual, and that they were immediately condemned by Anglo-India. And that is a complete falsehood.

The British in Punjab in 1919 were panicky. They feared a second Indian Mutiny. They had nightmares about rape. The court-martial may have condemned Dyer, but the colonists did not. He had taught the wogs a lesson; he was a hero. And when he returned to England, he was given a hero's welcome. An appeal fund launched on his behalf made him a rich man. Tagore, disgusted by the British reaction to the massacre, returned his knighthood.

In the case of Amritsar, artistic selection has altered the meaning of the event. It is an unforgivable distortion.

Another example: the assassination of Gandhi. Attenborough considers it important enough to place it at the beginning as well as the end of his film; but during the intervening three hours, he tells us nothing about it. Not the assassin's name. Not the name of the organization behind the killing. Not the ghost of a motive for the deed. In a political thriller, this would be merely crass; in *Gandhi* it is something worse. Gandhi was murdered by Nathuram Godse, a member of the Hindu-fanatic RSS, who blamed the Mahatma for the Partition of India. But in the film the killer is not differentiated from the crowd; he simply steps out of the crowd with a gun. This could mean one of three things: that he *represents* the crowd—that the people turned against Gandhi, that the mob threw up a killer who did its work; that Godse was 'one lone nut', albeit a lone nut under the influence of a sinister-looking sadhu in a rickshaw; or that Gandhi is Christ in a loincloth, and the assassination is the crucifixion, which needs no explanation. We know why Christ died. He died that others might live. But Godse was *not* representative of the crowd. He did *not* work alone. And the killing was a political, not a mystical, act. Attenborough's distortions mythologize, but they also lie.

Ah, but, we are told, the film is a biography, not a political work. Even if one accepts this distinction (surely spurious in the case of a life lived so much in public), one must reply that a biography, if it is not to turn into hagiography, must tackle the awkward aspects of the subject as well as the lovable side. The *brahmacharya* experiments, during which Gandhi would lie with young naked women all night to test his will-to-abstain, are well known, not without filmic possibilities, and they are, of course, ambiguous events. The film omits them. It also omits Gandhi's fondness for Indian billionaire industrialists (he died, after all, in the house of the richest of them, Birla House in Delhi). Surely this is a rich area for a biographer to mine: the man of the masses, dedicated to the simple life, self-denial, asceticism, who was financed all his life by super-capitalist patrons, and, some would say, hopelessly compromised by them? A written biography which failed to enter such murky waters would not be worth reading. We should not be less critical of a film.

Gandhi presents false portraits of most of the leaders of the independence struggle. Patel comes across as a clown, whereas he was one of the hardest of hard men. And it was witty to portray Jinnah as Count Dracula. But the important changes are in the personality of Nehru and in the decision to erase Bose from history.

In both cases, dramatic interest has been sacrificed in the interests of deification. Nehru was not Gandhi's disciple. They were equals, and they argued fiercely. Their debate was central to the freedom movement—Nehru, the urban sophisticate who wanted to industrialize India, to bring it into the modern age, versus the rural, handicraft-loving, sometimes medieval figure of Gandhi: the country lived this debate, and it had to choose. India chose Gandhi with its heart, but in terms of practical politics, it chose Nehru. One can understand nothing about the nature of India's independence unless one understands the conflict between these two great men. The film, by turning Nehru into Bapuji's acolyte, manages to castrate itself.

And Bose is selected out. Bose the guerrilla, who fought with the Japanese against the British in the war, Bose whose views could have provided another sort of counterweight to Gandhi's, and so improved the film. But Bose was violent, and the film, if it means anything, seeks to mean that non-violence works, and that it could work anywhere, in any revolution. All counter-arguments are therefore rigorously excluded. The message of *Gandhi* is that the best way to gain your freedom is to line up, unarmed, and march towards your oppressors and permit them to club you to the ground; if you do this for long enough, you will embarrass them into going away. This is worse than nonsense. It is dangerous nonsense. Non-violence was a strategy chosen for a particular people against a particular oppressor; to generalize from it is a suspect act. How useful would non-violence have been against, say, the Nazis? Even in India, the leaders of the independence movement did not succeed because they were more moral than the British. They won because they were smarter, craftier, better fighting politicians than their opponents. *Gandhi* shows us a saint who vanquished an Empire. This is a fiction.

All devotees of unintentional comedy will relish the scenes in *Gandhi* in which Bapu re-enacts his marriage for the benefit of a Western journalist; in which one man's hunger strike pacifies a rioting Calcutta, and repentant hooligans promise Gandhi that they will adopt Muslim orphan children; in which Mirabehn is played as a woman in a permanent hypnotic trance; or in which the Partition is sorted out during a two-minute break in the independence negotiations. If this is the Best Film of 1983, God help the film industry.

What it is, is an incredibly expensive movie about a man who was dedicated to the small scale and to asceticism. The form of the film, opulent, lavish, overpowers and finally crushes the man at its centre, in spite of Ben Kingsley's luminous performance (at least *he* deserved his Oscar). It is as if Gandhi, years after his death, has found in Attenborough the last in his series of billionaire patrons, his last Birla. And rich men, like emperors, have always had a weakness for tame holy men, for saints.

1983

SATYAJIT RAY

'I can never forget the excitement in my mind after seeing it,' Akira Kurosawa said about Satyajit Ray's first film, *Pather Panchali* (*The Song of the Little Road*), and it's true: this movie, made for next to nothing, mostly with untrained actors, by a director who was learning (and making up) the rules as he went along, is a work of such lyrical and emotional force that it becomes, for its audiences, as potent as their own, most deeply personal memories. To this day, the briefest snatch of Ravi Shankar's wonderful theme music brings back a flood of feeling, and a crowd of images: the single eye of the little Apu, seen at the moment of waking, full of mischief and life; the insects dancing on the surface of the pond, prefiguring the coming monsoon rains; and above all the immortal scene, one of the most tragic in all cinema, in which Harihar the peasant comes home to the village from the city, bringing presents for his children, not knowing that his daughter has died in his absence. When he shows his wife, Sarbajaya, the sari he has brought for the dead girl, she begins to weep; and now he understands, and cries out, too; but (and this is the stroke of genius) their voices are replaced by the high, high music of a single *tarshehnai*, a sound like a scream of the soul.

Pather Panchali was the first Ray movie I ever saw, and, like many cinema-addicted Indians, I saw it not in India but in London. In spite of having grown up in the world's number-one movie city, Bombay ('Bollywood' in those days produced more movies per annum than Los Angeles or Tokyo or Hong Kong), I knew less about India's greatest film-maker than I did about 'international cinema' (or, at any rate, the movies of Robert Taylor, the Three Stooges, Francis the Talking Mule and Maria Montez). It was at the old Academy in Oxford Street, and at the National Film Theatre, and at the Arts Cinema in Cambridge that, with mixed feelings of high elation and shame at my own previous ignorance, I filled in this lamentable gap. By the middle 1960s, when the *Nouvelle Vague* hit the cinemas like a tidal wave, and the names of Truffaut and Godard and Resnais and Malle and Antonioni and Fellini and Bergman and Wajda and Kurosawa and Buñuel became more important to us than any mere novelist, and when the new movie in a given week might be called *Jules et Jim* or *Alphaville* and might be followed, a week later, by *Ashes and Diamonds* or *Yojimbo* or *Le Feu Follet* or *L'Eclisse* or *8½* or *The Seventh Seal* or *The Exterminating Angel* or *The Saragossa Manuscript*—when, that is to say, the cinema was ablaze with innovation and originality, I took real pride in the knowledge I gained from Ray's films: that this explosion of creative genius had its Indian dimension, too.

This was not an opinion shared by all Indians. Because Ray, a Bengali, made films in his own language, his films were not distributed outside Bengal. His international success brought predictable sniping at home. Andrew Robinson records, in *Satyajit Ray: The Inner Eye*, a paradigmatic expression of this resentment, which also brings the vulgar, energetic (and, it must be said, sneakily appealing) Bombay cinema into direct conflict with the highbrow, uncompromising, 'difficult' Ray. The Bombay movie star Nargis (Nargis Dutt), star of the 1957 mega-weepie *Mother India*, was by the beginning of the 1980s a member of the Indian Parliament, from which exalted position she launched an amazing attack on Ray:

NARGIS: Why do you think films like *Pather Panchali* become popular abroad? . . . Because people there want to see India in an abject condition. That is the image they have of our country and a film that confirms that image seems to them authentic.

INTERVIEWER: But why should a renowned director like Ray do such a thing?

NARGIS: To win awards. His films are not commercially successful. They only win awards . . . What I want is that if Mr Ray projects Indian poverty abroad, he should also show 'Modern India'.

INTERVIEWER: What is 'Modern India'?
NARGIS: Dams . . .

She was answered by a letter from the Forum for Better Cinema: 'Do you honestly believe that [Modern India] is portrayed in the so-called commercial films of Bombay? In fact, the world of commercial Hindi films is peopled by thugs, smugglers, dacoits, voyeurs, murderers, cabaret dancers, sexual perverts, degenerates, delinquents and rapists, which can hardly be called representative of modern India.' Soon afterwards, Mr Robinson tells us, 'the government informed Ray it could not grant him permission to make a film about child labour since this did not constitutionally exist in India.' (Indian governments often demonstrate a weakness for the ostrich position. My own 1987 documentary, *The Riddle of Midnight*, ran into trouble because, among other things, I mentioned that all the Kashmiri Muslims I spoke to were highly disaffected with India, and wanted to join Pakistan. This was officially unsayable at the time, and so I was accused of fundamentalist sympathies; less than three years later, the lid that New Delhi pushed down over the Kashmir issue for so long may finally have blown off.)

The exchange between Nargis Dutt and Ray's supporters, the quarrel between the philistine/commercialist/jingoistic position and the aesthete/purist/open-eyed view, can be seen in a number of different ways: as a quarrel between two definitions of patriotic love, because while Nargis all but calls Ray anti-Indian, his love for India is, as Mr Robinson asserts, powerfully evident throughout his *œuvre*; and, more interestingly perhaps, as a dispute between two very different urban cultures, the cosmopolitan, brash bitch-city of Bombay versus the old intellectual traditions of Calcutta. Ray himself is, with much justification, scathing about the Bombay talkies. 'India,' he says, 'took one of the greatest inventions of the West with the most far-reaching artistic potential, and cut it down to size.' Endless Bollywood remakes of *Love Story*, *The Magnificent Seven*, etc., go a long way to proving his point.

However, being a Bombaywallah myself, I can't avoid

observing that in the battle between Bombay and Calcutta, Andrew Robinson seems more emphatically on Ray's side than Ray himself. He makes a number of unfairly dismissive remarks about the 'new' or 'middle' cinema now growing up in Bombay, Kerala and elsewhere. This attempt to steer a course between mandarin and moneybags attitudes to the movies is, we are told, 'lacking in commitment' to its subject matter, a vague sort of assertion and one that demeans the solid achievements of the directors he names, Benegal, Gopalakrishnan and Aravindan. 'There is a superficiality and dullness in most of the work of the "new" cinema that seems to derive from the fake urban culture of modern India, and which arises ultimately from the failure of imagination in the Indian "synthesis" of the last century,' Mr Robinson suggests, in one of the few over-the-top passages in an otherwise scrupulous book. The films he attacks are better than he admits; and while it's undeniable that Indian urban culture, Bombay above all, is full of fakery and gaudiness and superficiality and failed imaginations, it is also a culture of high vitality, linguistic verve, and a kind of metropolitan excitement that European cities have for the most part forgotten. And this is true of that over-painted courtesan, Bombay, as it is of Ray's Calcutta.

The case of Ray's movie *Shatranj ke Khilari* (*The Chess Players*) represents the lowest point in the uneasy relationship between Satyajit Ray and the Bombay film industry. This film, Ray's first (and to date only) feature film in Hindi, was a deliberate attempt to enter the mainstream of Indian culture. According to legend, the movie bosses of Bombay ruined the film's chances by putting pressure on national distributors not to book it. Mr Robinson sheds little light on the incident, remarking only that 'Ray refuses to be drawn on the point and has avoided wasting his time trying to find out the truth; but Shama Zaidi, who knows Bombay's film world well, thinks the existence of a conspiracy against the film "quite probable".' Gossip is no substitute for investigation. My own memory of talking to Satyajit Ray about this matter is that he was a more open believer in the conspiracy theory than Mr Robinson allows; but that, in spite of it all, he had found the experience of working in Hindi very stimulating, above all because he had been able to choose from a much larger group of gifted actors than were to be found in the smaller Bengali-language cinema. He was interested in making more Hindi movies; ill health may now have made that impossible.

A highbrow *auteur* who is nevertheless appreciative of the talents of Bollywood movie stars, Satyajit Ray is also, for a man who disapproves of the movies of Buñuel because of 'the surrealist element', a man with a strong streak of fantasy. His fairy-tale movie, *Goopy Gyne Bagha Byne* (*The Adventures of Goopy and Bagha*), is, in Bengal, as well-loved as *The Wizard of Oz* is here. 'It really is extraordinary how quickly [*Goopy and Bagha*] has become part of popular culture,' Ray wrote soon after the movie's release. 'Really, there isn't a child in the city who doesn't know and sing the songs.' So it seems that Ray's work has been quite capable of doing more than winning awards; but every one of Ray's fabulist movies—*Hirak Rajar Dese* (*The Kingdom of Diamonds*), *Sonar Kella* (*The Golden Fortress*), *Joi Baba Felunath* (*The Elephant God*) as well as *G&B*— has failed, outside India, to attract the plaudits accorded to his more realist films. Mr Robinson puts this down to 'the West's historic disinterest [*sic*] in the legends of India', which may be true. Certainly, when I mentioned to Satyajit Ray that *The Golden Fortress* was one of my favourite movies, he leapt up from his breakfast and made huge gesticulations of delight, turning into the epitome of the proud parent whose least-appreciated child has just been lavished with unlooked-for praise.

Goopy and Bagha, Andrew Robinson rightly says, 'released the vein of pent-up fantasy in Satyajit Ray, that is given free rein in his grandfather's and father's work.' By far the strongest section of *Satyajit Ray: The Inner Eye* is the opening seventy-page biographical study. Ray came from a family of fantasists, creators of nonsense verse and fabulous hybrid animals—Stortle, Whalephant, Porcuduck—and both Ray's father Sukumar and his grandfather Upendrakishore were famous for their children's stories and illustrations, published in the family's magazine, *Sandesh*, which means, as Mr Robinson tells us, both Sweetmeat and Information. But this was also a family of dazzling and varied intellectual and spiritual gifts. Upendrakishore was a printer whose innovations in half-tone screenprinting were stolen by a British company; Sukumar had a visionary side, and saw his own death before it happened. Ray has been deeply affected by his family's recurring mystical streak (his great-great-grandfather Loknath had it, too); he even attributes his own artistic gifts to it. 'This whole business of creation . . . cannot be explained by science.' Once again, close examination reveals Satyajit Ray to be something other than the realistic artist he seems, even claims, to be.

The rest of the Ray clan was no less brilliant. His great-uncle, Hemendranath Bose, was a perfumer, and also 'a pioneer of the bicycle in India, one of the first people in India to own a motor-car, and the first to make phonogram recordings . . . his fourteen children included, in due course, a famous singer, a painter and connoisseur of music, a film sound recordist, four cricketers (one of whom was *the* name of his time), and a well-known film director, Nitin Bose, who would later tell Satyajit he should take up art direction and forget directing.' With a family like this to live up to, Ray had to start early. He was 'highly sensitive as a child to sounds and lighting. Half a century later, he can remember various vanished street cries and the fact that in those days you could spot the make of a car from inside the house by the sound of its horn.' Among the car horns he learned to identify was the one belonging to his aunts' Lancia, which 'had a glass cricket perched on its bonnet which glowed pink as the car cruised along.' Even his friends seemed to develop magical gifts; his college chum Pritwish Neogy, for example, 'had the extraordinary ability to identify a painting by looking at one square inch of it' and, according to Satyajit, he could 'immediately spot the fake from the genuine.'

Mr Robinson maintains his biographical approach up to the making of *Pather Panchali*, of which he provides an absorbing account. Then, somewhat regrettably, he switches to a movie-by-movie account of Ray's career, and only occasionally attempts to weave the story of the movies into the larger story of Ray's personal and intellectual development. It is as if Ray's own famous reticence on personal matters has permeated the book.

Such attempts at contextualization as are made are unfailingly interesting. Sukumar Ray's commitment to the movement that 'swept Bengal from 1903 in reaction to Lord Curzon's proclaimed intention of partitioning the province' sheds valuable light on his son Satyajit's later decision to film the novel Rabindranath Tagore wrote about that movement, *Ghare Baire* (*The Home and the World*); and Ray's own family associations with Tagore himself provide equally valuable sidelights on the film director's lifelong engagement with the writer's work. Again, Ray's reactions to the great Bengal Famine of 1943–4, his sense of shame at having done nothing to help the dying, powerfully informs our knowledge of the great film he later made on the subject, *Asani Sanket* (*Distant Thunder*). There is much interesting information about the films and their reception, too: the story of how *Devi* (*The Goddess*) was attacked by religious extremists as anti-Hindu is one such snippet. One cannot avoid saying, however, that the film-by-film approach does reduce the interest of this book for non-movie buffs; which is a pity because, as those opening pages demonstrated, a full-blooded biography could not have failed to be of wide general appeal.

The book deserves to be welcomed nevertheless. It is extremely thorough, often perceptive and at times highly entertaining. It is good to have a sympathetic portrait of one of the giants of the cinema. After a heart attack and bypass surgery in 1984, Satyajit Ray's ability to work has been restricted; his latest film, *Ganashatru*, a version of Ibsen's *An Enemy of the People*, has perforce been filmed in the studio, with Ray's son assisting his father. It is to be hoped that Ray will manage to complete many more movies, but his already-completed achievement is astonishing; and you could say that the entire *œuvre* is, like the very first film, a 'song of the little road', because Ray has invariably preferred the intimate story to the grand epic, and is the poet *par excellence* of the human-scale, life-sized comedy and tragedy of ordinary men and women, journeying, as we all journey, down little, but unforgettable, roads.

1990

HANDSWORTH SONGS

In *The Heart of a Woman*, volume four of her famous autobiography, Maya Angelou describes a meeting of the Harlem Writers' Guild, at which she read some of her work and had it torn to pieces by the group. It taught her a tough lesson. 'If I wanted to write, I had to be willing to develop a kind of concentration found mostly in people awaiting execution. I had to learn technique and surrender my ignorance.'

It just isn't enough to be black and blue, or even black and angry. The message is plain enough in Angelou's self-portrait, in Louise Meriwether's marvellous *Daddy Was A Numbers Runner*, in Toni Morrison and Paule Marshall; if you want to tell the untold stories, if you want to give voice to the voiceless, you've got to find a language. Which goes for film as well as prose, for documentary as well as autobiography. Use the wrong language, and you're dumb and blind.

Down at the Metro cinema there's a new documentary starting a three-week run, *Handsworth Songs*, made by Black Audio Film Collective. The 'buzz' about the picture is good. *New Socialist* likes it, *City Limits* likes it, people are calling it multi-layered, original, imaginative; its makers talk of speaking in metaphors, its director John Akomfrah is getting mentioned around town as a talent to watch.

Unfortunately, it's no good, and the trouble does seem to be one of language.

Let me put it this way. If I say 'Handsworth', what do you see? Most Britons would see fire, riots, looted shops, young Rastas and helmeted cops by night. A big story; front page. Perhaps a West Side Story: Officer Krupke, armed to the teeth, versus the kids with the social disease.

There's a line that *Handsworth Songs* wants us to learn. 'There are no stories in the riots,' it repeats, 'only the ghosts of other stories.' The trouble is, we aren't told the other stories. What we get is what we know from TV. Blacks as trouble;

blacks as victims. Here is a Rasta dodging the police; here are the old news-clips of the folks in the fifties getting off the boat, singing calypsos about 'darling London'. Little did they know, eh? But we don't hear about their lives, or the lives of their British-born children. We don't hear Handsworth's songs.

Why not? The film's handouts provide a clue. 'The film attempts to excavate hidden ruptures/agonies of "Race".' It 'looks at the riots as a political field coloured by the trajectories of industrial decline and structural crisis.' Oh dear. The sad thing is that while the film-makers are trying to excavate ruptures and work out how trajectories can colour fields, they let us hear so little of the much richer language of their subjects.

When Home Secretary Hurd visits Handsworth, looking bemused, just after the riots, a black voice is heard to say: 'The higher monkey climb, the more he will expose.' If only more of this sort of wit and freshness could have found its way into the film. But the makers are too busy 'repositioning the convergence of "Race" and "Criminality",' describing a living world in the dead language of race-industry professionals.

I don't know Handsworth very well, but I do know it's bursting with tales worth telling. Take a look at John Bishton and Derek Reardon's 1984 photo-and-text essay, *Home Front*. There are Vietnamese boat people in Handsworth, where Father Peter Diem, a refugee himself, runs a pastoral centre to which they come for comfort. There's an Asian businessman in Handsworth who made his pile by employing his fellow-Asians in sweatshops to make, of all things, the Harrington jackets beloved by the skinheads who were also, as it happened, fond of bashing the odd Paki.

Here are two old British soldiers. One, name of Shri Dalip Singh, sits stiffly in his army tunic, sporting his Africa Star with pride; the other, a certain Jagat Singh, is a broken old gent who has been arrested for drunkenness on these streets over three hundred times. Some nights they catch him trying to direct the traffic.

It's a religious place, Handsworth. What was once a

Methodist chapel is now one of many Sikh *gurdwaras*. Here is the Good News Asian Church, and there you can see Rasta groundations, a mosque, Pentecostal halls, and Hindu, Jain and Buddhist places of worship. Many of Handsworth's songs are hymns of praise. But there's reggae, too; there are toasters at blues dances, there are Punjabi *ghazals* and Two Tone bands.

These days, the kids in Handsworth like to dance the Wobbler. And some of its denizens dream of distant 'liberations', nurturing, for example, the dark fantasy of Khalistan.

It's important, I believe, to tell such stories; to say, this is England. Look at the bright illuminations and fireworks during the Hindu Festival of Lights, Divali. Listen to the Muslim call to prayer, 'Allahu Akbar', wafting down from the minaret of a Birmingham mosque. Visit the Ethiopian World Federation, which helps Handsworth Rastas 'return' to the land of Ras Tafari. These are English scenes now, English songs.

You won't find them or anything like them, in *Handsworth Songs*, though for some reason you will see plenty of footage about troubles in Tottenham and Brixton, which is just the sort of blurring you know the Harlem writers would have jumped on, no matter how right-on it looked.

It isn't easy for black voices to be heard. It isn't easy to get it said that the State attacks us, that the police are militarized. It isn't easy to fight back against media stereotypes. As a result, whenever somebody says what we all know, even if they say it clumsily and in jargon, there's a strong desire to cheer, just because they managed to get something said, they managed to get through. I don't think that's much help, myself. That kind of celebration makes us lazy.

Next time, let's start telling those ghost-stories. If we know why the caged bird sings, let's listen to her song.

1987

THE LOCATION OF *BRAZIL*

In N. F. Simpson's play *One Way Pendulum*, one of the very few competent British contributions to the Theatre of the Absurd, a man receives, by mail order, a full-sized replica of an Old Bailey courtroom in kit form. He assembles it in his living room and shortly afterwards finds himself on trial in it. A clerk announces that on the day in question, the defendant, our hero, 'was not in this world'. The judge, frowning, inquires, 'Which world was he in, then?' And the clerk explains: 'It seems he has one of his own.'

It is not easy, you see, to be precise about the location of the world of the imagination. Even the legal system (especially the legal system) is unaware of its whereabouts. The French, these days, would have us believe that this world, which they call 'the text', is quite unconnected to the 'real' world, which they call 'the world'. But if I believe (and I do) that the imagined world is, must be, connected to the observable one, then I should be able, should I not, to locate it; to say how you get there from here. And it is not easy, you see, to be precise . . .

These reflections have been prompted by Terry Gilliam's magnificent film of future totalitarianism, *Brazil*. Because the more highly imagined a piece of work, the more ticklish this problem of location becomes. Let me put it this way: we can all agree, without too much argument, that the climax of *North by Northwest* takes place on Mount Rushmore, or that *All the President's Men* was set in Washington, DC. Progressing beyond such reassuring clarities, we arrive in a murky zone about which we could argue until the small hours: was *Apocalypse Now* 'really' set in Vietnam, or in some 'fictional' heart of darkness? Is *Amadeus* history or bunk? And, still further down this road, the surface turns to yellow brick, white rabbits scurry past, Lemmy Caution chews a Gauloise. My point is: where have we come to? What kind of place is Oz, or Wonderland? By what route, with or without a Ford

Galaxy, may one arrive at Alphaville? Specifically—for the purposes of this essay—where is *Brazil*?

Where it is not, is in South America. (Although that Brazil, like this one, has in the past been known for attaching high-voltage electrodes to the anatomies of its dissident citizens.) The film takes its title from an old Xavier Cugat melody.

> *Brazil, where hearts were entertained in June,*
> *We stood beneath an amber moon*
> *And softly murmured: Someday soon.*

So are we to say that this is a film that is somehow located in a song? Well, there's an ironic sense in which that might be true. The lush innocence of the old tune, when set against Gilliam's tale of State terror, does indeed embody much of the film's spirit, a combination, as Gilliam has said, of Franz Kafka and Frank Capra.

'Someday soon,' softly murmurs the song, and in the light of Gilliam's story, it sounds like a threat. Which leads us to a second way of locating the film, that is, in time. George Lucas's *Star Wars* cycle begins with a coy paradox, a subtitle informing us that what we are about to see happened not only far away but also long ago. However, Lucas's 'past' looks so much like a conventional space-opera future that we quickly disregard his little opening joke. A much more interesting time-location is to be found in Michael Radford's recent film of *Nineteen Eighty-Four*. If Lucas makes the past look like the future, Radford chooses to make his 'future' (an odd term to use about a film released in the year after which it was named, and which is already past) look consciously old-fashioned; such a future as might have been envisioned by a designer from 1948, the year in which Orwell wrote his book. It's an effective, if somewhat literal idea. The future in *Brazil* is a far more ambiguous and disturbing place.

Here elements of past and future combine to disorient us. The TV sets look oddly quaint. Messages are sent (as they are in the Radford movie) in those little metal canisters one pops into suction tubes, the kind they used to have in department stores. In other ways, though, the film looks marvellously futuristic, sometimes very comically so, as in the scene set in the restaurant festooned with great intestinal metallic pipework, where the food depicted so lavishly on photographic menus turns out to be coloured mush. The conflation of past and future is unsettling; it creates, instead of Radford's archaic future, an air of something very like nostalgia. (Once again, the title music is apposite.)

It feels as though, in these days when, as at the last millennium and with better reason, we fear we may be near the end of time, our dreams of the future—even of such a dark future as this one—must necessarily be tinged with nostalgia and regret. It may not be too fanciful to suggest that the other Star Wars programme, the one that isn't at all far away or long ago, has turned the future into a fiction, or rather, heightened its fictionality. Nowadays tomorrow is not only a place that hasn't arrived yet, but one that may never arrive at all. Like the clothes Jonathan Pryce (who plays Sam, the anti-hero of *Brazil*) wears in the movie, the idea of the future is somewhat out of date. And if this cancelled future is the location of Gilliam's movie, then we see that that location is an even more elusive place than we previously suspected.

At the most obvious level, the film is set in Dystopia, Utopia's dark opposite, the worst of all possible worlds. Unseen terrorist bombers oppose the violence of the police state. Ordinary citizens get killed in large quantities by both parties, but that's life. Amid the mayhem, two stories intertwine. One is the sad tale of Mr Buttle and Mr Tuttle, which begins deep in the bowels of the State, when a thought-policeman swats a fly, which falls into a computer printer and induces a spelling mistake. In place of the dangerous subversive and freelance air-conditioning engineer, Harry Tuttle (Robert de Niro, dressed like a cigar-smoking version of the old cartoon character The Phantom), the machine fingers the innocent family man Mr Buttle, and the cops accordingly carve a hole in his ceiling and haul him off, to be slowly carved into pieces with blunt scissors, or something like that. *As flies to wanton boys are we to the gods.* Meanwhile, as they say, a Winston Smith-ish clerk named Sam dreams of being winged and soaring free above the earth amid fleecy clouds, pursuing a blonde vision wrapped, like Renaissance Virgins, in floating folds of shimmering fabric. This turns out to be Jill (Kim Greist), who drives a monster truck and with whom, eventually, Sam revolts against the State, with predictable and nasty results.

It might seem, then, that the film can be 'placed' as a visually brilliant reworking of Orwellian themes. The ending of the version I saw—when Sam's escape from the torture chamber, with the help of Harry Tuttle, turns out to have been the wish-fulfilment dream of his maddened brain (he ends up back in the torture chair, gazing inwardly upon green fields, while his tormentors grin ironically: 'Looks like he's got away from us')—emphasized this Orwellian connection, and made me want to raise against *Brazil* the same criticism I would make of Orwell: that it is too easy, too pat, to create a Dystopia in which resistance is useless; that by offering only token individual resistance to the might of the State one falls into a sort of romantic trap; that there has never in the history of the world been a dictatorship so overpowering that it became impossible to fight against. But, for a number of reasons, it seems to me that to locate *Brazil* too close to Orwell's Airstrip One would not be quite cartographically accurate.

For one thing, audiences in the United States will see a rather different ending. Sam is still, at the last, in the grip of the torturers; but now, in the last scene, they do not have the last, leering words. Now the torture chamber slowly fills up with clouds, the same fleecy white clouds amongst which, in his winged dreams, he used to fly (and with which the American cut of the film, again unlike the British, also opens). This rather changes the meaning of the ending. It becomes a scene about the triumph of the imagination, the dream, over the shackles of actuality. It becomes clear that this, rather than the political allegory, may in fact be what the film has been about. It seems, at last, that we are getting closer to where, and what, the film is 'at'.

Other elements in the film also suggest a vision more complex than the bleak simplicities of *Nineteen Eighty-Four*, notably the role of Robert de Niro as Tuttle the Phantom-handyman. Sam may be destroyed, but Tuttle swings on, like an urban Tarzan, from skyscraper to skyscraper, munching his cheery cigar. Because he, too, 'flies', if only with the aid of ropes, he can be seen as a street-wise version of Sam's dream of himself as an angel. In *Brazil*, flight represents the imagining spirit; so it turns out that we are being told something very strange about the world of the imagination—that it is, in fact, *at war* with the 'real' world, the world in which things inevitably get worse and in which centres cannot hold. Angelic Sam and devilish Mr Tuttle represent the power of dream-worlds to oppose this dark reality. In an age in which it seems impossible to create happy endings; in which we seem to make Dystopias the way earlier ages made Utopias; in which we appear to have lost confidence in our ability to improve the world, Gilliam brings heartening news. As N. F. Simpson revealed in *One Way Pendulum*, the world of the imagination is a place into which the long arm of the law is unable to reach.

This idea—the opposition of imagination to reality, which is also of course the opposition of art to politics—is of great importance, because it reminds us that we are not helpless; that to dream is to have power. And I suggest that the true location of Brazil is the other great tradition in art, the one in which techniques of comedy, metaphor, heightened imagery, fantasy and so on are used to break down our conventional, habit-dulled certainties about what the world is and has to be. Unreality is the only weapon with which reality can be smashed, so that it may subsequently be reconstructed. (I once worked in an office building in which some troubled anonymous soul took to destroying the lavatories. It seemed like motiveless, insane destruction, until one day, on a wall next to a wrecked water-closet, we read these scribbled words: *If the cistern cannot be changed, it must be destroyed. Brazil's* radical repairman, Harry Tuttle, would have been proud of him.)

Play. Invent the world. The power of the playful imagination to change for ever our perceptions of how things are has been demonstrated by everyone from Laurence Sterne, in *Tristram Shandy*, to a certain Monty Python in his *Flying Circus*. Our sense of the modern world is as much the creation of Kafka, with his unexplained trials and unapproachable castles and giant bugs, as it is of Freud, Marx or Einstein. But there lies, in this approach, a terrible danger which is not faced by the realist artist. This danger is whimsy. When there are no rules except the ones you make up, don't things get too easy? When pigs can fly, do they remain pigs, and if not, why should we care about them? Can a work of art grow into anything of value if it has no roots in observable reality?

One answer to such questions is 'Lewis Carroll'. (We recall that Terry Gilliam is the director of *Jabberwocky*.) There are artists whose gift is to put down roots within the world of dreams, the logic of whose work is the logic of the dreaming and not the waking mind. James Joyce did it in *Finnegans Wake*. Terry Gilliam, I believe, does something very like it in *Brazil*.

And there is a second answer. It has been said that the basic difference between the American and the British approach to comedy is that American comedy begins with the question, 'Isn't it funny that . . .?' (that MASH doctors existed to mend soldiers so that the army could damage them again; that New Yorkers, as embodied by Woody Allen, are driven by anxiety and guilt; or that the poor—Chaplin eating his boots—are poor) . . . whereas British comedy's starting-point is the question, 'Wouldn't it be funny if . . .?' (if a pet shop sold dead parrots; if brain surgeons were mentally defective; if men in pinstriped suits did silly walks). Terry Gilliam, an American living in Britain and looking back at America—because he says clearly that *Brazil* is about America, and while we're trying to locate the film we really ought to pay a little attention to what its maker says—manages to make a synthesis of both approaches.

One of the keys to his method is Kafka. A story like 'Metamorphosis' appears, at first glance, to fall into the

'British' camp: wouldn't it be funny if Gregor Samsa woke up one morning to find himself metamorphosed into a giant insect? But in fact it derives its (very black) humour from a rather more serious question: Isn't it funny that a man's family reacts with fear, embarrassment, shame, love, boredom and relief when the son of the house becomes something they do not understand, suffers terribly and finally dies? The humour in *Brazil* is similarly black—isn't it funny that bourgeois women have face-lifts that go horribly wrong? Isn't it funny that people about to be killed look so ridiculous with their heads hidden inside bags? And like Kafka, it uses 'surface' techniques of the Absurdist/Python type: giant Samurai warriors; typists, writing down a condemned man's confession while he's being tortured, and including every aargh and sob. By darkening his humour, Gilliam avoids the trap of whimsy. Monty Python goes to *Metropolis* and the result is that rarity, a seriously funny movie.

It is also relevant that Terry Gilliam is a migrant. 'America bombards you with dreams and deprives you of your own,' he says, and *Brazil* is about that, too: the struggle between private, personal dreams (flying, love) and the great mass-produced fantasies, eternal youth, material wealth, power. But Gilliam's migrant status is not important just because of his alienation from the American consumer society. *Brazil* is the product of that odd thing, the migrant sensibility, whose development I believe to be one of the central themes of this century of displaced persons. To be a migrant is, perhaps, to be the only species of human being free of the shackles of nationalism (to say nothing of its ugly sister, patriotism). It is a burdensome freedom.

The effect of mass migrations has been the creation of radically new types of human being: people who root themselves in ideas rather than places, in memories as much as in material things; people who have been obliged to define themselves—because they are so defined by others--by their otherness; people in whose deepest selves strange fusions occur, unprecedented unions between what they were and where they find themselves. The migrant suspects reality: having experienced several ways of being, he understands their illusory nature. To see things plainly, you have to cross a frontier.

The controlling imagination of *Brazil* is born of a fusion between the type of Britishness exemplified by Lewis Carroll, Sterne or Swift, and an Americanness that understands intuitively how to avoid parochialism, how to pace an epic, how to use a superstar's persona to surprising effect. De Niro has rarely been so eccentrically, but confidently, employed. Through the film, we find images with roots on both sides of the Atlantic. The end, for example, when Sam's fantasy of escape fizzles out, leaving him back in the hot seat (with or without clouds) is reminiscent of *Pincher Martin*, in which a drowning sailor fantasizes an island on which he imagines himself to be washed up; but, equally, it is an echo of *Incident at Owl Creek*, the film based on an Ambrose Bierce story, in which a man about to be hanged fantasizes his escape into a deliriously happy future, only to end up dangling from his rope.

Migrants must, of necessity, make a new imaginative relationship with the world, because of the loss of familiar habitats. And for the plural, hybrid, metropolitan result of such imaginings, the cinema, in which peculiar fusions have always been legitimate—in which, for example, casting directors have taught us to accept Peter Sellers as a French detective, and a French actor as Lord Greystoke, Tarzan of the apes—may well be the ideal location. And if I am to conclude with the simple (but also, perhaps, not so simple) observation that the location of *Brazil* is the cinema itself, because in the cinema the dream is the norm, then I should add that this cinematic *Brazil* is a land of make-believe of which all of us who have, for whatever reason, lost a country and ended up elsewhere, are the true citizens. Like Terry Gilliam, I am a Brazilian.

1985

5

THE NEW EMPIRE WITHIN BRITAIN

AN UNIMPORTANT FIRE

HOME FRONT

V. S. NAIPAUL

THE PAINTER AND THE PEST

THE NEW EMPIRE WITHIN BRITAIN

Britain isn't South Africa. I am reliably informed of this. Nor is it Nazi Germany. I've got that on the best authority as well. You may feel that these two statements are not exactly the most dramatic of revelations. But it's remarkable how often they, or similar statements, are used to counter the arguments of anti-racist campaigners. 'Things aren't as bad as all that,' we are told, 'you exaggerate, you're indulging in special pleading, you must be paranoid.' So let me concede at once that, as far as I know, there are no pass laws here. Inter-racial marriages are permitted. And Auschwitz hasn't been rebuilt in the Home Counties. I find it odd, however, that those who use such absences as defences rarely perceive that their own statements indicate how serious things have become. Because if the defence for Britain is that mass extermination of racially impure persons hasn't yet begun, or that the principle of white supremacy hasn't actually been enshrined in the constitution, then something must have gone very wrong indeed.

I want to suggest that racism is not a side-issue in contemporary Britain; that it's not a peripheral minority affair. I believe that Britain is undergoing a critical phase of its post-colonial period, and this crisis is not simply economic or political. It's a crisis of the whole culture, of the society's entire sense of itself. And racism is only the most clearly visible part of this crisis, the tip of the kind of iceberg that sinks ships.

Now I don't suppose many of you think of the British Empire as a subject worth losing much sleep over. After all, surely the one thing one can confidently say about that roseate age of England's precedence, when the map of half the world blushed with pleasure as it squirmed beneath the Pax Britannica, is that it's over, isn't it? Give or take a Falkland Island, the imperial sun has set. And how fine was the manner of its setting; in what good order the British withdrew. Union Jacks fluttered down their poles all round the world, to be replaced by other flags, in all manner of outlandish colours. The pink conquerors crept home, the boxwallahs and memsahibs and bwanas, leaving behind them parliaments, schools, Grand Trunk Roads and the rules of cricket. How gracefully they shrank back into their cold island, abandoning their lives as the dashing people of their dreams, diminishing from the endless steaming landscapes of India and Africa into the narrow horizons of their pallid, drizzled streets. The British have got other things to worry about now; no point, you may say, in exhuming this particular dead horse in order to flog the poor, decomposed creature all over again.

But the connection I want to make is this: that those same attitudes are in operation right here as well, here in what E. P. Thompson has described as the last colony of the British Empire. It sometimes seems that the British authorities, no longer capable of exporting governments, have chosen instead to import a new Empire, a new community of subject peoples of whom they think, and with whom they can deal, in very much the same way as their predecessors thought of and dealt with 'the fluttered folk and wild', the 'new-caught, sullen peoples, half-devil and half-child', who made up, for Rudyard Kipling, the White Man's Burden. In short, if we want to understand British racism—and without understanding no improvement is possible—it's impossible even to begin to grasp the nature of the beast unless we accept its historical roots. Four hundred years of conquest and looting, four centuries of being told that you are superior to the Fuzzy-Wuzzies and the wogs, leave their stain. This stain has seeped into every part of the culture, the language and daily life; and nothing much has been done to wash it out.

For proof of the existence of this stain, we can look, for instance, at the huge, undiminished appetite of white Britons for television series, films, plays and books all filled with nostalgia for the Great Pink Age. Or think about the ease with which the English language allows the terms of racial abuse to be coined: wog, frog, kraut, dago, spic, yid, coon, nigger, Argie. Can there be another language with so wide-ranging a vocabulary of racist denigration? And, since I've mentioned

Argies, let me quote from Margaret Thatcher's speech at Cheltenham on the third of July, her famous victory address: 'We have learned something about ourselves,' she said then, 'a lesson which we desperately need to learn. When we started out, there were the waverers and the fainthearts . . . The people who thought we could no longer do the great things which we once did . . . that we could never again be what we were. There were those who would not admit it . . . but—in their heart of hearts—they too had their secret fears that it was true: that Britain was no longer the nation that had built an Empire and ruled a quarter of the world. Well, they were wrong.'

There are several interesting aspects to this speech. Remember that it was made by a triumphant Prime Minister at the peak of her popularity; a Prime Minister who could claim with complete credibility to be speaking for an overwhelming majority of the electorate, and who, as even her detractors must admit, has a considerable gift for assessing the national mood. Now if such a leader at such a time felt able to invoke the spirit of imperialism, it was because she knew how central that spirit is to the self-image of white Britons of all classes. I say white Britons because it's clear that Mrs Thatcher wasn't addressing the two million or so blacks, who don't feel quite like that about the Empire. So even her use of the word 'we' was an act of racial exclusion, like her other well-known speech about the fear of being 'swamped' by immigrants. With such leaders, it's not surprising that the British are slow to learn the real lessons of their past.

Let me repeat what I said at the beginning: Britain isn't Nazi Germany. The British Empire isn't the Third Reich. But in Germany, after the fall of Hitler, heroic attempts were made by many people to purify German thought and the German language of the pollution of Nazism. Such acts of cleansing are occasionally necessary in every society. But British thought, British society, has never been cleansed of the filth of imperialism. It's still there, breeding lice and vermin, waiting for unscrupulous people to exploit it for their own ends. One of the key concepts of imperialism was that military superiority implied cultural superiority, and this enabled the British to condescend to and repress cultures far older than their own; and it still does. For the citizens of the new, imported Empire, for the colonized Asians and blacks of Britain, the police force represents that colonizing army, those regiments of occupation and control.

Now the peoples whom I've characterized as members of a new colony would probably be described by most of you as 'immigrants'. (You'll notice, by the way, that I've pinched one of Mrs Thatcher's strategies and the You to whom I'm talking is a white You.) So now I'd like to ask you to think about this word 'immigrant', because it seems to me to demonstrate the extent to which racist concepts have been allowed to seize the central ground, and to shape the whole nature of the debate. The facts are that for many years now there has been a sizeable amount of white immigration as well as black, that the annual number of emigrants leaving these shores is now larger than the number of immigrants coming in; and that, of the black communities, over forty per cent are not immigrants, but black Britons, born and bred, speaking in the many voices and accents of Britain, and with no homeland but this one. And still the word 'immigrant' means 'black immigrant'; the myth of 'swamping' lingers on; and even British-born blacks and Asians are thought of as people whose real 'home' is elsewhere. Immigration is only a problem if you are worried about blacks; that is, if your whole approach to the question is one of racial prejudice.

But perhaps the worst thing about the so-called 'numbers game' is its assumption that less black immigration is self-evidently desirable. The effect of this assumption is that governments of both parties have eagerly passed off gross injustice as success. Let me explain. The immigration laws of this country have established a quota system for migration of UK passport holders from various countries. But after Idi Amin drove out the Ugandan Asians, and Britain did her best to prevent those British citizens from entering this country, that African quota was never increased; and, as a result, the total number of black immigrants to Britain has fallen. Now you might think that natural justice would demand that the already lamentably low quotas for British citizens from Africa would be made available to those same citizens, many of whom are now living as refugees in India, a desperately poor country which can ill-afford to care for them. But natural justice has never been much in evidence in this field. In fact, the British tax system now intends to withhold tax relief from wage-earners here whose dependants are trapped abroad. So first you keep people's families away from them and then you alter your laws to make it twice as hard for those people to keep their families fed. They're only 'immigrants', after all.

A couple of years ago the British press made a huge stink about a family of African Asians who arrived at Heathrow airport and were housed by the very reluctant local authority. It became a classic media witch hunt: 'They come over here, sponge off the State and jump the housing queue.' But that same week, another family also landed at Heathrow, also needing, and getting, housing from the same local authority. This second family barely made the papers. It was a family of white Rhodesians running away from the prospect of a free Zimbabwe. One of the more curious aspects of British immigration law is that many Rhodesians, South Africans and other white non-Britons have automatic right of entry and residence here, by virtue of having one British-born grandparent; whereas many British citizens are denied these rights, because they happen to be black.

One last point about the 'immigrants'. It's a pretty obvious point, but it keeps getting forgotten. It's this: they came because they were invited. The Macmillan government embarked on a large-scale advertising campaign to attract them. They were extraordinary advertisements, full of hope and optimism, which made Britain out to be a land of plenty, a golden opportunity not to be missed. And they worked. People travelled here in good faith, believing themselves wanted. This is how the new Empire was imported. This country was named 'perfidious Albion' long ago; and that shaming nickname is now being earned all over again.

So what's it like, this country to which the immigrants

came and in which their children are growing up? You wouldn't recognize it. Because this isn't the England of fair play, tolerance, decency and equality—maybe that place never existed anyway, except in fairy-tales. In the streets of the new Empire, black women are abused and black children are beaten up on their way home from school. In the run-down housing estates of the new Empire, black families have their windows broken, they are afraid to go out after dark, and human and animal excrement arrives through their letter-boxes. The police offer threats instead of protection, and the courts offer small hope of redress. Britain is now two entirely different worlds, and the one you inhabit is determined by the colour of your skin. Now in my experience, very few white people, except for those active in fighting racism, are willing to believe the descriptions of contemporary reality offered by blacks. And black people, faced with what Professor Michael Dummett has called 'the will not to know—a chosen ignorance, not the ignorance of innocence,' grow increasingly suspicious and angry.

A gulf in reality has been created. White and black perceptions of everyday life have moved so far apart as to be incompatible. And the rift isn't narrowing; it's getting wider. We stand on opposite sides of the abyss, yelling at each other and sometimes hurling stones, while the ground crumbles beneath our feet. I make no apology for taking an uncompromising view of the reasons for the existence of this chasm. The will to ignorance of which Professor Dummett speaks arises out of the desire not to face the consequences of what is going on.

The fact remains that every major institution in this country is permeated by racial prejudice to some degree, and the unwillingness of the white majority to recognize this is the main reason why it can remain the case. Let's take the Law. We have, in Britain today, judges like McKinnon who can say in court that the word 'nigger' cannot be considered an epithet of racial abuse because he was nicknamed 'Nigger' at his public school; or like the great Lord Denning, who can publish a book claiming that black people aren't as fit as whites to serve on juries, because they come from cultures with less stringent moral codes. We've got a police force that harasses blacks every day of their lives. There was a policeman who sat in an unmarked car on Railton Road in Brixton last year, shouting abuse at passing black kids and arresting the first youngsters who made the mistake of answering back. There were policemen at a Southall demonstration who sat in their vans, writing the letters NF in the steam of their breath on the windows. The British police have even refused to make racial discrimination an offence in their code of conduct, in spite of Lord Scarman's recommendations. Now it is precisely because the law courts and the police are not doing their jobs that the activities of racist hooligans are on the increase. It's just not good enough to deplore the existence of neo-Fascists in society. They exist because they are permitted to exist. (I said every major institution, so let's consider the government itself. When the Race Relations Act was passed, the government of Britain specifically exempted itself and all its actions from the jurisdiction of the Act.)

A friend of mine, an Indian, was deported recently for the technical offence known as 'overstaying'. This means that after a dozen or so years of living here, he was found to be a couple of days late sending in the forms applying for an extension to his stay. Now neither he nor his family had ever claimed a penny in welfare, or, I suppose I should say, been in trouble with the police. He and his wife financed themselves by running a clothes stall, and gave all their spare time and effort to voluntary work helping their community. My friend was chairman of his local traders' association. So when the deportation order was made, this association, all three of his borough MPs and about fifty other MPs of all parties pleaded with the Home Office for clemency. None was forthcoming. My friend's son had a rare disease, and a doctor's report was produced stating that the child's health would be endangered if he was sent to India. The Home Office replied that it considered there were no compassionate grounds for reversing its decision. In the end, my friend offered to leave voluntarily—he had been offered sanctuary in Germany—

and he asked to be allowed to go freely, to avoid the stigma of having a deportation order stamped into his passport. The Home Office refused him this last scrap of his self-respect, and threw him out. As the Fascist John Kingsley Read once said, one down, a million to go.

The combination of this sort of institutional racism and the willed ignorance of the public was clearly in evidence during the passage through Parliament of the Nationality Act of 1981. This already notorious piece of legislation, expressly designed to deprive black and Asian Britons of their citizenship rights, went through in spite of some, mainly non-white, protests. And because it didn't really affect the position of the whites, you probably didn't even realize that one of your most ancient rights, a right you had possessed for nine hundred years, was being stolen from you. This was the right to citizenship by virtue of birth, the *ius soli*, or right of the soil. For nine centuries any child born on British soil was British. Automatically. By right. Not by permission of the State. The Nationality Act abolished the *ius soli*. From now on citizenship is the gift of government. You were blind, because you believed the Act was aimed at the blacks; and so you sat back and did nothing as Mrs Thatcher stole the birthright of every one of us, black and white, and of our children and grandchildren for ever.

Now it's possible that this blindness is incurable. One of the SDP's better-known candidates told me recently that while he found the idea of working-class racism easy to accept, the parallel notion of widespread prejudice in the middle classes was unconvincing to him. Yet, after many years of voluntary work in this field, I know that the management levels of British industry and business are just as shot through by the threads of prejudice as are many unions. It is believed for instance, that as many as fifty per cent of all telephone calls made by employers to employment agencies specify no blacks. Black unemployment is much, much higher than white; and such anomalies don't arise by accident.

Let me illustrate my point by talking about television. I once earned my living by writing commercials, and I found the prejudice of senior executives in British industry quite appalling. I could tell you the name of the chairman of a leading building society who rejected a jingle on the grounds that the off-screen singer sounded as if he had a black voice. The irony was that the singer was actually white, but the previous year's jingle *had* been sung by a black man who obviously had the good fortune not to sound like one. I know the marketing director of a leading confectionery firm who turned down all requests to cast a black child—as one of an otherwise white group of children—in his commercial. He said his research showed such casting would be counter-productive. I know an airline advertising manager who refused to permit the use, in his TV ads, of a genuine air stewardess employed by his own airline, because she was black. She was good enough to serve his customers their drinks, but not good enough to be shown doing so on television.

A language reveals the attitudes of the people who use and shape it. And a whole declension of patronizing terminology can be found in the language in which inter-racial relations have been described inside Britain. At first, we were told, the goal was 'integration'. Now this word rapidly came to mean 'assimilation': a black man could only become integrated when he started behaving like a white one. After 'integration' came the concept of 'racial harmony'. Now once again, this sounded virtuous and desirable, but what it meant in practice was that blacks should be persuaded to live peaceably with whites, in spite of all the injustices done to them every day. The call for 'racial harmony' was simply an invitation to shut up and smile while nothing was done about our grievances. And now there's a new catchword: 'multiculturalism'. In our schools, this means little more than teaching the kids a few bongo rhythms, how to tie a sari and so forth. In the police training programme, it means telling cadets that black people are so 'culturally different' that they can't help making trouble. Multiculturalism is the latest token gesture towards Britain's blacks, and it ought to be exposed, like 'integration' and 'racial harmony', for the sham it is.

Meanwhile, the stereotyping goes on. Blacks have rhythm, Asians work hard. I've been told by Tory politicians that the Conservative Party seriously discusses the idea of wooing the Asians and leaving the Afro-Caribbeans to the Labour Party, because Asians are such good capitalists. In the new Empire, as in the old one, it seems our masters are willing to use the tried and trusted strategies of divide-and-rule.

But I've saved the worst and most insidious stereotype for last. It is the characterization of black people as a Problem. You talk about the Race Problem, the Immigration Problem, all sorts of problems. If you are liberal, you say that black people have problems. If you aren't, you say they are the problem. But the members of the new colony have only one real problem, and that problem is white people. British racism, of course, is not our problem. It's yours. We simply suffer from the effects of your problem.

And until you, the whites, see that the issue is not integration, or harmony, or multiculturalism, or immigration, but simply the business of facing up to and eradicating the prejudices within almost all of you, the citizens of your new, and last, Empire will be obliged to struggle against you. You could say that we are required to embark on a new freedom movement.

And so it's interesting to remember that when Mahatma Gandhi, the father of an earlier freedom movement, came to England and was asked what he thought of English civilization, he replied: 'I think it would be a good idea.'

1982

AN UNIMPORTANT FIRE

There was an unimportant fire in the London Borough of Camden on 20 November. Nothing spectacular; just a cheap bed-and-breakfast establishment going up in flames. The fire was at 46 Gloucester Place, owned by London Lets, whose proprietor is one Mr J. Doniger. When it started, no alarm rang. It had been switched off. The fire extinguishers were empty. The fire exits were blocked. It was night-time, but the stairs were in darkness, because there were no bulbs in the lighting sockets. And in the single, cramped top-floor room, where the cooker was next to the bed and where they had been housed for nine months, Mrs Abdul Karim, a Bangladeshi woman, and her five-year-old son and three-year-old daughter died of suffocation. They had been housed in London Lets by Camden Council, at a cost that one councillor estimated at £280 a week. Death-traps are not always economical, it would appear.

Those of us who do not live in slum housing get used with remarkable ease to the fact that others do. It is by now reasonably well known that councils all over the country are putting people into substandard B&B accommodation. The councils admit that this accommodation is way below their own standards, and conforms to just about no public health and safety regulations. They will even admit, if pressed, that black and Asian families are far more likely than white ones to be placed in such 'temporary' places. (I use the inverted commas because I have met many families who have been in these slums, without hope of a move, for well over a year.) Hard statistics are not easy to come by, but it seems safe to say that between a third and a half of all families put into London Lets-type establishments are black. We know all this; and sighing sympathetically about the problem, we pass by on the other side. This time, however, the maltreated families have decided not to make things so easy for the council, or for us. On 22 November, they came to Camden Town Hall to ask for a public inquiry. When it was refused, they occupied the council chamber. As I write this, they are still there, and intend to remain until kingdom come, if need be, although they would prefer just to be rehoused in safe, decent, permanent accommodation.

The occupying families are representative of the eighty or so families housed by Camden in London Lets properties. They are demanding a commitment from the council that it cease to use such accommodation. And there are plenty of horror stories, if you want them. One mother told us how her baby died of infections contracted because they were living in a room into which sewage kept pouring. Another told us that she had been stuck in a B&B for three years now. Two pregnant mothers, past their due dates, have been sleeping on the council chamber floor for over a week, thinking it preferable to, and safer than, their appalling homes. And, over and over again, I was told of staircases with rotten floorboards, of toilets that did not flush, of damp and mould, and of infestation by insects. In their single room at 42 Gloucester Place, Mr and Mrs Ali and their son are obliged to share their quarters with large numbers of 'whitish, crawling insects, like earthworms'.

It gives me no pleasure to attack a socialist local authority like Camden Council, already high on Nanny's hit list. But nor do I derive much pleasure from the way I have seen supposed socialists behaving and talking over the last week or so. I asked Councillor Bob Latham, Chair of Camden's Race Committee, what would happen if the families in the slums took the council to court for being in breach of their statutory duty to house the citizens of the borough according to public standards. He said that many of the B&B places were in fact outside Camden; so he didn't think Camden could be sued. Councillor Sandy Wynn, Deputy Leader of the council and a woman with an unfortunate, high-handed manner, loudly proclaimed that the homeless families were being 'manipulated by people with other things in their minds.' Councillor Richard Sumray has implied in his media interviews that the occupation is part of an attempt by Bengali families to jump the housing queue. (It's worth pointing out that by no means all the families involved are black.) Presumably not enough people have been burned to death yet. Priorities are priorities, after all. How does the old song go? *The people's tape is deepest red* . . .

On the second night of the occupation, the families formed a ring around a group of councillors who were trying to walk out of a discussion. Camden's radical response was to send in the police. While a police superintendent was negotiating with the families' lawyer, his men took matters into their own hands and stormed the council chamber. There are three entrances to this room. Two were completely unguarded and unlocked. By the third, there was a crowd of people. The police came in by the crowded entrance, and they came in roughly. One young man had to go to hospital and returned with his arm in a sling. I asked Sumray what had happened. 'Somebody grazed an elbow,' he told me.

The police are now treating the deaths of Mrs Karim and her children as a murder investigation. There is apparently evidence that the fire was started deliberately. And at once the hints and innuendoes have started flying: the homeless families started the fire themselves, the insinuations say, to force the council to rehouse them. It sounds like the New Cross fire all over again: how much neater life gets when you make the victims responsible for the crime.

Since the deaths and the beginning of the occupation, there have been numerous stories of an increase in the harassment of slum-housed families by their landlords, and by the police, under the cover of 'investigating the Karim murders'. There has been an attempt by councillors to divide and rule: they offered to rehouse the families actually in the council chamber, and leave it at that. But solidarity still means something in Britain, even if Labour councillors have forgotten the word: the occupiers refused to negotiate except on the basis that all eighty families should be considered together.

And there has been one very moving moment. On Wednesday 29 November, the Leader of the council, Phil Turner, came to listen to the families describing the horrors of their lives, and to discuss what the council could do; and he burst into tears, an honourable man driven to weeping by the frustrations of his position. The occupying families believe Turner to be sympathetic to their case. They say his problem is that he is not getting much support either from the housing department's officers or from the majority Labour Group. So the families have been offered, and rejected, a whole series of vague promises and inadequate new homes, that is, more B&B housing or more 'temporary' accommodation.

This is why the council is so nervous of giving the eighty families the commitment they are asking for: London Lets is by no means the end of the story. I have heard people describing many other B&B establishments which sound even worse. Again, it's hard to be certain about the figures, but there may be as many as 700 families—about 2,000 human beings—housed by Camden in disease-infested firetraps. No wonder the councillors are nervous. The mice have started biting back.

Let me say again, at the end, it's no fun to bash Camden. Many members of the council, and many of its employees, are dedicated folk doing their best. Think how much worse the plight of the homeless must be in less 'enlightened' boroughs.

The trouble is, Camden's best has been nothing like good enough. It is time people stopped having to die to prove to local authorities that they live in hideously unsatisfactory conditions. If the deaths of Mrs Karim and her children are to be treated as murders, then many of us would say that the murderers are to be found in Camden Town Hall; and no, I am not talking about the families occupying the council chamber to protest non-violently and to demand their long-denied rights.

1984

HOME FRONT

ome Front, by John Bishton and John Reardon, is a book of images; and imagination, the process by which we make pictures of the world, is (along with the idea of the self and the development of the opposable thumb) one of the keys to our humanity. So well-made pictures are of importance to us all; they tell us not only what we have previously seen, but what it is possible to begin seeing. They *open our eyes*. There are many such pictures to be found in this photographic portrait of everyday reality as it is experienced by Britain's Asians and blacks—many memorable images of happiness, turbulence, defiance, childhood, death. In a Handsworth *gurdwara*, or Sikh temple, an old man sits on a white-sheeted floor and clutches at a radiator for warmth. Or in a scrap of urban waste land, a child's head appears at the peak of a pyramid of rubble, while behind him rises the irony of a brick wall on which is painted a lurid scene of tropical paradise.

But the significance of such a photographic essay as *Home Front* is not only aesthetic. For these are images of people who have for centuries been persecuted by images. The imagination can falsify, demean, ridicule, caricature and wound as effectively as it can clarify, intensify and unveil; and from the slaves of old to the British-born black children of the present, there have been many who could testify to the pain of being subjected to white society's view of them.

Fortunately, 'white society' is no homogeneous mass. After all, we have here the work of two white men, and it is sensitive, knowledgeable work. In *The Black Jacobins*, C. L. R. James wrote: 'The blacks will know as friends only those whites who are fighting in the ranks beside them. And whites will be there.' And so they are.

Let us say, then, that this book should be seen as part of the struggle. Its title implies as much, with its echoes of wartime privations and vigilance, as well as the growing comradeship and solidarity of the people—in this case the black communities. It seeks to set new, truer images against the old falsehoods, so that the world and its attitudes may be enabled to move forward a millimetre or two.

An honourable enterprise; but what forces are still arrayed against it! The trouble began, one might almost say, at the very Beginning:

> God made the little nigger boys
> He made them in the night
> He made them in a hurry
> And forgot to paint them white.

Yes, perhaps it started with Creation. Darkness, you recall, preceded light; but 'God saw the light, that it was good: and God divided the light from the darkness.' Then the fear of melanin-darkened skin is really the fear of the primal Dark, of the Ur-Night. It is the instinctual hostility of day-beings for the creatures of night. Maybe so. And maybe all this is connected also to the idea of the Other, the reversed twin in the looking-glass, the double, the negative image, who by his oppositeness tells one what one is. God cannot be defined without the Devil, Jekyll is meaningless without Hyde. Clearly the Other is to be feared. Images of him-her-it often use motifs of night, or of invisibility, which is a night of the watching eye; or of sexual threat (Beauty and the Beast); or of malformation (Frankenstein's monster). Very frequently the Other is foreign; only very, very rarely is it presented as an object of sympathy. Two notable exceptions are Kafka's 'Metamorphosis' and the film *King Kong*. Kafka shows us elsewhere that the Other can be a Castle, or a nocturnal knock at the door; but it can also be a helpless bug, that is to say Gregor Samsa, that is to say ourselves. And Kong is allowed to love Fay Wray, which earns him a kind of tragedy: ' 'Twas Beauty killed the Beast.'

However, it will not suffice to blame racism and the creation of lying images of black peoples on some deep-bubbling, universal failing in humanity. Even if prejudice has roots in all societies, each malodorous flowering of the plant occurs in specific historical, political and economic circumstances. So each case is different, and if one wishes to fight against such triffids of bigotry, it is the differences that are important and useful. Interestingly, the universality of racial prejudice is often used to excuse it. (Whereas few people would try to condone—for example—murders on the grounds that aggression and violence are also universal to the species.) And, while it is obviously true that blacks and Asians need to face up to and deal with our own prejudices, it seems equally clear that the most attention must be paid to the most serious problem, and in Britain, that is white racism. If we were speaking of India or Africa, we would have other forms of racism to fight against. But you fight hardest where you live: on the home front. That's human nature, too.

British racism—and by that I mean a fully developed ideology, complete with the trappings of pseudo-science and 'reason'—first flowered as a means of legitimizing the lucrative slave trade, and was patently economic in origin. It expanded, during the Asian and African colonial experience, into a rationale for world domination. These are the specific circumstances without which the British variation of the disease cannot be understood. But it is often argued that those old days, those old ideas are long dead, and play no significant part in the events of contemporary Britain. If only that were true. If only history worked so cleanly, erasing itself as it went forward.

If only the ideas of the past did not rot down into the earth and fertilize the ideas of the present. In the nineteenth century, it was the Irish who were criticized for their rabbit-like breeding and their cooking smells; a hundred years later, the same slanders, in just about the same words, were being hurled at the 'Pakis'. And many of the myths, the false pictures against which blacks still struggle, date from the early days of the slave trade—the myth, for instance, of their insatiable animal desires, of the sexual aggression of black women and the huge, threatening members of black men. In 1626, Francis Bacon wrote in *New Atlantis* that the 'Spirit of Fornication' was 'a little foul ugly Aethiope'. It was just one of many such remarks.

It is impossible in this brief piece to catalogue all the concocted imagery and received ideas which work both on the conscious and unconscious mind to create the environment in which racism can thrive. Minstrel shows, old-movie mammies shuffling and bopping across the screen wearing head-kerchiefs and carpet slippers, pantomime Orientals in harem-pants, yashmaks, turbans. Yes, the golliwog, too; at football grounds, black players are taunted with the cry, 'Get back on your jamjar.' Television and newspaper images: because blacks and Asians, whether in Britain or abroad, more or less disappear from the news except in times of crisis. Violence, riot, assassination, famine, flood, disease, mugging: the operation of 'news values' subliminally links blacks to trouble. Well, no, not entirely. Blacks have natural rhythm, Asians don't. Blacks are good at athletics, Asians at studies. (This stereotypical contrast is still at work in many schools.) Asians are thrifty, interested in business, naturally conservative; blacks throw their money around, are lazy, disaffected from the State. Blacks take drugs; Asians can't speak English.

The point about stereotypes is that, in spite of their banality, in spite of their seemingly evident wrongness, they work. They have effects. They are at work in Britain today. And they are hard to combat, because nobody readily admits to being influenced by them. Of course you can see how other people might be—but not you—no!—ridiculous. And while the great power of false perceptions is being denied, Britain's blacks and Asians go on living in the worst available public housing, suffering from a far higher unemployment rate than their white neighbours, facing street-armies of neo-Fascists, fearing the police, being harassed at immigration points, and, when they protest, being told that there is no reason for them to stay here if they don't like it; as if the ethnic minorities' British citizenship were conditional on their never making a fuss.

We live in ideas. Through images we seek to comprehend our world. And through images we sometimes seek to subjugate and dominate others. But picture-making, imagining, can also be a process of celebration, even of liberation. New images can chase out the old. This book is one, notable contribution to that process, the process of getting off the jamjar.

1984

V. S. NAIPAUL

A few years ago, V. S. Naipaul said that he still thought of himself as a comic writer, and that his highest ambition was to write a comedy to equal his magnificent 1961 novel, *A House for Mr Biswas*. To read this was to feel heartened; if the author could find a way of uniting the warmth and energy of the early work that culminated in *Biswas* with the technical mastery of his later writing, we might be in for something rather special.

But there were doubts. The dark clouds that seemed to have gathered over Naipaul's inner world would not, one feared, be easily dispelled; his affection for the human race appeared to have diminished, and the comedy of *Miguel Street*, *The Mystic Masseur*, *The Suffrage of Elvira* and *Biswas*, cutting and unsentimental as those books were, had been essentially affectionate.

The Enigma of Arrival, Naipaul's first novel in eight years, suggests that the clouds have not lifted, but deepened. The book lacks the bitter taste of some of his recent writing, but it is one of the saddest books I have read in a long while, its tone one of unbroken melancholy. 'This melancholy penetrated my mind while I slept,' says the narrator whom it is impossible not to see as the author, 'and then, when I awakened . . . I was so poisoned by it . . . that it took the best part of the day to shake it off.'

It's a strange book, more meditation than novel, autobiographical in the sense that it offers a portrait of the intellectual landscape of one who has long elevated 'the life of the mind' above all other forms of life. Its subject is the narrator's consciousness, its reformation by the act of migration, of 'arrival', and its gradual turning towards James's 'distinguished thing', death. There are other characters here, but they are observed from a distance, the main events in their lives—an elopement, a sacking, a death—taking place off-stage. As a result of this emptying, the writer becomes the subject; the story-teller becomes the tale.

Interestingly, and unlike most of his fellow-migrants, Naipaul has chosen to inhabit a pastoral England, an England of manor and stream. The book's first segment deals with what he calls his 'second childhood' in this piece of Wiltshire. The notion of migration as a form of rebirth is one whose truths many migrants will recognize. Instantly recognizable, too, and often very moving, is the sense of a writer feeling obliged to bring his new world into being by an act of pure will, the sense that if the world is not described into existence in the most minute detail, then it won't be there. The immigrant must invent the earth beneath his feet.

So Naipaul describes: this lane, this cottage, this gardener, this view of Stonehenge, this tiny patch of the planet in which his narrator must learn, once more, to see. It is a kind of extreme minimalism, but it becomes almost hypnotic. And slowly the picture is built, figures arrive in the landscape, a new world is won.

Through the story—well, the account—of the farm labourer Jack and his garden, we are shown how the narrator's view of rustic England changes. At first idyllic—'Of literature and antiquity and the landscape Jack and his garden . . . seemed emanations'—it develops along more realistic lines. Jack's health fails, his garden decays, he dies, the new occupants of his cottage pour concrete over his garden. The idea of timelessness, of Jack as being 'solid, rooted in his earth', turns out to be false. *Change and decay in all around I see.*

So the new world begins to be seen for what it is, but at what a price! It's as if Naipaul expended so much of his energy on the effort of creating and comprehending his piece of Wiltshire that he had no strength left with which to make the characters breathe and move. They manage only tiny flutters of activity; even the story of Brenda, the country wife who expected too much from her beauty, and Les, the husband who murdered her after she returned, tail between legs, from her failed attempt at an affair with another man, is told in an oddly enervated, inconsequential manner.

The narrator speaks often of his spirit being broken, of illness, of exhaustion. He once wanted to write a story based on Chirico's painting 'The Enigma of Arrival', he says, and then, in less than a page, gives us a summary of this untold tale. It is quite brilliant, a traveller's tale set in the classical world of the surrealist painting, utterly unlike anything Naipaul has ever written.

The painting shows a port, a sail, a tower, two figures. Naipaul makes one of the figures a traveller who arrives at a 'dangerous classical city'. 'Gradually . . . his feeling of adventure would give way to panic . . . I imagined some religious ritual in which, led on by kindly people, he would unwittingly take part and find himself the intended victim. At the moment of crisis he would come upon a door, open it, and find himself back on the quayside of arrival . . . Only one thing is missing now . . . The antique ship has gone. The traveller has lived out his life.'

The book we have is at once more honest and direct, and less vibrant and engaging, than the first-imagined fantasy, and, especially in the drawn-out second half of the novel, one frequently wishes that Naipaul had been able to write the discarded tale. Exhaustion again; when the strength for fiction fails the writer, what remains is autobiography.

After an interesting, and courageous, account of his formation as a writer, Naipaul returns to his Wiltshire microcosm, and it turns out that his narrator's exhaustion and turning-towards-death is mirrored in his tiny world. A version of England is dying, too, the manor no longer as economically powerful as it was, its owner sunbathing plump-thighed amid the decay. Just about all the book's personages are in some way in thrall to the manor—a second gardener, Pitton, the estate manager Phillips and his wife, a driver, a failed writer, even the narrator himself—and they, too, are going down with the ship. Death and failure stalk them all.

All this is evoked in delicate, precise prose of the highest quality, but it is bloodless prose. The idea that the British have lost their way because of 'an absence of authority, an organization in decay', that the fall of the manor encourages ordinary folk 'to hasten decay, to loot, to reduce to junk', is an unlikeable, untenable one. But if only the book occasionally sparked into some sort of life! As it stands, the portrait of exhaustion becomes, eventually, just exhausting.

Why such utter weariness? We are told of a dream of an exploding head, of ill health, of family tragedy. There may be more to it. I think it was Borges who said that, in a riddle to which the answer is *knife*, the only word that cannot be employed is *knife*. There is one word I can find nowhere in the text of *The Enigma of Arrival*. That word is 'love', and a life without love, or one in which love has been buried so deep that it can't come out, is very much what this book is about; and what makes it so very, very sad.

1987

The Painter and the Pest

It looks very much as though a new paragraph needs to be added to the history of Abstract Expressionist painting. A new name, it appears, must henceforth be mentioned, if not in the same breath as those of Jackson Pollock and Willem de Kooning, then in the breaths following: the name of Harold Shapinsky, sixty years old this month, an artist of Russian extraction presently living in New York City, where for most of the past four decades his work has been completely ignored. Now, after all the years of neglect, there has been a remarkable reversal of fortunes, and Mr Shapinsky is experiencing an *annus mirabilis*, with a major retrospective of his work at London's Mayor Gallery, loads of publicity on both sides of the Atlantic, and several important European galleries reportedly queuing up to buy his work.

The story of the belated 'discovery' of Harold Shapinsky must surely be one of the most extraordinary in the history of modern art. It is hard enough to believe that a painter who is now attracting lavish praise from every corner of the European art establishment could have languished so long in Manhattan, the undisputed capital of the art world, without gaining any sort of real recognition. Even less plausible, perhaps, is the identity of his 'discoverer'; because the man who has singlehandedly worked the miracle is not an art expert at all, and has no links with either the American or European art establishments. He describes himself variously as 'some crazy Indian' and 'a pest'.

This man is Akumal Ramachander, thirty-five, a teacher of elementary English at an agricultural college in Bangalore in southern India—a suitably improbable background for the hero of a shaggy-dog story whose saving grace is that it happens to be quite true.

Professor Ramachander—Akumal—is an amateur in the real sense: a man of passions. In fact, he is quite possibly the most enthusiastic individual on the face of the planet, as I discovered a couple of years ago when I was on a lecture tour of India. Akumal, then a complete stranger, arrived at my Bangalore hotel room, introduced himself, and proceeded to overwhelm me with the unstoppable frenzy of garlands, vast smiles, flashing eyes, unceasing monologues and emphatic gesticulations to which those who find themselves in his vicinity rapidly grow accustomed. He struck me as a bit of an operator, but it was impossible not to warm to his openness and affection for life, as well as his obviously genuine love for literature, art, cinema and many other things, including butterflies. (He also sings.) This inexhaustible, 'crazy' energy needed something to focus on. That necessary sense of purpose was provided when Akumal met, by chance—though one sometimes wonders if anything in his life really happens by chance—the son of the painter Harold Shapinsky.

In September 1984, Akumal, visiting the Indian poet A. K. Ramanujan in Chicago, was taken to a party where he met David Shapinsky, and heard about Harold for the first time. At David's home he saw a few examples of the father's work and became, as he put it, 'alerted'. He travelled to New York— it should be pointed out here that Akumal is no zillionaire, jetsetting Indian; he has never had much money, and during this period went quite some way into debt—and met Harold and Kate Shapinsky for the first time.

He was impressed and moved by the paintings, and also by the dignity with which the Shapinskys lived, in spite of their considerable poverty. The apartment was minute. There was, Akumal found, no liquid soap with which to do the washing-up; they used a cake of hard soap placed at the bottom of a jar of water instead. The painter had been so short of funds for so long that he was unable to afford canvases, and was obliged to work, as a result, on thick sheets of paper. (So the paintings are all rather small, and, to my eye at least, one of Shapinsky's most impressive achievements has been to paint epic, 'big' concepts on this artificially constricted scale.)

Kate Shapinsky is a dancer by profession, a contemporary of Martha Graham's. Now, while Shapinsky paints, she makes quilts, sweaters and pullovers and sells them to boutiques, and the small income from this work is what has, for many years, enabled the Shapinskys to live and Harold to paint.

Akumal discussed with David Shapinsky the possibility of his, Akumal's, trying to promote Harold's work, and it was agreed that he should try. Now the professor from Bangalore made a bet with the painter's son—that within twelve months he would get Harold Shapinsky a major exhibition in Europe, in London, perhaps, or Amsterdam; and that the *Encyclopaedia Britannica* would have to rewrite its section on Abstract Expressionism, to make room for the achievement of the long-neglected master.

But Harold Shapinsky had spent most of his career in total isolation from the art marketplace, unnoticed by galleries and dealers. In 1950 his work had been included in a new talent exhibition, and even praised by the *New York Times*, but since then there had been virtually nothing, except for a few obscure group shows. Indifference had forced him into seclusion. And any establishment hates to admit to a mistake.

It was this wall of indifference and scepticism that Akumal had to scale, or to demolish. He had slides of Shapinsky's work made at his own expense, and began a frontal assault on the Manhattan art world. He had no success; the wall held firm. After all, how was it possible that the crazy Indian from the Bangalore agricultural college had spotted something that the New York mandarins had missed? After about thirty galleries had refused even to look at the slides, Akumal decided to try Europe. And now his luck—and Shapinsky's—changed.

In London in December 1984 Akumal arrived at the Tate Gallery, without an appointment, clutching his box of slides. A few minutes later Ronald Alley, the Keeper of the Modern Collection, was telephoned from the front hall and told that an Indian gentleman had arrived, in rather an agitated state, and was insisting on showing somebody a group of slides that he claimed were a major discovery. Alley agreed to look at the slides. Akumal had broken through the wall.

When Ronald Alley saw the slides, he says, 'I was amazed that a real Abstract Expressionist painter of such quality should be unknown,' and he put Akumal in touch with the Mayor Gallery. He also put in writing his feelings about Shapinsky's work. In the next few weeks many European experts followed suit. Professor Norbert Lynton, Professor of Art History at Sussex University, wrote: 'He is certainly a painter of outstanding quality . . . the slides suggest a rare quality of fresh and vivid (as opposed to mournfully soulful) abstract expressionism, a marvellous sense of colour and also a rare feel for positioning marks and areas of colour on the canvas or paper.' The leading modern-art galleries of Cologne and Amsterdam also expressed enthusiasm. And James Mayor of the Mayor Gallery flew to New York, was impressed and excited, and made a selection for the Shapinsky retrospective. The bet was won.

One suspects that, as well as the genuine enthusiasm all over Europe for the quality of Shapinsky's work, there has been a certain amount of gleeful hand-rubbing going on, because the Shapinsky case reflects so badly on the New York art scene. And New York has been ruling the roost for so long that this piece of European revenge must taste sweet indeed.

As for Professor Ramachander, he, too, should now benefit from the 'launch' of Harold Shapinsky. But what was it that enabled Akumal to see what everyone had failed to see? The answer, it seems, is those butterflies: 'My art school was a small field near my house. I would spend quite a long time there, chasing butterflies. Hundreds of thousands of them, you know, in all their brilliant hues. I would never destroy a butterfly, just chase them and wonder at that great profusion of colours. And I think all that colour sank into me . . . all those permutations and combinations, they were already there in me. All that had to happen was to get someone's work, and see if I could get back all the colours I saw in my childhood. And Shapinsky seemed to come very close to that.'

For centuries now, it has been the fate of the peoples of the East to be 'discovered' by the West, with dramatic and usually unpleasant consequences. The story of Akumal and Shapinsky is one small instance in which the East has been able to repay the compliment, and with a happy ending, too. And if we are asked to believe that it all began in a field in Calcutta, where an Indian boy ran with butterfly-colours swirling all around him, then why not? It's as likely as anything else in this story, after all.

1985

6

A General Election

Charter 88

On Palestinian Identity:
A Conversation with Edward Said

A GENERAL ELECTION

I returned to England only recently, after spending two months in India, and was feeling pretty disorientated even before the general election was called. Now, as successive opinion polls inform us of the near-inevitability of a more or less enormous Tory victory, my sense of alienation has blossomed into something close to full-scale culture shock. "'Tis a mad world you have here, my masters.'

Have they been putting something in the drinking water while I've been away? I had always thought that the British prided themselves on their common sense, on good old-fashioned down-to-earth realism. But the election of 1983 is beginning to look more and more like a dark fantasy, a fiction so outrageously improbable that any novelist would be ridiculed if he dreamed it up.

Consider this fiction. A Tory Prime Minister, Maggie May, gets elected on the basis of her promises to cut direct taxation and to get the country back to work ('Labour isn't working'). During the next four years she increases direct taxation and contrives to add almost two million people to the dole queues. And she throws in all sorts of extra goodies: a fifth of the country's manufacturing industry lies in ruins, and (although she claims repeatedly to have vanquished the monster Inflation) she presides over the largest increase in prices of any British Prime Minister. The country's housing programme grinds to a halt; schools and hospitals are closed; the Nationality Act robs Britons of their 900-year-old right to citizenship by virtue of birth; and the great windfall of North Sea oil money is squandered on financing unemployment. Money is poured into the police force, and as a result notifiable crimes rise by twenty-eight per cent.

She constantly tells the nation that cash limits are tight, but finds untold billions to spend on a crazy war whose legacy includes the export of drinking water to the South Atlantic at a cost to the British taxpayer of five pence a pint;

159

and, speaking of peace, she earmarks further untold billions for the purchase of the latest weapons of death, although common sense, not to mention history, clearly indicates that the more such weapons exist, the more likely they are to be used.

So far, the story of Prime Minister May is almost credible. The fictional character does come across as unusually cruel, incompetent, unscrupulous and violent, but there have just occasionally been Tory politicians of whom such a description would not be wholly inaccurate. No, the story only falls apart when it gets to the end: Maggie May decides to go to the country, and instead of being hounded into the outer darkness, or at least Tasmania, like her namesake, it seems that she is to receive a vote of confidence; that five more years of cruelty, incompetence, etc., is what the electorate wants.

The hapless novelist submits his story, and is immediately submerged in a flood of rejection slips. Desperately, he tries to make his narrative more convincing. Maggie May's political opponents are presented as hopelessly divided. The presence of alleged 'full-time socialists' amongst her foes alarms the people. The leader of the Labour Party wears a crumpled donkey-jacket at the Cenotaph and keeps falling over his dog. But still (the rejection slips point out) the fact remains that for Mrs May to hold anything like the lead that the polls say she holds, the unemployed—or some of them, anyway—must be planning to vote for her; and so must some of the homeless, some of the businessmen whose businesses she has destroyed, some of the women who will be worse off when (for instance) her proposal to means-test child benefits becomes law, and many of the trade unionists whose rights she proposes so severely to erode.

At this point, our imaginary novelist (compromising the integrity of his vision for the sake of publication) would, in all probability, agree to rewrite his ending. The trumpets sound, the sleeping citizenry awakes, *le jour de gloire* arrives, and Maggie May gets, in 1983, the same sort of bum's rush given to her hero Winston Churchill in 1945.

Is it not passing strange that this, the plausible and happy ending, is the one that looks, in the cold light of real-life Britain, like the one in which it's almost impossible to believe?

I find myself entertaining Spenglerian thoughts about how there can be times when all that is worst in a people rises to the surface and expresses itself in its government. There are, of course, many Britains, and many of them—the sceptical, questioning, radical, reformist, libertarian, non-conformist Britains—I have always admired greatly. But these Britains are presently in retreat, even in disarray; while nanny-Britain, straight-laced Victoria-reborn Britain, class-ridden know-your-place Britain, thin-lipped, jingoist Britain, is in charge. Dark goddesses rule; brightness falls from the air. 'The Ancient Britons,' says the best of history books, *1066 and All That*, 'painted themselves true blue, or woad, and fought heroically under their dashing queen, Woadicea.' The Britons are even more Ancient now, but they have been fighting once again, and that blue dye takes a long time to wear off. Woadicea rides again.

What an achievement is hers! She has persuaded the nation that everything that goes wrong, from unemployment to the crime rate, is an Act of God or someone else's fault, that the forces of organized labour are actually the enemies of organized labour; that we can only defend ourselves by giving the United States the power of life and death over us; that to be an 'activist' is somehow far worse than being an inactivist, and that the left must once more be thought of in Latin, as sinister. She propounds what is in fact an ideology of impotence masquerading as resolution, a con-trick, and it looks as though it's going to work: Maggie's sting.

And it was as recently as 1945 that the British people, politicized by their wartime experiences, threw off the yoke of the true-blue ruling class . . . How quickly the wheel has turned, how quickly faith has been lost in the party they forged as their weapon, how depressingly willing the nation seems to be to start touching forelocks once again. The worst thing about this election is that nobody seems really angry about what has happened, is happening, and is sure to go on happening if Mrs Thatcher is standing on the steps of No. 10

on the morning of 10 June. (What will she quote from this time? St Francis of Assisi again? St Joan? The Hitler Diaries?)

I believe the absence of widespread anger matters enormously, for this reason: that democracy can only thrive in a turbulent climate. Where there is acquiescence, cynicism, passivity, resignation, 'inactivism', the road is clear for those who would rob us of our rights.

So, finally, and in spite of all the predictions and probabilities, I refuse to accept that the cause is lost. Despair brings comfort to one's enemies. And elections are not, at bottom, about reasoned arguments; they are about passions. It is just conceivable that even now, in this eleventh hour, a rage can be kindled in the people, rage against the dying of the light that Thatcherism represents. The electorate, we are told, has never been so volatile; so maybe the miracle can still be worked. Maybe, on the day, real life will turn out to obey the same laws of probability as fiction, and sanity will return.

If not, we can look forward to five more years of going to the dogs. *Guardian* readers will no doubt remember these unappealing canines; a few years ago, they used to be known as the running dogs of capitalism.

1983

CHARTER 88

It used to be believed that philosophies of social justice, arguments over the definition of the good, indeed all discussion of the shape of the society in which we wished to live, were *anterior to politics*, that, in fact, politics was a secondary and subservient branch of ethics. You could argue that this was as true for Karl Marx as it had been for Aristotle. It is apparently true no more. 'Nothing in Britain is these days permitted to be apolitical,' Hugo Young tells us in a *Guardian* article accusing the Charter 88 campaign of being the SDP in disguise, an appeal to the 'apolitical classes'. The only 'real' target of such campaigns, he says, is 'to convert the Labour Party to this kind of thinking.' So new ideas must now go cap in hand to political overlords (and 'politics' is equated with 'party politics'). These are narrow days.

In the mind of one of these overlords, Mr Roy Hattersley, an even more remarkable fusion of the ethical and political has occurred, one which enables him to define 'positive freedom' as 'government action'—this in an article whose immediately preceding paragraph refers, without any seeming awareness of the contradiction involved, to the denial, 'by government action', of the rights of ethnic minorities and women.

'True liberty requires action from the government,' says Mr Hattersley in authentically Orwellian tones, ignoring the entire history of freedom movements the world over, to say nothing of the distinguished record of extra-governmental citizens' movements in the increase of liberty—a record which suggests that, in the matter of freedom, governments do not act until they are pushed.

It will clearly take quite a push to move Mr Hattersley, for whom democracy means the 'absolute sovereignty' of Parliament. Quoting a Mori report of what proportional representation would have meant in the 1987 election (the Tories would have won 279 seats, not 375; Labour 202, not

229; the Alliance 149 instead of just 22), he insists that because this would have created a hung parliament, resulting in the 'destruction of the major parties', it must never be allowed to happen. Thus we see that the Deputy Leader of the Labour Party believes not only in the absolute sovereignty of Parliament, but *of the major parties*; further proof, if further proof were needed, that the true conservatives in Britain are now in the Labour Party, while there are plenty of radicals in blue.

Charter 88 is an attempt to renew the debate about the kind of country we want to live in, precisely because our 'absolute sovereigns' seem no longer capable of giving expression to such concerns; precisely because it is becoming difficult to believe in the inviolability of our rights, or even in their existence, until we see them enshrined in a written constitution. As Ian McEwan puts it, if we in Britain are the proud possessors of fundamental freedoms denied to so many other peoples, what could be the objection to writing them down?

I would certainly not describe the Charter 88 campaign as 'apolitical', because it must clearly seek eventually to enter the political, even the party-political field; but as *pre-political*, as one of those initiatives which, like the civil rights movement, the anti-Vietnam movement, the women's movement, the nuclear disarmament movement, the greens, seeks initially to work as a movement of citizens, not leaders, and requires politicians to listen, for a change, to other voices than their own.

What differentiates Charter 88 from the movements I've just listed is that it is not a single-issue campaign, but an attempt at a radical critique of the way we are presently governed; and that, for its aims ever to be achieved, it would need support from all parts of the political spectrum. A lasting constitution must be above the sectarianism of party politics.

Roy Hattersley is contemptuous of written constitutions. Even the European Convention on Human Rights is dismissed as a means of protecting the public schools. Anyway, he tells us, the thing can't be done. 'What Parliament has given away,

Parliament can take back.' Absolute sovereigns lack, it seems, absolute power only over themselves. All this is hogwash. Yes, Charter 88 proposes something very like a constitutional revolution, but constitutional revolutions have happened before. Yes, it would require, for example, Parliament voting for its own, momentary abolition, so that—perhaps at a constitutional convention—the law could finally be placed above our rulers' heads. Yes, we're talking about changing the legal form of the nation. Nations can do such things if they deem them necessary. Mr Hattersley's hatred of change condemns him, I fear, to the fate of the dinosaurs.

The simple truth is that just about every other democratic society possesses, and cherishes, a written constitution; that the British insisted that all their former colonies should, at the moment of independence, acquire such a document; and that increasing numbers of British citizens no longer have faith in the untrammelled powers of this, or any other over-mighty, British government.

'The very idea of human rights—particularly *universal* ones—is a comparatively novel, recent development,' Steve Platts writes in the *New Statesman & Society*. It is valuable to be reminded by him 'just how revolutionary a development' the UN's Universal Declaration of Human Rights, just forty years ago, really was. Even the most cursory study of the history of the twentieth century indicates that it's really very hard indeed to pin down what may or may not be a 'human' or a 'civil' right, and that it's correspondingly easy for governments to act as if such rights did not, or need not, exist. But we all know what we mean by a 'constitutional right'. The Fifth Amendment of the US constitution makes it impossible for an American Thatcher to remove a defendant's right to silence in a court of law. The Charter 88 signatories believe that it's high time we had such rights; and it may just be possible to achieve a national—and, at first, extra-parliamentary—consensus that agrees.

1988

ON PALESTINIAN IDENTITY: A
CONVERSATION WITH EDWARD SAID

SALMAN RUSHDIE: For those of us who see the struggle between
Eastern and Western descriptions of the world as both an
internal and an external struggle, Edward Said has for
many years been an especially important voice. Professor
of English and Comparative Literature at Columbia and
author of literary criticism on, among others, Joseph
Conrad, Edward has always had the distinguishing feature
that he reads the world as closely as he reads books. We
need only think of the major trilogy which precedes his
new book, *After the Last Sky*. In the first volume, *Orientalism*,
he analysed 'the affiliation of knowledge with power',
discussing how the scholars of the period of Empire helped
to create an image of the East which provided the
justification for the supremacist ideology of imperialism.
This was followed by *The Question of Palestine*, which
described the struggle between a world primarily shaped
by Western ideas—that of Zionism and later of Israel—and
the largely 'oriental' realities of Arab Palestine. Then came
Covering Islam, subtitled 'How the Media and the Experts
Determine How We See the Rest of the World', in which
the West's invention of the East is, so to speak, brought up
to date through a discussion of responses to the Islamic
revival.

After the Last Sky is a collaborative venture with Jean
Mohr—a photographer who may be known to you from
John Berger's study of immigrant labour in Europe, *A
Seventh Man*. Its title is taken from a poem, 'The Earth is
Closing on Us', by the national poet of Palestine,
Mahmoud Darwish:

*The earth is closing on us, pushing us through the last
passage, and we tear off our limbs to pass through.*

> *The earth is squeezing us. I wish we were its wheat so we*
>   *could die and live again. I wish the earth was our*
>   *mother*
> *So she'd be kind to us. I wish we were pictures on the*
>   *rocks for our dreams to carry*
> *As mirrors. We saw the faces of those to be killed by the*
>   *last of us in the last defence of the soul.*
> *We cried over their children's feast. We saw the faces of*
>   *those who will throw our children*
> *Out of the window of this last space. Our star will hang*
>   *up mirrors.*
> *Where should we go after the last frontiers? Where should*
>   *the birds fly after the last sky?*
> *Where should the plants sleep after the last breath of air?*
>   *We will write our names with scarlet steam,*
> *We will cut off the hand of the song to be finished by our*
>   *flesh.*
> *We will die here, here in the last passage. Here and here*
>   *our blood will plant its olive tree.**

After the last sky there is no sky. After the last border there is no land. The first part of Said's book is called 'States'. It is a passionate and moving meditation on displacement, on landlessness, on exile and identity. He asks, for example, in what sense Palestinians can be said to exist. He says: 'Do we exist? What proof do we have? The further we get from the Palestine of our past, the more precarious our status, the more disrupted our being, the more intermittent our presence. When did we become a people? When did we stop being one? Or are we in the process of becoming one? What do those big questions have to do with our intimate relationships with each other and with others? We frequently end our letters with the motto "Palestinian love" or "Palestinian kisses". Are there really such things as Palestinian intimacy and embraces, or are they simply intimacy and embraces—

---

*'The Earth is Closing on Us', translated by Abdullah al-Udhari, in *Victims of a Map*, Al Saqi Books, London, 1984, p. 13.

experiences common to everyone, neither politically significant nor particular to a nation or a people?'

Said comes, as he puts it, from a 'minority inside a minority'—a position with which I feel some sympathy, having also come from a minority group within a minority group. It is a kind of Chinese box that he describes: 'My family and I were members of a tiny Protestant group within a much larger Greek Orthodox Christian minority, within the larger Sunni Muslim majority.' He then goes on to discuss the condition of Palestinians through the mediation of a number of recent literary works. One of these, incorrectly called an Arab *Tristram Shandy* in the blurb, is a wonderful comic novel about the secret life of somebody called Said, *The Ill-Fated Pessoptimist*. A pessoptimist, as you can see, is a person with a problem about how he sees the world. Said claims all manner of things, including, in chapter one, to have met creatures from outer space: 'In the so-called age of ignorance before Islam, our ancestors used to form their gods from dates and eat them when in need. Who is more ignorant then, dear sir, I or those who ate their gods? You might say it is better for people to eat their gods than for the gods to eat them. I would respond, yes, but their gods were made of dates.'

A crucial idea in *After the Last Sky* concerns the meaning of the Palestinian experience for the form of works of art made by Palestinians. In Edward's view, the broken or discontinuous nature of Palestinian experience entails that classic rules about form or structure cannot be true to that experience; rather, it is necessary to work through a kind of chaos or unstable form that will accurately express its essential instability. Edward then proceeds to introduce the theme—which is developed later in the book—that the history of Palestine has turned the insider (the Palestinian Arab) into the outsider. This point is illustrated by a photograph of Nazareth taken from a position in what is called Upper Nazareth—an area which did not exist in the time of Arab Palestine. Thus

Arab Palestine is seen from the point of view of a new, invented Palestine, and the inside experience of the old Palestine has become the external experience in the photograph. And yet the Palestinians have remained.

It would be easier
to catch fried fish in the milky way
to plough the sea
or to teach the alligator speech
*than to make us leave.**

In part two, 'Interiors', which greatly develops the theme of the insider and the outsider, Edward refers to a change in the status of the Palestinians who are inside Palestine. Until recently, among the Palestinian community in general, there was a slight discounting of those who remained inside, as if they were somehow contaminated by the proximity of the Jews. Now, however, the situation has been inverted: those who go on living there, maintaining a Palestinian culture and obliging the world to recognize their existence, have acquired a greater status in the eyes of other Palestinians.

This experience of being inside Palestinianness is presented as a series of codes which, though incomprehensible to outsiders, are instantly communicated by Palestinians when they meet one another. The only way in which to show your insiderness is precisely through the expression of those codes. There is a very funny incident in which Professor Said receives a letter, via a complete stranger, from a man who has built his *Palestinian* identity as a karate expert. 'What was the message to me?' Said asks. 'First of all he was inside, and using the good offices of a sympathetic outsider to contact me, an insider who was now outside Jerusalem, the place of our common origin. That he wrote my name in English was as much a sign that he too could deal with the world I lived in as it was that he followed what I did. The time had come to

---

*From the poem 'The Twenty Impossibles', by Tawfiq Zayyad, cited by Said in *After the Last Sky*.

demonstrate that the Edward Saids had better remember that we were being watched by karate experts. Karate does not stand for self-development but only for the repeated act of being a Palestinian expert. A Palestinian—it is as if the activity of repeating prevents us and others from skipping us or overlooking us entirely.'

He then gives a number of other examples of repeating behaviour in order to make it Palestinian behaviour, and thus existing through that repetition. There also seems to be a compulsion to excess, illustrated in various ways, both tragic and comic, within the book. One of the problems of being Palestinian is that the idea of interior is regularly invaded by other people's descriptions, by other people's attempts to control what it is to occupy that space—whether it be Jordanian Arabs who say there is no difference between a Jordanian and a Palestinian, or Israelis who claim that the land is not Palestine but Israel.

The third part, 'Emergence', and the fourth part, 'Past and Future', turn to a discussion of what it actually is or might be to be a Palestinian. There is also an account of the power to which Palestinians are subject, of the way in which even their names have been altered through the superimposition of Hebrew transliteration. As a mark of resistance, Palestinians are now seeking to reassert their identity by going back to the old Arabic forms: Abu Ammar, for example, instead of Yasser Arafat. On various occasions the very meaning of names has been changed. Thus the largest refugee camp in Lebanon, Ein el Hilwé, which is written with an 'h' in the Arabic transliteration, has become Ein el Khilwé in the Hebrew transliteration: a name which means 'sweet spring' has been turned into something like 'spring in the empty place'. Said sees in this an allusion to mass graves and the regularly razed and not always rebuilt camps. 'I also register the thought,' he writes, 'that Israel has indeed emptied the camp with its Palestinian wellspring.'

The text goes on to talk about Zionism, which he addressed in his earlier book *The Question of Palestine*. We should note the difficulty in making any kind of critique of Zionism without being instantly charged with anti-Semitism. Clearly it is important to understand Zionism as a historical process, as existing in a context and having certain historical functions. A further idea in these later sections of the book is that, in the West, everyone has come to think of exile as a primarily literary and bourgeois state. Exiles appear to have chosen a middle-class situation in which great thoughts can be thought. In the case of the Palestinians, however, exile is a mass phenomenon: it is the mass that is exiled and not just the bourgeoisie.

Finally Said poses a series of questions which come down to the original one of Palestinian existence: 'What happens to landless people? However you exist in the world, what do you preserve of yourselves? What do you abandon?' I find one passage particularly valuable, as it connects with many things I have been thinking about. 'Our truest reality,' he writes, 'is expressed in the way we cross over from one place to another. We are migrants and perhaps hybrids, in but not of any situation in which we find ourselves. This is the deepest continuity of our lives as a nation in exile and constantly on the move.' He also criticizes the great concentration of the Palestinian cause on its military expression, referring to the dangers of cultural loss or absence.

Professor Said periodically receives threats to his safety from the Jewish Defense League in America, and I think it is important for us to appreciate that to be a Palestinian in New York—in many ways *the* Palestinian—is not the easiest of fates.

One of my sisters was repeatedly asked in California where she came from. When she said 'Pakistan' most people seemed to have no idea what this meant. One American said: 'Oh, yes, Pakestine!' and immediately started talking about his Jewish friends. It is impossible to overestimate the consequences of American ignorance on world affairs. When I was at the PEN Congress in New York in 1986, the American writer Cynthia Ozick took it upon herself to circulate a petition which described Chancellor Kreisky of Austria as an anti-Semite. Why was he an anti-Semite—this man who is himself a Jew and has given refuge to tens, perhaps hundreds, of thousands of Jews leaving the Soviet Union? Because he had had a conversation with Yasser Arafat. The alarming thing is that this petition, on the face of it quite absurd, should have been taken so seriously by participants at the congress. There was even a moment when I felt nervously that since no one else seemed to be speaking for Palestine, I might have to myself. But the defence came from Pierre Trudeau of all people, who spoke very movingly about the Palestinian cause. These are some of the extraordinary things that happen in New York. Edward, you are the man on the spot. Is it getting worse or better? How does it feel?

EDWARD SAID: Well, I think it is getting worse. First of all, most people in New York who feel strongly about Palestine and Palestinians have had no direct experience at all. They think of them essentially in terms of what they have seen on television: bomb scares, murders and what the Secretary of State and others call terrorism. This produces a kind of groundless passion, so that when I am introduced to someone who may have heard of me, they react in a very strange way that suggests 'maybe you're not as bad as you seem.' The fact that I speak English, and do it reasonably well, adds to the complications, and most people eventually concentrate on my work as an English professor for the rest of the conversation. But you do feel a new kind of violence around you which is a result of 1982. An important break with the past occurred then, both for people who have supported Israel in the United States, and for people like us, for whom the destruction of Beirut, our Beirut, was the end of an era. Most of the time you can feel that you are leading a normal life, but every so often you are brought up against a threat or an allusion to something which is deeply unpleasant. You always feel outside in some way.

SALMAN RUSHDIE: Has there been any change in your

ability to publish or talk about the Palestinian issue?

EDWARD SAID: To some extent. This is one issue on which, as you know, there is a left–right break in America, and there are still a few groups, a few people—like Chomsky or Alexander Cockburn—who are willing to raise it publicly. But most people tend to think that it is better left to the crazies. There are fewer hospitable places, and you end up publishing for a smaller audience. Ironically, you also become tokenized, so that whenever there is a hijacking or some such incident, I get phone-calls from the media asking me to come along and comment. It's a very strange feeling to be seen as a kind of representative of terrorism. You're treated like a diplomat of terrorism, with a place at the table. I remember one occasion, though, when I was invited to a television debate with the Israeli ambassador—I think it was about the *Achille Lauro* incident. Not only would he not sit in the same room with me; he wanted to be in a different building, so as not to be contaminated by my presence. The interviewer said to the national audience: 'You know, Professor Said and Ambassador Netanyahu refuse to speak to each other, the Israeli ambassador won't speak to him and he won't . . .' But then I interrupted and said: 'No, no, I am perfectly willing to speak to him, but he won't . . .' The moderator replied: 'Well, I stand corrected. Mr Ambassador, why won't you speak to Professor Said?' 'Because he wants to kill me.' The moderator, without batting an eyelid, urged: 'Oh really, tell us about it.' And the ambassador went on about how Palestinians want to kill the Israelis, and so on. It was really a totally absurd situation.

SALMAN RUSHDIE: You say you don't like calling it a Palestinian diaspora. Why is that?

EDWARD SAID: I suppose there is a sense in which, as one man wrote in a note to me from Jerusalem, we are 'the Jews of the Arab world'. But I think our experience is really quite different and beyond such attempts to draw parallels. Perhaps its dimension is much more modest. In any case the idea that there is a kind of redemptive homeland doesn't answer to my view of things.

SALMAN RUSHDIE: So let me put to you your own question. Do you exist? And if so, what proof do you have? In what sense is there a Palestinian nation?

EDWARD SAID: First of all, in the sense that a lot of people have memories or show great interest in looking into the past for a sign of coherent community. Many, too—especially younger-generation scholars—are trying to discover things about the Palestinian political and cultural experience that mark it off from the rest of the Arab world. Secondly, there is the tradition of setting up replicas of Palestinian organizations in places as far afield as Australia or South America. It is quite remarkable that people will come to live in, say, Youngstown, Ohio—a town I don't know, but you can imagine what it's like—and remain on top of the latest events in Beirut or the current disagreements between the Popular Front and Al Fatah, and yet not even know the name of the mayor of Youngstown or how he is elected. Maybe they will just assume that he is put there by somebody rather than being elected. Finally, you can see from Jean Mohr's pictures that the Palestinians are a people who move a lot, who are always carrying bags from one place to another. This gives us a further sense of identity as a people. And we say it loudly enough, repetitiously enough and stridently enough, strong in the knowledge that they haven't been able to get rid of us. It is a great feeling—call it positive or pessoptimistic—to wake up in the morning and say: 'Well they didn't bump me off.'

SALMAN RUSHDIE: To illustrate this point that things could be worse, you tell the story of a mother whose son died very soon after his wedding. While the bride is still mourning she says: 'Thank God it has happened in this way and not in another way!' The bride then gets very angry and says: 'How dare you say that! What could possibly be a worse way?' But the mother-in-law replies: 'Well, you know, if he grew old and you left him for another man and then he died, that could be worse. So it's better that he dies now.'

EDWARD SAID: Exactly. You are always inventing worse scenarios.

SALMAN RUSHDIE: It's very difficult to work out whether this is optimism or pessimism. That's why it is called pessoptimism. Would you like to say something now about the codes by which Palestinians exist and recognize each other and about the idea of repetition and excess as a way of existing?

EDWARD SAID: Let me tell you another story that will show you what I mean. A close friend of mine once came to my house and stayed overnight. In the morning we had breakfast, which included yogurt cheese with a special herb, za'atar. This combination probably exists all over the Arab world, and certainly in Palestine, Syria and Lebanon. But my friend said: 'There, you see. It's a sign of a Palestinian home that it has za'atar in it.' Being a poet, he then expatiated at great and tedious length on Palestinian cuisine, which is generally very much like Lebanese and Syrian cuisine, and by the end of the morning we were both convinced that we had a totally distinct national cuisine.

SALMAN RUSHDIE: So, because a Palestinian chooses to do something it becomes the Palestinian thing to do?

EDWARD SAID: That's absolutely right. But even among Palestinians there are certain code words that define which camp or group the speaker comes from; whether from the Popular Front, which believes in the complete liberation of Palestine, or from the Fatah, which believes in a negotiated settlement. They will choose a different set of words when they talk about national liberation. Then there are the regional accents. It is very strange indeed to meet a Palestinian kid in Lebanon who was born in some refugee camp and has never been to Palestine but who carries the inflections of Haifa, or Jaffa, in his Lebanese Arabic.

SALMAN RUSHDIE: Let us turn to the idea of excess. You talk

about how you find yourself obliged to carry too much luggage wherever you go. But more seriously, I remember that dialogue between a captured Palestinian guerrilla and an Israeli broadcaster in which the guerrilla appears to be implicating himself in the most heinous crimes but is in fact sending up the entire event by a colossal excess of apologies. The broadcaster is too tuned into his own set of attitudes to realize what is going on.

EDWARD SAID: Yes. It was in 1982 in southern Lebanon, when Israeli radio would often put captured guerrillas on the air as a form of psychological warfare. But in the case you are talking about, no one was deceived. In fact, the Palestinians in Beirut made a cassette recording of the whole show and played it back in the evening as a way of entertaining people. Let me translate a sample:

Israeli broadcaster: Your name?

Captured Palestinian: Ahmed Abdul Hamid Abu Site.

Israeli: What is your movement name?

Palestinian: My movement name is Abu Lell [which in English means Father of Night, with a rather threatening, horrible sound to it].

Israeli: Tell me, Mr Abu Lell, to which terrorist organization do you belong?

Palestinian: I belong to the Popular Front for the Liberation . . . I mean terrorization of Palestine.

Israeli: And when did you get involved in the terrorist organization?

Palestinian: When I first became aware of terrorism.

Israeli: What was your mission in South Lebanon?

Palestinian: My mission was terrorism. In other words, we would enter villages and just terrorize the occupants. And whenever there were women and children in particular, we would terrorize everything, and all we did was terrorism.

Israeli: And did you practise terrorism out of belief in a cause or just for money?

Palestinian: No, just for money. What kind of cause is this anyway? Is there still a cause? We sold out a long time ago.

Israeli: Tell me . . . where do the terrorist organizations get their money?

Palestinian: From anyone who has spare money for terrorism.

Israeli: What is your opinion of the terrorist Arafat?

Palestinian: I swear that he is the greatest terrorist of all. He is the one who sold us and the cause out. His whole life is terrorism. [Of course, to a Palestinian this could mean that he is the most committed of all, but it sounds as if he is just a total sellout.]

Israeli: What is your opinion of the way in which the Israeli defence forces have conducted themselves?

Palestinian: On my honour, we thank the Israeli defence forces for their good treatment of each terrorist.

Israeli: Do you have any advice for other terrorists, who are still terrorizing the IDF?

Palestinian: My advice to them is to surrender their arms to the IDF. What they will find there is the best possible treatment.

Israeli: Lastly, Mr Terrorist, would you like to send a message to your family?

Palestinian: I would like to assure my family and friends that I am in good health. I would also like to thank the enemy broadcasting facility for letting me speak out like this.

Israeli: You mean the Voice of Israel?

Palestinian: Yes, yes, sir. Thank you, sir. Yes of course, sir.

SALMAN RUSHDIE: And this went out over the air?

EDWARD SAID: Absolutely. It was put out on a daily basis, and recorded in Beirut and played back to the guerrillas. It's a very funny and wonderful story.

SALMAN RUSHDIE: You also talk about a photo article in

a fashion magazine, under the headline 'Terrorist Culture', which claims that the Palestinians are not really Palestinians because they have simply hijacked Arab dress and renamed it Palestinian.

EDWARD SAID: We do it all the time!

SALMAN RUSHDIE: The article also claims that this supposedly distinctive dress is not that of the people but of the upper middle class. Referring to the American author of the article, Sharon Churcher, you write: 'In the larger scheme of things . . . she is somebody doing a hack job on a hack fashion magazine.' And yet, you say you feel the need to go right back to the beginning, to explain the whole history of Palestine in order to unmake Sharon Churcher's lie and show that this is in fact genuinely popular Palestinian dress. Doesn't this need to go back again and again over the same story become tiring?

EDWARD SAID: It does, but you do it anyway. It is like trying to find the magical moment when everything starts, as in *Midnight's Children*. You know midnight, and so you go back. But it is very hard to do that because you have to work out everything and get past a lot of questions in the daily press about why Palestinians don't just stay where they are and stop causing trouble. That immediately launches you into a tremendous harangue, as you explain to people: 'My mother was born in Nazareth, my father was born in Jerusalem . . .' The interesting thing is that there seems to be nothing in the world which sustains the story: unless you go on telling it, it will just drop and disappear.

SALMAN RUSHDIE: The need to be perpetually told.

EDWARD SAID: Exactly. The other narratives have a kind of permanence of institutional existence and you just have to try to work away at them.

SALMAN RUSHDIE: This is one of the things that you criticize from within Palestinianness: the lack of any serious effort to institutionalize the story, to give it an objective existence.

EDWARD SAID: That's right. It is interesting that right up

to 1948, most of the writing by Palestinians expressed a fear that they were about to lose their country. Their descriptions of cities and other places in Palestine appeared as a kind of pleading before a tribunal. After the dispersion of the Palestinians, however, there was a curious period of silence until a new Palestinian literature began to develop in the fifties and, above all, the sixties. Given the size of this achievement, it is strange that no narrative of Palestinian history has ever been institutionalized in a definitive masterwork. There never seems to be enough time, and one always has the impression that one's enemy—in this case the Israelis— are trying to take the archive away. The gravest image for me in 1982 was of the Israelis shipping out the archives of the Palestine Research Centre in Beirut to Tel Aviv.

SALMAN RUSHDIE: In the context of literature rather than history, you argue that the inadequacy of the narrative is due to the discontinuity of Palestinian existence. Is this connected with the problem of writing a history?

EDWARD SAID: Yes. There are many different kinds of Palestinian experience, which cannot all be assembled into one. One would therefore have to write parallel histories of the communities in Lebanon, the occupied territories, and so on. That is the central problem. It is almost impossible to imagine a single narrative: it would have to be the kind of crazy history that comes out in *Midnight's Children*, with all those little strands coming and going in and out.

SALMAN RUSHDIE: You have talked of *The Pessoptimist* as a first manifestation of the attempt to write in a form which appears to be formlessness, and which in fact mirrors the instability of the situation. Could you say some more about this?

EDWARD SAID: It's a rather eccentric view, perhaps. I myself am not a scholar of Palestinian and certainly not Arabic literature in general. But I am fascinated by the impression made on everyone by, for instance, Kanafani's novel *Men in the Sun*, whose texture exemplifies the uncertainty whether one is talking about the past or the present.-One story of his, called, I think, 'The Return to Haifa', follows a family who left in 1948 and resettled in Ramallah. Much later they return to visit their house in Haifa, and to meet again the son they had left behind in a panic and who was adopted by an Israeli family. Throughout the novel there is a powerful sense of endless temporal motion, in which past, present and future intertwine without any fixed centre.

SALMAN RUSHDIE: Perhaps we could now turn to the lengthy discussion in *After the Last Sky* about the unheard voices of Palestinian women. You write: 'And yet, I recognize in all this a fundamental problem—the crucial absence of women. With few exceptions, women seem to have played little more than the role of hyphen, connective, transition, mere incident. Unless we are able to perceive at the interior of our life the statements women make: concrete, watchful, compassionate, immensely poignant, strangely invulnerable—we will never fully understand our experience of dispossession.' The main illustration you then give is a film, *The Fertile Memory*, by the young Palestinian director Michel Khleifi, which deals with the experience of two Palestinian women.

EDWARD SAID: Yes. This film made a very strong impression on me. One of the most striking scenes revolves around the older woman, who is actually Khleifi's aunt. She has a piece of property in Nazareth which a Jewish family has been living on for many years, but one day her daughter and son-in-law come with the news that this family now wants to buy up the title deeds. She makes it clear that she is not interested. 'But what do you mean?' they insist. 'They are living on it; it's their land. They just want to make things easier for you by giving you money in return for the deeds.' 'No, I won't do that,' she replies. It is a totally irrational position, and Khleifi registers the expression of stubbornness, almost transcendent foolishness, on her face. 'I don't have the land now,' she explains. 'But who knows what will happen? We were here first. Then the Jews came and others will come after them. I own the land and I'll die, but it will stay there despite the comings and goings of people.' She is then taken to see her land for the first time—it had been left to her by her husband, who went to Lebanon in 1948 and died there. Khleifi records her extraordinary experience of walking on the land that she owns but does not own, treading gently and turning round and round. Then suddenly her expression changes as she realizes the absurdity of it all and walks away. This scene typified for me the persistent presence of the woman in Palestinian life—and, at the same time, the lack of acknowledgement which that presence has elicited. There is a strong misogynist streak in Arab society: a kind of fear and dislike existing alongside respect and admiration. I remember another occasion when I was with a friend looking at a picture of a rather large and formidable yet happy Palestinian woman, her arms folded across her chest. This friend summed up the whole ambivalence with his remark: 'There is the Palestinian woman, in all her strength . . . and her ugliness.' The picture of this woman, by Jean Mohr, seems to say something that we have not really been able to touch upon. That experience is one that I, as a man, in this Palestinian sort of mess, am beginning to try to articulate.

SALMAN RUSHDIE: In *After the Last Sky* you say that, having lived inside Western culture for a long time, you understand as well as any non-Jew can hope to do what is the power of Zionism for the Jewish people. You also describe it as a programme of slow and steady acquisition that has been more efficient and competent than anything the Palestinians have been able to put up against it. The problem is that any attempt to provide a critique of Zionism is faced, particularly nowadays, with the charge that it is anti-Semitism in disguise. The retort that you are not anti-Semitic but anti-Zionist is always, or often, greeted with: 'Oh yes, we know that code.' What you have done in this book and in *The Question of Palestine* is to offer a very useful, emotionally neutral critique of Zionism as an historical phenomenon. Perhaps you could say a few words about this.

EDWARD SAID: In my opinion, the question of Zionism is the touchstone of contemporary political judgement. A lot of people who are happy to attack apartheid or US intervention in Central America are not prepared to talk about Zionism and what it has done to the Palestinians. To be a victim of a victim does present quite unusual difficulties. For if you are trying to deal with the classic victim of all time—the Jew and his or her movement—then to portray yourself as the victim of the Jew is a comedy worthy of one of your own novels. But now there is a new dimension, as we can see from the spate of books and articles in which any kind of criticism of Israel is treated as an umbrella for anti-Semitism. Particularly in the United States, if you say anything at all, as an Arab from a Muslim culture, you are seen to be joining classical European or Western anti-Semitism. It has become absolutely necessary, therefore, to concentrate on the particular history and context of Zionism in discussing what it represents for the Palestinian.

SALMAN RUSHDIE: The problem, then, is to make people see Zionism as being like anything else in history, as arising from sources and going somewhere. Do you think that Zionism has changed its nature in recent years, apart from the fact that it has become subject to criticism?

EDWARD SAID: One of my main concerns is the extent to which people are not frozen in attitudes of difference and mutual hostility. I have met many Jews over the last ten years who are very interested in some kind of exchange, and events in the sixties have created a significant community of Jews who are not comfortable with the absolutes of Zionism. The whole notion of crossing over, of moving from one identity to another, is extremely important to me, being as I am—as we all are—a sort of hybrid.

SALMAN RUSHDIE: I would like to ask you a couple of more personal questions. You say that to be a Palestinian is basically to come from a Muslim culture, and yet you are not a Muslim. Do you find that a problem? Have there been any historical frictions in this respect?

EDWARD SAID: All I can say is that I have had no experience of such frictions. My own sense is that our situation as Palestinians is very different from Lebanon, where conflicts between Sunnis, Shiites, Maronites, Orthodox and so forth have been sharply felt historically. One of the virtues of being a Palestinian is that it teaches you to feel your particularity in a new way, not only as a problem but as a kind of gift. Whether in the Arab world or elsewhere, twentieth-century mass society has destroyed identity in so powerful a way that it is worth a great deal to keep this specificity alive.

SALMAN RUSHDIE: You write: 'The vast majority of our people are now thoroughly sick of the misfortunes that have befallen us, partly through our own fault, partly because of who the dispossessors are, and partly because our cause has a singular ineffectuality to it, capable neither of sufficiently mobilizing our friends nor of overcoming our enemies. On the other hand, I have never met a Palestinian who is tired enough of being a Palestinian to give up entirely.'

EDWARD SAID: That's rather well put!

SALMAN RUSHDIE: This brings me to my final point that, unlike your previous three books, which centred on the dispute between Eastern and Western cultures, *After the Last Sky* focuses much more on an inner dispute or dialectic at the heart of Palestinianness. After a period of extroversion, you suggest, many Palestinians are themselves experiencing a certain turning inwards. Why is this so? What has been your own experience?

EDWARD SAID: Well, obviously much of it has to do with disillusion. Most people in my own generation—and I can't really speak for others—grew up in an atmosphere of despondency. But then in the late sixties and early seventies, a tremendous enthusiasm and romantic glamour attached to the rise of a new movement out of the ashes. In a material sense it accomplished very little: no land was liberated during that period. Moreover, the excitement of the Palestinian resistance, as it was called in those days, was a rather heady atmosphere, forming part of Arab nationalism and even—in an ironic and extraordinary way—part of the Arab oil boom. Now all that is beginning to crumble before our eyes, giving way to a sense of disillusionment and questioning about whether it was ever worthwhile and where we are to go from here. It was as an expression of this mood that I wrote *After the Last Sky*. The photographs were important in order to show that we are not talking just of our own personal, hermetic disillusionment. For the Palestinians have become a kind of commodity or public possession, useful, for example, to explain the phenomenon of terrorism. I found myself writing from the point of view of someone who had at last managed to connect the part that was a professor of English and the part that lived, in a small way, the life of Palestine. Luckily Jean Mohr had built up quite a large archive of pictures since he worked for the Red Cross in 1949. We came together under strange circumstances: he was putting up some pictures and I was working as a consultant for the United Nations. Since they would not let us write what we wanted, we said: 'Let's have a book and do it in our own way.' It represented a very personal commitment on both our parts.

SALMAN RUSHDIE: The picture on the cover is really quite extraordinary—a man with a kind of starburst on the right lens of his glasses. As you say, he has been blinded by a bullet in one eye, but has learned to live with it. He is still wearing the spectacles . . . and still smiling.

EDWARD SAID: Jean told me that he took the photo as the man was en route to visit his son, who had been sentenced to life imprisonment.

1986

7

NADINE GORDIMER

RIAN MALAN

NURUDDIN FARAH

KAPUŚCIŃSKI'S ANGOLA

NADINE GORDIMER

Something Out There

Great White sharks, killer bees, werewolves, devils, alien horrors bursting from the chests of movie spacemen: the popular culture of our fearful times has provided us with so many variations on the ancient myth of the Beast, the 'something' lurking out there that hunts us and is hunted by us, as to make it one of the defining metaphors of the age. In the jungle of the cities, we live amongst our accumulations of things behind doors garlanded with locks and chains, and find it all too easy to fear the unforeseeable, all-destroying coming of the Ogre—Charles Manson, the Ayatollah Khomeini, the Blob from Outer Space. Clearly, many of these forebodings are the product of affluence and of power. The haves and the powerful, fearing the uprising of the have-nots and the powerless, dream of them as monsters.

There is a wild animal roaming around the affluent white suburbs of Johannesburg in the long novella which gives its title to Nadine Gordimer's new collection; but Gordimer is the least lurid of writers, and her creature's worst offence is to bite a woman on the shoulder. Her prose is cool and meticulous, and the sightings of her Beast—probably a baboon, it is said—are for the most part low-key, even domestic: a leg of venison stolen from its hook in Mariella Chapman's kitchen; a photograph of thrashing tree-tops taken by the thirteen-year-old schoolboy Stanley Dobrow at his bar mitzvah; a shape, a pair of eyes seen in the vegetation at the edge of an exclusive golf course. And at the end of the piece the creature is quite matter-of-factly demystified; dead in a lane, it is no nightmare monster, but 'only a baboon, after all; not an orang-utan, not a chimpanzee—just a native species.' White South Africans have no need of dream-ogres: it is reality that they fear, and the something out there is the future. The Naas Kloppers, the van Gelders and all the other rather stupid, somewhat caricatured bigots with whom

Nadine Gordimer populates her tale go to some trouble to protect themselves, but the baboon shows them a most uncomfortable truth: 'The Bokkie Scholtz's house is burglar-proofed, has fine wires on windows and doors which activate an alarm . . . They have a half-breed Rottweiler who was asleep, apparently, on the front step, when the attack came. It just shows you—whatever you do, you can't call yourself safe.'

This quality of subversion, this deliberate use of banality in order to disturb, is what sets Ms Gordimer's version of the Beast myth apart. The pulp fiction and cinema which exploit this theme usually offer no more than an enjoyable scare, a sanitized *frisson*; they actually reassure us while pretending to terrify. *Something Out There* concentrates, by contrast, on the minutiae of the real world. The art lies in the refusal of all exaggeration, all hyperbole. From this refusal springs the story's authority, its unsettling menace. 'Whatever you do, you can't call yourself safe.'

A second narrative counterpoints that of the baboon. The other 'something' out there beyond the white suburbs is a cell of four terrorists, two black men and a white couple or rather, a white man and woman who are no longer lovers. Here again, Nadine Gordimer's purpose is to demystify a kind of twentieth-century Beast. The four insurgents, listening to anti-terrorist rhetoric on the radio, 'were accustomed to smile as people will when they must realize that those being referred to as monsters are the human beings drinking a glass of water, cutting a hang-nail, writing a letter, in the same room; are themselves.'

While the terrorists wait for the right time to blow up a power station, Ms Gordimer brings them expertly to life, not as beasts, not orang-utans or chimpanzees. Just a native species. She gives us, in effect, portraits of two rather differently odd couples: the white man and woman, Charles and Joy, awkward both with their black colleagues and with each other; and the black men, Eddie, the outgoing one, who jeopardizes their mission by hitching a ride into town for a night among the bright lights, and Vusi, the battle-hardened one, the still centre of the group. The stilted, damaged humanity of this foursome is set against the bluff inhumanity of the inhabitants of the rich suburbs. Mr and Mrs Naas Klopper, the estate agent and his biscuit-making wife, with their split-level lounge and their arsenal of labour-saving devices and their impala-skin bar stools, are perhaps the story's real beasts.

The tone remains muted to the very end. The climax of the terrorist plot is made to happen, so to speak, off-stage; the lives of Charles and Joy and Eddie and Vusi fade into hints, rumours, readings between the lines of the news. And the baboon, as we have seen, is simply shot. But then, in the last couple of pages, comes a brilliant stroke. Rising above its characters' essential unknowability ('Nobody really knows . . . whom they believed themselves to be'), and also their ignorance of their own histories and genealogies, the narrative, in a kind of rage against this excess of unknowing, places them all upon the map of history—puts them firmly in their context, or place. And just as Dr Grahame Fraser-Smith, when he looked into the baboon's eyes on a golf course, fancied himself to be looking 'back into a consciousness from which part of his own came,' to be closing a circle, so the novella at its conclusion closes a circle, joining the far-off past to the approaching future; and both of them (ominously for all the Kloppers caught within the circle's closing jaws) are black.

There are nine other stories in this collection, not all of them of the same distinction as the novella. One seems to me an unmitigated disaster. Ms Gordimer has taken upon herself the task of writing, on Hermann Kafka's behalf, a reply to his son's famous and never-sent 'Letter to His Father'. 'Letter from His Father' is a twenty-page arch embarrassment, full of Homely Wisdom ('Well, we had to accept what God gave'), Literary Nudging ('Some say you were also some kind of prophet') and occasional fits of Thigh-Slapping ('Hah! I know I'm no intellectual, but I knew how to live'). It may well be the case that Franz was unfair to Papa, but I am afraid Ms Gordimer has not done the old man any favours, either.

A second story, 'Rags and Bones', fails to escape the trap of inconsequentiality. It begins casually: 'A woman named Beryl Fels recently picked up an old tin chest in a junk shop.' And it remains desultory to the end. In the tin chest is a bundle of letters; they draw Beryl Fels into the story of an affair, in the 1940s, between a distinguished male scientist and an equally distinguished woman writer. The lovers feel obliged to keep their affair secret, because 'we are both people in the public eye; it's the price or the reward, God knows, of what we both happen to be.' But when Beryl Fels looks into their lives, she can find no trace of either of them. The writer is unknown, not one of her books in print; the scientist has likewise vanished from the record. This is intended, I take it, as a cruel irony: the pain of the secrecy rendered absurd by the disintegration of their public status. But the story's casual tone, its reluctance to allow any heightening of feeling, prevents the irony from being felt by the reader.

Fortunately, the other seven stories are excellent. 'Blinder' is about Rose, an old family retainer with a weakness for going on alcoholic binges, who suddenly has to cope with a different sort of befuddlement, a different 'blinder'—that is, the death of her lover, Ephraim. This brief story is passionate, moving and beautiful. 'A Correspondence Course' describes the friendship that grows between a young woman and a political prisoner, through the letters they write to each other. But the important character is Pat Haberman, the mother of the young woman, Harriet. While the man is safely in jail, she encourages the correspondence, even talks about it proudly to others, as proof of her liberalism. But then the man escapes, and comes to the house and, in an extraordinary final paragraph, 'Liquid flashes like the sweeps of heat that had gone through her blood at fifty took Pat to her bedroom. She locked that door, wanting to beat upon it, whimper . . . To do something with her hands she filled a tooth-glass at the wash-hand basin and, a prisoner tending his one sprig of green, gave water to the pot of African violets for what she had done, done to her darling girl, *done for.'* The game has turned real, and, as we have seen, reality in Ms Gordimer's world is a thing of which to be afraid.

The remaining stories can be read as variations on the theme of betrayal. (And, of course, in the Kafka story, Ms Gordimer's Hermann is accusing Franz of betrayal, too: of betraying his family and his Judaism; and Pat Haberman in 'A Correspondence Course' comes to feel she has betrayed her daughter.) In 'Sins of the Third Age', the treachery is sexual. The carefully laid retirement plans of an elderly couple, Peter and Mania, are irrevocably altered when Peter has an affair; even when he chooses to put this affair behind him, the damage cannot be undone. Paradise has been lost. 'Terminal' presents another version of the treason of lovers. A woman dying of an incurable disease makes a pact with her husband that he will not prevent her suicide. Her last act is to leave him a note: 'Keep your promise. Don't have me revived.' But he does; and when, after taking the pills, she has the 'terror of feeling herself waking from it', the traitor is holding her hand.

And inevitably there are the betrayals of politics. In 'A City of the Dead, A City of the Living', in which Ms Gordimer magnificently describes life in the black ghetto, a poor woman, oppressed by the tension of having a wanted man hiding in her cramped home, squeals to the police. Her treason teaches her nothing; she longs to tell everyone, 'I don't know why I did it,' but nobody asks. Instead, people spit. In 'Crimes of Conscience', conversely, we see that betrayal can be a kind of education. The story is about a government-paid infiltrator, Felterman, who seduces a radical woman in order to spy on her group. He senses a reserve in her, as if she were waiting for him to speak some password. Finally he discovers it: 'I've been spying on you,' he confesses, and she takes his head into her hands.

'At the Rendezvous of Victory' is a classic cameo portrait—of the guerrilla 'general' for whom, after the success of his revolution, his old friend, now the Prime Minister of the newly liberated nation, has less and less time. Ms Gordimer's portrait of Sinclair 'General Giant' Zwedu, the discarded hero who will not toe the line and who becomes an embarrassment, is very deeply felt and imagined; and from Che Guevara, kept at a distance by Castro after their triumph, to the revolutionary fighters of present-day Black Africa, it is a portrait with many echoes in real life. Like most of the stories in what is, in spite of a couple of false notes, a distinguished collection, it makes its point and creates its resonances not by any exaggeration or flashiness, but by the scrupulous depiction of what all Nadine Gordimer's readers will instantly recognize as the unvarnished truth.

1984

The Essential Gesture: Writing, Politics, Places

Like most of her South African white contemporaries, the young Nadine Gordimer was a sort of sleepwalker: 'I led an outward life of sybaritic meagreness that I am ashamed of. In it I did not one thing that I wanted wholeheartedly to do . . . My existential self was breathing but inert.' She has, of course, left that somnambulist self far behind. 'I live at 6,000 feet in a society whirling, stamping, swaying with the force of revolutionary change,' she said at the New York Institute of the Humanities in 1982, demonstrating, as her editor and collaborator Stephen Clingman suggests, her full realization that the South African revolution was no longer merely potential; that it had already begun. One way of characterizing The Essential Gesture: Writing, Politics, Places would be to call it the story of an artist's awakening; to literature, to Africa, and to the great ugly reality of apartheid.

In André Brink's book Mapmakers, he tells us that his awakening happened 'on a bench in the Luxembourg Gardens in Paris', where the meaning of the recent massacre at Sharpeville (this was in 1960) came home to him, and changed his view of his country for ever. For Gordimer, the process was more inward, more literary. 'The "problems" of my country did not set me writing; on the contrary, it was learning to write that sent me falling, falling through the surface of the "South African way of life".' This volume of essays, skilfully selected and introduced by Clingman, is the record of that lifelong creative plunge. And if some of the early material can sound, at times, a little plaintive—'Where do whites fit in in the New Africa? *Nowhere*, I'm inclined to say, in my gloomier and least courageous moods'—it is never less than wholly truthful. Nadine Gordimer has been radicalized by her time—or, rather, by her attempt to *write* her time—and it's fascinating to watch history happening to her prose.

'It is not for nothing,' she tells us, 'that I chose as an epigraph for my novel *July's People* a quotation from Gramsci: "The old is dying, and the new cannot be born; in this interregnum there arises a great diversity of morbid symptoms."' Now many people would include among these symptoms the fact that white experiences of the South African reality, as evoked by white novelists, playwrights and film-makers, continue to command a degree of international attention that black descriptions of black experience only rarely receive. Steve Biko's story is subsumed, on film, into the story of Donald Woods; Chris Menges's fine, humane new movie *A World Apart* is praised by the *Observer*'s John Coleman for forcing us 'into some realization of what it must be like, day in, day out, for those middle-class whites *there*, brave enough to buck the system'; and while Brink, Gordimer, Breyten Breytenbach, Athol Fugard and J. M. Coetzee have well-deserved worldwide reputations, very few of their admirers could name more than (perhaps) one or two of their black counterparts.

Nadine Gordimer is fully aware of the paradoxes of her situation: a central figure in world literature who is also, in her own estimation, peripheral to her country's political and even cultural life, dependent for the ethical validity of her position on the willingness of some South African blacks to concede that whites who reject apartheid have a genuine role to play in the struggle for freedom. It is a great strength of her writing that she recognizes this vulnerability, and yet (or perhaps *and therefore*) succeeds in writing with immense confidence, openness and an entirely unromantic clearness of sight. She is a writer who finds it absurd that South African writers are praised around the world for their 'courage', because she knows, as Camus knew, that courage is a value not of literature but of life.

The literary value of these essays derives not only from their testamentary power, but also from the range and depth of their preoccupations. 'Why Did Bram Fischer Choose Jail?' (1966) deals with the communist leader around whom, thirteen years later, she built her finest novel, *Burger's Daughter*. 'One Man Living Through It' is a moving portrait of the young black writer Nat Nakasa, who committed suicide in exile in the USA. The 'Letter from Johannesburg' (1976) is a brilliant description of the time of the Soweto riots.

However, some of the most potent pieces are not directly, or at any rate primarily, 'political'. The section entitled 'A Writer in Africa' contains Gordimer's reckonings with, among other places, Botswana, Egypt, Madagascar, and especially the Congo River. The quality of the prose is uneven: sometimes little more than conventional magazine travel writing, it can suddenly take glorious flight; for example when considering the beautiful Malagasy word *lolo*, which means both 'soul' and 'butterfly'. Here she is, unforgettably, on the Congo:

> Begin with a stain in the ocean. Three hundred miles out to sea, off the west coast of Africa, the mark of a presence the immensity of seas has not been able to swallow . . . the stain of land; a massive land, a continent, giving rise to and feeding a river great enough to make a dent in the sea.

That immensity is Gordimer's chosen subject, and she has grown to match it. The writers she quotes and draws strength from—Brecht, Mann, Pasternak, Solzhenitsyn, Achebe—have taught her that the only important thing for a writer is 'to go on writing *the truth as he sees it*.' Such an effort inevitably brings the artist into the arena of public affairs, and not only in totalitarian states; nor does such a fierce engagement with life necessarily involve creative compromise. Gordimer (who is good at quoting) quotes Turgenev: 'Without freedom in the widest sense of the word—in relation to oneself . . . indeed, to one's people and one's history—a true artist is unthinkable; without that air it is impossible to breathe.'

And she adds her own, indisputable last word: 'In that air alone, commitment and creative freedom become one.'

1990

RIAN MALAN

Los Angeles, 1979. A young South African, Rian Malan, who has fled South Africa because 'I wouldn't carry a gun for apartheid, and because I wouldn't carry a gun against it,' lands a job writing rock'n'roll reviews for a small music magazine. He is in the United States illegally and so, as a precaution, uses a pen-name. The pen-name is 'Nelson Mandela'. Nobody recognizes it. 'The ESTians who owned the magazine mistook the word for *mandala*,' Malan tells us. It is one of the few genuinely funny moments in an otherwise enraged, remorseless (and magnificent) book, and like all the best comedy, it contains a truth. During his imprisonment, and even more so since his release, Mr Mandela has been elevated to the level of spiritual symbol. He really is Nelson Mandala now.

To worry about whether this is entirely a Good Thing is in no way to detract from Mr Mandela's qualities of humanity and leadership. But Nelson Mandela is a politician involved in one of the cruellest struggles of modern times. The understandable Wembley euphoria should not blind us to the inevitable moral ambiguities of such a struggle. These gut-wrenching ambiguities, black South African as well as white Afrikaner ambiguities, are the subject of Rian Malan's *My Traitor's Heart*.

Mr Malan is the black sheep of one of the very whitest of families in the White Tribe of Afrikaners. His ancestor D. F. Malan, who came to power in 1948, was the first architect of apartheid. And further back in time, his eighteenth-century forebear Dawid Malan lived a life which, we are told, remains a truthful metaphor for present-day South Africa. Dawid Malan fell in love with a black woman, gave up everything for her, and fled with his Sara into Xhosa country across the Great Fish River. He reappeared in history years later, without Sara, transformed into a white supremacist, with a white wife and sons, 'willing to die rather than accord black people equality before the law.' He was now one of the ringleaders of a Boer revolt against the British, who had been 'interfering with their right to chastise and slaughter the dark-skinned heathen as they deemed necessary.' This is the moment, Rian Malan suggests, at which the Boers became Afrikaners, 'arrogant, xenophobic, and "full of blood", as the Zulus say of tyrants.' And he adds that nothing has changed, that 'it all leads us back, in the end, to Dawid Malan and a law formulated on the banks of the Great Fish River two hundred years ago: You have to put the black man down, plant your foot on his neck, and keep him that way for ever, lest he spring up and slit your throat.'

The book that Rian Malan set out to write was altogether more conventional than the one he has written. It was supposed to be a history of the great and detested Malan family, as told by its *kafferboetie* (that is, 'brother of blacks', 'nigger-lover') renegade. But along the way he ran into, and faced up to, the truth that is the making of his book—that for all his nigger-loving, leftist views, for all his long hair and days smoking *zol* (dope) on the hillsides in the mystical Tolkienish company of 'wise old Afs', for all his daubing of pro-black slogans on the walls of Johannesburg's northern suburbs, where scarcely a black would ever see them, *he was still a Malan*; that he could only write about the atrocity of South Africa by admitting the atrocity hidden in his own traitorous heart.

The source of it all is fear. *Lest he spring up and slit your throat.* Even for a radical journalist like Rian Malan, walking in Soweto at night can be terrifying. *When the day comes, you'll still be whitey.* And along with the fear comes incomprehension: of the necklace killings, of the burning alive of thirty-two black 'witches' by fellow-blacks in Sekhukuniland, of the things which human beings, black and white, are capable of. Malan is excellent and unforgiving about the naïveties and hypocrisies of white leftists like himself. 'When the chips were down . . . and the killing started, there were no whites on the black side of the barricade. None. Ever.'

For all Rian Malan's clear-sightedness and truth-telling, his testament is not without unresolved problems. 'We white people couldn't really talk to Africans,' he writes. 'They lived on the far side of a barrier of language and culture, so when we tried to look into their hearts, all we saw was darkness. Who knows what lurks in darkness? We feared the worst.' One of the strengths of *My Traitor's Heart* is precisely this portrait of South Africa as a place of mutual incomprehension, of struggling languages. But if one perceives that the issue is at bottom linguistic, might one not make some effort *to learn black languages*? If such an idea has ever occurred to Rian Malan, it isn't evident from these pages; which is puzzling and one of the book's few false notes. (The repeated protestation about 'loving blacks' is, to my ear at any rate, another.)

However, the presence of a few ragged edges does little to undermine the book's immense power. Perhaps that rawness, that sense of a *cri de cœur* too painful to be controlled fully, is actually the source of the writing's energy. And, in truth, one of the book's greatest triumphs is linguistic. Here, as in nothing I've read before, is the demotic voice of black and Afrikaner South Africa. In Malan's pages, blacks and whites go *jolling* ('a very important South African concept, connoting kamikaze debaucheries'), indulging in *'drank, dagga, dobbel en vok'*—'drink, dope, dice and fucking'. They speak the street patois, *tsotsi-taal*: to buy dope from a black dealer, you *'gooi* [give] the double-horned devil's hand sign and *charf* [say], *"Level with the gravel, ek se"*.' An English South African is a *soutpiel*, 'salt dick', because he has one foot in South Africa and the other in England, 'a straddle so broad that his cock dangled in the sea'. Most evocative of all, perhaps, are the terms used for the two rival black camps: the ANC/UDF supporters who 'say Mandela'; and the remnants of the Black Consciousness movement, the ones who 'say Biko'. The Biko people are called 'Zim-zims' because their heads are full of 'isms'—socialism, racism, capitalism, colonialism. The Mandela men are 'Wararas', from the Afrikaans *waar-waar* ('where-where'), because the UDF's doctrine of non-racialism is thought by its opponents to be confused. 'They were groping around in the dark in search of their true enemy, crying, "Where? Where?"'

Malan is excellent on the still uncompleted war between the Zim-zims and Wararas; but the main thrust of his book is its attempt to reach the heart of the South African tragedy by exploring 'tales of ordinary murder'. Murder is different in South Africa, Malan says. In most parts of the world, murder is an intimate crime; killers and victims are usually well known to each other. In South Africa, murder is a relationship of strangers, brought about by race, or ideology, or darker, crueller motivations (the witch-burnings of Sekhukuniland) for which all explanations seem inadequate.

The central section of *My Traitor's Heart* is full of such tales. Two stand out. A black man, Dennis Mosheshwe, is savagely beaten to death by a poor white, Augie de Koker. Malan calls this 'a completely traditional South African death. There is even a traditional word for it in Afrikaans: *kafferpak*, meaning a "kaffir hiding".'

And then there is the story of Simon the Hammerman, the multiple murderer of Empangeni, who struck terror into white hearts until he simply surrendered. Rian Malan's investigation of the Hammerman case is superb. First he tells us of Simon's prison quarry days, where Simon witnessed the deliberate beating to death of fellow-prisoners, and found that, as he smashed rocks with a hammer, 'it is not long before the rocks are the white man's head.' But Malan does not stop here. 'Something is hiding in this story.' He discovers crueller truths. Simon the Hammerman was the child of an incestuous union, an outcast, a source of horror among his own Zulu people, because incest 'causes harrowing turbulence in the spirit world.' His hideous crimes were as much a response to his experience of rejection by blacks as of maltreatment by whites. Ambiguity: the kind of truth that is beyond politics, that is hard to tell because people don't wish to hear it. *My Traitor's Heart* is full of such invaluable, awkward, unpackaged truth.

Its final section, when Rian Malan goes to sit at the feet of an old white woman living among Zulus in a remote corner of the country, is the least successful, because here Malan seems to be straining for the metaphorical resonance which, elsewhere in his book, comes naturally out of his material. But it is here that we find the key to this tormented book. The old woman, Creina Alcock, tells Rian Malan: 'Love is worth nothing until it has been tested by its own defeat . . . Love is to enable you to transcend defeat.' *My Traitor's Heart*, which tells us of the defeat of its author's illusions, his ideals, his sense of his own goodness, his courage, and his ability to comprehend his fellow South Africans as they dance their death-dances, which is full of bitterness, cynicism, anger and storms, is a triumphant instance of this type of defeated love.

1990

NURUDDIN FARAH

ere is a starving child, there is a mad dog; feed her, bomb him . . . information about Africa reaches us, most of the time, through a series of filters which, by reducing the vast continent to a cluster of emotive slogans, succeed in denying us any sense of complexity, context, truth. But then, as Nuruddin Farah reminds us in his new novel (his sixth), the West was always rather arbitrary about the names it pinned to Africa: Nigeria was named for an imperialist's mistress, Ethiopia lazily derived from the Greek for 'a person with a black face'.

For many years Farah, one of the finest of contemporary African novelists, has been bringing us a very different world. His Africa, most particularly his native Somalia, is in revolt against the long hegemony of cartographers and bestowers of names. To be a Somali is to be a people united by a language and divided by maps. *Maps* is a book about such political divisions, and the wars they cause (the conflict in the Ogaden is central to the story); but what makes it a true and rich work of art is Farah's knowledge that the deepest divisions are those between men and women, and the rifts within the self. *Maps* charts the chasms of the soul.

An orphaned Somali baby, Askar, is found and raised in the Ogaden village of Kallefo by a non-Somali woman, Misra. The book's first movement—the musical term seems necessary—is a meditation on their relationship. He is a preternaturally wise child, and his growing up is at once mythical and sensual, punctuated by such strange images as the discovery of a man violating a hen. The passion and intimacy of what develops between Askar and Misra culminates in a surreal rite of blood, when the boy, just once, and inexplicably, menstruates.

Later, as a young man in Mogadiscio (its local name, *Xamar*, the red city, echoes and underlines the importance in the novel of blood), he encounters Misra again. Now she is a woman under a dark cloud, accused of an act of treason that led to 600 people in Kallefo being executed by the Ethiopians. Askar, who is being drawn to the life of a Somali revolutionary fighter, is set at war with himself: will he find her guilty or not? She denies the treason; and, as Askar's uncle points out, 'throughout history, men have blamed women for the ill luck they themselves have brought on their heads.' The struggle inside Askar is that ancient struggle, and it is also an echo of the 'real' war, and of his own divisions and doubts. The resolution is ambiguous, but Askar does arrive at a certainty of sorts, a characterization of life as sacrifice, as blood.

Around the central narrative, Farah weaves a web of leitmotifs drawn from folk-tales and from dreams; and in the end it is this web in which the novel's strength is seen to reside, as the meaning of names, the remaking of history, meshes with nightmare and myth to form the basis of a new description of the world, and offers us new maps for old.

1986

KAPUŚCIŃSKI'S ANGOLA

What kinds of life should we call 'ordinary', here in the late twentieth century? What is 'normal' in these abnormal days? For many of us, any definition of the quotidian would still include notions of peace and stability. We would still, perhaps, wish to picture everyday life as rhythmic, based on settled and repeating social patterns. Ryszard Kapuściński's work seems to be based on his knowledge that such conventional descriptions of actuality are now so limited in application that they have become, in a way, fictions.

There's this 'spry old dame' whom Kapuściński meets in the emptiness of Luanda, Angola, during the civil war of 1975. She's worried that the white race is about to enter 'the vestigial phase. Barely two per cent (of the inhabitants of earth) will have naturally blond hair. Blondes: . . . a rarity of rarities.' You could say that humdrum, predictable lives are getting to be as abnormal as those blondes.

Kapuściński's own life hasn't been dull. He's been to twenty-seven revolutions in fifty-five years, which could be a record. The statistic reveals more than just his line of work. It suggests that the revolution, that thing of rumours and broken rhythms, amorphous, bloody, fitful, is now one of the normative processes of human affairs. When peace becomes abnormal, combat fatigues, automatic rifles, missiles, hostages, hunger, fear become the building blocks of a new, uncomfortable definition of the real.

In such a brave new world, it's not surprising that the foreign correspondent has become a myth-figure. He goes out there, doesn't he, and sends us the bad news. And when we've had too much reality, we turn the page, we switch channels, enough is enough.

Alas, our intrepid correspondents tend to run into brick walls. The situation is too confused, they can't find anything out, it's time to file a story. In these stories Ryszard

Kapuściński is able to admire 'the opulence of human fantasy.' One hundred thousand Cubans were in Angola according to the world's press, whereas in truth the total fighting strength of the leftist MPLA was about 30,000 soldiers, 'of whom about two thirds were Angolans.' The MPLA's Cuban allies had brought over lots of extra uniforms, because a Cuban uniform scared the pants off the right-wing FNLA and UNITA troops.

If war reportage is so often make-believe, from whom are we to hear reliable accounts of the horrific, metamorphosed reality of our age? To answer this question is to understand the profound importance of Kapuściński's writing. There is a difference between invention and imagination, and Kapuściński possesses in abundance the gifts of the true imaginative writer.

In his books on Haile Selassie and the Shah, and now in *Another Day of Life*, his descriptions—no, his *responses*—do what only art can manage: that is, they fire our own imaginations. One Kapuściński is worth a thousand grizzled journofantasists; and through his astonishing blend of reportage and artistry we get as close to what he calls the incommunicable image of war as we're ever likely to by reading.

Another Day of Life is about the birth-crisis of independent Angola. It is also a superlative, vivid piece of writing, containing many of the resonant surreal visions that have become Kapuściński's trademark.

In the opening section, the capital, Luanda, is emptying rapidly, its inhabitants convinced that Holden Roberto's FNLA forces, backed by Zaire and the West, are about to devastate the city. 'Everybody,' Kapuściński notes, 'was busy building crates.' From this prosaic beginning he launches into a rhapsodic account of the emptying of the city's stone buildings into the wooden crates. 'Gradually . . . the stone city lost its value in favour of the wooden city . . . Nowhere else in the world had I seen such a city . . . But afterward, [it] sailed away on the ocean . . . I don't know if there had ever been an instance of a whole city sailing across the ocean, but that is

204

exactly what happened. The city sailed out into the world, in search of its inhabitants.'

The seagoing crate-city belonged to the Portuguese who had fled Angola. Kapuściński finally traced the crates to their destinations: Rio, Capetown, Lisbon. His ode to the wooden Luanda is perhaps a shade too long, but it's still a little bit of genius. Of all those who wrote about Luanda, only Kapuściński saw the wooden city. It was there under everybody's noses, but it still needed eyes to see.

In this Angola, a roadblock uses 'a ceiling-high wardrobe built in the form of a huge triptych with a movable crystal-glass mirror mounted on the central section. By manipulating this mirror . . . so that it reflected the rays of the sun, they blinded drivers.' At such roadblocks, death is always close. It can come when you greet the guards with the word *camarada*, not knowing that this is the faction that uses the greeting *irmão*.

After a journey down one of Angola's many dangerous roads, past the Russian roulette of roadblocks and the constant probability of ambush, Kapuściński's companion Nelson murmurs, 'Another day of life.' He is celebrating their survival, *good, so we live until tomorrow at least.* But Kapuściński appreciates that the phrase has a secondary meaning: this is how life is now, this is just the way of it, it is what living has become: a daily escape from death, until the day you don't.

Kapuściński counterpoints his portrait of this shifting, uncertain, terrified world with his telexes home, setting up a tension between the rich, ambiguous truth of life in war-crazed Angola and the need of newspapers for facts. For most of the book, his portrayal of the nightmare seems far more important than what might 'really' be going on. But in the book's last movement, facts do begin to emerge. History takes centre stage, the MPLA comes to power, the poet Neto becomes President, a page turns, a day of life ends.

This concluding, albeit temporary, victory of facts over uncertainty shows us that Kapuściński is not the kind of purely 'literary' writer who might have been content with an open-ended, unresolved portrait of life as chaos, studded with many brilliant metaphors of unknowing. The truth may be hard to establish, but it still needs establishing.

'Overseas, they don't know,' Kapuściński writes, but he often does. He knows that the whole war has depended on two men: the pilot Ruiz, who flies ammunition to besieged border cities, and the engineer Alberto Ribeiro, who manages to keep Luanda's water supply going. Without these two, the cities would have had to surrender to the South Africa-backed enemy forces.

Such details are, like the wooden crate-city, proof that Kapuściński's is a very piercing eye. He hears well, too. Of an MPLA commissar, he says: 'Ju-Ju's communiqués are brief and calm when things are going well . . . But when something turns rotten, [they] become prolix and crabbed, adjectives proliferate, and self-praise and epithets scorning the enemy multiply.' Ours is the most cryptic of centuries, its true nature a dark secret. Ryszard Kapuściński is the kind of codebreaker we need.

1987

8

JOHN BERGER

GRAHAM GREENE

JOHN LE CARRÉ

ON ADVENTURE

AT THE ADELAIDE FESTIVAL

TRAVELLING WITH CHATWIN

CHATWIN'S TRAVELS

JULIAN BARNES

KAZUO ISHIGURO

JOHN BERGER

The young John Berger was memorably described by Stephen Spender as being like 'a foghorn in a fog.' The remark was intended to be derogatory—in those days Berger's art criticism in the *New Statesman* was getting up a lot of distinguished noses—but Berger wrote to Spender thanking him for the compliment. 'What could be more useful in a fog than a foghorn?' he wondered.

Over thirty years later the fog is thicker than ever, and the foghorn is still working. Berger's great gift has always been his ability to help us see how what we see can be manipulated. At the end of the influential first programme of *Ways of Seeing*, he said: 'I am controlling and using for my own purposes the means of reproduction needed for these programmes. I hope you will consider what I arrange—*but be sceptical of it.*'

Ways of Telling by Geoff Dyer is the first book-length study of Berger's work, and its author, who calls it 'an extended response from an interested and grateful reader', writes primarily in celebration of that keen but sceptical eye. And why not? 'All his work,' as Dyer rightly says, 'is criticism in the sense, noted by Barthes, of *bringing into crisis*, and the intellectual stimulation of such an approach reminds me of a very different manner of critic, Kenneth Tynan, because they both put themselves on the line, at risk, in the manner of all artists and very few other writers of criticism.'

Berger is, of course, not only a critic but a creative artist (albeit one of disputable quality). His novels *G.*, about whose 'strikingly cinematic' structure Geoff Dyer is particularly good, and *Pig Earth*, the first part of a trilogy in which Berger proposes to examine nothing less than 'the intricate movement from peasant society to metropolis', bear witness to his imaginative gifts. But to me, and to a generation of the left, his ideas have meant more than his dreams.

E. P. Thompson has reminded us that political discourse in this country was not always the narrow, managerial thing it is today, but an argument about morals, about what kind of world we wished to live in. For John Berger, politics remains an ethical discourse; so does art. He is a formidable protagonist in one of the most crucial battles of our age: the war over the nature of reality.

Walter Benjamin and Bertolt Brecht understood long ago that 'realism' is not an aesthetic concept. It is not a set of rules to write or paint by. It is, rather, an attempt to respond as fully as possible to the circumstances of the world in which the artist works. Realism depends, Berger says, 'upon the nature of the conclusions drawn about the subject', and not on any particular technique. Mimetic naturalism, which Berger calls a 'thoughtless, superficial goggling at appearances', is a very different affair. The technologized nightmares of a J. G. Ballard are, to me at least, a deal more realistic than the cool, poised worlds of an Anita Brookner.

Migration, and the situation of the émigré as worker and as artist, has been another of Berger's long-standing concerns. In his novel *A Painter of Our Time*, and later in *A Seventh Man*, the study of European migrant labour undertaken in collaboration with the photographer Jean Mohr, he looked at, respectively, the bourgeois and working-class variants of the phenomenon. In both books, the experience of cultural displacement results in forms of degradation. The painter in the novel feels crippled by his émigré status, capable only of 'a very limited art'; the workers of *A Seventh Man* are 'homeless' and 'nameless', and in their eyes we see the effects of centuries of 'infernal' history.

One can appreciate the compassion of Berger's vision, and admire the brilliant originality of *A Seventh Man*, and still wish to start pushing beyond such apparent despondency. To migrate is certainly to lose language and home, to be defined by others, to become invisible or, even worse, a target; it is to experience deep changes and wrenches in the soul. But the migrant is not simply transformed by his act; he also transforms his new world. Migrants may well become mutants, but it is out of such hybridization that newness can emerge.

Ways of Telling is a good, solid job of work. Geoff Dyer is no hagiographer, quite capable of pointing up the utter humourlessness of Berger's work, and of taking his hatchet to the unsuccessful early novels. He takes us on what is, for the most part, a skilfully conducted voyage round John Berger that manages to be both readable and scholarly.

He is particularly sharp when he discusses Berger's present idea of himself as story-teller, a role which Berger interprets as a submerging of self: 'Story-tellers lose their own identity and are open to the lives of other people.' Dyer, shrewdly, comments that Berger is not the right type to remain simply a witness, suggesting that there is 'something so eager in Berger's witnessing as to turn it into an overly participatory activity . . . Berger is simply too self-conscious to write as a detached observer.'

A few niggles creep in. In the passage on *The Foot of Clive*, the dully dog-ridden novel, I waited in vain for some comparison to Grass's majestic *Dog Years*, published within months of the Berger book. And when Dyer discusses the failure of *Corker's Freedom* and its attempt to write about people who 'are deprived of the means of translating what they know into thoughts which they can think,' it is extraordinary that the master of inarticulacy, Harold Pinter, remains unmentioned.

Dyer is also far too bothered about the opinions of the egregious Auberon Waugh and Graham Lord. John Berger can do without their praise. The book reads at times like a plea for Berger's inclusion in that very establishment which he has opposed all his life, for all Dyer's disclaimers. I think this is because Dyer, exactly like Berger, has terrible trouble with such words as 'greatness', 'genius' and 'masterpiece'.

Berger himself admitted that his failure to deal with the idea of genius was the 'immense theoretical weakness' of *Ways of Seeing*. He has continued to need, and to employ, such descriptions of exceptionality, but, as Dyer says, 'has never applied himself to developing a systematic theory of the aesthetic.'

Like master, like pupil. What does 'masterpiece' mean when it can be used like this: 'Boucher's image is one of the great what-the-butler-saw masterpieces in painting'? Which, one wonders, are the others?

It is when our ideas of quality, of transcendence, even, are ill-defined, that one gets to worrying about the approval of the 'literary establishment'. There is work to be done here, because such worries are faintly absurd. The foghorn does not desire the good opinion of the fog.

1987

GRAHAM GREENE

The Captain and the Enemy

G raham Greene's new novel begins with the figure of a twelve-year-old boy, Victor Baxter—'Baxter Three'— fleeing across his boarding school quad to escape from his enemies. Baxter is one of nature's 'Amalekites', an outsider, intended, as the Bible suggests, for slaying. So when the mysterious, piratical 'Captain' arrives with a note from the boy's father and permission to take him out, young Baxter looks upon him as a saviour: a view he will, in a way, never lose, for it is the Captain who enables him to stop being an Amalekite almost for ever, by abducting him and so changing the course of his life.

'Will you be sure to know the good side from the bad, the Captain from the enemy?' reads the novel's epigraph, and within a page or two Greene has enmeshed us in just such a moral tangle: Were the boy's schoolfellows his real foes? Is his abductor truly on the good side? Did the Captain really win Baxter Three from his father in a game of backgammon? Or was it, as his father later insists, actually chess? Can the father be what he is called through the book: viz., 'the Devil'? And is the Captain justified, that is to say right, to have captured this boy for the sake of the woman he purports to love, a certain Liza, who longs for a child—particularly as Liza, when the Captain first met her, was recovering from an abortion, which was itself the outcome of her liaison with the elder Baxter, the Devil himself?

For seventy-nine pages, as he explores such questions with a miraculous, zany lightness of touch, Greene writes like a dream. There can rarely have been a less probable fictional family—helpless Liza and her crook of a beau, looking after the Devil's child—but their story is pure delight. The Captain, also known as Colonel Claridge, the Major, the Sergeant, Señor Smith and Mr Brown, gives Baxter Three an education in the slipperiness and mutability of things. The boy quickly becomes 'Jim', while 'Victor' is added to the Captain's list of names. Geography, under the Captain's tutelage, becomes a war game. And there's economics, too: 'If you're a bit short of cash . . . never drink at the bar, unless you've booked a room first, for otherwise they want their money straight away.' Whereas, once you've booked a room, you can eat a hearty dinner and then abscond, leaving behind a cheap suitcase containing two stout bricks.

Most problematic of all, however, are the Captain's lessons in love. He takes him to see the film *King Kong*, and the boy is puzzled. '"Why doesn't he drop her?" I asked. I suppose I sounded very heartless to the Captain, for he replied harshly, "He loves her, boy. Can't you understand that—he loves her?" But of course I couldn't understand.' *Of course*, because it is Jim's tragedy to be unable to love any human being. (Even more bewildering to him is the Captain's assertion that the woman's kicking out at Kong does not mean she doesn't like him. 'It's a woman's way.')

The unloving child, the pale, needy woman and the cut-price corsair who needs her are as haunting (and, I suppose one ought to say, 'seedy') a trio as Greene has come up with in a long time. And while we're seeing through twelve-year-old Jim's cold eyes, the novel works. Then we leap ahead ten years. Jim is now twenty-two, Liza dies an accidental death while the Captain is away in Panama, and the spell breaks.

Part of the problem is technical. Greene has described the fitful manner in which the novel was written over a period of some thirteen years, and his fictional Jim's narrative method now acquires something of the same stop–go quality. Jim becomes a self-conscious narrator, revising and updating his text as we go along; until at length he throws the whole thing into a waste-paper basket, whence it is retrieved by one Colonel Martinez, an associate of the Captain's, who considers having it recommended for a Cuban literary prize. After the lightness of the novel's early pages, this comes across as heavy-handed stuff.

But the biggest disappointment is the weakening of emotional tension that results from Liza's death. With the woman out of the way, the book becomes something like a ripping yarn, in which the old, male and somewhat exhausted theme of the betrayal of the (fake) father by the (false) son moves ponderously to centre stage.

Jim, lusting for adventure, has decided to join the Captain in Panama, where, it transpires, he's busy airlifting weapons to the Sandinistas (the action takes place before the 1979 Nicaraguan revolution). Geography is, once again, a war game, but Jim is blithely ignorant of Latin America ('Where's Estelí? What country are you talking about?' And, a little later: 'What Canal treaty?'). He lies to the Captain, not daring to tell him that Liza is dead; and at last, after a bitter quarrel, spills the beans about his surrogate father's secret plane to Mr Quigly, an Englishman with a bit of an American accent, who poses as a financial correspondent but is actually the ghost of many such shadowy spooks from Greeneland long ago, drinking Pisco Sours and arranging for the Captain to be shot down and killed.

The Captain turns out to be King Kong, after all. He has held on to Liza's memory for years, writing to her every day, and when she is freed from his grasp it's the aeroplanes that get him. (But not really the aeroplanes, as we know from the film's famous last line: ''Twas Beauty killed the Beast.') And Jim, remorseless Jim, turns out to be an Amalekite after all: an enemy, fit to be slain.

Goodish news, then, from Greeneland. After the damp squib of *Doctor Fischer of Geneva* and the Don Camillo-like flatness of *Monsignor Quixote*, half a novel's worth of vintage Greene is not to be sneezed at. We should be grateful for that initial champagne, and tolerant of what follows, even if much of it is a rather plain Panamanian plonk.

1988

Yours Etc.: Letters to the Press 1945-1989

If you glance through the index of this sprightly volume, in which is to be found a most entertaining celebration of Graham Greene's lesser-known career as a prolific author of letters to newspapers, you will find unarguable proof of his total addiction to everything about his time, from the greatest issues of the day to the humblest subject imaginable. Under 'E' you will find, in close proximity, El Salvador, Eliot, T. S., Elizabeth II, Queen, and Eltham Laundry Supplies Ltd. The letter *G* offers the equally remarkable sequence: God, sex of, Goddard, Lord Rayner, Gonzi, Archbishop, and Gorbachev, Mikhail; while, amongst the *M*s, Matisse rubs shoulders with Mau Mau rebellion and Maudling; and *My Fair Lady* (musical) is followed by My Lai (massacre). Here is evidence of that most un-English of characteristics, an eclectic and frontierless engagement with the world; engagement not in the narrow sense of overt political affiliation, but in the broader sense of finding oneself possessed of a huge and consuming need to report on the reality of real life.

Greene has always acted upon the assumption that a writer might have a public role as well as a purely literary one; that there is much that an artist might legitimately comment on outside the confines of his art. His letters keep up a running commentary on a number of issues, notably the nature of the Sandinista government in Nicaragua and of its opponents, the 'contra' insurgents and their puppet-masters in the United States; and the folly of NATO's commitment to the nuclear 'first strike'; and, at a somewhat less elevated level, the postal service itself (there are letters on fair pay for postmen, and letters containing apparently contradictory schemes to bankrupt the Post Office entirely).

The inevitable effect of such meddling is that Greene has been regularly reviled in the public prints, accused of blasphemy, bizarrerie, Communism, Jansenism and other capital offences. One of the most remarkable aspects of this collection is its demonstration of Greene's perfect equanimity and good-humoured perseverance in the face of such opposition. When accused of becoming 'increasingly left wing in his old age' by Alexander Chancellor, on account of his friendship with Nicaragua's Tomás Borge, Greene replied: 'I am, I hope you will agree, a friend of Alexander Chancellor. Does this mean that I am seeing Blue?' Or, when the American right-winger William F. Buckley took serious issue with Greene's frivolous suggestion that 'it would be equally true, or equally false' to call the Nicaraguan government Catholic as Communist, Greene rejoined: 'Alas, these English jokes! I must try to avoid them.'

Journalists in general appear to be the only human beings for whom Graham Greene has little time or respect. 'A petty reason perhaps why novelists more and more try to keep a distance from journalists is that novelists are trying to write the truth and journalists are trying to write fiction,' he says sharply before demolishing one Stephen Pile. Other journos who get the treatment in these pages include Bernard Levin, Penelope Gilliatt, Nicholas Wapshott, Marina Warner and Bernard Levin again. On rarer occasions, such as the fairly well-known tiff with Anthony Burgess, he quarrels with fellow-novelists as well, though in this case Burgess's habit of telling interviewers that Greene 'was living with a woman whose husband walks by at night and shouts up at the window "*Crapaud! Salaud!*"' might be thought a sufficient provocation. (Typically, Greene quarrels only with the yelling. 'But I live on the fourth floor. And with the traffic, how can her husband come shouting through the window?')

Some vendettas are friendlier. The verbal swordplay between Greene and Evelyn Waugh is one of the features of this book. When an American dramatization of *The Heart of the Matter* flopped, Waugh wrote: 'I long to hear an account of your Boston disaster.' Greene, in his turn, is capable of referring to a piece of Waugh correspondence as 'a little castrated letter'. But the friendship was a deep one, and when Waugh died Greene defended him fiercely against an attack by Beverley Nichols in the *Spectator*. He likens Nichols to the 'oldest unmarried woman' customarily employed by an unnamed West African tribe to spit upon a dead chief's grave.

'Evelyn never waited till a man died to release his venom,' Greene finely remarks. 'He would always have chosen to spit in a man's face rather than on his grave.'

Yours Etc., in which Greene's letters are placed in context by the excellently witty Christopher Hawtree (who remarks, at one point, in true Greene journalist-hating fashion, that 'a haddock never looks best pleased at being squashed against a mugshot of Paul Johnson'), is a book studded with gems. Here you will learn of Greene's addiction to practical jokes, to the formation of satirical societies and to *New Statesman* and *Spectator* competitions, particularly those asking for parodies of Graham Greene. Several of his books, including the most recent novel *The Captain and the Enemy*, had their origins in such competition entries. Here, too, are Greene's letters championing Charlie Chaplin, anatomizing Indo-China, defending Nabokov's *Lolita*, resigning from the American Academy over the Vietnam War, and fulminating against the outrageous decision by the British government to seize and burn books and music imported from Argentina during the Falklands War. Contraception, the Pope, liberation theology and voodoo also figure prominently. A long life, and an argumentative one; and while there have been those who wondered, as Kingsley Martin informed Greene during the course of a dispute in 1958, 'why anyone so successful and creative as you should have become so "bitter, rude and disgruntled",' most readers will, I'm sure, agree that while Greene is quite capable of rudeness he is never bitter and seems a most enviably gruntled individual. Gruntlement is likewise his readers' happy lot.

1989

John le Carré

If your characters have to hide behind façades for a living, the world of your novel can all too easily look more like a cheap stage set than the real thing. But readers read spy novels to be persuaded that they're getting an authentic insight into the closed world on the far side of the looking-glass. It is this problem (How do you create a satisfyingly rounded portrait of Flatland? How to give faces to necessarily faceless men?) which the spy novelist must solve if he wants his work to transcend the genre and be treated as Serious Literature.

John le Carré, who wants to be taken very seriously indeed, has in the past tried two solutions to what could be called the 'human factor' problem. His best book, *Tinker Tailor Soldier Spy*, was a brilliantly plotted procedural thriller in which the secret world was shown not to be flat but composed of different dimensions. Here character was no longer destiny. Deception and power had supplanted it. This was a theatre of masks, whose spook-world, its economy and morals in decay, became a perfect metaphor for Britain as a whole. Earlier, in *The Spy Who Came in from the Cold*, the technique was different. In this variation, an agent burdened with residual human values (love, ethics, etc.) found himself at odds with the anti-ethic of the 'espiocrats'. The 'round' world of the emotions struggled against the 'flat' world of power. This is the method to which *The Russia House* returns.

Love and war have long been incompatible in le Carré. His most proficient cold warriors, like George Smiley, have emotional lives that are not so hot. Whereas those who permit themselves human attachments, the ones who come in from the cold, tend to become casualties of the loveless, endless war of shadows from which they can't really escape. To put it more simply: women usually mean trouble. Mr Palfrey, the spies' lawyer who is the ostensible narrator of *The Russia House*, is Smileyishly unhappy in love; while at the centre of the novel is the love affair of an English publisher, Barley Blair, perhaps the unlikeliest spy of all le Carré's honourable schoolboys, and a Russian woman, Katya Orlova. And from this love affair all kinds of trouble flows.

Much of the trouble is, I'm afraid, literary. There is something unavoidably stick-figure-like about le Carré's attempts at characterization. Here, for example, is Katya's entry into the story: 'She was earnest. She was intelligent. She was determined. She was scared, even though her dark eyes were lit with humour. And she had that rare quality which Landau in his flowery way liked to call the Class That Only Nature Can Bestow. In other words, she had quality as well as strength.' This is pretty close to schlockbusterese, and the novel's male characters are not much better done by. All that public-school chatter, all those insufferable Americans and poetic/tormented/drunk Russians! And if one is going to send a fully formed human being down the mean streets of the inhuman secret world, one ought to be able to make his declaration of love more convincing than, oh, 'It's a mature, unselfish, absolute, thrilling love,' or, 'I love you so profoundly that I am ashamed to be articulate . . . I look at you, and I am absolutely sick of the sound of my own voice.' At which Katya, displaying the Class That Only Nature Can Bestow, suffers herself to be kissed.

The truth is that le Carré's strengths do not include profound characterization. He is at his best telling a terrific, mystifying story peppered with the special vocabulary that he has taught us all and which may be his greatest gift to us— mole, lamplighter, tradecraft. The human factor brings out what is most naïve and sentimental in his prose. And the biggest problem with *The Russia House* is that the love story takes up so much of the foreground that the spy story is almost perfunctorily simple—a Russian scientist wants his work published in the West, it turns out to contain sensational information about the limitations of Russian weaponry, the Brits recruit the Russian's chosen publisher, the above Barley Blair, to get more out of the source, the Americans take over, Barley falls in love, things begin to go wrong . . . For admirers of the myriad subtle convolutions of le Carré's plotting at its best, this is disappointingly plain fare.

Those who have liked *The Russia House*—and it has already acquired many distinguished admirers, including Russian ones—have praised it primarily for its portrait of the USSR in the third summer of the *perestroika*, for its attempts to adapt the rules of the spy genre to the requirements of what one character calls 'glasnostics'. And there's no doubt that the novel is full of information about the Soviet Union, from the price of notebooks to the elaborate system of barter by which people obtain the things they want; while there are glasnosticians of every type to be found within these pages, from committed believers to unreconstructed cold warriors for whom nothing has really changed. But the knowledge the book imparts is head-knowledge; there's not much here to illumine the spirit. One page, one paragraph of Tatyana Tolstaya gives you more of Russia than all 344 pages of le Carré. What a shame that le Carré's Western readers will outnumber readers of Tolstaya's wicked, magical collection of stories, *On the Golden Porch*, by several thousands to one.

The shadow world is evidently a good deal more fascinating than the one most people inhabit. Unfortunately, few serious writers have ever penetrated it, Graham Greene being the great contemporary exception. Le Carré is as close to a serious writer as the spy genre itself has thrown up. Close, but—this time, anyway—no cigar.

1989

ON ADVENTURE

'The true adventurer,' wrote O. Henry in *The Green Door*, 'goes forth aimless and uncalculating to meet and greet unknown fate. A fine example was the Prodigal Son—when he started home.'

Among the most remarkable qualities of the words *adventure* and *adventurer* is their capaciousness. Any idea that can encompass the Prodigal Son and Indiana Jones, that finds common ground between the Pilgrim Fathers' voyage to America and the journey of the Darlings with Peter Pan to the Neverland, that suggests a connection between Alice's step through the looking-glass and Crick and Watson's discovery of the double helix of DNA, is clearly one of the most resonant notions in the culture. We often think of adventure as a metaphor of life itself, and not only of life: 'To die,' Peter Pan muses, 'will be an awfully big adventure.'

Closely connected with this version of the idea of adventure are notions of danger, of a journey, of the unknown. And, of course, of heroism: he (or she) who would voyage into the secret night, who would step off the edge of the earth because it is there, must clearly be made of the Right Stuff. Sam Shepard as Chuck Yeager is perhaps a modern archetype of this myth; Huck Finn its antithesis, adventure's anti-hero. Heroic adventure is, typically, an individualist affair. There are of course adventurer-heroes who travelled in groups—Argonauts, Everest climbers, the Magnificent Seven—but the myth more often seems to require the existentialist purity of a single human being pitted against the immensity of the universe, to prefer the lone sailor in the small boat traversing the liquid Andes of Cape Horn to any team effort, to elevate the lone gunman (Clint Eastwood in most of his Western roles) above the Wild Bunch.

Contemporary literary travellers tend, it being an anti-heroic age, to be more Huck than Chuck. Their true ancestors are not, perhaps, so much the wandering heroes of the classical epoch (Jason, Ulysses, unspeakably pious Aeneas) as the *picaros* of the novel. Many of the most appealing pieces of twentieth-century 'travel writing' read very like picaresque novels, offering us the notion of adventure-as-mad-quest. Even Italo Calvino's fictional Marco Polo, in *Invisible Cities*, has a whole series of such quests in mind: he travels through his wondrous cities in search of his past, his future, Venice, memory, and stranger things: 'This is the aim of my explorations: examining the traces of happiness still to be glimpsed. I gauge its short supply.' Such conceits, exquisite and comic, suggest parodies of the ancient myth of the Holy Grail.

To invoke the Grail is to realize that adventure, as it is understood today, has lost a certain high-minded grandeur, and that the loss lies in the area of purpose. Once upon a time the journey, the quest, the adventure was not so much a private, or idiosyncratic, or crazy enterprise as a spiritual labour. The Knights of the Round Table sought the Sangreal in God's name. The *Pilgrim's Progress*, like its Islamic counterpart, Farid-ud-din Attar's *Conference of the Birds*, is an adventure of purification, of winning through to the divine. The voyages of Sindbad the Sailor have been explicated in religio-mystical terms. Like the line of sight in a Gothic cathedral, the adventuring spirit was swept forwards and upwards in the direction of God. This allegorical, transcendent adventuring is, these days, more or less completely defunct.

There are good reasons for feeling relieved that adventure is nowadays the province of the determined, the curious and the idiosyncratic. The adventuring spirit, when ruled by faith or ideology, has not been an entirely Good Thing. The behaviour of the Crusader knights, Spanish conquistadors and the like bears witness to this. Like all important ideas, adventure has a dark side as well as a light. For every Christopher Columbus there is also a Captain Hook, for every lamp-genie there is a fiend. The world of the adventurer contains at least as many mercenary 'soldiers of fortune' as idealistic knights-errant, and for every Vasco da Gama there is also an *Aguirre, Wrath of God*. When the spirit of adventure invades the historical process—when States or their leaders or representatives go adventuring—the results are usually catastrophic. From Genghis Khan to Napoleon and Mussolini, history is littered with examples of what happens when adventurers come to power: disaster, rapine, fire and the sword, Bad Things galore. Adventure and politics are best kept far apart, rather like uranium and plutonium.

On the whole, then, the Candide/Quixote model of adventure seems preferable to older versions. In our increasingly vicarious culture, the adventurers are the people who perform marvels on our behalf. Escaping from their own roots, from the prison of everyday reality, they enable us to experience, if at one remove, something of the exhilaration of the successful jailbreaker. If urban society be a confining chain, then the adventurers are our necessary Houdinis, reminding us that change, difference, strangeness, newness, risk and achievement really do still exist, and can, if we wish, be attained.

This kind of adventuring has become, or so it seems to me, a pretty well exclusively Western phenomenon. Once there was an Ibn Battuta to set against Marco Polo, and even an Islamic empire to liken to the Christian ones. But it's hard to conceive of, say, an Indian Paul Theroux becoming obsessed with the railways of the United States, or a black African Karen Blixen heading for Scandinavia. I offer the theory that adventuring is, these days, by and large a movement that originates in the rich parts of the planet and heads for the poor. Or a journey from the crowded cities towards the empty spaces, which may be another way of saying the same thing. I recently watched a television documentary in which a group of British adolescents on Honda motor-trikes roared across the perfection of the Saharan sand-dunes, boasting that the crossing of the Erg had never been done before 'on motorized transport'. I was left with the memory of the bemused courteous faces of the locals they encountered, many of whom had very probably crossed that desert on admittedly non-motorized camels; and I fretted about the ethnocentric narrowness of vision of some who venture forth into the exotic South. To a Saharan nomad, after all, the journey is the point, the shaping fact of existence; arriving at some notional destination—'conquering the desert'—is a kind of fiction, the illusion of an end. Adventures tend to be linear narratives, but in life, as in literature, that's not the only way of seeing things.

As all writers know, you don't have to leave home to embark on an adventure. The poet Basho, in Edward Bond's play *Narrow Road to the Deep North*, returns from his dangerous northward pilgrimage in search of enlightenment, claiming to have found what he sought. And what was enlightenment? 'I saw there was nothing to learn in the deep north . . . You get enlightenment where you are.' Many of the greatest adventurers of our age, Marie Curie, Freud, Marx, Einstein, Proust, Kafka, Emily Dickinson and the rest, didn't travel much further than a laboratory, a library, a consulting room. Adventure may have much to do with the pushing back of frontiers, but few topographical boundaries can rival the frontiers of the mind.

Even in the case of travel-adventures, the best of all are those in which some inner journey, some adventure in the self, is the real point. *Peter Pan* would not be the same if Wendy and the Lost Boys didn't discover that they wanted to grow up, that Paradise has to be lost. The real plot of *Moby Dick* takes place inside Ahab; the rest is a fishing trip. And even Quixote, maddest of *picaros*, sees himself ridiculous at last: 'For there are no birds this year in last year's nests. I was mad, but I am sane now.'

So it turns out that Basho is both right and wrong; that the travelling adventurer can, after all, gain knowledge that is not available elsewhere, and then, by living to tell the tale, offer that knowledge to us. Enlightenment is certainly to be had at home, but it's still worth making the long, arduous trip, in spite of the storms and brigands, into the remote fastnesses of the deep north.

1985

AT THE ADELAIDE FESTIVAL

The first time I went to an international literary festival, I was bullied into playing centre-forward for the World against Finland (our host nation) in a football match that began at midnight by the light of the midnight sun—that is, in semi-darkness. The Finnish writers took the game very seriously, rehearsing wall passes and bicycle kicks, and warning us casually that their goalkeeper was also the country's harshest literary critic, so it might not be wholly advisable to make him cross. Meanwhile, the World, whose representatives did not have so much as a language in common, concentrated on trying to spot the ball through what Flann O'Brien would have called the accretions of black air. My own troubles were increased by my complete lack of footballing talent, by my decision not to wear my glasses in case they broke, and by D. M. Thomas, who convinced a gullible reporter that I had once won an Olympic medal at football for India. The final score—no thanks to the World's Olympic Star—was Finland 1, the World 6, and the Finns never really forgave us. Such international encounters can be risky.

At literary festivals you can hear J. P. Donleavy lamenting the present shortage of women who can both cook and sew. You can be instructed by Ted Hughes in the use of vitamins. Scandinavian novelists will read translations of novels about father–daughter incest, or science-fiction tales in which eight Swedes are marooned in a space station for fifty years. At literary festivals there will be drink, and a rare opportunity for writers to feel important. There will be interminable speeches by the Russian delegate about how Art is much to do with the passions, and is not rationalistic or objectivist in process. An earnest Yugoslav woman will demand the floor and inform her colleagues that they are all the victims of Positivism, after which there will be a low, polyglot buzz of writers' voices, asking in Dutch and Arabic and Gikuyu if anyone knows what this Positivism *is*. At literary festivals it is important not to be lured into sitting down to poker with Al Alvarez, unless you play approximately as well as Steve McQueen in *The Cincinnati Kid*.

What is valuable for audiences—for readers—about these rather strange events is that for some reason they find it interesting to look at and listen to authors as well as read their books. What is most valuable to the writers is, I think, the informal talk, the off-stage stuff. Writers know they will probably not meet each other very often and so, when they do, they tend to come directly to the point, and, usually, to talk a great deal. This aspect of literary gatherings is reminiscent of what I was told on my first night at university by the Provost of my college. 'The most valuable part of your education,' he said in an after-dinner speech to us freshmen, 'will be what you do when you sit privately in each other's rooms at night, fertilizing one another.'

This year, seeking fertilization, I travelled ten thousand miles to the Adelaide Festival's Writers' Week. I arrived knowing very little about Adelaide: capital of South Australia, close to the Barossa Valley where German migrants established many excellent vineyards, site of one of the most attractive cricket grounds on earth. Not much else, except that both David Hare, whose play *A Map of the World* was premiered at an earlier Adelaide Festival, and the actor Roshan Seth who played the lead in it, had spoken very highly of the place. Within hours of arriving, however, I was offered a memorable summary of the city by one of my hosts. 'It's called the City of Churches, Adelaide,' he said. 'But one of the churches is now a discothèque, and what's more it's the first disco in Australia to show porno films.'

It was a useful clue, a hint that there was more to Adelaide than met the eye. What met the eye was conservative, spacious, pretty and a little bland. Adelaide was designed from scratch by South Australia's first Surveyor-General, Colonel William Light, in 1836. 'Light's Vision' was of a grid set in a garden, and that's the way the city still looks. But for all its parkland and wide avenues it retains an air of being somehow unrooted, or unexplained, which is perhaps common to all planned cities. It is attractive enough, with its greenery and its 'Adelaide lace' filigree wrought-iron ornamentation on many porches and balconies, but it tells you nothing. The city's shape does not contain the history or unveil the nature of its people. It is a kind of disguise.

At times during my stay I would be afflicted by odd feelings of disorientation. I felt as though something were blurring my vision, or preventing me from focusing my eyes properly. No doubt jet lag and flu had something to do with this. But it wasn't just that: I kept thinking I was somewhere in North America. It was an illusion created by the furniture of the streets—the neon, the poster art, the traffic lights all derive from American, not European models. And then Adelaide is a new city, a city without much of a past, nothing in it more than 150 years old, and that's certainly American. And it also has to do with a choice made by white Australians. They may make anti-American jokes all the time, but they have chosen to turn their faces towards the New World and away from the old. There is something unreal, something *grafted* about Adelaide. It is America driving on the left. But— as that image indicates—there is still a great deal of British and European influence around. No wonder, then, that visitors occasionally suffer from double vision.

A delaide was an enigma, and I was getting interested in breaking its codes. Meanwhile, though, Writers' Week was proceeding fertilely enough. The distinguished South African novelist André Brink arrived, having been obliged to sit throughout his flight from Africa next to an Australian farmer who had assured him he would enjoy Australia, 'because we've got our blacks well under control, you follow me, sport?' However, Brink's meeting with the exiled black South African writer Bessie Head was the week's most moving encounter. Bessie, a tough woman with a tiny, singsong voice issuing from an ample frame, said it had been worth coming all the way from Botswana to Adelaide just to meet André, 'because, for the first time in my life, I have met a good white South African.'

Writers' Week takes place in and around a large marquee set in pleasant, palm-fringed lawns across the road from the main Festival Centre; half-establishment, half-fringe, it has in the past irritated some of the more pompous visiting writers by its informality. But that seemed to me to be its chief virtue. All week, writers and readers meandered in and out of the marquee, strolled on the lawns, dipped into the book-tent and even, from time to time, stopped by the bar for a tinnie of Swan. The audiences are mostly friendly, but they do sometimes heckle: Adelaide's own Barbara Hanrahan had to put up with one well-lubricated gentleman's repeated advice to 'shut up and give someone else a chance.'

No hecklers, however, while Morris West, Australia's best-selling novelist, spoke for an hour without once getting off the absorbing subject of his extremely high income.

Everywhere you looked you saw excellent Australian writers. Elizabeth Jolley, deceptively frail to look at, with a profile uncannily close to Virginia Woolf's, read what she called a couple of dances. 'I don't really dance myself,' she told the audience, 'but for some reason my characters often do.' The dances were subtle, courtly, graceful. Later in the week Rodney Hall read from his magnificent novel *Just Relations*, winner of the Miles Franklin award: it was so good that you wished you had written it yourself. And there was Blanche d'Alpuget, the acute, level-headed biographer of Bob Hawke, the Prime Minister with the seventy-eight per cent popularity rating, a Labour leader who misses no opportunity of beating up the left. 'His physical appeal is huge,' Blanche d'Alpuget told me. 'Men write to him to say they carry his photograph in their wallets and it gives them strength.' What does that do to a man, I wondered, that adulation. When he arrives at rock concerts and walks through the crowd, people stand up as he passes. 'Bob, it's Bob. G'day Bob, good on yer, Bob.' It seemed alarming to me, this leader-worship.

'Well, of course,' Blanche said, 'what's happening to him is totally corrupting.'

Jolley, Hall, d'Alpuget; Thomas Keneally beaming at everyone and standing them drinks; and Patrick White, David

229

Malouf, Peter Carey and Murray Bail weren't even there . . .
Australian literature seemed to be in extremely good shape. I
was ashamed to have arrived knowing so little; I left knowing
a little more; it was a good week.

'Don't you find,' Angela Carter said one evening, 'that
there's something a little exhausted about the place
names around here? I mean, Mount Lofty, Windy Point.' On
another occasion, Bruce Chatwin said something similar: 'It's
a tired country, not young at all. It tires its inhabitants. It's too
ancient, too old.'

I was looking for the keys to Adelaide. And gradually
things did come bubbling up from under that smooth, solid
façade. On an excursion into the Adelaide Hills I was told how
fires regularly devastated the region. I heard about the famous
blaze on 'Ash Wednesday'. Freak effects—as the flames
surged over a road on which there were two petrol pumps,
one blew up and the other was unharmed. And finally, almost
casually, I was given hints about arson. What sort of people
are these that burn the landscape? There is strangeness here.

Hindley Street, Adelaide, looks lively when you first
walk down it. Young people, nightspots, restaurants, street
life. Then you notice the brothels and the winos. And one
night a trail of blood along the pavement. Shoeprints in
blood staggering along, ending up in a dark doorway.
Another clue. And a couple of days later I hear about the
vanishing youngsters. Sixteen-year-old girls and boys,
disappearing into thin air. The police do nothing, shrug;
teenagers are always leaving home. But they never turn up. I
am told that parents of these dematerialized children have
formed their own search organizations. Adelaide seems more
eerie by the minute.

On my last night in town, many of us go to a party
thrown by Jim, a local sheep king. It is a housewarming: his
last house with its priceless art collection was destroyed in
the Ash Wednesday fire. The new place is in ritzy North
Adelaide. An excellent party, and Jim is a generous and literate
host. But then I am buttonholed by someone who wants to

reminisce about his days in an English public school, and the double vision begins again. Later in the evening, a beautiful woman starts telling me about the weirdo murders. 'Adelaide's famous for them,' she says, excitedly. 'Gay pair slay young girls. Parents axe children and inter them under lawn. Stuff like that. You know.'

Now I begin to understand Adelaide. Adelaide is the ideal setting for a Stephen King novel, or horror film. You know why those films and books are always set in sleepy, conservative towns? Because sleepy, conservative towns are where those things happen. Exorcisms, omens, shinings, poltergeists. Adelaide is Amityville, or Salem, and things here go bump in the night.

Bruce Chatwin and I flew out from Adelaide at the end of Writers' Week, heading for Alice Springs. Very quickly the greenery of Adelaide was replaced by the desert. The great, red infinity of that awesome moonscape set the previous week in its proper context. The desert, the harsh pure desert, was the reality, was Australia, was the truth; the town I was leaving stood revealed as a mirage, alien, a prevarication. I settled back into my seat, eager to reach the Alice.

1984

1991: A postscript. When this essay was first published, some of the citizens of Adelaide were upset by its reference to 'weirdo murders', even though I'd been told about such crimes by more than one resident of the city. A few days after the Mayor attacked me in the local paper, however, a group of unknown crazies climbed into the Adelaide Zoo at night and systematically, viciously, murdered just about all the animals . . .

Travelling with Chatwin

Afew memories of my travels with Bruce in Central
Australia in early 1984:

We are driving down a wide red-dirt road when a dingo
emerges from nowhere and stands by the roadside, staring.
We stop the car and stare back. The dingo is unperturbed.
Bruce starts telling it sick dingo jokes. 'What's a baby in a
pram next to a dingo?—Meals on wheels.' The dingo,
disgusted, lopes off. (I discover later that sick dingo jokes
infect all visitors to Alice Springs. The producers of the recent
film about the Lindy Chamberlain case had trouble settling on
a title for the movie. Among the titles they considered were
'Foetal Attraction' and 'Full Matinée Jacket'.)

The idea of the 'dreaming tracks' or 'songlines' captivates
me as much as it does Bruce. How could writers fail to love a
world which has been mapped by stories? I find myself
envying him his subject. He talks about it constantly and we
go in for long arcane passages of supposition. What happens
when two songlines cross? Do the songs acquire common
lines? Or does one line 'burrow' while another 'flies'? The
London Underground map appears in my mind. I keep
nagging away at the idea of junctions: the Piccadilly
Circuses and King's Crosses of these strange, walking
poems. But so many of the songlines are lost, their people
exterminated by white settlers, that it's impossible to rebuild
the whole map.

Each aboriginal tribesperson 'owns' a piece of the local song.
Bruce and I get stuck into another futile discussion: which
came first, the urge to narrate or the urge to own? Imagination
or possession? Chicken or egg? I listen, Bruce talks. I am a
fairly garrulous person myself, but in Bruce's company I don't

manage more than a few interruptions. I start becoming rather proud of these.

Bruce talks about everything under the sun. I remember a long disquisition about the writer Eça de Queiroz. I remember many etymological snippets. 'The word bugger comes originally from the pejorative French verb, bougrir—to make love like a Bulgarian.'

At this stage, Bruce thought his book would be called *Arkady*, and would take the simple form of a Platonic dialogue. Two men sitting under a tree in Alice Springs, letting their talk range across time and space. In our four-wheel-drive Toyota, he is, I realize, using me to help him have a kind of rough draft of this talk.

Later, after the book is published, Bruce tells someone that 'of course' I am Arkady. This isn't true. I know one person in Alice Springs, like Arkady an Australian of Russian descent, also highly knowledgeable about aboriginal religion, who is a much more obvious model. Nor do I recognize a single line of our conversation in *The Songlines*. The truth is, 'of course', that Bruce is Arkady as well as the character he calls Bruce. He is both sides of the dialogue.

An impressive fact. Bruce made a great many telephone calls from various motels. In his famous moleskin notebooks he seemed to have the phone numbers of everyone on the planet. When he called someone he invariably said simply, 'Bruce here'. Amazingly, in that country stuffed with Bruces, I never heard anybody ask: 'Bruce who?' No other Bruce ever sounded quite like Bruce.

Bruce takes me to meet a Lutheran pastor who looks like a cowboy; weatherbeaten face, wrinkled eyes. This man offers us tea and cakes and begins to chat with gentle craziness about the genetic differences that make aboriginal peoples unable to hold their liquor. 'Their intestines are not like ours.'

Apparently no white Australians ever get drunk. Bruce treats the man like an old friend. When we leave I ask him why. 'He knows a vast amount of stuff.' Later I discover that many of the young white radicals I meet in Alice Springs, people working as lawyers for the Land Rights movement, or people working with the various tribes 'out bush', distrust Bruce for his apparent political conservatism and his 'anthropological' orientation. Bruce is untroubled, walking through the minefield of black Australian politics with unconcern. (When I read *The Songlines* I said, 'You realize many of the sort of people you've written about will be pretty cross about some of this?' He said he knew, but what could one do? You had to tell it as you saw it.)

At Glen Helen we hear the story of the crooked pub owner who filled the hollow tubes of his car's roofrack with sweet sherry and made a fortune driving around the bush selling the stuff to 'the boongs'. Again, the stories of genetic inferiority recur.

At Hermannsburg, a Lutheran mission settlement for aboriginal peoples, we go out beyond the township's limits to meet a man running a car mechanics' workshop with a wholly aboriginal workforce. Out here cars are endlessly cannibalized to make other equally ancient cars run. When the mechanic sees us coming he yells, 'Look! It's the bookies!' We have brought copies of our books as presents. When his wife is offered these, she adopts a wide-eyed, reverential expression, caresses the Picador paperbacks and says, 'You mean we can have them to look at for a bit?' 'No,' says Bruce, 'please keep them, they're gifts.' She can't believe it, and then, as if handling sacred objects, wraps *In Patagonia* and *Midnight's Children* in a bit of cloth and puts them up on a high shelf.

At the Inland Motel near Ayers Rock we hear about the truck-driver, Douglas Crabbe, who was thrown out of the pub one night and went outside and reversed his truck into the bar, killing and maiming a number of people. The locals rebuilt the pub even though they knew the whole motel was going to be demolished a year later anyway.

Later we are in Alice Springs and hear that Crabbe's trial is under way and he is in the witness-box. Bruce and I grab our notepads and go off to play court reporter. Crabbe is softly spoken, dapper, with a little brown moustache and button-down blue shirt with dark blue knotted tie. While giving evidence he keeps his eyes cast down. His line is that he didn't know what he was doing, he has no memory of it: a temporary insanity plea, I suppose. He says repeatedly that he's not the sort of man to commit such a crime. When pressed about this, he says: 'I've been driving trucks now for four and a half years, and treating them as if they were my own.' (He doesn't quite add 'children'.) 'So for me to half destroy a truck is completely against my personality.' I look at the jury and see them all begin to sort of hiss and grind their teeth and decide to send him away and throw away the key. Afterwards I say to Bruce, 'Wasn't that an amazing piece of self-destruction?' Bruce is genuinely puzzled, betraying an unexpected innocence. 'I don't see what was so wrong with that. He was actually telling the whole truth about himself. He was being honest.'

I come to think of Bruce's unwritten book as the burden he's been carrying all his writing life. Once he's done this, I think, he'll be free, he'll be able to take flight in all sorts of directions.

The thing I find saddest about *Utz* is that is suggests to me that Bruce was indeed beginning that new, light-spirited phase of flight. *Utz* is all we have of what had become possible for him once his Australian odyssey helped him express the ideas which he'd carried about for so many years.

There is in the centre of Alice Springs a brave woman trying to run a proper literary bookshop. After I left Bruce in the

Alice, this lady persuaded him to do a lunchtime signing session. She said Alice Springs was full of fans of his, and she would advertise, and so forth. Out of friendship and admiration for her, Bruce agreed. The advertisement appeared in the small-ads section of the paper, next to notices about animal provender and camel rearing. Bruce went to the bookshop with his Mont Blanc pen at the appointed hour.

Not a single person came into the shop.

What happened in Australia was that Bruce and I became friends. If you spend that much time talking that much with another person, locked up inside a Toyota station wagon and a succession of motel rooms, you find out a great deal about each other. At the end of such a journey you either hate each other passionately or you discover you're in love.

Speaking for myself, I fell in love.

1989

CHATWIN'S TRAVELS

Bruce Chatwin and I drove around Central Australia in a four-wheel-drive station wagon, a vehicle which, we were repeatedly informed, 'must be Toyota's Answer to the Little Subaru.' Bruce puzzled over this curious phrase, trying to invent a mythology that might explain it. The Little Subaru was plainly some sort of Dreamtime Ancestor, but if our car was the 'answer' then what, Bruce wanted (like Gertrude Stein) to know, could possibly have been the question?

To be with Bruce Chatwin was, usually, to be his willing audience. His conversation would soar up Mount Everest (we were halfway up Ayers Rock, and I was half dead and turning purple, when he mentioned that he'd recently made it to the Everest base camp), and just as swiftly plummet to a discussion of the diseases one might contract from divers European and African whores. He was a magnificent raconteur of Scheherazadean inexhaustibility, a gilt-edged name-dropper, a voracious reader of esoteric texts, a scholar-gypsy, a mimic—his Mrs Gandhi was perfect—and a giggler of international class. He was as talkative as he was curious, and he was curious about everything, from the origins of evil to the question asked by the Little Subaru. His words about the ex-Chamberlain of King Zog of Albania are truer of himself: 'People of his kind will never come again.' What a voice we lost when his fell silent! How much he still had to say.

What Am I Doing Here (could the fastidious Chatwin really have agreed to the omission of the question mark?) is what we have left. His last book, a 'personal selection' of essays, portraits, meditations, travel writing and other, unclassifiable, Chatwinian forms of prose, was put together during his final, terrible year of wasting away, and it is inevitably a little patchy in places; but one of its chief delights is that it contains so many of its author's best anecdotes, his choicest performances.

Here is Bruce's 'snake story', as told to him by the
cleaning lady from Palermo, and Assunta's monologue is
really Bruce 'doing' Assunta, all waving arms and flashing
eyes, a figure not from life but from a comic opera. And here
is Bruce's encounter with the footprints of the Yeti, and
Bruce's visit to a Mansonesque hippy family in Boston. His
campier performances are here, too: a delicious snatch of
Diana Vreeland, and my own favourite Chatwin story, the
one about his meeting with Noel Coward, who told him: 'I
have very much enjoyed meeting you, but unfortunately, we
will never meet again, because very shortly I will be dead. *But*
if you'll take one parting word of advice, "Never let anything
artistic stand in your way."'

There are, it should swiftly be said, many more
substantial pleasures to be had from this collection. Bruce
Chatwin was often at his best when furthest afield, and *What
Am I Doing Here* contains some superb pieces from Russia—
an unforgettable Nadezhda Mandelstam, carelessly stuffing
her errant breasts back into her blouse; a concise, brilliant
account of the decline of the Leftist Movement in post-
revolutionary Russian art, and of its excavation and
preservation by the collector George Costakis; a trip down the
Volga that is a classic of 'travel writing'. Bruce was planning a
large-scale Russian novel when he died; he might have
proved to be a kind of Nabokov in reverse. We'll never know.

Africa, in which that 'desert mutation', *homo sapiens*, the
nomad, the walker, first evolved, is the setting for some
equally fine pieces: the account of the coup Chatwin stumbled
into in Benin while researching *The Viceroy of Ouidah*, and the
very different (comic rather than scary) account of how
Werner Herzog and Klaus Kinski set about filming *Viceroy*
(re-titled *Cobra Verde*) some years later, in Ghana. In this latter
essay, Bruce has untypically, and kindly, censored himself,
omitting the no doubt libellous accounts of sexual shenanigans
on location, and also his less than complimentary view of the
finished film, both of which were included with relish in the
oral version of the tale.

Bruce's politics could be, to put it politely, a little innocent.

He could bang on about how things were really getting a lot better in South Africa, and he could fail to understand why Nadine Gordimer was irritated by his insistence on referring to Namibia as 'South West Africa'. But he could also get things magnificently right, and the essay in this collection entitled 'The Very Sad Story of Salah Bourguine', which uses the inter-racial murder in Marseilles as a way of opening up the unsavoury subject of French colonialism in North Africa, is one of the most vivid things ever written on this difficult topic.

Bruce was much attracted (and attractive) to formidable ladies of a certain age, and this volume offers us quite a gallery of them: the aforesaid Nadezhda Mandelstam and Diana Vreeland, but also Madeleine Vionnet, 'the Architect of Couture', who designed her clothes on a doll because she didn't dare tell her father the extent of her business (he worried, as a result, that she might be retarded); and Maria Reiche, spending her life trying to decode the mystery of the lines and patterns on the Peruvian pampa. And the piece on Mrs Gandhi is as wonderful in writing as it was when he told it aloud. '"How that woman wants to be PM!" Mrs G. says of Mrs Thatcher. "I felt like telling her, if you want to be PM that badly, you'll never make it."' Which just goes to show that even Mother Indira could be wrong.

What Am I Doing Here is indeed, as the blurb suggests, a sort of autobiography, but it is an autobiography of the mind. In this book, as in life, Bruce Chatwin is secretive about the workings of his heart. I wish it were not so, for he was a man of great heart and deep feeling, but he rarely let it into his prose. Exceptions here are a moving vignette of his father; and an elegy for the Afghanistan known to Robert Byron and trampled by Russian troops, that will read, to Bruce Chatwin's many admirers, like a lament for what we have lost through his untimely death:

We will not sleep in the nomad tent, or scale the Minaret of Jam. And we shall lose the tastes—the hot, coarse, bitter bread; the green tea flavoured with

cardamoms . . . Nor shall we get back the smell of the
beanfields, . . . or the whiff of a snow leopard at
14,000 feet.

1989

JULIAN BARNES

A History of the World in 10½ Chapters, by Julian Barnes, is not a history but a fiction about what history might be: 'just voices echoing in the dark; images that burn for a few centuries then fade; stories, old stories that sometimes seem to overlap; strange links, impertinent connections.' Overlapping stories, strangely linked, is what we're given: a post-modern, post-Christian series of variations on the theme of Noah's Ark. Barnes is in his *Flaubert's Parrot* mode, only more so. In this vein he's like a worldly, secular reincarnation of a medieval gloss-writer on sacred texts, and what he offers us is the novel as footnote to history, as subversion of the given, as brilliant, elaborate doodle around the margins of what we know we think about what we think we know. This is fiction as critique, which is its limitation as well as its strength, because for all its high intelligence and formal elegance it proceeds (except for one brief, redeeming parenthesis) from the brain rather than the heart.

There's no denying the ingenuity, though, and at its best Barnes's *History* offers much high and some low comedy as well. The quality of the early episodes makes one anticipate a feast of inventiveness. There's a woodworm's-eye-view of the Ark story, featuring a drunken Noah who thinks of his menagerie as a 'floating cafeteria' and eats many species into extinction, and a God described as an 'oppressive role model' who drove poor Noah to drink. The playful irreverence of this chapter would make instructive and no doubt shocking reading for some of today's hardline religionists. (Sorry, Julian.) The woodworms crop up again in the hilarious proceedings of a medieval French court; this time they're the accused in a surreal trial, charged with eating a church until it fell down.

A church, being a ship of souls, is also a sort of ark. And the *Titanic* was an ark, and so, for Jonah, was the Whale, and so was the raft of the survivors of the *Medusa* that Géricault painted. And just as Noah ate his animals, so the *Medusa*'s survivors turned to cannibalism; and there are woodworm, it is suggested, in the Géricault picture's frame . . . the stories proliferate and cross-connect and Noah's tub becomes an ever more protean image. We are all, it seems, riders of Barnes's lost ark.

Not all the stories convince, however. In particular, 'Upstream', the epistolary account of the making of a film something like *The Mission*, told by a notably self-regarding actor, and containing a notably self-indulgent, in-jokey reference to the author's buddy, Redmond O'Hanlon, is a real turkey. And several times the connections between the tales offer no enrichments; they're just links. In chapter six, a religious zealot, Amanda Fergusson, dies on Mount Ararat in 1839; in chapter nine, another religious zealot, an astronaut, who believes he's been spoken to by God when he was on the moon, goes to Ararat to find Noah's Ark and, finding Amanda's skeleton, claims to have discovered old Noah himself. You get the point, but not the message.

The key to this strange, ambitious novel lies in that 'Parenthesis' I mentioned, the ½ of its 10½ chapters. Here the author gazes at us directly, like El Greco staring out of his masterpiece *The Burial of Count Orgaz*, and talks to us about love. Barnes's view of history (voices echoing in the dark, etc.: near meaninglessness upon which we try to impose meanings) is, finally, what lets this book down; it's just too thin to support the whole fabric; but his view of love almost saves the day. His beautiful idea is that history 'is ridiculous without love'; that 'love teaches us to stand up to history,' to reject its stupid, martial terms. Love, too, is a kind of ark, he says, on which two people might just be saved. I don't know if he's right, if this is *true*, any truer than Auden's 'We must love one another or die,' any truer than history, but the idea that *the opposite of history is love* is worth hanging on to, like a lifebelt, like a raft.

But even here one wishes that Barnes the essayist had stepped aside for Barnes the full-blooded novelist; that instead of a disquisition on love, we could have been given the thing itself. 'Don't talk of love,' as Eliza Doolittle sang, 'show me.'

Julian Barnes has written a book that is frequently brilliant, funny, thoughtful, inventive, daring, iconoclastic, original, and a delight to read. What more, he might legitimately inquire, could anybody ask for? I can only reply that, for me, the bits of *A History of the World in 10½ Chapters* didn't quite add up; that, although they possess in abundance the high literary virtue of lightness, they fail to acquire, by cumulation, the necessary weight: it being the paradox of literature that you need the pair of them on the voyage, weight and lightness, and, as with lovers and animals, you can't afford to leave half the couple off your ark.

1989

KAZUO ISHIGURO

The surface of Kazuo Ishiguro's novel, *The Remains of the Day*, is almost perfectly still. Stevens, a butler well past his prime, is on a week's motoring holiday in the West Country. He tootles around, taking in the sights and encountering a series of green-and-pleasant country folk who seem to have escaped from one of those English films of the 1950s in which the lower orders doff their caps and behave with respect towards a gent with properly creased trousers and flattened vowels. It is, in fact, July 1956; but other, timeless worlds, the world of Jeeves and Bertie Wooster, the upstairs-downstairs world of Hudson, Mrs Bridges and the Bellamys, are also in the air.

Nothing much happens. The high point of Mr Stevens's little outing is his visit to Miss Kenton, the former housekeeper at Darlington Hall, the great house to which Stevens is still attached as 'part of the package', even though ownership has passed from Lord Darlington to a jovial American named Farraday who has a disconcerting tendency to banter. Stevens hopes to persuade Miss Kenton to return to the Hall. His hopes come to nothing. He makes his way home. Tiny events; but why, then, is the ageing manservant to be found, near the end of his holiday, weeping before a complete stranger on the pier at Weymouth? Why, when the stranger tells him that he ought to put his feet up and enjoy the evening of his life, is it so hard for Stevens to accept such sensible, if banal, advice? What has blighted the remains of his day?

Just below the understatement of the novel's surface is a turbulence as immense as it is slow; for *The Remains of the Day* is in fact a brilliant subversion of the fictional modes from which it at first seems to descend. Death, change, pain and evil invade the Wodehouse-world; the time-hallowed bonds between master and servant, and the codes by which both live, are no longer dependable absolutes but rather sources of ruinous self-deceptions; even the gallery of happy yokels turns out to stand for the post-war values of democracy and individual and collective rights which have turned Stevens and his kind into tragicomic anachronisms. 'You can't have dignity if you're a slave,' the butler is informed in a Devon cottage; but for Stevens, dignity has always meant the subjugation of the self to the job, and of his destiny to his master's. What then is our true relationship to power? Are we its servants or its possessors? It is the rare achievement of Ishiguro's novel to pose Big Questions (What is Englishness? What is greatness? What is dignity?) with a delicacy and humour that do not obscure the tough-mindedness beneath.

The real story here is that of a man destroyed by the ideas upon which he has built his life. Stevens is much preoccupied by 'greatness', which, for him, means something very like restraint. (The greatness of the British landscape lies, he believes, in its lack of the 'unseemly demonstrativeness' of African and American scenery.) It was his father, also a butler, who epitomized this idea of greatness; yet it was just this notion which stood between father and son, breeding deep resentments and an inarticulacy of the emotions that destroyed their love.

In Stevens's view, greatness in a butler 'has to do crucially with the butler's ability not to abandon the professional being he inhabits.' This is linked to Englishness: Continentals and Celts do not make good butlers because of their tendency to 'run about screaming' at the slightest provocation. Yet it is Stevens's longing for such 'greatness' that wrecked his one chance of finding romantic love; hiding within his role, he long ago drove Miss Kenton away, into the arms of another man. 'Why, why, why do you always have to *pretend*?' she asked in despair. His greatness is revealed as a mask, a cowardice, a lie.

His greatest defeat was brought about by his most profound conviction—that his master was working for the good of humanity, and that his own glory lay in serving him. But Lord Darlington ended his days in disgrace as a Nazi collaborator and dupe; Stevens, a cut-price St Peter, denied him at least twice, but felt for ever tainted by his master's fall. Darlington, like Stevens, was destroyed by his own code of ethics; his disapproval of the ungentlemanly harshness of the Treaty of Versailles is what led him towards his collaborationist doom. Ideals can corrupt as thoroughly as cynicism.

But at least Lord Darlington chose his own path. 'I cannot even claim that,' Stevens mourns. 'You see, I trusted . . . I can't even say I made my own mistakes. Really, one has to ask oneself, what dignity is there in that?' His whole life has been a foolish mistake; his only defence against the horror of this knowledge is that same facility for self-deception which proved his undoing. It's a cruel and beautiful conclusion to a story both beautiful and cruel.

Ishiguro's first novel, *A Pale View of Hills*, was set in post-war Nagasaki but never mentioned the Bomb; his new book is set in the very month that Nasser nationalized the Suez Canal, but fails to mention the crisis, even though the Suez débâcle marked the end of a certain kind of Britain whose passing is a subject of the novel. Ishiguro's second 'Japanese' novel, *An Artist of the Floating World*, also dealt with themes of collaboration, self-deception, self-betrayal and with certain notions of formality and dignity that recur here. It seems that England and Japan may not be so very unlike one another, beneath their rather differently inscrutable surfaces.

1989

9

MICHEL TOURNIER

ITALO CALVINO

STEPHEN HAWKING

ANDREI SAKHAROV

UMBERTO ECO

GÜNTER GRASS

HEINRICH BÖLL

SIEGFRIED LENZ

PETER SCHNEIDER

CHRISTOPH RANSMAYR

MAURICE SENDAK AND WILHELM GRIMM

MICHEL TOURNIER

In one of the key texts of Surrealism, *Paris Peasant*, Louis Aragon spoke of his 'sense of the marvellous suffusing everyday life.' Defining reality as 'the apparent absence of contradiction,' he explained: 'The marvellous is the eruption of contradiction within the real.' The surrealist's task of revealing these contradictions—literally 'against-sayings', or denials of what is commonly held to be the case—requires a relentless intensity of vision, powered by an innately iconoclastic form of intellectual energy. It is this task which Michel Tournier has set himself in *Gemini*. Echoing Aragon's fifty-five-year-old thesis, Tournier makes one of his characters reflect that 'Under its apparent banality, the world is decidedly full of barely concealed wonders—just like Ali Baba's cave.' On the enormous loom of *Gemini*, Tournier weaves banalities into wonders: rubbish dumps, tapeworm, Venetian honeymoons, even the weather, are here transmuted into the stuff of marvels. (This is not a random metaphor: near the centre of Tournier's web of symbols stands the tall shape of an old Jacquard machine.)

Gemini is about a pair of identical twins, collectively known as Jean-Paul. This is something like saying that *Ulysses* is about a man walking around Dublin. Because Tournier uses the theme of twinship to explore a near-infinity of dualities: heterosexuality and homosexuality, city and countryside, Heaven and Hell. Here we discover the profound opposition of chronology and meteorology: on the one side, the fixed, regulated march of the hours, and on the other, the wild, unpredictable fluctuation of the seasons; and, in a passage of startling metaphysical originality, we are told that *'Christ has to be superseded'*—not by any Manichean Satan, but by the Spirit, the Holy Ghost.

It will be clear that *Gemini* is not light reading; and yet, such is the electricity of Tournier's intelligence, so skilfully does he weave his shimmering web, that for the greater part of this mammoth book the reader is mesmerized by the sheer daring of the conception and the audacity with which the author carries it off. The magic wanes in the last third, but by then the momentum which has been built is strong enough to sweep us on to the finale.

Gemini begins in a small community on the Breton coast. It opens, significantly, with a description of the weather conditions. The book was originally called *Les Météores*, and Tournier insists on reviving the true meaning of the word: as meteorologists know, it refers to any atmospheric phenomenon at all. The element of most interest to Tournier is the air: in *Gemini*, the air is truly everywhere. It is a gale which pushes the young homosexual Daniel to his death in a foul pit full of rats; and it is 'wind, tempest, breath' which, for the priest Thomas, is the Earthly manifestation of the Holy Ghost. No breeze, in these pages, blows by accident, whether for good or ill.

In 'Les Pierres Sonnantes'—the 'Sounding Stones'—live the twin-children, Jean and Paul, so alarmingly identical that their parents cannot tell them apart; and, in one memorable incident, when their father Édouard mixes up photographs of the pair, Jean himself fails to separate himself from his Other half. They are a complete organism: they speak their own language, 'Aeolian' (named after Aeolus, the wind god); their private game of Bep is their abiding interest; they often join, head to tail in 'geminate communion', an echo of their position in the womb, to which is added a rite of semen. For Paul, the dominant twin, to whom twinship is unquestionably superior to 'normal' humanity, his twinned life is a treasure to be preserved at all costs. 'Every pregnant woman carries two children in her womb,' he imagines. 'But the stronger will not tolerate the presence of a brother . . . and, having strangled him, he eats him . . . Mankind is made up of ogres . . . We alone, you understand, are innocent. We alone came into this world hand in hand, a smile of brotherhood on our lips.'

But Jean, the other twin, rebels. Twinship, for him, has become a cage. His early attempts at asserting his independence sometimes misfire: insisting on going shopping for clothes separately, he returns home, having chosen garments identical in every respect to those selected by his brother. Later, he attempts to marry; but Paul drives Sophie away, first seducing her and then horrifying her when she realizes that Jean, her fiancé, has come to her from his brother's bed. But Jean does break away, and this break represents a moment of transformation for the novel itself.

Before that, however, we have spent a good deal of time away from the twins, from their weak father Édouard and their earth-mother, Maria-Barbara; away, too, from the mentally handicapped children at St Brigitte's next door—children whose enforced enclosure in a solipsistic world forms a wholly unsentimentalized echo of the twins' self-absorption.

This time is spent in the company of the twins' 'shocking uncle', Alexandre, who makes of his homosexuality a totem almost as powerful as Paul's theory of twinship. (World War Two, when it comes, is to Alexandre a heterosexual business, nothing to do with him, except of course for the fact that Hitler is exterminating his kind.) Alexandre's exuberance gives the first half of the book much of its drive and verve; he lives dangerously, walking the street with his trusty swordstick 'Fleurette' in search of conventionally oriented males: 'Heterosexuals are my women,' he reveals. He is the manager of a garbage firm called TURDCO (The Urban Refuse Disposal Company), and in the sections of the book narrated by him he turns this 'lunar landscape' of refuse into a world of revelations, the truth of which society seeks to disguise, but which it cannot hide from its garbage-men. These passages in praise of faeces are kissed with genius; in them, Tournier performs the vertiginously difficult feat of imbuing the worst things in the world with a kind of radiance and meaning. (It is easy to see why Jean Genet thinks so highly of this book.) At the Saint-Escobille dump outside Paris during the war—to take just one instance—the rubbish-train from Paris brings Alexandre strange, resonant symbols of the time; dogs, for instance. 'Hundreds of thousands of dead dogs! Thirty-five wagonloads of them!' Because the fleeing Parisians had abandoned their pets, and the Nazis had had them massacred.

Alexandre is, in a way, killed by the twins. He sees them in Casablanca and, not knowing that there are two of them, or recognizing them as his nephews, he falls in love with this 'ubiquitous boy', like an Aschenbach of shit; and when he stumbles across the two performing their rite of union, and sees that there is no chance for him against such completeness, he goes deliberately into the murderous docks at night and is killed. As a homosexual, he is, after all, only a counterfeit twin: 'he is usurping a condition which does not belong to him.'

Alexandre dies. Maria-Barbara is sent to Buchenwald. Édouard doesn't last much longer. Sophie is chased away, but this deed splits the twins for good. Jean takes off on a long odyssey around the world, 'throwing himself', to escape from Paul, 'into the arms of anyone he meets.' Paul, of course, pursues him. And the book changes. Mirroring its characters' eruption out of the egg of geminate completeness into this global quest, the novel becomes linear, sequential, episodic— and a good deal less gripping. Intellectually, it remains rigorous and satisfying, showing how what began as a pursuit changes, for Paul, into a determination to have all Jean's experiences after him, to prevent their drifting apart; and then, when he begins to accept that he may never find Jean again, his journey—which goes from Venice to North Africa, Japan, Vancouver, until the linear quest becomes circular, a two-dimensional mirror-image of the geminate egg, as it heads back home across Canada—turns into the physical expression of what Alexandre's friend, Thomas the priest, describes as *universal didymy*: 'the unpaired twin died and a brother to all men was born in his place.' The quest contains many gripping images, too: a whole series of gardens, for example, represent Jean's search for Eden, and the amputation of Paul's left limbs in an accident beneath the Berlin Wall (itself a symbol of lost unity, the city as a divided egg) is the physical expression of his loss of twinship.

What this section lacks is more traditionally novelistic

satisfactions. The global journey cannot avoid sounding like a travelogue; the characters encountered are inevitably minor, rarely gripping and in one instance—the gardener-sage, Shonin, in Japan—like a pretentious echo of that monk who used to teach David Carradine ('Grasshopper') the meaning of life in the *Kung Fu* TV series.

The ending, however—in which Paul surmounts the loss of his limbs by a sort of act of supranatural will—is worth waiting for; and there is no doubt that this is a book of rare intelligence, originality and that intensity of sight of which Aragon was also a master. Tournier and Aragon are far from being twins, however: *Gemini* is a novel impregnated with theology, after all, and Aragon's view of God was that he was 'a disgusting and vulgar idea'.

1981

ITALO CALVINO

At the beginning of Italo Calvino's first book for six years, an entirely fictional personage named You, the Reader, buys and settles down with a novel which he firmly believes to be the new Calvino. 'You prepare to recognize the unmistakable tone of the author. No. You don't recognize it at all. But now that you think about it, who ever said this author had an unmistakable tone? On the contrary, he is known as an author who changes greatly from one book to the next.' One of the difficulties with writing about Italo Calvino is that he has already said about himself just about everything there is to be said.

If on a winter's night a traveller distils into a single volume what is perhaps the dominant characteristic of Calvino's entire output: his protean, metamorphic genius for never doing the same thing twice. In the space of 260 pages, we are given the beginnings of no fewer than ten novels, each of which is a transmogrified avatar of the previous one; we also have a more or less fully developed love story between the above-mentioned You and Ludmilla, the Other Reader; plus, for good measure, a conspiracy-theory fiction about a secret organization known as the Organization of Apocryphal Power, run by a fiendish translator named Ermes Marana, whose purpose may or may not be the subversion of fiction itself. The OAP is vaguely reminiscent of Thomas Pynchon's underground postal service, the Tristero System, and almost certainly has covert links with Buñuel's Revolutionary Army of the Infant Jesus, the only comic terrorist organization in the history of the cinema. (Buñuel's film *The Phantom of Liberty*, with its almost infinite sequence of plots which take over the movie, one after the other, with astonishing casualness, and are then themselves supplanted with hilarious ease, is the work of art which most closely resembles *If . . .*)

It is entirely possible that Calvino is not a human being at all, but a planet, something like the planet Solaris of

Stanislaw Lem's great novel. Solaris, like Calvino, possesses the power of seeing into the deepest recesses of human minds and then bringing their dreams to life. Reading Calvino, you are constantly assailed by the notion that he is writing down what you have always known, except that you've never thought of it before.

The first message from the planet Calvino was received on Earth as long ago as 1947. This was *The Path to the Nest of Spiders*, a war story sired by Ernest Hemingway out of Italian neo-realist cinema about a cobbler's apprentice who joins the partisans and who finally finds the friend he has always longed to have. In spite of its marvellous title, the novel is no better than worthy, and the last sentence appears to have dipped its feet in slush: 'And they walk on, the big man and the child, into the night, amid the fireflies, holding each other by the hand.'

I have quoted this line in full because it is the last example on record of a bad sentence by Italo Calvino. After *Spiders*, he tells us, 'Instead of making myself write the book I *ought* to write, the ['neo-realistic'] novel that was expected of me, I conjured up the book I myself would have liked to read, the sort by an unknown writer, from another age and another country, discovered in an attic.'

Instant metamorphosis, caterpillar into butterfly, Samsa into giant bug. In 1952, he published *The Cloven Viscount*, which, along with its successors *The Baron in the Trees* and *The Non-Existent Knight*, he has now collected in the volume entitled *Our Ancestors*. *The Cloven Viscount* is about a cloven viscount, vertically bisected by a cannonball in medieval Bohemia. The two halves continue to live, the one fiendishly evil, the other impossibly good. Both halves are unbearable. In the end they fight a duel; the Bad 'Un and the Good 'Un each manage to slice each other at the very edges, reopening the terrible wounds of their bisection, and are sewn back together by the story's most appealing character, his name a homage to Calvino's favourite writer, R. L. Stevenson: Dr Trelawney it is who performs the operation. This is a happy ending, but for the story's youthful narrator it is also the moment of childhood's end; Dr Trelawney, the tippling medic, leaves on a British ship, 'hitched on board astride a barrel of *cancarone* wine,' 'and I was left behind, in this world of ours full of responsibilities and wills-o-the-wisp.'

The Baron in the Trees is the story of Cosimo Piovasco di Rondo, who refuses to eat the repellent snail soup prepared by his sister Battista (who also cooks 'some pâté toast, really exquisite, of rats' livers; . . . and some grasshoppers' claws, . . . laid on an open tart in a mosaic; and pigs' tails roasted as if they were little cakes'), is ordered from the table by his crusty father, climbs a tree at the age of twelve and never sets foot on solid ground for the rest of his life. His affair with the capricious Viola, his adventures with the local bandits, his encounter with a group of exiled Spanish grandees and his meticulous strategies for making a successful life in the trees twine and intertwine to form thick forests of marvellous ideas, and make *The Baron in the Trees* one of the most haunting images of rebellion, of determined nay-saying, that exists in the literature of this rebellious century.

In *The Baron*, and in the third book in the trilogy, *The Non-Existent Knight*, Calvino is also getting interested in narration as a process. To continue with my presentation of last sentences, here is *The Baron*'s:

> Ombrosa no longer exists . . . perhaps it was . . . embroidered on nothing, like this thread of ink which I have let run on for page after page, swarming with cancellations, corrections, doodles, blots and gaps, bursting at times into clear big berries, coagulating at others into piles of tiny starry seeds, then twisting away, forking off, surrounding buds of phrases with frameworks of leaves and clouds, then interweaving again, and so running on and on and on until it splutters and bursts into a last senseless cluster of words, ideas, dreams, and so ends.

The Non-Existent Knight, which is the story of an empty suit of armour that thinks it's a knight of the Emperor Charlemagne and keeps itself/himself going by sheer

willpower, discipline and devotion to duty, is also a very
'narrated' tale, told by Sister Theodora, a nun locked up in a
convent, who can have no possible experience, as she is very
well aware, of the scenes of chivalry she is required to describe.
As she says: 'Apart from religious ceremonies, triduums,
novenas, gardening, harvesting, vintaging, whippings,
slavery, incest, fires, hangings, invasions, sacking, rape and
pestilence . . . what can a poor nun know of the world?'

And yet, heroically, she writes on and on, inventing the
unknown and making it seem truer than the truth, and
providing Calvino with a marvellous metaphor for himself.
This growing preoccupation with the Book as opposed to the
World will come to its true fruition in *If on a winter's night a
traveller.*

'World conditions were still confused in the era when this
took place,' writes Theodora/Calvino. 'It was not rare then to
find names and thoughts and forms and institutions that
corresponded to nothing in existence. But at the same time
the world was pullulating with objects and capacities and
persons who lacked any name or distinguishing mark. It was
a period when the will and determination to exist, to leave a
trace . . . was not wholly used up.' But six years later, Calvino
published a collection of stories about an even more fluid
time. The twelve *Cosmicomics* take, for their modest theme,
nothing more or less than the creation of the universe, as
narrated by a polymorphous, immortal being masquerading
under the muffled, spluttering title of Qfwfq. In the
Cosmicomics, we discover that the Moon was, in fact, made of
cheese: 'Moon-milk was very thick, like a kind of cream
cheese. It formed . . . through the fermentation of various
bodies and substances of terrestrial origin which had flown
up from the prairies and forests and lakes, as the Moon sailed
over them. It was composed chiefly of vegetal juices,
tadpoles, bitumen, lentils, honey, starch crystals, sturgeon
eggs, moulds, pollens, gelatinous matter, worms, resins,
pepper, mineral salts, combustion residue.' (Like all fabulists,
Calvino loves lists.) We see the galaxies form, we see life
crawl out of the waters of the earth; but the miracle of these

stories is that somehow Calvino gives it all a richly comic, human scale. In 'The Aquatic Uncle', for instance, Qfwfq and his family have just 'abandoned aquatic life for terrestrial,' and Qfwfq is in love with a fellow-land creature. But: 'Yes, we had a great-uncle who was a fish, on my paternal grandmother's side, to be precise, of the Coelacanthus family of the Devonian period'; and this Uncle N'ba N'ga obstinately refuses to give up his watery life. What's more, when an embarrassed Qfwfq is forced by his loved one to introduce her to his stubbornly primitive relative, the aquatic uncle seduces her back into the water.

What do you do when you've just reinvented the world? What Calvino did was to turn himself into Marco Polo and go travelling in it. *Invisible Cities* is not really a novel at all, but a sort of fugue on the nature of the City. Polo and Kublai Khan are the only attempts at 'characters' in this book; but its true star is Calvino's descriptive prose. Gore Vidal has called this Calvino's 'most beautiful work', and so it is.

Here the reader may discover Octavia, a city hung like a spider's web between two mountains: 'The life of Octavia's inhabitants is less uncertain than in other cities. They know the net will last only so long.' And Aria, which 'has earth instead of air.' And Thekla, the eternally unfinished city, for which the star-filled sky is the blueprint, and whose completion is eternally delayed 'so that its destruction cannot begin.'

Next, Calvino turned himself into two packs of Tarot cards and used them as the bases of the stories in *The Castle of Crossed Destinies*, the only one of his books which succeeds in being too clever to like. Travellers meet by chance, in the first part, in a castle and in the second, in a tavern, and fall miraculously dumb, so that they are obliged to tell their travellers' tales by laying out the Tarot cards. Calvino uses these card-sequences as text which he then interprets for us, telling us the stories which the cards may or may not be intending to tell: a form, I suppose, of mystical structuralism.

If on a winter's night a traveller, however, is a book to praise without buts. This is Calvino rampant in the world of books, Calvino joyously playing with the possibilities of fiction, of story-telling, which is, after all, also a nursery euphemism for lying; You, the Reader, is (or are) a sort of dogged Lemmy Caution figure trying to find Your way through the literary labyrinths of Calvino's city of words, his Alphabetaville.

You buy 'the new Calvino'. You begin reading a story called 'If on a winter's night a traveler'. (I note that an 'l' has fallen out of this last word in its journey from the dustjacket.) The story is a thriller set at a train station. But suddenly You have to stop reading: there is a binding error in Your copy. You take it back to the bookshop and find that the story You began wasn't the new Calvino at all. The wrong pages, the bookseller tells You, were bound between the wrong covers. What You started (and now want to finish) was *Outside the town of Malbork* by one Tazio Bazakbal. You, and Your new friend Ludmilla, who has had the same problem with her copy of the Calvino, go off to read this second book. But it turns out to be an entirely different story, some kind of rural novel, and then another binding mistake is discovered just when You're getting interested: blank pages have been bound in by mistake. You ring Ludmilla, speak first to her sister Lotaria, eventually to this girl in whom You have become very interested indeed. You find that what you believed to be *Outside the town of Malbork* is in fact (another publisher's cock-up) a part of an old book written in Cimmerian, the language of an extinct East European culture. You go off to Professor Uzzi-Tuzii at the University and he tells You the original was called *Leaning from a steep slope*. Painfully, he begins to translate for you. Then he gets more and more fluent as the story weaves its spell. It is, of course, a completely different story, nothing to do with Malbork, about a young man of excessive soulfulness who gets caught up in a prison escape plot. Suddenly Uzzi-Tuzii stops reading. He tells You that the author, Ukko Ahti, committed suicide after reaching this point in the story. But now Lotaria appears with one Galligani, Professor of Erulo-Altaic languages. Galligani, an enemy of Uzzi-Tuzii's, claims that *Leaning from a steep slope* is in fact derived from a Cimbrian original, *Without fear of wind or vertigo*, by Vorts Viljandi.

Without fear, etc., turns out to be yet another, and completely unrelated work, about spies and counterspies in a city in the throes of a coup. But again, only a fragment remains, because Lotaria has given away most of the pages.

Two things need to be said right away: first, that all the fragments are wonderfully readable, and somehow don't seem fragmentary at all; second, that You, the Reader, have been getting less and less peripheral, and Your involvement with Ludmilla and Lotaria more and more important.

You now cease to be merely a passive reader. You act. You go to the publishers themselves, determined to find a copy of *Without fear of wind or vertigo*, which is what you now want to continue with. Here you meet Mr Cavedagna, who speaks, for the first time, the ominous name of Ermes Marana, translator, who has apparently been passing off as Polish, Cimmerian, Cimbrian what is actually a Belgian novel, *Looks down in the gathering shadow*, by Bertrand Vandervelde. You go off to read this new book, which inevitably bears no relationship to any of the other fragments you've seen, but is so exciting that it doesn't matter. *Looks down . . .* is a sort of film noir spoof, about a crook and his moll trying to get rid of a body in a plastic bag. You (the real you this time) will probably agree with You (not the real . . .) and Ludmilla that this is the most gripping thing you've read yet. But this, too, breaks off . . . Cavedagna hasn't lent You the whole typescript. You return to see him. 'Ah,' he tells You, 'Heaven knows where it's got to.'

Now, in despair, Cavedagna shows You the file on Ermes Marana, who has managed to throw the entire affairs of this publishing house into turmoil . . . and, because I don't want to give away the whole plot, I will content myself with telling you that there are five more extracts from stories, and that the story of You, Ludmilla and Lotaria now becomes deeply embroiled in the fictions You are trying to read.

If on a winter's night a traveller is quite possibly the most complicated book you (and You, too) will ever read. But Calvino's conjuring trick works because he makes the complications so funny, and makes you (though not You) share the joke. The ten transformations of the eternally beginning story are carried off with an inventiveness that never becomes tiresome; the gradual inweaving of the texts and their readers is nothing less than—to use an appropriately archaic piece of slang—wizard. Calvino has left Stevenson far behind; he has avoided sounding like imitation Borges, which is what happens to him when he isn't on peak form; and his great gift, the ability to give credibility to the most extravagant of his inventions, has never been more in evidence. In *If . . .* , the most outrageous fiction about fiction ever conceived, we stumble in every paragraph over nuggets of hard, irreducible truth:

> 'Nobody these days holds the written word in such high esteem as police states do,' Arkadian Porphyrich says. 'What statistic allows one to identify the nations where literature enjoys true consideration better than the sums appropriated for controlling it and suppressing it?'

Why, finally, should we bother with a Calvino, a word-juggler, a fantasist? What does it mean to write about non-existent knights, or the formation of the moon, or how a reader reads, while the neutron bomb gets the go-ahead in Washington, and plans are made to station germ-warfare weaponry in Europe? Not escapism, because although the reader of Italo Calvino will be taken further out of himself than most readers, he will also discover that the experience is not a flight from, but an enrichment of himself. No, the reason why Calvino is such an indispensable writer is precisely that he tells us, joyfully, wickedly, that there are things in the world worth loving as well as hating; and that such things exist in people, too. I can think of no finer writer to have beside me while Italy explodes, while Britain burns, while the world ends.

1981

STEPHEN HAWKING

The most appealing account of the Big Bang I've ever read was written by Italo Calvino in his marvellous *Cosmicomics*. In the beginning, we're told by Calvino's narrator, the proto-being Qfwfq, 'Every point of each of us coincided with every point of each of the others in a single point, which was where we all were . . . it wasn't the sort of situation that encourages sociability.' Then a certain Mrs Ph(i)Nk$_0$ cried out, 'Oh, if only I had some room, how I'd like to make some noodles for you boys!' And at once—bam!—there it was: spacetime, the cosmos. *Room*.

The idea that the universe might have been set in motion by the first truly generous impulse, the first expression of love, is rather wonderful, but it's certainly unscientific, and these days the creation of Creation is primarily the work of scientific, rather than literary or theological, imaginations. It's a hot story, and Professor Hawking's book, *A Brief History of Time*, is only the latest of a string of popularizing bestsellers on the subject—fascinating books, full of exclamations.

To read this rapidly expanding universe of books is to come to see physicists as a highly exclamatory breed, longing above all for the moment when they get to cry 'Eureka!' It's tempting to use a variant of the anthropic principle (the world is what it is because were it otherwise we wouldn't be here to observe that it was so) and propose that it's not surprising that such persons should have created a cosmos that begins with the biggest exclamation of them all.

Let us quickly concede, however, that there have been many astonishing discoveries, many genuine Eureka-opportunities, since Einstein's General Relativity Theory changed the world. Professor Hawking, striking a fine balance between the need to address himself to non-scientists and the danger of condescending over-simplification, takes us for a canter over the territory. Here is General Relativity itself, and Hubble's discovery of the expanding universe. Over there is the defeat of the Steady-state Theory by the Big-Bangers, and to the right (or maybe to the left) is Heisenberg's Uncertainty Principle. Just ahead are the great voyages into the heart of the atom, and out towards the black holes.

Hawking's near-legendary status confers immense authority on the text. Not only is he the fellow who showed that black holes leak, but it was his 1970 paper that 'proved' that the universe must have begun as a *singularity*, that is, a thing not unlike Calvino's single point. But the reason that this book gets steadily more engrossing as it approaches the heart of the subject is that it turns out that on the question of Genesis, the Professor has changed his mind. Having applied the ideas of quantum mechanics—the study of the frequently irrational world of infinitely tiny things—to the condition of the universe before the Bang, he has decided that the singularity whose existence he 'proved' in 1970 needn't really have existed at all.

He now proposes that instead of a 'beginning' there was what Richard Feynman called a 'sum over histories'—a situation in which time was indistinguishable from directions in space, making redundant the concept of something out of nothing, of before and after. If this were so, he tells us, 'the universe . . . would neither be created nor destroyed. It would just BE.' It's a dazzling argument, ending with the dismissal of God himself: 'What place, then, for a creator?' Man proposes, God is disposed of; and Hawking is, as he makes clear, making no more than a proposal, a theory about a theory which he thinks will soon be worked out.

He is prepared, however, to draw an astonishing conclusion from his survey of his field. He suggests that we're actually quite near the end of 'humanity's intellectual struggle to understand the universe.' There's a good chance, apparently, that a complete unified theory of everything will be found 'within the lifetime of some of us who are around today, always presuming we don't blow ourselves up first.'

This sounds, I'm afraid, like a particularly bad case of Premature Eurekitis. Anyone who has followed Professor Hawking through his own changes of mind; who has learned, through him, the implications of the Uncertainty Principle ('one certainly cannot predict future events exactly if one cannot even measure the present state of the universe precisely') or who has even the most rudimentary awareness of the history of human knowledge, will find this notion of the proximity of the Ultimate Truth hard to swallow.

And, anyway, to all of us who aren't scientists—who are lay readers, or even writers—the real value of the ideas of the new physics and of quantum mechanics is precisely the same as that of Calvino's stories: namely, that they make it possible for us to dream new dreams, of ourselves as well as the universe.

It is impossible, however, not to admire the grand Quixotic conviction of Stephen Hawking's quest for the end of knowledge; while continuing to believe that the only permanent discoveries are those of the imagination. All theories eventually pass away, and are replaced by new ones; only Mrs Ph(i)Nk$_0$ lives for ever.

1988

Andrei Sakharov

Compared to the might of a State, especially a State as ruthless as the Soviet Union has been for most of this century, it is easy to think of the individual as a ridiculously weak, even helpless entity. Even when the individual in question is as distinguished and influential a scientist as Andrei Sakharov, he can be scooped up out of his life, the way the KGB seized Sakharov after he criticized the Soviet invasion of Afghanistan, and hurled on to the garbage heap of history, in this case the remote town of Gorky.

And yet the meaning of a life like Sakharov's is that individual weakness can be turned to strength, if one has the will and moral courage to do so. Now that the power of Soviet communism is crumbling, while the ideas and principles to which Sakharov dedicated his days are changing the face of Europe, the great physicist's endurance and refusal to be broken give his autobiography the status of an exemplary life.

This first volume of Sakharov's memoirs takes the story up to his release from internal exile by President Gorbachev in 1986; a second book, detailing his last years, including his frequent clashes with Gorbachev in the Congress of People's Deputies, is promised. Sections of the typescript were confiscated on four occasions (one time he lost 1,400 pages of work). That it exists at all is proof of the determination with which its author kept at it.

It isn't easy to live a symbolic, even iconic, life; it isn't easy to write about one either. Andrei Sakharov's rather flat style can be heavy going. His desire to write as a witness, to detail just about every dissident cause in which he participated, every battle he fought, results in many turgid (if unfailingly noble) passages. It was clearly difficult for him to write about personal matters, and that reticence, too, can be frustrating, as can its opposite, the understandably idealizing gushiness which sometimes overcomes him when he writes about his beloved second wife, 'Lusia', the formidable Elena

Bonner. He speaks at one point in these memoirs of his dislike of books thick enough to be used as doorstops. This extremely thick doorstop would have been a more vivid self-portrait, though a less complete testament, at half the length. As it is, what we're given is an account 'for the record', a thorough, often plodding version of a great life.

The Sakharov who emerges from these pages is a boy who loved science-fiction novels, *Uncle Tom's Cabin* and Mark Twain, who was something of an awkward character and made few friends. The boy grew up to be, like many scientists, better at his work than at his private life. In one of the relatively rare intimate passages in his book, he faces up to this: 'In my private life, in my relations with Klava [his first wife] and with the children after she died, I always tended to avoid confrontations, feeling myself psychologically unable to cope with them . . . in all honesty, I never spared my time or my physical strength. Afterwards I suffered. I felt guilty, and then made new mistakes, since guilt hardly improves one's judgement.' After Klava's death, his growing involvement with human rights and his new love for 'Lusia' were the things that turned him outwards toward the world, and made him whole. His description of falling in love is, however, characteristically laconic. 'For months, Lusia and I had been drawing closer and it was becoming more and more dificult for us to hide our feelings. Finally . . . we confessed our love.' That's it.

Alexander Solzhenitsyn, among others, has suggested that Sakharov was an innocent, unworldly figure who was manipulated by the ferociously articulate and highly motivated Elena Bonner, and Sakharov repeatedly defends her against these charges. Perhaps the truth lies somewhere in the middle. It is impossible to read these memoirs without believing that Sakharov knew exactly what he was doing when he espoused human rights causes in the USSR; but one also gains a strong impression of a reserved, inward personality who needed, or felt he needed, his wife to help him with his public utterances.

It was Elena Bonner who insisted, 'My husband is a

physicist, not a dissident,' but of course he was both. His memoirs fall roughly into two halves, the physicist's book and the dissident's book, and each half really needs a different reviewer. As a scientist, Sakharov was in the same league as Stephen Hawking, but as a writer he makes far fewer concessions to the lay reader. As a result, his long and important descriptions of the Soviet nuclear weapons programme, and also of his theoretical work, can be bewildering, even for those non-scientists with a keen interest in such matters. Nevertheless, these chapters are in many ways the most informative in the book, in the sense of opening up to us a world we knew almost nothing about—for example, the secret city, 'The Installation', where the Soviet hydrogen bomb was built. It's also clear that the theories Sakharov developed around the notion of 'baryon asymmetry'—crudely, the relationship between matter and antimatter—prefigured the Grand Unified Theories of the 1970s. (Sakharov plainly regretted not having become involved in the GUTs.)

Sakharov was, in a sense, a Russian version of J. Robert Oppenheimer. The 'father of the Russian hydrogen bomb', he came passionately to oppose the testing and proliferation of these weapons. What makes him fascinating is that there was also a part of him that was a Russian version of Edward Teller, Oppenheimer's more hawkish colleague and opponent, who believed that in the late 1940s and 1950s 'only American military strength could restrain the socialist camp from an expansion that . . . might trigger a third world war.' Sakharov is almost lyrical about the theoretical beauty of thermonuclear explosions. For him, to participate in such work was to be able to witness, in microcosm, the unleashing of the same forces that created the universe. The cruel paradox that these might also be the forces by which life could be destroyed was not lost on him; but the ambiguity of his position allows us a richer understanding of nuclear issues than any simple hawk/dove antithesis. Sakharov was both hawk and dove.

There is much more information of great value, both scientific and political, in these pages: Sakharov's attack on the absurd Stalin-endorsed theories of Trofim Lysenko, who believed that 'modified' plants and animals could pass on their new characteristics to succeeding generations, thus offering a 'quick fix' for Soviet agriculture; his campaign to save Lake Baikal from pollution; portraits of Beria, Khrushchev and other Soviet bosses; and a notably unsentimental account of the dissident movement, especially of the emergence of a breed of 'professional dissidents' with whom Sakharov plainly felt he had little in common. His dispute with Solzhenitsyn in which he rejects the writer's ultraist religious ideas and dissents from Solzhenitsyn's contempt for Western values, is one in which this reviewer's sympathies, at least, are firmly on the Sakharov side.

Ultimately, however, this book is a monument to the triumph of the human spirit over adversity. But Sakharov's victory was not complete (perhaps no individual victories ever are). There are many Russians today who blame President Gorbachev for the scientist's death in December of last year. They say that Gorbachev may have ended Sakharov's long exile in Gorky, but that he then hastened the great man's demise by his harsh and humiliating public criticisms of Sakharov in the Congress of People's Deputies. We'll have to wait for volume two of these memoirs to find out how Sakharov felt about Gorbachev's behaviour. But whether the story is true or not, the fact that people believe it emphasizes the widespread Russian distrust of Gorbachev, and also the extent of public sympathy for the élite academician who became the Soviet system's most distinguished dissident, the boy who made friends with difficulty but who grew up to be, as the Estonian deputy Marju Lauristin said at his funeral service, 'the incarnation of intellectual courage and conscience, of the true Russian spirit'.

1990

UMBERTO ECO

About twenty years ago the bookshops seemed to be full of volumes with titles like *Illuminatus*, in which it was suggested that the world was run by this or that occult conspiracy. In the aftermath of the Kennedy assassination, the notion that 'visible' history was a fiction created by the powerful, and that these 'invisible' or subterranean histories contained the 'real' truths of the age, had become fairly generally plausible. The only writer who ever managed to transmute the base metal of the illuminatus-novel into art was Thomas Pynchon, who succeeded in making the necessary connections between the occult and political worlds, and who constructed a rich metaphorical framework in which two opposed groups of ideas struggled for textual and global supremacy: on the one hand, Entropy (the idea that things fall apart, which we can call 'pessimism', but which is also connected, in Pynchon, to the profane, democratic spirit); and in the opposite corner, Paranoia (the idea that everything has a meaning, a Plan, it's just that we don't know what it is . . . which we can call 'optimism' because of its opposition to meaninglessness; but which is also linked to the religious, even totalitarian spirit, because meaning, in Pynchon, is in the hands of the hidden adepts).

What gave Pynchon the edge over all the other cabalistic babblers was that he was funny, he could create vivid, belching, hilariously unstrung characters (Benny Profane, Tyrone Slothrop), and that his awareness of genuinely suppressed histories—of the genocide of the Herero people in southern Africa, for example, or of the collaboration between US and Nazi industrialists during World War II—always informed his treatment of even his most lunatic fictional conspiracies.

Pynchon once wrote a short story called 'Under the Rose', its title an Englishing of the Latin *sub rosa*. *Foucault's Pendulum*, the obese new volume from Umberto Eco, is an illuminatus-novel for the end of the eighties, a post-modernist conspiracy fiction about, I suppose, the world under the name of the rose. It is, I regret to report, a very faint Eco indeed of those old Pynchonian high jinks. It is humourless, devoid of characterization, entirely free of anything resembling a credible spoken word, and mind-numbingly full of gobbledygook of all sorts. Reader: I hated it.

The plot of *Foucault's Pendulum* (which begins on page 367 of this 629-page book) is surprisingly uncomplicated. Three weird publishers, Belbo (named after a typeface), Diotallevi and Casaubon ('wasn't he a character in *Middlemarch*?'), are employees of a two-faced publishing house, Garamond/Manutius, whose visible Garamond face is that of a straight, up-market company, but whose true Manutius nature is that of a vanity press for self-financing authors ('SFAs'). Tired of receiving an endless stream of cranky manuscripts about Templars and Rosicrucians and suchlike twaddle, our three heroes decide to make up the ultimate conspiracy theory, their own private totalization of occult knowledge. 'If the Plan exists, it must involve everything,' they decide. Their invention, the bad fiction within this fiction, is fed into a computer named Abulafia after a medieval Jewish cabalist. Then, in a ridiculously melodramatic finale involving the eponymous pendulum (no relation, incidentally, to the philosopher) and massed hordes of crazed mystics, the fictional Plan starts to come true . . . Edgar Allan Poe is among the myriad references in this book, but it doesn't help. This Pendulum is the pits.

It's just possible that, inside this whale, there's an enjoyable smaller fish trying to get out. The unscrupulous world of the vanity press and the fleecing of its feeble authors is depicted with some verve, and there are moments when the ponderous narrative sparks into life. But the spark is instantly snuffed out by page after page of Higher Bullshit. Here is a typical paragraph:

> 'So those are the Massalians, also known as Stratiotics and Phibionites, or Barbelites, who are made up of

Nasseans and Phemionites. But for other fathers of
the church, the Barbelites were latterday Gnostics . . .
and their initiates in turn called the Borborites Hylics,
or Children of Matter, as distinct from the Psychics,
who were already a step up, and the Pneumatics, who
were the truly elect . . . But maybe the Stratiotics were
only the Hylics of the Mithraists.' 'Sounds a bit
confused,' Belbo said.

And this is what passes for dialogue: '"Are you saying I'm
superficial?" "No . . . what others call profundity is only a
tesseract, a four-dimensional cube."' And this, I assure you, is
a love scene:

'Amparo, the sun's coming up.'
'We must be crazy.'
'Rosy-fingered dawn gently caresses the waves . . .'
'Yes, go on. It's Yemanjà. Listen. She's coming.'
'Oh, Tintinnabulum!'
'You are my Atalanta Fugiens . . .'
'Oh, Turris Babel . . .'

I rest my case.

Eco, the consummate post-modernist, is perfectly aware
of all possible criticisms of his text, and lets us know that he
knows. 'We're talking in stereotypes here,' one of his
characters astutely observes. And, 'Maybe only cheap fiction
gives us the measure of reality,' Belbo muses; that's Eco
hinting that he intends to play deliberately with the form of
the penny dreadful. And, because he's enough of an
intellectual to know that hokum is hokum, he has not written
an 'innocent' late-sixties illuminatus-novel, but a 'knowing'
version, a fiction about the creation of a piece of junk fiction
that then turns knowingly into that piece of junk fiction.
Foucault's Pendulum is not a novel. It is a computer game.

One way of playing it is to spot the references. Apart
from Pynchon, *Middlemarch* and Poe, there are touches of *The
Maltese Falcon*, *Raiders of the Lost Ark*, *Ghostbusters*, *The Lord of
the Rings* (Belbo/Bilbo), *Gone with the Wind*, *The Magus*, 007

and a classic SF story entitled 'The Nine Billion Names of God'. And at the very end, in Casaubon's conclusion ('I have understood. And the certainty that there is nothing to understand should be my peace, my triumph'), there's more than a touch of the ancient Japanese poet Basho who travelled to the seat of wisdom, the Deep North, to learn that there was nothing to learn in the Deep North.

Unfortunately, the journey to this truth is so turgid that it's impossible to care about reaching the goal. This is Spielbergery without the action or bullwhips, and if, as Anthony Burgess threatens on the jacket, 'this is the way the European novel is going,' we should all catch a bus in the opposite direction as soon as possible.

1989

GÜNTER GRASS

The Meeting at Telgte

When the Thirty Years War ended, one word was sufficient to describe Germany: rubble. And in our own century, after a war which did its work at approximately six times the speed: once again, nothing to be seen but rubble. 'The thing that hath been tomorrow,' reads the opening sentence of Günter Grass's new novel, 'is that which shall be yesterday.'

Grass's subject is how German writers responded to ruination; how, after Hitler, German pens re-wrote Genesis to read: After the end was the word. How they tore their language down and rebuilt it anew; how they used words to assault, excoriate, accept, encompass and regenerate; how the phoenix poked its beak out of the fire. Rubble, after World War Two, gave birth to what was at first disparagingly termed 'rubble literature'. Heinrich Böll, defending these books of war and homecoming, wrote: 'We have no reason to be ashamed of this label . . . we see things the way they are, with a human eye that normally is not quite dry and not quite wet, but damp, for let us not forget that the Latin for dampness is *humor*.' And now Günter Grass has taken the story of a group of writers who set about the task of seeing sharply, but with a sense of *humor*, and projected it three hundred years backwards in time; which of course, Grass being Grass, enables him to tell the tale more humorously.

On the cover of his book, drawn by himself, is the image of a hand holding a goose quill rising triumphant from a heap of stones . . . taking arms, so to speak, against that sea of rubble.

In 1947, such a meeting of writers did in fact take place: that was when H. W. Richter first convened the famous Group 47. Its mirror-meeting, the one Grass describes, never happened, at Telgte or anywhere else except in his own Croesus-rich imagination; but it seems none the less actual for that.

There assemble, in the Bridge Tavern at Telgte, a town located in the midst of the 1647 peace negotiations, divers writers, publishers and even musicians, 'for the purpose of giving new force to the last remaining bond between all Germans, namely the German language . . . Everything had been laid waste, words alone kept their lustre.' As a matter of fact, even the words themselves are somewhat tarnished: the great composer Schütz tells the Meeting, 'When the fatherland was laid low, poetry could hardly be expected to flower.' And in a comic-opera parallel to the twentieth-century pollution of Germany by the terrible dead language of Nazism, we find the tongue of the seventeenth century polluted, too: all manner of armies, tramping and Babeling across the land, have left their bootmarks on the common speech, so thoroughly that the landlady, Libuschka, in *The Meeting at Telgte* is moved, at one point, to ask the assembled bards 'whether the *signores* would care for a *boccolino* of *rouge*.'

The Bridge Tavern is, of course, symbolically named; Grass the snail, the Social Democrat, the 'irenicist', has always been a man for bridges. And when the inn burns down, its destruction seems to signify the failure of the writers' hopes. But before the fire, we have been given a marvellously credible portrait of a bunch of bitching, pedantic, devout, bawdy, gloomy and innocent men struggling to build a new world from the flawed fabric of their minds.

At the centre of the book stands Christoffel Gelnhausen, a version of the writer Grimmelshausen, whose novel *Simplicissimus* is the rumbustious, iconoclastic ancestor of *The Tin Drum*; riotous, self-taught, amoral, Stoffel is also Grass himself in green doublet and feathered hat. In *The Flounder*, Grass gave himself the starring role and popped up, disguised as all sorts of folk, throughout German history; in *The Meeting*, which is a sort of chip off that mighty fish, he is once again his own best character. Stoffel lies, cheats, steals, punches women in the eye; he empties the Bridge Tavern to make room for the poets by telling its residents that the scribblers have the plague, which is 'no respecter of wealth'.

But after the book's great set-piece, a feast provided by Gelnhausen which turns out to be the product of a looting trip, he defends himself against the rage of the rhymers by pointing out that they are, in fact, also corrupt, and precisely because they do respect wealth too much: 'He and his horsemen had acted in the spirit of the times, just as the gentlemen here assembled . . . when they wrote poems in praise of princes to whom murder and arson came as naturally as their daily prayers.' What enrages the poets most of all about Stoffel, of course, is neither his lying nor his looting but his decision to compete with them at writing.

To balance Gelnhausen, we have the landlady Libuschka, or Courage, veteran of umpteen battles, giver and receiver of the pox (the German *Courasche* is an old slang term for syphilis), literary know-all and provider of much poorer fare than we're used to in Grass novels. (Stoffel complains bitterly about the food.) This Courage is also a visitor from Grimmelshausen; Brecht has borrowed her before. The explosive relationship of Courage and Stoffel ('what stirred them together was an excess of love, or call it hate') is what breathes genuine, Grassy life into an otherwise astonishingly restrained book.

Because *Telgte* is Günter Grass in second gear. The book is written in honour of the seventieth birthday of H. W. Richter; *The Flounder* was Grass's fiftieth birthday present to himself. Perhaps it's time all these celebrations stopped; Grass—unthinkable thought—is in danger of sounding a wee bit cosy. But enough carping; even in a minor key, he's still one of the few great ones around, and has written a fascinating, entertaining book. You may wish to consider, while reading it, why the rubble of the German cities yielded up the likes of Grass, Böll and Lenz, while British rubble produced only car parks.

1981

Essays

In the summer of 1967, when the West was—perhaps for the last time—in the clutches of the optimism disease, when the microscopic invisible bacilli of optimism made its young people believe that they would overcome some day, when unemployment was an irrelevance and the future still existed, and when I was twenty years old, I bought a paperback copy of Ralph Manheim's English translation of *The Tin Drum* from a bookshop in Cambridge, England. In those days everybody had better things to do than read. There was the music and there were the movies and there was also, don't forget, the world to change. Like many of my contemporaries I spent my student years under the spell of Buñuel, Godard, Ray, Wajda, Welles, Bergman, Kurosawa, Jancsó, Antonioni, Dylan, Lennon, Jagger, Laing, Marcuse and, inevitably, the two-headed fellow known to Grass readers as Marxengels. In spite of all these distractions, however, Oskar Matzerath's autobiography had me hooked, and I stayed hooked all the way from grandmother Anna Koljaiczek's wide skirt, past fizz powder and horse's head full of eels, right up to Anna's dark opposite, the wicked Black Witch.

There are books that open doors for their readers, doors in the head, doors whose existence they had not previously suspected. And then there are readers who dream of becoming writers; they are searching for the strangest door of all, scheming up ways to travel through the page, to end up inside and also behind the writing, to lurk between the lines; while other readers, in their turn, pick up books and begin to dream. For these Alices, these would-be migrants from the World to the Book, there are (if they are lucky) books which give them permission to travel, so to speak, permission to become the sort of writers they have it in themselves to be. A book is a kind of passport. And my passports, the works that gave me the permits I needed, included *The Film Sense* by Sergei Eisenstein, the *Crow* poems of Ted Hughes, Borges's *Fictions*, Sterne's *Tristram Shandy*, Ionesco's play *Rhinoceros*—and, that summer of 1967, *The Tin Drum*.

This is what Grass's great novel said to me in its drumbeats: Go for broke. Always try and do too much. Dispense with safety nets. Take a deep breath before you begin talking. Aim for the stars. Keep grinning. Be bloody-minded. Argue with the world. And never forget that writing is as close as we get to keeping a hold on the thousand and one things—childhood, certainties, cities, doubts, dreams, instants, phrases, parents, loves—that go on slipping, like sand, through our fingers. I have tried to learn the lessons of the midget drummer. And one more, which I got from that other, immense work, *Dog Years*: When you've done it once, start all over again and do it better.

Günter Grass, Danzig's most famous son (Lech Walesa, the only other contender for the title, inhabits—it is important to insist—not Danzig but Gdańsk), who now lives partly in Berlin, a city which itself seems to have migrated to a new and starker location, and partly in a North German landscape which reminds him of the wide, diked vistas of his writing and his youth, is a figure of central importance in the literature of migration, and the migrant is, perhaps, the central or defining figure of the twentieth century. Like many migrants, like many people who have lost a city, he has found it in his luggage, packed in an old tin box. Kundera's Prague, Joyce's Dublin, Grass's Danzig: exiles, refugees, migrants have carried many cities in their bedrolls in this century of wandering. And let nobody underestimate the obstinacy of such writers; they will not tolerate the Gdansking of their past. In Grass's transported city, Labesweg is still Labesweg and the shipyard which saw the birth of Solidarity is not called Lenin, but Schichau. (Here, once again, I feel a small affinity. I grew up on Warden Road, Bombay; now it's Bhulabhai Desai Road. I went to school near Flora Fountain; now the school is near Hutatma Chowk. Of course, the new decolonized names tell of a confident, assertive spirit in the independent State; but the loss of past attachments remains a loss. What to do? Shrug. And pickle the past in books.)

In one sense, Grass is only approximately half a migrant. A full migrant suffers, traditionally, a triple disruption: he loses his place, he enters into an alien language, and he finds himself surrounded by beings whose social behaviour and codes are very unlike, and sometimes even offensive to, his own. And this is what makes migrants such important figures: because roots, language and social norms have been three of the most important parts of the definition of what it is to be a human being. The migrant, denied all three, is obliged to find new ways of describing himself, new ways of being human.

Well, Grass certainly lost his place (and, as I suggested, found that he'd brought it along with him). It's possible to argue that he lost a part of his language, the Kashubian dialects of his youth which he attempted to preserve in his literature; but here I'm on thin ice, as my knowledge of German is probably about as great as Grass's knowledge of Urdu. At any rate, apart from the dialects, it seems difficult to suggest that Grass is a writer out of language, and certainly he has remained within a society whose social mores are known to him. Indeed, as his essays show, his dedication to the idea of a German civilization which embraces both West and East Germany and which finds its true expression in the German language, is complete. One may therefore legitimately ask how useful this notion of a half-migrant Grass, a maybe-only-one-third-migrant Grass, really is.

I think it is useful, because there are other senses in which Grass seems to me to be very much more than merely a fragment or percentage of a migrant writer. Migration across national frontiers is by no means the only form of the phenomenon. In many ways, given the international and increasingly homogeneous nature of metropolitan culture, the journey from, for example, rural America to New York City is a more extreme act of migration than a move from, say, Bombay. But I want to go further than such literalistic discussions; because migration also offers us one of the richest metaphors of our age. The very word *metaphor*, with its roots in the Greek words for *bearing across*, describes a sort of migration, the migration of ideas into images. Migrants— borne-across humans—are metaphorical beings in their very essence; and migration, seen as a metaphor, is everywhere around us. We all cross frontiers; in that sense, we are all migrant peoples.

Günter Grass is a migrant from his past, and now I am no longer talking about Danzig. He grew up, as he has said, in a house and a *milieu* in which the Nazi view of the world was treated quite simply as objective reality. Only when the Americans came at the war's end and the young Grass began to hear how things had really been in Germany did he understand that the lies and distortions of the Nazis were not the plain truth. What an experience: to discover that one's entire picture of the world is false, and not only false, but based upon a monstrosity. What a task for any individual: the reconstruction of reality from rubble.

I am suggesting that we can see this process as an act of migration, from an old self into a new one. That the end of World War Two was for Grass, as it was for Germany, as tough and disrupting a frontier to cross as anyone can imagine. And if we call Grass a migrant of this type, we quickly discover that the triple dislocation classically suffered by migrants has indeed been in operation in the case of Migrant Grass, the man who migrated across history. The first dislocation, remember, is the loss of roots. And Grass lost not only Danzig; he lost—he must have lost—the sense of home as a safe, 'good' place. How could it retain that feeling in the light of what he learned about it at the war's end? The second dislocation is linguistic. And we know—and Grass has written often and eloquently—of the effect of the Nazi period on the German language, of the need for the language to be rebuilt, pebble by pebble, from the wreckage; because a language in which evil finds so expressive a voice is a dangerous tongue. The practitioners of 'rubble literature'— Grass himself being one of the most prominent of these—took upon themselves the Herculean task of reinventing the German language, of tearing it apart, ripping out the poisoned parts, and putting it back together.

And the third disruption is social. Once again we can argue that the transformation in German society, or, rather, in the Germany that the growing Grass knew and experienced, was of the same order as the change in social codes that a migrant from one country to another experiences: that Nazi Germany was, in some ways, another country. Grass had to unlearn that country, that way of thinking about society, and learn a new one.

I see Grass, then, as a double migrant: a traveller across borders in the self, and in Time. And the vision underlying his writing, both fiction and non-fiction, is, I believe, in many ways a migrant's vision.

This is what the triple disruption of reality teaches migrants: that reality is an artefact, that it does not exist until it is made, and that, like any other artefact, it can be made well or badly, and that it can also, of course, be unmade. What Grass learned on his journey across the frontiers of history was Doubt. Now he distrusts all those who claim to possess absolute forms of knowledge; he suspects all total explanations, all systems of thought which purport to be complete. Amongst the world's great writers, he is quintessentially the artist of uncertainty, whose symbol might easily have been the question mark if it were not the Snail. To experience any form of migration is to get a lesson in the importance of tolerating others' points of view. One might almost say that migration ought to be essential training for all would-be democrats.

About that Snail. This social-democratic mollusc, under whose spiralling shell are housed the ideas of hurrying slowly, caution, circumspection, and gradualism, has served Grass well, and also earned him his share of brickbats from those who advocate more rapid rates of advance. I don't want to enter that dispute here, noting only that there are times—for instance during his advocacy of nuclear disarmament—when Grass himself appears far from Snailesque. But I should like to use the Snail as evidence that Grass lives more comfortably in images, in ideas, than in places. This, too, is a characteristic of migrants. He is, after all, a metaphorical being.

The migrant intellect roots itself in itself, in its own capacity for imagining and reimagining the world. This can lead to difficulties: Is it because the United States is a migrants' culture that its citizens can, at times (election campaigns, for instance), appear to prefer image to substance? But the love of images also contains great potential. When the world is seen through ideas, through metaphors, it becomes a richer place. When Grass looks at Czechoslovakia through the writing of Kafka, or contemporary Japanese urban sprawl through the images of Alfred Döblin, he helps us see more, and more clearly.

A writer who understands the artificial nature of reality is more or less obliged to enter the process of making it. This is perhaps why Grass has so determinedly sought a public role, why he has used his great fame as a novelist as a platform from which to speak on the many issues—the bomb, the invasion of our privacy by data banks, the relationship between the nations of the rich North and the poor South— which concern him. And since to argue about reality is to be at once creative and political, it is not surprising that when Grass writes about literature he finds himself writing about politics, and when he discusses political issues, the quirky perspectives of literature have a habit of creeping in.

In his essay 'The Destruction of Mankind Has Begun' Grass makes the point that, for the first time in the history of the species, writers can no longer assume the existence of posterity. He says that, as a result, 'The book I am planning to write . . . will have to include a farewell to the damaged world, to wounded creatures, to us and our minds, which have thought of everything and the end as well.' And the composition of elegies is indeed one of the proper responses for a writer to make when night is drawing in. But outside his fiction, in his political activities and writings, Grass is also making a second, and equally proper response. What this work says is: we aren't dead yet. We may be in deep trouble but we aren't done for. And while there is life, there must be analysis, struggle, persuasion, argument, polemic, rethinking, and all the other longish words that add up to one very short word: hope.

1984

Heinrich Böll

einrich Böll has never lacked courage. When most good German burghers were reacting to the words 'Baader–Meinhof' as if they were the names of Hell's most fearsome demons, Böll attempted to explain, in print, why some of Germany's most brilliant people had chosen the left-hand path of terrorism. It's always easier to condemn than to understand, and Böll took a fair amount of flak for having assumed the role of devil's advocate (although he never condoned the violence of the Baader–Meinhof group, or of anyone else, for that matter). Andreas Baader, Ulrike Meinhof, Gudrun Ensslin, Holger Meins and the rest had given the German ruling class its biggest fright in years; the burghers didn't enjoy being told that incomprehensible acts may arise out of comprehensible, even rational motivations.

The Safety Net is about the effects of that fright on the frightened. Baader and Meinhof appear in it, thinly disguised as 'Heinrich Beverloh' and 'Veronica Tolm'; but until the novel's chillingly orchestrated, thriller-like climax, they hover high above the action, like circling Furies, waiting to strike. (The central character, Fritz Tolm, actually speculates on the possibility of his being assassinated by an airborne bomb disguised as a bird.) The foreground is occupied by more or less 'respectable' people and by the security forces—the 'safety net' of the title—who must protect them; and Böll's message, for this is certainly a message-novel, is that this security system is as destructive a force as the terrorists it seeks to resist. If Beverloh and Veronica are the novel's devils, the security police are its deep blue sea.

The plot is pretty simple, even schematic. Tolm, a newspaper owner, becomes President of 'the Association' and thus a prime target for the assassins. He is obliged to submit to the ministrations of the security police, although he remains convinced that absolute security does not exist, and that the killers will certainly get him. The safety net closes around his whole family, tapping telephones, destroying privacy, suspecting everyone, turning the most trivial events into a kind of battle against an invisible enemy—a visit to an art gallery is referred to by the security chief as 'the Madonna front'. All the lives held in this net are corrupted in profound and subtle ways.

Meanwhile Tolm knows that his newspaper empire will shortly be gobbled up by his rival Zummerling (an Axel Springer figure), while his own house and lands will be swallowed by the open-cast mining machines that are already nibbling at his horizon—so that he is doomed to end up the victim of that same omnipotent force, Money, which is precisely the entity against which the terrorists are struggling. This is one of the novel's darkest ironies.

And in the end, of course, the terrorists . . . but it would be wrong to spoil a climax as gripping as this one.

This fine, meticulous novel shows Böll at his most effectively ruminant. His method has always been to chew away at people, details, places, turning them over and over until they yield up every last iota of meaning. The Tolm family is perhaps a little too representative a cross-section of the German middle classes: Tolm himself is a weary fellow gripped by 'capitalist melancholy'; then there's his 'ultra-capitalistic' daughter Sabine; his reformed radical son Rolf and Rolf's communist wife; even a hippie-ish son, Herbert, rather quaintly described in the List of Characters as 'one of the "alternate society"'. But Böll worries away at them all to such revealing effect that it's easy to forgive the too-programmatical structure of the book.

'It's the era of nice monsters, Käthe,' Tolm tells his wife, 'and we must count ourselves amongst them.' And really, just about everyone here is alarmingly nice. The security policemen are nice. (When Sabine has an affair with one of her guards, Böll goes to great pains to present him as a decent, troubled chap. In his fair-minded way, he's making the useful point that the guardians, too, are damaged by their roles.) Bleibl, the ex-Nazi newspaper man, turns out to have a human side. Only Zummerling, the media czar, and

his creature, Amplanger, are not nice. Even Beverloh and
Veronica seem nice enough, particularly Veronica, who keeps
ringing up with warnings about her own group's activities.
Too much niceness, you may think; but it has the advantage of
allowing Böll to present, sympathetically, a very wide range
of points of view. *The Safety Net* is a sort of interior panorama:
its primary purpose is not to judge, but to understand.

There is, however, a judgement. 'It is Beverloh's era and
Amplanger's era . . . figuring, figuring, figuring,' says Tolm,
and you sense that Böll agrees; that the real tragedy for Böll is
the replacement of the old kindnesses, of human values, by
the remorseless, amoral world of the technologists. The press,
the police and the bombers are all aspects (or victims) of this
sickness; and it is in bringing us to this perception that the
achievement of this brave, pained novel really lies.

1982

SIEGFRIED LENZ

'Pardon me? A detestable word? A word with a dark history? . . . I realize that the word has a bad reputation, that it has been so seriously abused that one can hardly use it nowadays . . . But could we not try to rid the word of its bad connotations? Give it back a sort of purity?'

The word is *Heimat*, 'Homeland', and the speaker is Zygmunt Rogalla, master weaver both of rugs and of the narrative of Siegfried Lenz's epic fable, *The Heritage*, whose original title, literally translated, was *The Homeland Museum*, and whose theme is the creation of a vast gulf between Germany's past and present: a gulf created by the unscrupulous use of the sense of home, roots and history to justify and legitimize xenophobia, tyranny and the dread syntax of ethnic purity. The Nazis dirtied many words, but Siegfried Lenz is not willing to leave it at that. *The Heritage* is, among many other things, an attempt to rescue the past from its exploiters: a fable of reclamation, the very writing of which is a kind of heroism, and which reveals Lenz as being a good deal more optimistic than his narrator. For the novel begins when Rogalla deliberately burns down the irreplaceable museum in which, for most of his life, he has nurtured the relics of his homeland's past, in order, as we finally learn, 'to bring the collected witnesses . . . into safety . . . from which they would never again issue forth, but where they could never again be exploited for this cause or that.' This seems like a deeply pessimistic conclusion; but then again, 'in our memory things lead a purer existence,' and through Zygmunt Rogalla's feat of total recall, history, the lost homeland, is indeed restored to us, neither sentimentalized nor distorted, made neither quaint nor risible; the heritage is given back its innocence.

Siegfried Lenz's novel is a colossal achievement in every sense. It contains a seemingly endless parade of striking images, vivid detail and characters who seem mythical and larger than life precisely because they are so beautifully rooted in real life. We meet Jan Rogalla, Zygmunt's father, the elixir man, closeted in his laboratory like a German José Arcadio Buendia, dreaming of inventing a universal panacea, half-asphyxiating his family with his vapour clouds and trying to sell the Russian Army a potion which prevents funk on the battle-field; the jailbird Eugen Lavrenz who knows a story for each one of his homeland's ninety-two lakes; and Zygmunt's blood brother, Conny Karrasch, who as a child was fond of sabotaging history plays; and Zygmunt's Uncle Adam, digging for relics in the local peat bogs, who grows up to believe the homeland idea is 'nothing but the sanctuary of arrogance', and whose transformation, after the war, into an unlikely recruit to the ranks of nostalgia is one of the book's few unconvincing notes. (Another is the too-coincidental chapter in which Conny discovers the racially impure past of a local Nazi by bumping into his long-lost brother at a horse fair.)

The homeland of *The Heritage* is called Masuria, and is made as real to us, in these pages, as Grass's Kashubia. Good news, incidentally, for all fans of that marvellous trinity of pagan gods, Perkunos, Pikollos and Potrimpos: having presided over the outrageous comedy of Grass's Danzig novels, they have now turned up in Lenz's pages, to preside over wedding rituals in which people's shoes are hidden but vast numbers of hats are brought out and displayed, in which train-loads of Polish geese are dive-bombed by the Luftwaffe, and a vest made from the hair of a hound called Hoggo is capable of warning its wearer of imminent danger, because all the hair stands up on end. It's true to say that the prevailing mood of *The Heritage* is more sombre than Grass ever gets, however. Which is not to say it's less memorable: I defy anyone who reads the description of Lucknow in the last, dark days of the Second World War to get it out of their heads: 'The horses bucked and sank knee-deep into the drifts . . . One wagon after another lurched off the road . . . People were pinned underneath, loads landed in the snow . . . the cracking of whips was drowned out by shouts . . . Ah, all those losses, that long trail of ruins and lost possessions! You could trace the fortunes of the refugees by the goods they left behind.'

I see that the English-language edition has been 'shortened with the co-operation of the author'; perhaps this accounts for the occasional jerkiness of the story-line, and for certain unsolved mysteries, such as why Zygmunt calls Conny 'the great Konrad Karrasch' without ever really justifying the epithet. It seems a shame to have gone at this book with scissors; it feels like being in a museum from which some of the exhibits have been arbitrarily removed.

The book has survived the surgery, however. It remains a genuinely fabulous tale, another demonstration of the fact that the fable is now the central, the most vital form in Western literature; and it should be read by anyone who takes pleasure in entering a world so beautifully and completely realized that, for all its apparent alienness, it rapidly becomes our own.

1981

PETER SCHNEIDER

In Berlin, they even exhibit walls in the museums. In East Berlin's Pergamum Museum, the astonished visitor is faced with huge Roman triumphal arches and a vast segment of the walls of Babylon, containing the blue-and-gold-tiled Ishtar Gate. Walls and gates: antiquity prefiguring the city's partitioned present. Berlin wears German history in the form of a concrete and wire scar, 'the only structure on earth,' as Peter Schneider says, 'apart from the Great Wall of China, that can be seen from the moon with the naked eye.'

I was told, in West Berlin, the story of the couple who got divorced and decided, instead of selling the marital home and moving to new addresses, that they would build a wall. The house was sliced in two from top to bottom and the couple still live in it, on either side of the new partition, more or less ignoring each other's existence. Berliners, it seems, like telling each other parables of the city and swearing that they are true stories. Mr Schneider's book *The Wall Jumper* is full of such truths.

The Wall Jumper is described on its title page as a novel. If it is a novel, it is trying very hard not to look like one. It purports to be an account by a West Berlin writer, an anonymous 'I' whom it is impossible not to identify with Peter Schneider, of his attempt to write a novel about the Berlin Wall; of his relationship with and vision of the divided city in which he has lived for twenty years; and of his friendships with three East Berliners, two of whom, Robert and Lena, now live in the West, while the third, Pommerer, is still in the East. It is a book about the invisible walls as well as visible ones: 'It will take us longer to tear down the Wall in our heads,' Schneider writes, 'than any wrecking company will need for the Wall we can see.'

Robert and Pommerer tell the nameless narrator a number of 'Wall stories'. About Kabe, who jumped the Wall fifteen times, apparently for no reason except that, like Everest, it was there: 'Sometimes it's so quiet in the apartment and so grey and cloudy outside and nothing's happening and I think to myself: Hey, let's go and jump the Wall again.' About the three moviegoers, Lutz and the two Willys, who jumped the Wall to see Western movies and then jumped back East again after the show. About Michael Gartenschläger, who found a way to dismantle the robot mines he called his '22,000 comrades'. These stories are marvellous, balanced between the mythic and the plausible, boundary-walking tales that create, in very few words, the unreal reality of Berlin.

Schneider is excellent, too, at describing 'the Wall in our heads'. To East Berliners, even those settled in the West, like Robert and Lena, everything on both sides of the Wall seems 'pre-programmed, monitored, controlled'. A demonstration in the streets, an ice-hockey game between the USA and the Soviet Union, newscasts about Afghanistan, all prove the point. Lena also hates irony. It seems to her to be a kind of trick.

But Schneider is nothing if not even-handed, and he analyses his own 'delusion' as well as his friends'. His Western belief in spontaneity, personal initiative, free choice is, as he knows, no more or less real than the beliefs of Robert and Lena. This even-handedness is vital; it is what prevents *The Wall Jumper* from turning into a mere tract.

Perhaps the best things in the book are Schneider's many acute insights into the life of the city. On the cramped atmosphere of Berlin, an island in a sea of land: 'Berliners drive like murderers. They seem in the centre of the city to be seized by the need for movement that West German drivers work out on their highways and turnpikes.' On city maps, he points out that Western maps indicate the Wall only by a delicate pink dotted band. Whereas 'on a city map in East Berlin, the world ends at the Wall . . . untenanted geography sets in.' On the Wall as language: he tells us that Pommerer's first English sentence was 'Ami [Yankee], go home.' His narrator's was: 'Have you chewing-gum?' There is a fine moment when Lena visits her family in the East and the narrator, accompanying her, is at once aware that 'the family had become Lena's homeland'—its loss had never been compensated for. And to her family, Lena's restlessness during her visit proved that 'she had returned empty-handed' from the Wall.

The trouble with *The Wall Jumper* is that Peter Schneider will not let it take off. He can describe, he can analyse, he can evoke place, he can create mythic images and credible characters; but he scarcely ever lets the fiction rip. The result is a maddening book: maddening because of the hints it contains of the book it might have been. The narrator tells us at one point that he thinks he has found the story he is looking for, the story of a boundary-walker, a 'man who feels at home only on the border.' And he goes on: 'If the philosopher is right that a joke is always an epitaph for a feeling that has died, the boundary-walker's story must turn out to be a comedy.' I wish we had had that story. There's not much comedy in *The Wall Jumper*, although there is the odd good, bleak gag ('You know the Russian formula for concrete: a third cement, a third sand, a third microphone.') And we never really get the boundary-walker's tale.

So, finally, *The Wall Jumper* remains unsatisfying, in spite of all the good things it contains. The casual, random tone, the distrust of the narrative, undermines all the intelligence, all the image-making, all the evocative anecdotes. I was, however, pleased to learn that even after the East German authorities had banned all sports that might lead to border crossing—scuba diving, ballooning, etc.—the human impulse to rise to such challenges has resulted in the availability of excellently improvised, homemade diving masks.

1983

CHRISTOPH RANSMAYR

Of all the opposed pairs of ideas by which human beings have sought to understand themselves, perhaps the oldest and deepest-rooted are the eternally warring myths of stasis and of metamorphosis. Stasis, the dream of eternity, of a fixed order in human affairs, is the favoured myth of tyrants; metamorphosis, the knowledge that *nothing holds its form*, is the driving force of art.

We do not know why Augustus Caesar banished Ovid to a lifetime of bitter exile in Tomis on the shores of the Black Sea, but the destruction of the great author of the *Metamorphoses* by the Emperor-God can be seen as one battle in the war of the myths for which they stood. It is one of the great paradoxes of this war that the Sword wins almost all the battles, but the Pen eventually rewrites all these victories as defeats. Which is not, of course, much consolation for the author in the ruin of his life; not even when, like Ovid, he is proud and defiant enough to end his masterpiece with the words:

> But through this Work
> I will live on and
> lift myself high above the stars
> and my Name
> will be Indestructible.

Christoph Ransmayr's The Last World is a reimagining of the smashing of Ovid, a parable of the ability of art to survive the breaking of the artist. It takes place in a hybrid time in which the Empire of the Caesars holds sway over a rusting iron city visited by travelling movie projectionists and the occasional clattering bus. The city, de-Latinized, has changed from Tomis to Tomi, and its people are dirt-poor, often brutal peasants leading narrow, violent lives. But they are also figures from the legends around which Ovid wove his *Metamorphoses*. Arachne and Echo are here; Tereus is the local butcher, and the bloody story of his rape and mutilation of his sister-in-law

Philomela is re-enacted in Tomi's mean streets.

Ransmayr's time-jumbling may seem excessively tricksy to some readers, but it's no more than a literary version of the common theatrical device of playing the classics in modern dress. Ransmayr is suggesting that we live in a debased, rotting, rusting time (a time after the death of art, perhaps); a time in which the only possibilities that remain to us are these harshly unpoetic shreds of old poetic glories. Like the citizens of Tomi, we are the rotten echoes of our pasts. Even our stories can only be crude effigies of the great works of long ago.

A young Roman, Cotta, comes to Tomi in search of Ovid. In Ransmayr's version, the poet is banished because he begins a public oration, standing in front of a 'bouquet of microphones', by omitting the usual verbal genuflections to the Emperor, and simply saying 'Citizens of Rome'. This Ovid is an accidental democrat, who responds to his banishment by burning his masterpiece, the *Metamorphoses*. (The 'real' Ovid probably did burn his book, but it wasn't the only copy.) Ransmayr calls him throughout by his surname, Naso, and suggests that this was a nickname given him on account of his big nose, thus placing him in a long tradition of big-nosed tragic (and comic) heroes including Cyrano and Pinocchio. But the poet remains off-stage throughout the novel except for one brief, phantom appearance. Cotta finds only his traces, the marks he has left upon his rock-hard, barren world of exile and defeat.

Cotta is a young dissident, one of a group known as *fugitives of the state*, who hopes to rediscover the *Metamorphoses*, which is, for him, the ultimate dissident work. He finds no book, but discovers its imprint on everyone he meets. One of Tomi's inhabitants remembers all Naso's stories of transformations of living beings into stones; another recalls only his visions of flight, of people turning into birds. The travelling projectionist shows movies in which more Ovidian tales are recounted. And the very lives of the people, too, have been infected by the great book. The Fama of this story is not the Ovidian goddess of rumours, but she is an incessant gossip, and her son Battus does turn, one day, to stone, just like the shepherd of that name in the *Metamorphoses* who could not keep Mercury's secrets.

Ransmayr's book is distinguished by the lyricism with which it explores the world's ugliness, but dissatisfactions creep in. The trouble with his method is that the reader works out what's going on long before the protagonist, Cotta; so that when at length Cotta understands that Naso has transformed 'this barren, craggy coast . . . into *his* coast, these barbarians . . . into *his* characters', and thus gained his immortality, you can't help being irritated that it's taken him so long to come up with so little.

Behind *The Last World* there stands a far greater work of literature; behind Christoph Ransmayr, a fine novelist, there stands one of the most important figures in the whole of literature. Too much of the power of this novel is borrowed; too much depends on the intimate network of allusions and references that connect the two works. (There's a twenty-five-page 'Ovidian repertory' at the back of the book to help non-classical readers pick some of these up.) This web becomes a trap; it ties down the characters and prevents them from coming fully to life. It is a brilliantly clever artifice, and full of the pain of rejected art, but it is more stone than bird.

As for Ransmayr's vision of art conquering defeat by remaking the world in its own image, one can celebrate its optimism, while continuing to feel more concerned about Publius Ovidius Naso, banished from his own people, buried by a strange sea in an unknown grave. Art can look after itself. Artists, even the highest and finest of all, can be crushed effortlessly at any old tyrant's whim.

1990

MAURICE SENDAK
AND WILHELM GRIMM

In 1816, Wilhelm Grimm wrote a most unusual letter of condolence to a young girl whose mother had just died. It begins with a lush Romantic passage suggesting that it is easier for flowers, floating down a stream, to 'kiss', or for birds to fly over mountains to meet each other, than it is for human beings to come together. 'But one human heart goes out to another, undeterred by what lies between. Thus does my heart go out to you . . . and thinks it is sitting beside you. And you say: "Tell me a story." And it replies: "Yes, dear Mili, just listen."' Now the sentimentality of all this may very well have been proper and comforting in such a letter, but in book form it's somewhat cloying. What follows, however, is as beautiful a tale as any in Wilhelm and Jakob's great collection of *Kinder- und Hausmärchen*.

The subject of the story is death: death as an ever-present fact of life. Of the two central characters to whom we are introduced at the start, one, the mother, is a widow, while the other, the daughter, is the sole survivor of many children, who has only survived, or so her mother believes, because she has a guardian angel. They live—where else?—in a village at the edge of the forest; and death is approaching them in the form of a war: clouds of smoke, cannon fire, wicked men. Not knowing how to save her daughter, the mother sends her into the forest with a piece of cake. 'Wait three days and come home; God in his mercy will show you the way.' But God seems not to oblige, and the little girl gets terribly lost.

At length, however, she comes upon a small house, in which she is cared for by St Joseph and by her guardian angel, who is a little girl just like herself, only with blonde hair. And after three days the guardian angel guides her back through the forest to her village, but not before St Joseph has given her a rosebud and a promise: 'When this blooms, you will be with me again.' She finds the village much changed, and her mother grown ancient; for in the world outside the forest, thirty years have passed in the three days between her entry into the forest (her 'death') and her return (or 'resurrection'). That night, the mother and daughter die together in their sleep, 'and between them lay St Joseph's rose in full bloom.' It is a part of the small miracle of this story that death becomes a happy ending, an act or pact of love.

A haunting tale intended, no doubt, to help a little girl look into the darkness of her orphaning and find in it something more than a void. One cannot know whether Wilhelm Grimm made it up, or whether he found it growing like a mushroom in the forest when he went gathering fictions with his brother. No matter; it's a small treasure, and good to have. But perhaps we would not have it, perhaps not in book form (as *Dear Mili*), certainly not in a printing of some 200,000 copies, were it not for Maurice Sendak. People will be attracted to this book by the skill and reputation of its illustrator; yet, in my view, the words may linger in their minds longer than Mr Sendak's illustrations.

This is not to say that Mr Sendak has lost any of his extraordinary gifts; the manner of these pictures will be familiar to all admirers of the brilliant *Outside Over There*, strangest of Sendak tales, with its explorations of the hatred and love that exists between siblings, its world of goblin babies and another absent father. Indeed Sendak has said that, for him, the girl in *Dear Mili* is none other than Ida's sister, grown up, and Ida is one of the children who died. The girl certainly has something of Ida's wise, old-young look.

And all around are the familiar motifs of Sendak's art: 'dogs and Mozart', to quote the man himself. That's some of the problem; there's just too much here that is familiar, done before, even a little stale. There are no surprises in the drawing, no babies made of ice; only Sendak coming dangerously close to imitating himself.

The greatest disappointment of all is Sendak's failure to create a fairy-tale forest possessed of genuinely magical power, and genuinely fearsome, too. The story's child-heroine is, after all, as scared as Hansel and Gretel: 'When thorns took hold of her dress, she was terrified, for she thought that wild beasts had seized her in their jaws and would tear her to pieces . . . at every step sharp stones cut her feet. She trembled with fear.' Yet in Sendak's pictures her dress remains untorn and clean; she loses her shoes, but her feet do not bleed; and instead of being scared *to death* she looks merely morose, while for some unaccountable reason, in one double-page picture, we see seven dwarfish, stick-carrying figures crossing a wooden bridge behind her (has she become Snow White?) amid trees that writhe and gnarl but do not manage to look fierce. This is too pretty a forest, and even though Sendak has spoken of the 'shadows' in what he does, it's precisely the darkness that's missing here.

'I feel that this is mine. I'll share *Dear Mili* with Wilhelm, but I swear I've gotten into his skin,' Sendak says; and again, 'Grimm comes close to being what I wish I had written.' This may be no more than forgivably enthusiastic empathizing, but the harsh truth is that Sendak has not 'gotten' into Wilhelm's skin, that—with the exception of the very last picture, in which the child returns to her aged mother—he has only very partially captured the sombre, glowing quality of the tale, and that it is probably time he gave up on Mozart and dogs.

1988

10

GABRIEL GARCÍA MÁRQUEZ

MARIO VARGAS LLOSA

GABRIEL GARCÍA MÁRQUEZ

Chronicle of a Death Foretold

We had suspected for a long time that the man Gabriel was capable of miracles, so that when the miracle of the printing presses occurred we nodded our heads knowingly, but of course the foreknowledge of his sorcery did not release us from its power, and under the spell of that nostalgic witchcraft we arose from our wooden benches and garden swings and ran without once drawing breath to the place where the demented printing presses were breeding books faster than fruit-flies, and the books leapt into our hands without our even having to stretch out our arms, the flood of books spilled out of the print room and knocked down the first arrivals at the presses, who succumbed deliriously to that terrible deluge of narrative as it covered the streets and the sidewalks and rose lap-high in the ground-floor rooms of all the houses for miles around, so that there was no one who could escape from that story, if you were blind or shut your eyes it did you no good because there were always voices reading aloud within earshot, we had all been ravished like willing virgins by that tale, which had the quality of convincing each reader that it was his personal autobiography, and then the book filled up our country and headed out to sea, and we understood that the phenomenon would not cease until the entire surface of the globe had been covered, until seas, mountains, underground railways and deserts had been completely clogged up by the endless copies emerging from the bewitched printing press . . .

It is now fifteen years since Gabriel García Márquez first published *One Hundred Years of Solitude*. During that time it has sold over four million copies in the Spanish language alone, and I don't know how many millions more in translation. The news of a new Márquez book takes over the front pages of Spanish-American dailies. Barrow-boys hawk copies in the streets. Critics commit suicide for lack of fresh superlatives. His latest book, *Chronicle of a Death Foretold*, had a first printing in Spanish of considerably more than one million copies. Not the least extraordinary aspect of the work of 'Angel Gabriel' is its ability to make the real world behave in precisely the improbably hyperbolic fashion of a Márquez story.

It seems that the greatest force at work on the imagination of Márquez himself is the memory of his grandmother. Many, more formal antecedents have been suggested for his art: he has himself admitted the influence of Faulkner, and the world of his fabulous Macondo is at least partly Yoknapatawpha County transported into the Colombian jungles. Then there's Borges, and behind the Borges the *fons* and *origo* of it all, Machado de Assis, author of three great novels, *Epitaph of a Small Winner*, *Quincas Borba* and *Dom Casmurro* that were far in advance of their times (1880, 1892 and 1900), light in touch and clearly the product of a proto-Márquezian imagination (see, for example, the use Machado makes of an 'anti-melancholy plaster' in *Epitaph*). And Márquez's genius for the unforgettably visual hyperbole—the Americans forcing a Latin dictator to give them the sea in payment of his debts, for instance, in *The Autumn of the Patriarch*: 'they took away the Caribbean in April, Ambassador Ewing's nautical engineers carried it off in numbered pieces to plant it far from the hurricanes in the blood-red dawns of Arizona'—may well have been sharpened by his years of writing for the movies. But the grandmother is more important than any of these.

In an interview with Luis Harss and Barbara Dohmann, Márquez gives her credit for his language. 'She spoke that way.' 'She was a great storyteller.' Anita Desai has said of Indian households that the women are the keepers of the tales, and the same appears to be the case in South America. Márquez was raised by his grandparents, meeting his mother for the first time when he was seven or eight years old. His remark that nothing interesting ever happened to him after the age of eight becomes, therefore, particularly revealing. Of his grandparents, Márquez said to Harss and Dohmann: 'They had an enormous house, full of ghosts. They were very superstitious and impressionable people. In every corner there were skeletons and memories, and after six in the evening you didn't dare leave your room. It was a world of fantastic terrors.' From the memory of that house, and using his grandmother's narrative voice as his own linguistic lodestone, Márquez began the building of Macondo.

But of course there is more to him than his granny. He left his childhood village of Aracataca when still very young, and found himself in an urban world whose definitions of reality were so different from those prevalent in the jungle as to be virtually incompatible. In *One Hundred Years of Solitude*, the assumption into heaven of Remedios the Beauty, the loveliest girl in the world, is treated as a completely expected occurrence, but the arrival of the first railway train to reach Macondo sends a woman screaming down the high street. 'It's coming,' she cries. 'Something frightful, like a kitchen dragging a village behind it.' Needless to say, the reactions of city folk to these two events would be exactly reversed. Márquez decided to elevate the village world-view above the urban one; this is the source of his fabulism.

The damage to reality in South America is at least as much political as cultural. In Márquez's experience, truth has been controlled to the point at which it has ceased to be possible to find out what it is. The only truth is that you are being lied to all the time. Márquez has always been intensely political; but his books are only obliquely to do with politics, dealing with public affairs only in terms of grand metaphors like Colonel Aureliano Buendia's military career or the colossally overblown figure of the Patriarch, who has one of his rivals served up as the main course at a banquet, and who, having overslept one day, decides that the afternoon is really the morning, so that people have to stand outside his windows at night holding up cardboard cut-outs of the sun.

El realismo magical, magic realism, at least as practised by Márquez, is a development out of Surrealism that expresses a genuinely 'Third World' consciousness. It deals with what Naipaul has called 'half-made' societies, in which the impossibly old struggles against the appallingly new, in which public corruptions and private anguishes are somehow more garish and extreme than they ever get in the so-called 'North', where centuries of wealth and power have formed thick layers over the surface of what's really going on. In the works of Márquez, as in the world he describes, impossible things happen constantly, and quite plausibly, out in the open under the midday sun. It would be a mistake to think of Márquez's literary universe as an invented, self-referential, closed system. He is not writing about Middle-earth, but about the one we all inhabit. Macondo exists. That is its magic.

It sometimes seems, however, that Márquez is consciously trying to foster a myth of 'Garcíaland'. Compare the first sentence of *One Hundred Years of Solitude* with the first sentence of *Chronicle of a Death Foretold*: 'Many years later, as he faced the firing squad, Colonel Aureliano Buendia was to remember that distant afternoon when his father took him to discover ice' (*One Hundred Years*). And: 'On the day they were going to kill him, Santiago Nasar got up at five-thirty in the morning to wait for the boat the bishop was coming on' (*Chronicle*). Both books begin by invoking a violent death in the future and then retreating to consider an earlier, extraordinary event. *The Autumn of the Patriarch*, too, begins with a death and then circles back and around a life. It's as though Márquez is asking us to link the books, to consider each in the light of the other. This suggestion is underlined by his use of certain types of stock character: the old soldier, the loose woman, the matriarch, the compromised priest, the anguished doctor. The plot of *In Evil Hour*, in which a town allows one person to become the scapegoat for what is in fact a crime committed by many hands—the fly-posting of satiric lampoons during the nights—is echoed in *Chronicle of a Death Foretold*, in which the citizens of another town, caught in the grip of a terrible disbelieving inertia, once again fail to prevent a killing, even though it has been endlessly 'announced' or 'foretold'. These assonances in the Márquez *œuvre* are so pronounced that it's easy to let them overpower the considerable differences of intent and achievement in his books.

For not only is Márquez bigger than his grandmother; he is also bigger than Macondo. The early writings look, in retrospect, like preparations for the great flight of *One Hundred Years of Solitude*, but even in those days Márquez was writing about two towns: Macondo and another, nameless one, which is more than just a sort of not-Macondo, but a much less mythologized place, a more 'naturalistic' one, insofar as anything is naturalistic in Márquez. This is the town of *Los Funerales de la Mamá Grande* (the English title, *Big Mama's Funeral*, makes it sound like something out of Damon Runyon), and many of the stories in this collection, with the exception of the title story, in which the Pope comes to the funeral, are closer in feeling to early Hemingway than later Márquez. And ever since his great book, Márquez has been making a huge effort to get away from his mesmeric jungle settlement, to continue.

In *The Autumn of the Patriarch*, the interminable sentences are the formal expression of the interminable tyranny that is the book's subject; a dictatorship so oppressive that all change, all possibility of development, is stifled. The power of the patriarch stops time, and the text proceeds to swirl and eddy around the stories of his reign, its non-linear form providing an exact analogy for the feeling of endless stasis. And in *Chronicle of a Death Foretold*, which looks at first sight like a reversion to the manner of his earlier days, he is in fact innovating again.

The *Chronicle* is about honour and its opposite, that is to say, dishonour, shame. The marriage of Bayardo San Roman and Angela Vicario ends on their wedding night when she names the young Arab, Santiago Nasar, as her previous lover. She is returned to her parents' house and her brothers, the twins Pedro and Pablo Vicario, are thus faced with the obligation of killing Santiago to salvage their family's good name. It is giving nothing away to reveal that the murder does take place. But the oddness and the quality of this unforgettable short fable lies in the twins' reluctance to do what must be done. They boast continually of their intentions, so that it is a sort of miracle that Santiago Nasar never gets to hear about it; and the town's silence eventually forces the twins to perform their terrible deed. Bayardo San Roman, whose honour required him to reject the woman with whom he was besotted, enters a terrible decline after he does so; 'honour is love,' one of the characters says, but for Bayardo this is not the case. Angela Vicario, the source of it all, appears to survive the tragedy with more calm than most.

The manner in which this story is revealed is something new for Márquez. He uses the device of an unnamed, shadowy narrator visiting the scene of the killings many years later, and beginning an investigation into the past. This narrator, the text hints, is Márquez himself—at least, he has an aunt with that surname. And the town has many echoes of Macondo: Gerineldo Márquez makes a guest appearance here, and one of the characters has the evocative name, for fans of the earlier book, of Cotes. But whether it be Macondo or no, Márquez is, in these pages, writing at a greater distance from his material than ever before. The book and its narrator probe slowly, painfully, through the mists of half-accurate memories, equivocations, contradicting versions, trying to establish what happened and why; and achieve only provisional answers. The effect of this retrospective method is to make the *Chronicle* strangely elegiac in tone, as if Márquez feels that he has drifted away from his roots, and can only write about them now through veils of formal difficulty. Where all his previous books exude an air of absolute authority over the material, this one reeks of doubt. And the triumph of the book is that this new hesitancy, this abdication of Olympus, is turned to such excellent account, and becomes a source of strength; *Chronicle of a Death Foretold*, with its uncertainties, with its case-history format, is as haunting and as true as anything Márquez has written before.

It is also rather more didactic. Márquez has, in the past, taken sides in his fictions only where affairs of State were concerned: there are no good banana company bosses in his stories, and the idea of the masses, 'the people', is occasionally—for instance in the last few pages of *The Autumn of the Patriarch*—romanticized. But when he has written about the lives of 'the people', he has thus far forborne to judge. In *Chronicle*, however, the distancing has the effect of making it clear that Márquez is launching an attack on the *macho* ethic, on a narrow society in which terrible things happen with the inevitability of dreams. He has never written so disapprovingly before.

Chronicle of a Death Foretold is speech after long silence. For a time Márquez abjured fiction; we can only be grateful that he is back, his genius unaffected by the lay-off. There will not be a better book published in England this year.

1982

Clandestine in Chile

The first time Márquez wrote the true story of a man's life, in *Story of a Shipwrecked Sailor*, the man, previously a national hero, lost his reputation, and the newspaper in which the story was published closed down.

It took a brave man to agree to be Márquez's second non-fictional subject. One can only suppose that after the dangers to which Miguel Littín had exposed himself during his Chilean adventure, this literary risk didn't seem so great.

'One's homeland is where one is born, but it's also the place where one has a friend, the place where there is injustice, the place where one can contribute with one's art,' Littín once said. After a dozen years in exile from Pinochet's Chile, this distinguished film director chose to make an unusual artistic contribution to his forbidden homeland. 'The important thing,' his children had told him, 'is for you to pin a great long donkey's tail on Pinochet.' He promised them he would, and that it would be a tail 20,000 feet long. He underestimated his abilities. The tail grew to 105,000 feet.

It was, of course, a film, an uncensored portrait of Chile

after over a decade of tyranny, made clandestinely by a man for whom discovery would have meant death. To make the film he had to change his appearance completely, remembering not to laugh (his laugh, he confesses, proved impossible to disguise). Littín worked in Chile for six weeks, helped by the resistance and by friends, and even managed to film inside Pinochet's private office, pinning his celluloid tail, so to speak, to the very seat of power.

It's easy to see how the outsize drama of Littín's story, the story behind the film, appealed to García Márquez, a writer who has turned exaggeration into an art form. *Clandestine in Chile* is not, however, written, as the blurb claims, 'in the voice we know from the novels.' (You can't entirely blame the blurbist; the author himself asserts something similar in his preface.) This is Márquez at his least baroque and most self-effacing; understanding that the story has no need of magical realist embellishment, he tells it plainly, in the form of Littín's first-person narrative. That is to say: he acts as Littín's ghost. It is a little strange that Littín doesn't even get to share the writing credit with his illustrious shadow, but there it is.

Anyhow, Márquez's restraint proves extremely effective. Littín's story comes across with startling directness and force. Littín, transformed into a Uruguayan businessman or *momio*— 'a person so resistant to change that he might as well be dead . . . a mummy'—bumps into his mother-in-law and, later, his mother, and in both cases the ladies fail to recognize him. He rebels constantly against the requirements of security, to the fury of his resistance 'wife' Elena and the tolerant irritation of the Chilean underground. And he completes his film.

This short, intense book offers a succession of extraordinary filmic images. There is a story of the man who burns himself to death to save his children from the government's torturers. There is a brief but potent account of the continuing cults of Allende and Neruda. 'This is a shitty government, but it's my government,' reads a sign paraded before Allende in a demonstration. Allende applauded, and went down to shake the protester by the hand. Even now, at Neruda's house at Isla Negra, the graffiti remember:

'Generals: Love never dies. Allende and Neruda live. One minute of darkness will not make us blind.' And there are, it is true, a couple of images we can recognize as classical Márquez, for example when Littín pays a surprise visit to his mother and finds that, without knowing why, she has prepared a great feast; or when Littín finds Santiago, formerly 'a city of private sentiments', full of highly demonstrative young lovers. 'I thought of something I had heard not long before in Madrid: "Love blossoms in times of the plague."'

Márquez once rashly swore never to publish a novel until Pinochet fell. Since then he has published *Chronicle of a Death Foretold*, *Love in the Time of Cholera* and a new work, *The General in his Labyrinth*, about Simón Bólivar. The broken promise will no doubt have made this book feel all the sweeter; he, too, had a tail to pin on the donkey. It clearly had the desired effect. 'On 28 November 1986, in Valparaiso,' we are told, 'the Chilean authorities impounded and burned 15,000 copies of this book.'

The book continues to exist, however; while Pinochet is, at long last, tottering on his plinth. To burn a book is not to destroy it. One minute of darkness will not make us blind.

1989

MARIO VARGAS LLOSA

The War of the End of the World

Peru's most important living novelist, Mario Vargas Llosa, has for many years played a significant part in his country's politics. In this respect he is like many writers of the South and unlike the great majority of his Northern colleagues. He may well, for example, be the only novelist to have been offered the post of Prime Minister, and to have turned it down—at any rate, the number of such writers must be very small—and he remains one of the most influential supporters of Peru's President, Belaùnde Terry. For backing Belaùnde, Vargas Llosa has come in for a certain amount of criticism, for instance from left groups and writers who have objected to his critique of the Sendero Luminoso guerrillas in the hills. He has in turn argued that while the world seems almost to expect the history of South America to be wholly composed of violent revolutions and repressive dictatorships, his own inclination is towards a less glamorous method of regulating human affairs—that is, some locally adapted variant of the old, flawed, battered idea of democracy, perhaps still the only idea by which the deadly cycle of coup and counter-coup can be broken. It is undeniably a persuasive point of view.

In his loudly acclaimed novel *The War of the End of the World*, which has arrived in English in a fine, fluent translation by Helen R. Lane, Vargas Llosa sets down with appalling and ferocious clarity his vision of the tragic consequences for ordinary people of millenarianism of whatever kind. He has written before, in the novel *Captain Pantoja and the Special Service*, about the emergence in remote rural parts of an ascetic figure who becomes a focus of resistance to a militaristic State; but that was primarily a comic novel, whereas the new book is as dark as spilled blood. And while it is most impressively got up as an historical novel—based, we are told, on a 'real' episode in Brazilian history—its value as a text is entirely contemporary. In an age such as ours, plagued by bloodthirsty armies and equally violent gods, an account of a fight to the finish between God and Mammon could be nothing else but contemporary, even though Vargas Llosa has placed his war in one of the most remote corners—the 'ends'—of the world, that is, the north-eastern part of Brazil in the nineteenth century. His imaginary Messiah, the Counselor, prefigures—to offer just one recent example—the Sikh leader, Sant Jarnail Singh Bhindranwale, shot dead by the Indian Army in Amritsar's famous Golden Temple, itself a real-life version of Vargas Llosa's fictive, Christian, Canudos.

The Counselor—Antonio Conselheiro—is a thin, awe-inspiring holy man who wanders the backlands of the province of Bahia in the last decade or so of the nineteenth century, advising the peons of their spiritual obligations in clear and comprehensible language, encouraging them to help him repair the region's many dilapidated and priestless churches, slowly gathering about himself an inner circle or band of apostles, and warning eloquently of the fearsome apocalypse that is to arrive with the millennium:

> In 1900 the sources of light would be extinguished and the stars would rain down. But, before that, extraordinary things would happen . . . In 1896 . . . the sea would turn into the backlands and the backlands into the sea . . . In 1898 hats would increase in size and heads grow smaller, and in 1899 the rivers would turn red and a new planet would circle through space. It was necessary, therefore, to be prepared.

The point of no return arrives, however, before any of these apparitions have had an opportunity to manifest themselves. Bahia, in which slavery has not been abolished for very long and which remains in the two-fisted grip of autocratic feudal landowners and extreme ignorance of the outside world, begins to hear about ominous developments. A Republic has been proclaimed, and it intends to make a census and, worse, to levy taxes. These are the last straws for the people of the backlands. Why would the Republic want everyone counted and described, if not to reimpose slavery? And, again, 'Animal instinct, common sense and centuries of experience made the townspeople realize immediately . . . that the tax collectors would be greedier than the vultures and the bandits.' The Counselor gives expression to their worst fears. He announces that 'the Antichrist was abroad in the world; his name was Republic.' Then he withdraws, with all who wish to follow him, to the fastness of Canudos, part of the lands of the Baron de Canabrava, the largest of the feudal landlords and chief of the Bahian Autonomist Party—which, ironically, is just as hostile to the new Republic, though for wholly profane reasons of self-interest.

In Canudos the Counselor sets about the construction and fortification of 'Belo Monte', a city and a church, a new Jerusalem against which the Antichrist must hurl his armies. There will be four fires, the Counselor tells his flock (which numbers, at its peak, more than 30,000 souls), and he will quench three and permit the fourth to consume them. So the four battles of the war of Canudos are prophesied in advance. What follows has the slow, sombre inevitability of a Greek tragedy—albeit one played out in a jungle—our knowledge of the end serves only to increase our pain.

Vargas Llosa's writing has, in a way, been working up to this book throughout his remarkable career; the prose has been getting simpler, the forms clearer. It's a long way from the structural complexities and the sometimes wilful-seeming obscurity of his very striking early novels *The Time of the Hero* and *The Green House* via the comic accessibility, even zaniness, of *Captain Pantoja* and *Aunt Julia and the Scriptwriter*, to the much more solid, crafted, traditional virtues of the present novel. It must not be supposed, though, that this represents some kind of descent into populism; rather that Vargas Llosa would appear to have been moving, gradually, from one form of complexity towards another. Or, to be precise, from complexity of form to that of ideas. *The War of the End of the World* does certainly offer many of the conventional satisfactions of the long, meticulous historical novel—the re-creation of a lost world; leisurely, well-paced exposition; a sense of elbow-room; and of being in safe hands—but it also gives us a fictional universe bursting with intellectual argument, one whose inhabitants are perfectly willing and able to dispute matters both political and spiritual at great length and with considerable verve.

But the greatest qualities of this excellent novel are, I believe, neither its inexorable Greek progress towards the slaughter of the innocents with which it climaxes, nor its intellectual rigour. They are, rather, its refusal ever to abandon the human dimension in a story that could so easily have become grandiose; also a sense of ambiguity, which enables Vargas Llosa to keep his characters three-dimensional, and not merely the representatives of Good, or Evil, or some such abstraction; and finally, a profound awareness of the tragic irony that makes tens of thousands of ordinary women and men die fighting against the Republic that was set up, in theory, precisely to serve them and to protect them against the rapacity of their previous, feudal overlords.

Much of the story is seen from the point of view of a group of characters centred on the peasant woman Jurema. She is the wife of the tracker Rufino, feudal bondsman of the Baron de Canabrava, and when she is raped by the naïf revolutionary Galileo Gall and taken off with him by a circus troupe, Rufino is obliged by the laws of honour to follow Galileo and kill him. When the two men have in fact done each other in, Jurema arrives at Canudos in the company of a dwarf, the teller of fairy-tales who is the sole survivor of the circus troupe; and of a character known only as 'the nearsighted journalist' whose growth from childlike innocence to bruised maturity is at the emotional heart of the novel. Jurema is thus accompanied by representatives of both oral and written literature, and neither is able to cope with Canudos. Nobody much wants to pay for the Dwarf's stories; and the journalist breaks his glasses and sees the great events as a series of shadows, or eventually of shards, because he pieces together a monocle from the broken lenses. An eyewitness deprived of his eyes is a sad image, and the journalist is indeed a moving figure. It is Jurema who keeps the men of words alive, partly because one of the chiefs of Canudos, the ex-bandit Pajeù, falls in love with her. Her place in the narrative is somewhat artificially centralized, it's true; towards the end, the Baron de Canabrava, hearing the tale of the fall of Canudos from the journalist, is amazed to learn that the fellow has married Rufino's wife (the two are among the handful of survivors of the massacre):

> All these happenstances, coincidences, fortuitous encounters . . . [The baron] suddenly had the absurd feeling that the former maidservant of Calumbí was the only woman in the *sertão*, a female under whose fateful spell all the men with any sort of connection to Canudos unconsciously fell sooner or later.

It is a bit like that; but perhaps just because Jurema is such an unlikely, even banal centre, the artifice does not jar too badly. And the benefits to the novel, in terms of keeping our eyes on individual lives, are considerable.

As to ambiguity: it was a fine stroke to make the Counselor's innermost disciples so badly flawed in so many ways. Some of them—scar-faced Pajeù, Pedrão, Abbot João— are former bandits and mass murderers; even holy Maria Quadrado, 'Mother of Men', turns out to be none other than the once-notorious Filicide of Salvador; and the closest disciple of all, the St Peter of this band, known as the Little Blessed One, finally (and like Peter) betrays his Christ, by breaking the solemn oath he himself made everyone take, that they would never reveal the dead Counselor's burial place. These flaws do more than make credible characters of the apostles: they make the important point that the leaders of this bizarre uprising are in no way 'better' than their followers; by being in many ways 'worse', they do not become the repositories of morality. That role is left to the mass of the faithful as a whole.

One ambiguity is less pleasing. The Baron de Canabrava's wife Estela goes mad when the rebels burn her beloved home, Calumbí, and for a while the falling feudalists seem almost sympathetic figures. Then the Baron quite forfeits the readers' sympathy (and to be honest, in the case of this reader, so, nearly, does the Baron's creator) when he rapes his wife's servant as a way of being close to dear Estela again. 'I always wanted to share her with you, my darling,' he 'stammers', and mad Estela makes no demur. The servant, Sebastiana, is not asked to comment. It is an ugly moment in a book which, for the most part, avoids coarseness at the most brutal of times.

The political vision of *The War of the End of the World* is bleak, and it would be possible to take issue with that absolute bleakness. But it is hard for a writer in the late years of this savage century not to have a tragic view of life, and Mario Vargas Llosa has written a modern tragedy on the grand scale, though not, mercifully, in the grand manner. At the end of its 550 pages, two images dominate its seething portrait of death, corruption and faith. One is of the tracker Rufino, and the anarchist Galileo Gall, each the somewhat absurd servant of an idea, hacking one another slowly to death; this image would seem to crystallize Vargas Llosa's political vision. The second is redemptive. Thirty thousand people die in Canudos, and it would be easy to think that a God who demanded such sacrifices was a God to avoid like the plague. But Vargas Llosa, with the generosity of spirit that informs the entire novel, is willing to allow the last word to someone who accepts that the catastrophe was also a kind of triumph.

The victorious soldiers, mopping-up after the levelling of Canudos, are anxious to account for the one leader whose body has not been found. An old woman asks Colonel Macedo if he wants to know what happened to Abbot João and the Colonel nods eagerly.

'"Archangels took him up to heaven," she says, clacking her tongue. "I saw them."'

1984

The Real Life of Alejandro Mayta

For a political 'moderate', Mario Vargas Llosa has been making some pretty immoderate remarks lately. To call Gabriel García Márquez 'the courtesan of Castro' was not exactly restrained. And when Günter Grass took issue with the use of such language, he, too, was lumped in with the extreme leftists who figure more and more in Vargas Llosa's personal demonology. That Grass the arch-gradualist, the political Snail, should seem extreme to Vargas Llosa is an indication of how far to the right the great Peruvian novelist's notion of the centre really lies.

Nevertheless, he *is* a great novelist. His last two books, *Aunt Julia and the Scriptwriter* and *The War of the End of the World*, were respectively comic and tragic masterpieces. He is also a public novelist of a type I have long admired, for whom literature is a quarrel with, and about, the world. I came to *Mayta* entirely prepared to disagree with all those, in Spain and in Central America, who had told me, sadly, that Vargas Llosa had written his first overtly right-wing tract. Having read it, I can't disagree with them after all. But in many ways the novel's literary weaknesses are more disappointing than the political slant.

Mayta takes place in a Peru of the near future, in which an apocalyptic confrontation between a Cuba-backed revolution and a government propped up by US marines is imminent. Vargas Llosa has gone to great, even exaggerated lengths to seem even-handed here. Government aircraft napalm the mountain community of Chunán; the guerrillas massacre the villagers at nearby Ricrán. A kind of balance of evil is implied.

Against this violent backdrop, an anonymous narrator, a writer about whom we learn little except that he's eminent enough to have a prison library named after him, is trying to piece together the story of a pathetic and calamitous earlier attempt at revolution, back in the 1950s, by his old schoolfellow, Alejandro Mayta. The novel moves seamlessly between investigation and flashback, sometimes in mid-sentence, our only guide being a change from present to past tense.

For at least half the novel, this is brilliantly done; the reader is never confused, and as reminiscence and re-creation mingle, Vargas Llosa's point about the impossibility of arriving at a 'real life' is perfectly demonstrated by his form. All versions of Mayta's life are suspect; the witnesses' histories are as unreliable as history itself has become in an age when falsification is the norm. The narrator himself is a self-declared liar, his purpose being to invent a fictional Mayta rather than to be the biographer of the 'real' one (a distinction made even more complex by our knowledge that there *is* no real one, anyway).

Within this *Citizen Kane*-like structure of retrospective investigation, a further balancing act is performed. Those witnesses who slander Mayta most virulently have their own motives called into question: the Senator who says the old Trot was a government informer, on the CIA payroll, turns out to be the youth, Anatolio, whom Mayta once taught to 'screw like a man', and who betrayed him even though they were lovers. Contradictory descriptions of the past struggle in the text; and the narrating 'I', camera-like, records them neutrally.

Alejandro Mayta, the ageing Trotskyist, is not drawn without sympathy. Most marginal of men, his chance meeting with an enthusiastic second lieutenant in the army, a certain Vallejos who is secretly planning an uprising in the mountain town of Jauja, seals his fate. For Mayta, Vallejos represents his only chance of real action after a lifetime spent in impotent theoretical disputes in rented garages, and in the debilitating faction-strife of the far-left grouplets of Peru. Needless to say, their plans go hopelessly, even comically wrong, and Mayta ends up a broken, betrayed figure, selling ice-cream and pretending to forget.

Vargas Llosa possesses a formidable gift for realism of the non-magical kind, a gift that can remind one of Stendhal. When Mayta arrives in the mountains for his life's greatest event, he is almost crippled by 'mountain sickness', a marvellous, ironic detail. The descriptions—of city and landscape alike—are unfailingly exact, and the machinations of the RWP(r), the minuscule, seven-man Trotskyist cell to which Mayta belongs, have the ring of truth. *The Real Life of Alejandro Mayta* ought to be a splendid novel. It isn't.

The failure is, unquestionably, in part polemic. That Vargas Llosa's lefties are without exception fanatics, weak, incurably romantic, party hacks, narrow ideologues, stupid, or opportunistic, is some of it. That he portrays the revolutionary impulse as being invariably divorced from the real lives (if I may use the term) of the people, is simply unhistorical. Whatever one's politics, it would be hard to look at twentieth-century Latin American history and come to such a conclusion.

For a novel about the nature of history, *Mayta* doesn't have much in the way of an historical sense. Why is the apocalypse imminent in this fictional Peru? What great forces are in collision? Only blind ideologies. It won't do. In *The War of the End of the World*, Vargas Llosa gave us a genuine historical tragedy, in which the economic and military power of a State collided with, and finally crushed, the religious fervour of the downtrodden poor. That 'end of the world' felt real; *Mayta*'s garbage-mountain Peru is a comic-strip.

No, it's worse. Because Vargas Llosa clearly lays the blame for the apocalypse at the feet of his hapless anti-hero. His feeble uprising 'charted the process that has ended in what we are all living through now.' So the revolutionaries are the reason why the State has to call in the marines. As a distortion of history, this takes some beating.

But such disputes are secondary. Mayta's clumsy adventure is not funny enough, sad enough or just plain exciting enough to hold our interest. As the novel progresses, Vargas Llosa seems to realize the thinness of his material, and the telling of the tale grows more frenzied. The witnesses proliferate, until almost every paragraph is told by a new voice; the distinction between past and present blurs, so that the 'I' is sometimes the narrator and sometimes, bewilderingly, Mayta himself. This is *Kane* without Kane

(Mayta is a rather hollow centre, after all), and—although the 'real' Mayta, in his last-chapter meeting with the narrator, does reveal a long-concealed secret, which inevitably shows up the novel's Trots as being even nastier than we had hitherto supposed—without Rosebud, either.

This final meeting between investigator and investigated uncovers what, for me, is the novel's deepest flaw. To change the Spanish *Historia de Mayta* to the English *Real Life of Alejandro Mayta* (and who, by the way, was responsible? The book names no translator) is to invite comparison with a very similar novel with a very similar name, Nabokov's *Real Life of Sebastian Knight*. Nabokov's narrator, too, pursues an elusive subject, and in fact never meets him. He, too, seeks to conceal himself from the reader. But Nabokov's genius reveals him anyway, and shows him, at the last, losing his identity in his subject. ('I am Sebastian, or Sebastian is I, or perhaps we are both someone whom neither of us knows.') The point is, *something happens to the narrator*. He is drawn into the tale he uncovers, and becomes its meaning. Vargas Llosa's narrator, never dropping the mask of objective neutrality while his creator loads the dice, opposes the hollowness of Mayta with an emptiness of his own. In place of Nabokov's merged identities, we have only a pair of badly crossed *I*s.

1986

11

THE LANGUAGE OF THE PACK

DEBRETT GOES TO HOLLYWOOD

E. L. DOCTOROW

MICHAEL HERR: AN INTERVIEW

RICHARD FORD

RAYMOND CARVER

ISAAC BASHEVIS SINGER

PHILIP ROTH

SAUL BELLOW

THOMAS PYNCHON

KURT VONNEGUT

GRACE PALEY

TRAVELS WITH A GOLDEN ASS

THE DIVINE SUPERMARKET

THE LANGUAGE OF THE PACK

Now it is a thing well known to any citizen who ever sits down to an evening of action that a deck of cards represents a vocabulary as supple as may be found in any dictionary; and, accordingly, that the playing of a little poker or gin is as absorbing a dialogue as any heated dispute over the burning issues of the day; and that, during such a dialogue, the citizen comes to discover a fair amount with regard to the innermost nature of his companions and himself also, including handy information as to which of them is the most foolhardy and which the most cautious, and who is a person of true sophistication and who, even though he is dressed to beat the band, is at bottom no more than a common rube. And as languages go a game of cards is superior in one respect to all other languages presently in employment, viz. that the person who speaks it best, demonstrating the greatest fluency and the fanciest subordinate clauses, most likely ends up going home holding a sizeable sack of potatoes, unless it happens that his less articulate colleagues pursue him to some shady quarter and beat him stupid and rob him blind.

And so it is natural that the language of cards spills over into our everyday speech, so that when we are shooting the breeze we can make mention of how a certain attribute, for example honesty, is not So-and-So's long suit; or if faced with a guy of an unpredictable disposition we can mark him down as the joker in the pack. Even citizens who get no action whatsoever can readily comprehend what it is to be dealt a bum hand in the game of life, or when some grand design for the future turns out to be a busted flush. The uninitiated civilian does not know that aces and eights are termed The Dead Man's Hand, as it is the hand held by Wild Bill Hickock when they drill him, but he is fully conversant with upping the ante and even finessing and when he is sitting pretty he knows he is holding all the aces or maybe coming up trumps.

What is more surprising, if you are given to being surprised by life, in which case you are very likely not a card-player, is that an activity wherein chance, skill, drama, intrigue, deception, crime, violence, money and wild fluctuations of fortune are so intimately conjoined, an activity at once literal, symbolic, and even allegorical, should feature so relatively rarely in literature. There is *The Rape of the Lock*, it is true, and there is *Alice in Wonderland*, and there is the character of Frankie Machine, the dope-fiend card-player, in Nelson Algren's *The Man with the Golden Arm*. There is Italo Calvino's *The Castle of Crossed Destinies*, in which tarot cards are used to tell stories, and there is Vladimir Nabokov's *King, Queen, Knave*. Then you start to scratch around. There is a Pushkin story of which I do not recall the title. In the cinema, there is *The Cincinnati Kid*, but *The Joker is Wild* is a movie that is not about cards, in spite of its name. *One-Eyed Jacks* likewise; also *Aces High*.

Gambling in general crops up now and again, in Dostoevsky and even in the *Mahabharata*, in which Prince Yudhisthira loses his entire kingdom to his arch-enemies because of his fondness for the tumbling dice. But cards? They are thin on the ground. It is as though these two languages, the language of cards and that of literature, are incompatible, and it is tougher to translate the one into the other than it seems.

The reason for this may be that the really interesting thing about cards is *cheating*. Damon Runyon (whose manner somewhat infected the opening of this piece, though it will be resisted henceforward) wrote what may be the two greatest stories about card-players, and cheating is central to both. In 'The Lacework Kid', the eponymous Kid, a genius at all card games except gin rummy, is obliged, during a wartime sojourn in a prison camp, to play gin against the German camp commandant. The Kid wins, the German is found with a bullet in his head, and the Kid uses his winnings to bribe the guards into letting all the prisoners escape. Years later, it turns out that the Kid used his magic dealing fingers in a less than straightforward way. 'In fact,' we are told by his old mentor, Kidneyfoot, 'The Lacework Kid is a rank sucker at gin until I instruct him in one manoeuvre that gives you a great advantage, which is to drop any one card to the floor accidentally on purpose.' Cheating at cards, the story suggests, can be thought of as a creative act. You achieve your end by stepping outside the frame. Which is OK as long as you get away with it.

Runyon's other great tale of cards and gambling, 'The Idyll of Miss Sarah Brown', which was the basis for *Guys and Dolls*, contains the most memorable cautionary passage ever written about card-sharping. Not surprisingly, it is quoted at length (twice!) by Anthony Holden in *Big Deal*, his entertaining account of a year spent playing professional poker:

> 'Son,' the old guy [Sky Masterson's father] says, 'you are now going out into the wide, wide world to make your own way, and it is a very good thing to do, as there are no more opportunities for you in this burg. I am only sorry,' he says, 'that I am not able to bankroll you to a very large start, but,' he says, 'not having any potatoes to give you, I am going to stake you to some very valuable advice . . . Son,' the old guy says, 'no matter how far you travel, or how smart you get, always remember this: Someday, somewhere,' he says, 'a guy is going to come to you and show you a nice brand-new deck of cards on which the seal is never broken, and this guy is going to offer to bet you that the jack of spades will jump out of this deck and squirt cider in your ear. But, son,' the old guy says, 'do not bet him, for as sure as you do you are going to get an ear full of cider.'

The Oxford Guide to Card Games, by David Parlett, has disappointingly little to tell us about cheating. It refers us to Girolamo Cardano's *Liber de ludo aleae* ('Book on Games of Chance'), written in 1564, and containing, apparently, a detailed examination of the 'inexorable logic' of cheating—alas, however, Parlett does not quote. He does tell us about the seventeenth-century view of whist as 'a low-class game . . .

wicked by association with cheating,' and quotes Charles Cotton (1674): 'There is a way to discover to their partners what Honours they have; as by the wink of one eye, . . . it signifies one honour; shutting both the eyes, two; placing three or four fingers on the table, three or four honours.' And in a later (1734) edition of Cotton, the editor, Seymour, added some more sophisticated variations: 'piping', a means of indicating the Honour cards held by the disposition of the cheat's fingers upon his pipe while smoking; and verbal cheating, too. '"Indeed" signifies diamonds; "truly", hearts; "Upon my word", clubs; "I assure you", spades.'

In spite of its relative reticence on this subject, *The Oxford Guide* is a handy and erudite volume. Parlett has absorbed the work of his great predecessors, ancient and modern, from Hoyle to Dummett, and written what is neither a rule-book nor a guide to better play, but a sort of eager meditation on the whole field of activity. He is excellent on history, demonstrating that cards did not arrive in Europe, as so often supposed, from China, possibly in Marco Polo's luggage, because trade with China had 'petered out long before John of Rheinfelden described [playing cards] as new' in 1377; nor were they brought back by crusaders returning from the East. The true source, as proved by the provenance and dating of a twelfth- or thirteenth-century pack now held in the Topkapi Museum in Istanbul, was Mameluke Egypt.

Parlett is strong on poker, sketchy on bridge, and fascinating on a vast range of minor games, which he groups into categories of technique—'Happy families', 'vying and bragging', 'matching and cribbing'. But for a portrait of card games in action, of the players as well as the play, it is Holden's book to which one must turn.

Holden is no Runyon or Algren, though clearly under the influence of both. He is an excellent journalist and a poker maniac, whose very name is so close in sound to the pro version of poker ('Hold'em') that he keeps thinking the public address systems of Las Vegas are calling it out. His book is vivid, engrossing, and, along with his friend A. Alvarez's book *The Biggest Game in Town* (1983), the best description of world-class poker we've been given. (Alvarez is the dedicatee of *Big Deal*, and also appears in it as The Crony.) Not much here about cheating, either, but nobody's perfect. What Holden captures superbly is the madness of the committed card-player, which Runyon, in 'The Lacework Kid', summarized thus:

> I will not attempt to describe gin rummy in any detail as you can call up any insane asylum and get any patient on the phone and learn about it in no time, as all lunatics are bound to be gin players, and in fact the chances are it is gin rummy that makes them lunatics.

There is a hilltop park in Karachi in which, as the heat of the day cools into evening, men gather in happy groups to sit cross-legged on the grass and break out the decks. The soft slaps of cards being played in triumph or resignation fill the air. Even at the height of the Zia dictatorship's puritanism, when night-clubs went out of business and the Karachi drive-in, that traditional site of youthful lust, was closed down, the moral guardians of the nation did not dare to prevent the people from playing their card-games. There could be no more striking tribute to the obdurate mania of the card-player, and to the enduring vitality of the language of cards.

1990

DEBRETT GOES TO HOLLYWOOD

In Times Square, a few years back, New Yorkers were alarmed by a gigantic poster that asked, in large white letters on a black background, a somewhat unsettling question: PATHETIC HUMANS, WHO CAN SAVE YOU NOW? A couple of weeks later, the answer went up in the question's place. It read: FLASH GORDON.

Hollywood always did see us as pathetic humans, didn't it, as lesser breeds in need of the profane demigods up there in VistaVision, Todd-AO or CinemaScope. Our place was a seat in the dark, from which we could look up to the stars and watch them shine. Banality made our lives unreal; *they* were the ones who were fully alive. So we munched our popcorn and grew confused about reality. As the modern city became the negation of nature, so the movies were the perfect metropolitan form, mythologies of the unreal, and they came complete with a new religion: fame.

'Fame! I wanna live for ever,' runs the song. The game is, has always been, immortality. Once you had to be a Roman emperor, a prophet, a hero, or at the very least a genius, to qualify for that particular curse. Hollywood pretended to democratize deification. If you were Lucille LeSueur, you could step away from your sleazy, poor, unhappy past, say the magic word, and shazam! There you were: Joan Crawford.

But the cinema is the least democratic, most hierarchical and status-ridden of worlds, and Hollywood has always been a place of despots (Goldwyn, Thalberg, Cohn), Kings (Gable) and Queens (Pickford). Of course the stars were snobs. Of course they wanted to be aristocrats. But maybe they never quite believed they really truly were, because when Rita Hayworth married Aly Khan, she cried, 'I'm so excited, I can hardly think, I'm sort of lost in a dream world.' And when Grace Kelly married Monaco's Rainier, an even dizzier pinnacle had been attained.

Debrett Goes to Hollywood sets out to chart the dynasties of Golden Age Hollywood, offering us both family trees and 'webs' at whose heart the sacred monsters sit: Elizabeth Taylor of the six husbands, Constance Bennett, Howard Hawks. It's a bizarre book, its nose at once high in the air and deep in the dirt. Its author, Charles Kidd, seems torn between the posh genealogical delights of revealing the connection between Tyrone Power and Evelyn Waugh, and the pleasures of gossip-column scandal-mongering.

That isn't surprising. Scandal and Hollywood were always difficult to separate. Maybe we always wanted the stars to fall. We wanted their divinity tarnished. So when Charles Kidd evokes 'an age of glamour never to return', he conjures up the Bennett sisters, who 'totalled twelve husbands, eight divorces and twelve children. Their stories include an unsolved mystery, the tragedy of mental illness, and a scandal that nearly ended a career.'

If that's glamour, his book is full of it: alcoholism, syphilis, suicide. 'Unhappy Sapphic affairs' were the undoing of one Pepi Lederer. Heterosexuality didn't have much better results. 'I hope they blast the living daylights out of that Elizabeth Taylor,' murmured Debbie Reynolds's mum after Liz ran off with Debbie's Eddie, whom she later ditched for Dick. 'Everyone knows exactly what she is.' Take *that*.

Who are the really pathetic humans, I thought more than once as I read; and who can save them now?

One of the (unintentional) revelations of *Debrett Goes to Hollywood* is, after all, that stars do dim, fade and go out; that, except in a very few cases, fame isn't for ever, and the promise of immortality is a con. Many of the 'legends' in this collection no longer seem quite so legendary. Does it interest you that Joan Bennett's daughter was once the sister-in-law of Gloria Swanson's daughter? How much do you care about Franchot Tone? Who on earth were the Rankin and Davenport dynasties? *Sic transit* Gloria Grahame, even if she does turn out to be descended from Edward III.

Many of the old-time stars whose immortality still seems assured are missing. No Mae West, no W. C. Fields, no Keaton. Even Monroe only rates a photograph. It's significant, too, that the most interesting connections Charles Kidd has managed to unearth catch the eye because they are links between the movie world and famous people from the 'real' world.

One of these connections is that between Humphrey Bogart and Princess Di (Bogey's mother was an eighth cousin of the Princess's great-grandmother; pretty close, no?). The other is even more startling. Groucho Marx's wife's sister's husband's ex-wife's ex-husband's ex-wife's husband was Randolph Churchill, whose father was, of course, Winston himself. Thus are two of the world's greatest cigar-smokers joined by indissoluble (well, sort of) ties.

Very few stars, nowadays, can generate enough power to dazzle us. TV has made them smaller than we are. We no longer go to their darkened temples; no longer larger than life, they visit us instead. We channel-hop while they kiss, we push the fast-forward button on our videos when they bore us. Even their scandals fail to raise our eyebrows.

But maybe Hollywood gets the last laugh, after all. The stars may no longer command our devotion, but the religion whose first deities they were has conquered the earth. In *The Big Room*, Michael Herr and Guy Peellaert's portraits of celebrity revealed that the real stars, today, can be gangsters (Meyer Lansky), gamblers (Nick the Greek) or hoteliers (Conrad Hilton). They can be used-car salesmen like Richard Nixon, or, like John Fitzgerald Kennedy, they can be President of the United States.

When murderers start becoming stars, you know that something has gone badly wrong. When ordinary folk queue up to submit to the diverse humiliations of game-shows just to get their five minutes in the spotlight, you realize how far the disease has spread. And when the techniques of starmaking, or image and illusion, become the staples of politics, you understand: we are all idolaters now, and there don't seem to be many iconoclasts around.

At least the old movie stars, flickering up there at twenty-four frames per second, were gods who knew themselves to be false. Come back, Flash Gordon; all is forgiven.

1986

E. L. DOCTOROW

The idea of the Star, of the human individual who radiates celestial light, is a quintessentially American one, because America is in love with light; just listen to its national anthem, star-spangled banner, dawn's early light, twilight's last gleaming, rocket's red glare, was there ever such an ode to illumination? But if America sees itself as the Light Incarnate it knows, too, its Darkness, and loves its dark stars also, loves them all the more because it fears them so: Al Capone, Don Corleone, Legs Diamond and the demon-god of E. L. Doctorow's *Billy Bathgate*, the barbarian Arthur Flegenheimer, who stole a dead man's name and became Dutch Schultz. A secular nation hungry for gods, America made of men like the Dutchman dark deities in whom it desperately wanted to believe, as fifteen-year-old Billy, Doctorow's narrator, wants to believe in Schultz. But what America loves most, needs most, more than light, more than darkness, more than gods or demons, is the myth of itself. Mythical America, its writers tell us constantly, is the real America, and myth demands, among other things, that heroes fall as well as rise. *Billy Bathgate* is the story of the Dutchman's long, last dive.

It's also the story of Billy's rise. Billy the punk, the 'capable boy' who catches the great hood's eye by juggling objects of different weight on the sidewalk outside one of the racketeer's beer drops. Billy with the crazy mother who nailed her departed husband's suit to the floor of her room, spread-eagled as if it were a man. Billy whose best friend is a scavenger named Arnold Garbage and who, at fifteen, takes fourteen-year-old Rebecca up to the roof of the orphanage and fucks her twice for a dollar. Billy who dreams of greatness, and pursues it the way he tells the story, in a great rush of language and scheming and love of danger and fear of death and determination to survive; and for whom his one chance of greatness lies with the Schultz gang and depends on the boss's

E. L. DOCTOROW

murderous whim. Knowing he could die at any moment, for seeing too much or learning too little, Billy seizes his chance with all the hunger of the street. 'I think these days for the real training you got to go right to the top,' he dares to say right into the Dutchman's face, and gets away with it.

He is apprenticed to the gang, and during one of the most unsentimental educations in literature he certainly sees much too much and learns plenty by way of compensation. What he sees includes the execution of the killer Bo Weinberg, whom Dutch takes out into New York harbour with his feet in a bowl of hardening cement, which slops back and forth in a 'slow-witted diagram of the sea,' and who goes to feed the fishes, singing 'Bye, Bye, Blackbird'. It includes the hideous murders of a fire inspector and a union boss, killed by Schultz out of the rage of his power's collapse. It includes the visit of the Mafia don with the drooping eye and bad skin and, later, the visit paid to Schultz by this gentleman's employees. What he learns: how to shoot a gun, and (from Schultz's financial genius Abbadabba Berman) the secrets of numbers, including the numbers racket, and what you feel when your god arranges to have your nose broken, and how some people feed on death, and what it means to a racketeer when the bent politicians refuse to take Schultz's money any more ('It is a momentous thing when the money won't flow'), and how dying gangsters, gasping out their last words, will give up their greatest secrets if you know how to listen right. He learns how to fall in love, and, above all, how to live to tell his tale.

Love comes to Billy in the form of Drew Preston, society beauty and tramp, inherited by Schultz from cemented Bo. Drew makes herself available to Billy as well, and although she is beautiful as all hell and the Dutchman is crazy about her and she almost splits the gang and Billy winds up saving her life at the Saratoga racetrack by an ingenious scheme involving bouquets of flowers and boxes of candy and also her husband Harvey, the fact is that she's the least convincingly drawn character in an otherwise flawless book; she reads like she's waiting for Michelle Pfeiffer to play her in the movie. The truth is the book does read at times too much

331

like the movie it will obviously be pretty soon but what the hell, the story is so terrific you really don't care to complain.

American novelists have always been readier than their European counterparts to demonstrate that the art of literature can adopt the form of the popular entertainment without losing an iota of seriousness, and *Billy Bathgate* is Doctorow's most brilliant proof of it to date. In fact, were it not as robustly vulgar as it is, it would fail as art, because Billy himself is in truth the incarnation of the street. He has named himself after Bathgate Avenue in the Bronx, 'this bazaar of life, Bathgate', and so it is right that he and his book should be as pellmell and clattering as that raucous thoroughfare. Doctorow's gift for evoking the actuality of street-life is unrivalled, and he brings to vivid life Bathgate, the market street, where the barrowboys sell grapefruit and Georgia peaches, and 'the aristocracy of the business' have real stores selling 'your chickens still in their feathers', and lox and whitefish and pickles and everything else as well. And just as vivid as Bathgate Avenue is the boy who takes its name, and is like it dedicated to money, to the pursuit of money in America, and to the gangsters who are the paradigms of that single-minded and ruthless pursuit, who are its most exalted and malign embodiments, who are to Bathgate Avenue as the monarch is to the punk.

'The city has always given me assurances,' says Billy Bathgate, 'whenever I have asked for them.' The gangsters in Doctorow's novel, like Jack Diamond in William Kennedy's equally potent *Legs*, draw their self-belief, their sense of solidity and permanence, from the metropolis itself, which suggests that only those who can believe in the permanence of the city are able to master it; or perhaps that it's only when you believe in that permanence that you can survive the city's transformations, its tricksy changes of light and lethal shadowplays, because it's belief that keeps you one step ahead, with money in your pocket and the world at your feet, until you come up against somebody who believes even harder than you.

1989

MICHAEL HERR: AN INTERVIEW

'Vietnam? Was that a war or what?' This is Sergeant Benson speaking. She's a character in a story by Richard Ford, and it's not that she doesn't know about Vietnam, it's that she doesn't want to know. She's talking to a Vietnam veteran on a train. 'You were probably on a boat that patrolled the rivers blindly in the jungle day and night, and you don't want to discuss it now because of your nightmares, right?' Who wants yesterday's papers, the Rolling Stones used to ask, and that's Vietnam: yesterday's apocalypse.

It's more than a decade, now, since Michael Herr finished work on the best book to come out of the madness, and reading *Dispatches* again after all this time I'm struck most of all by the language in it, because Vietnam was language as well as everything else: the dead language of jargon that lay over the event and tried to conceal it, *frontier sealing, census grievance, the Vietnam War will be an economy War*, and one I've never forgotten, a US military spokesman describing a bombing raid 'north of the Dee Em Zee' as having 'obtained a 100% mortality response.' Set against that language in *Dispatches* is the living argot of the enlisted men, the grunts. 'I been *scaled*, man, I'm *smooth* now,' a black paratrooper told Herr, 'leaving me to wonder where he'd been to get his language.' And then there's the third language. Rock 'n' roll. *The sixties . . . its war and its music had run power off the same circuit for so long they didn't even have to fuse.*

I'm sitting with Herr in his South Kensington apartment talking about how Vietnam was invaded by Hendrix, by Sam the Sham, by Zappa as well as soldiers, by General Waste-More-Land. He says: 'The grunts were conscious that they were involved in a drug-and-rock 'n' roll extension. Most of the combatants, black and white, came from the working class. For them, the war was an extension of their street lives. Rock 'n' roll had a currency in those days it hasn't had since

1970. The war didn't survive rock 'n' roll, in a way.' Those were the days of *heads* and *freaks*. And if *getting high* was where *it was at*, then Vietnam was the ultimate trip. When the grunts went into battle, Herr remembers, they 'put their guns on rock 'n' roll.'

It's easy to say that Vietnam was bad craziness, much harder to admit that the craziness was working inside you, you weren't just an observer. That honesty is what makes *Dispatches* special, what's made it last. 'I wanted to be intimate with the war,' says Herr. 'I also wanted to maintain control, as everyone does in the matter of intimacy, but I couldn't. Circumstances arose.' There were critical moments when he had to cross the line, pick up a gun, shoot. 'I felt I had almost certainly taken another life to preserve my own life.' In the book he wrote down his feelings as truthfully as he could. They included happiness. 'I was just happy I was alive. I went through an unbelievably terrible night and when the sun came up I was still there.' Now, ten years after the book, he is 'essentially a pacifist'. To take another human life was, as the saying went, a very heavy piece of karma. 'I think that somewhere along the line it's going to have to be accounted for.'

Accounting for Vietnam: and yes, Sergeant Benson, there are nightmares. When he worked on *Apocalypse Now*, and ten years later, writing *Full Metal Jacket*, the dreams returned. 'All the wrong people remember Vietnam. I think all the people who remember it should forget it, and all the people who forgot it should remember it.' Vietnam is a scar on the American psyche that has never been healed because 'the proper medication was never used.' And what's that? 'Meditation. The American media still deflect Americans from any true meditation about what happened there.' No collective act of understanding is possible in such a climate; only individual acts of understanding remain. 'I'm a hardcore Pascalian. All the suffering in the world comes from people not being able to be alone in a room.' A classic sixties solution, maybe, for a quintessential sixties crime.

He's worked on two of the best Vietnam movies, doesn't

think much of the others, but way back then, in Vietnam, the movies were already a way for him to experience the war. 'I'm a child of my time and a man of my culture. I grew up in the movies. Don Quixote experiences his travels in the language of romances. But when he dies, he knows what's happened to him. He's very clear. As many of us knew that the war was not a movie. It was real.' Nowadays, though, the Vietnam movies mostly create 'false representations. You know: wanting to look and not wanting to look. People want it authentic but not too authentic. They want their pain stirred up, but not too much, and then they want it taken away.'

The real tragedy is that there's 'no apparatus to deflect the guilt of the grunts. Those guys have been set adrift. They were simultaneously so innocent and evil out there, like Alden Pyle [Greene's 'quiet American']. There was no way to sort that out for them when they came back.'

Nowadays, he resists talking politics about the war. 'I was politicized by the war and then went to a stage beyond politics. It became critically nullified by the overwhelming experience of being there. The war was behaviour. Archetypal behaviour beyond judgement.' But is there such a thing? Isn't that a kind of exoneration? 'I don't want to exonerate them. It's just that from the outside the war was perceived as an exclusively political event. On the inside it was fundamentally and eternally a human event. And it's going to be a human event much longer than a political one.'

For the grunts, there was the World, and there was Vietnam. In Vietnam, after the death of Martin Luther King, there were race riots at many American bases. But then things quietened down. 'Men needed each other. They needed each other more than they needed their prejudice.' In Vietnam, Herr learned that true courage was refusing to fight. 'Once you've run in front of a machine-gun a few times, try facing your wife and kids.' In Vietnam, he accepted that war was glamorous, because of its intimacy with death. 'Nothing else can move that much adrenalin. I'm rather grateful that's so, because now I know how to avoid that level of drama.' Hardened foreign correspondents like Ryszard Kapuściński admit they need revolutions, wars; they're addicts. 'It's wonderful of Kapuściński to know and say that. But I'm no classic war correspondent. Vietnam was a one-off. I don't ever want to see war again, or to go back to Vietnam.' *Vietnam Vietnam Vietnam, we've all been there*, his book ends. But these days, the World is enough.

1988

RICHARD FORD

It is the summer of 1960 and all around the town of Great Falls, Montana, forest fires are burning. The forest wildlife flees the blaze. A bear is seen emerging from the fire, its fur blazing. A moose wanders into the main street of a small township, bewildered. The animals don't understand the fire. Its causes are mysterious. But it changes their lives.

Human beings are not so different. The fire changes things for them also. 'It was sometimes a good thing to be near a thing so uncontrollable and out of all scale that you felt reduced and knew your position in the world.' The fire draws men to fight it, and the women left behind accuse them of taking Indian women for lovers. The fire makes sudden, unpredictable changes of direction, and when it dies down to a smoulder it's still treacherous. It can blaze up again at any moment, without warning.

There's a sort of fire in people's hearts, too, and when it flares up it's too big a thing to resist, you feel reduced. Take Jerry. He's a golf pro who drifts into Great Falls with his wife Jeanette and sixteen-year-old son Joe. He loses his job, unjustly accused of putting his fingers in the club till, and falls into a slump, until the fire summons him to fight it. 'I've got this hum in my head now,' he says. 'I've got to do something about it.' Against his wife's wishes, in spite of his knowledge of her discontents, he goes.

Or take Jeanette. She's drifted with Jerry across America. 'We had lived in Coeur d'Alene and McCall, Idaho, and in Endicott and Pasco and Walla Walla.' She never expected to be living in Great Falls and to see her husband go off to risk his life like a child, standing up against a blaze. Jeanette has reached the end of some sort of line. She wants better. Better turns out to be a local rich guy, Warren Miller, and in the three days her husband's away she dresses up in her 'desperation dress' and goes to Miller's house to dance a drunken cha-cha and lets him into her marital bed at night and then goes to lie with him in his pink automobile. Things are changing for her, she lets them drift into irreversibility, she runs before the flames. She does all this in a dreamy sort of way, as if it's being done through her and not by her. 'I'm afraid of becoming somebody else now, I guess,' she says. 'That's probably how the world works. We just don't know it until it happens. "Ha-ha", I guess is what we should say. "Ha-ha."' Here's what Jerry says to his boy Joe when he finds out Jeanette has been stepping out on him: 'This is a wild life, isn't it, son?'

It's Joe who tells the story. And if the adults here don't fully understand why they do what they do, half-formed Joe, on the edge of the adult world, doesn't fully understand grown-ups, either. He is 'in limbo, between the cares of other people with only my own cares to show me what to do.'

Wildlife, Richard Ford's first novel-length fiction since the magnificent story collection *Rock Springs*, can't really be called an advance on that earlier volume. It's more like a continuation of the world he built there, an America without history, peopled by men and women of small ambition, small dreams, small disappointments. The town in this book may be called Great Falls but all the falls in it, Ford makes clear, are little ones. 'In the end, not very much happened' is a typical Ford sentence, but the not very much that happens is so well observed, felt and described that Ford effortlessly pulls off the trick of making us think that the lives he shows us mean a great deal, while also making us remember that they don't really mean much at all.

Ford's work has often been bracketed with and likened to the writing of his friend, the late Raymond Carver, and he hasn't always benefited by the comparison. 'Dirty realism' is a label that contains about as much truth as you can fit on to a label, but Ford and Carver's unlikenesses are more interesting than their similarities. The characteristic Ford tone of voice is a good deal more distanced than Carver's was, and the people he describes are likewise distanced from their own experience, like Jerry and Jeanette and Joe, all of them doing things without quite knowing they're going to, just waiting for things to reveal their need to be done. There's more passion in Carver; there's more dispassion in Ford.

Wildlife is a fine novel by a fine writer. At times it brought to mind David Byrne's movie about another American Nowheresville, *True Stories*, a movie which, like Ford's book, observes the human animal with friendship, understanding, and an almost clinical detachment. There's a scene in *True Stories* in which the people of the town take turns at a mike, singing brief verses of autobiography, trying, again like Ford's characters, to sing themselves into existence and significance, wearing their desperation dresses. The name of the song they sing is 'Wild, Wild Life'.

1990

RAYMOND CARVER

And did you get what
you wanted from this life, even so?
I did.

And what did you want?
To call myself beloved, to feel myself
beloved on the earth.

One Sunday last November, in some suitably 'high tacky' club in London, a bunch of us read out pieces for, and by, and in memory of, Raymond Carver. At one moment I looked along my row and the truth is we were all blubbering away, or close to it, anyhow, except for Ray's widow, the poet Tess Gallagher, who loved him most and who reminded me then of my grandmother refusing tears after my grandfather died. Tess gave out an iron serenity and even a kind of joy, and it's there again in *A New Path to the Waterfall*, their last book, in her beautiful, scrupulous, unflinching introduction and in his own last poems.

> *I'm a lucky man.*
> *I've had ten years longer than I or anyone*
> *expected. Pure gravy. And don't forget it.*

It's a hard fate to beat the booze and then lose out, a decade later, to the cigarettes, but then again ten years of good and plenteous work, ten years of feeling yourself beloved on the earth, that's more than most of us get, more, even, than we learn to expect. Raymond Carver was a great writer and, as *A New Path to the Waterfall* tells us he knew, a pretty lucky man.

'Memory doesn't care where it lives,' Carver writes. The memory of a slim, gay youth as a débutante who ran off to the Folies Bergères can survive in the dirty, 300-pound body of a dying baglady. The memory of old wretchedness and ruined love can haunt a happy man. Ray never stopped

340

writing about that old wretchedness, that ruined love, his first marriage. Manic calls on an answering machine, sudden beatings on an aeroplane, the loss of trust in the idea of love itself, the money problems, the terrible relationships with the children ('Oh, son, in those days I wanted you dead/a hundred—no, a thousand—different times'): this old violence, as much as the late serenity, creates the distinctive Carver voice, and universe. There's no censorship in Carver, which can lay him open to the charge of writing 'list poetry', but which recognizes, too, the dark and cluttered actuality of the heart. He is a poet of inclusion, of capaciousness:

> *The faint sound of rock and roll,*
> *The red Ferrari in my head,*
> *The woman bumping*
> *Drunkenly around in the kitchen . . .*
> *Put it all in,*
> *Make use.*

Scattered through this book are passages of Chekhov laid out as verse. The success of these arrangements guides us to see that in Carver's work, too, even the most narrative and 'prosaic' of his poems, even the ones that look most like chopped-up stories, gain added resonance from their form. 'Suspenders', which describes a nightmarish childhood moment, would 'work' as prose, but would lose its formal, distanced air, which seems almost like a truce, like the quiet that settles on the quarrelling family in the poem, the 'quiet that comes to a house/where nobody can sleep'.

In two consecutive poems, 'Miracle', the one about the beating he suffers on the aeroplane at the hands of his first wife, and 'My Wife', in which she has left him, we find the idea of having to 'account for' one's life: 'It's now/they have to account for, the blood/on his collar, the dark smudge of it/staining her cuff'; 'She left behind two nylon stockings, and/a hairbrush overlooked behind the bed . . . It is only the bed/that seems strange and impossible to account for.' The phrase contains both the idea of narration and that of balance sheets, and many of Carver's poems seem to use narration as a process of arriving at a profit-and-loss understanding of life, complete with bottom line.

The bottom line, for Ray, was lung cancer. The last group of poems in this volume, poems strong enough to turn inevitable death into art, have a simple, declaratory honesty that makes them almost unbearable to read. This is the beginning of 'What the Doctor Said':

> *He said it doesn't look good*
> *he said it looks bad in fact real bad*
> *he said I counted thirty-two of them on*
>   *one lung before*
> *I quit counting them*

And the ending is, if anything, even more shocking: 'I jumped up and shook hands with this man who'd just given me/something no one else on earth had ever given me/I may even have thanked him habit being so strong.'

But in writing the story of his death Raymond Carver also wrote the story of his love. There is a poem about getting married, Tess and Ray's Reno wedding, a wedding in that town of divorcees and gamblers, 'as if we'd found an answer to/that question of what's left/when there's no more hope.' There is a poem which sets love explicitly against death: 'Saying it then, against/what comes: *wife*, while I can, while my breath, each hurried petal/can still find her'. And there are poems of farewell, of which at least one, 'No Need', is a great poem, of a perfection that makes me unwilling to quote. Read it. Read everything Raymond Carver wrote. His death is hard to accept, but at least he lived.

1989

ISAAC BASHEVIS SINGER

In a writer who has just been made painfully aware of the extreme intolerance of some members of his own religious tradition, the easy irreverence with which Isaac Bashevis Singer continues to treat the great subjects of God and the Devil arouses a kind of envy: no fundamentalists are after *him*, no government has banned *his* book for blasphemy. Look at what the fellow gets away with! This, for instance, in the brief Author's Note with which he prefaces his new collection of stories: 'Art . . . can also in its small way attempt to mend the mistakes of the eternal builder in whose image man was created.' God's mistakes? That's dirty talk.

Nor is Singer's version of Satan by any means all bad. (Religious or not, he seems like many writers, from Milton onwards, to be somewhat 'of the devil's party'.) In the title story of this superb collection, 'The Death of Methuselah', the 969-year-old Methuselah is taken on a visit to Hell, 'Cain's city', and finds that it has its positive side: 'Satan and his brother Asmodeus are gods of passion, and so is their spouse, the goddess Lilith. They enjoy themselves and allow others their enjoyment.' While, at the other end of the book, a certain Kaddish, 'The Jew from Babylon', who has spent his life casting out demons, is captured by them at the moment of his death and borne off to the depths, where he actually gets to marry Lilith, the 'Queen of the Abyss'.

God's work and the Devil's, Singer suggests here, aren't all that far apart. Gehenna itself, in the comic parable 'Sabbath in Gehenna', is a distinctly worldly spot, in which the condemned of the earth talk about demanding improvements in their condition, dream of revolution, contemplate starting a magazine. ('When you sign a petition the angels throw it away . . . But a magazine they would read. The righteous in paradise expire from boredom.') There is even a 'liberal group among the angels' who want the condemned to have weekends off and a week's vacation in the World of Illusions.

Singer has obviously not heard that the smart money now considers this type of magic realism to be yesterday's horse. This, too, is fortunate, both for him and for us, because *The Death of Methuselah* is the most sheerly enjoyable book I've read all year, full of wisdom, history and wit. In the majority of the stories, a version of the author appears not as the story-teller but as the recipient of stories; these are tales compulsively told by their characters, a gallery of human beings for whom the act of story-telling is akin to that of coming-to-be. They talk that they might exist.

The frustrated painter Max Stein confesses his penchant (shared, one gathers from elsewhere, by George Bernard Shaw) for becoming a 'house friend', the 'other man' in a *ménage à trois*. Prisoners in jail tell each other the story of another triangle that goes murderously wrong on a boat to America, and at the end 'burst into the hilarious laughter of those who have nothing left to lose'; for them the story of the misfortunes of others is a way of briefly, bleakly, cheering themselves up. On a steamer to South America, a chance acquaintance tells the 'author' the tale of how an accidental glimpse of his fiancée kissing another man poisoned the rest of his life. This last story, 'A Peephole in the Gate', is to my mind the very finest in this fine collection.

What happens between men and women in this book is, mostly, trouble. The men cheat but cannot stand it if they think the women are doing the same; the very women with whom they cheat destroy their faith in womankind as a whole; although their own actions do not, naturally, make them think any the worse of their own sex. Jealousy, treachery, abandonment, cuckoldry: all human life is here. In one beautiful story, a woman's life is ruined by the discovery, after her marriage, that her husband has no sense of humour. In another, a certain Zeinvel, who is a frequenter of whorehouses, rediscovers his old friend Shmerl (who isn't), only to find that Shmerl's perfect and demure wife was once the 'most salacious of strumpets'. Heartbreakingly, Zeinvel is obliged to leave his friend for ever rather than tell him the truth, condemned by friendship to the tedium and loneliness of his paltry life.

Many of these stories are structures like old-fashioned fables, even down to the capsule of wisdom at the end: 'A day after the wedding both sides begin to search, the husband as well as the wife.' 'Of one thing I'm convinced—that here on earth truth and justice are for ever and absolutely beyond our grasp.' And in many of them there is trouble between Man and God as well as men and women; but behind the trouble there is a mischievous serenity, a disenchanted joy in life that compensates for all the difficulties life creates. This is an irresistible book.

1988

PHILIP ROTH

In Borges's story 'The Garden of Forking Paths', the garden turns out to be a fantastic and impossible novel by a certain Ts'ui Pen in which the characters live out all their possible lives: 'In all fiction, when a man is faced with alternatives he chooses one at the expense of the others. In the almost unfathomable Ts'ui Pen, he chooses—simultaneously—all of them. He thus *creates* various futures, various times which start others that will in their turn branch out and bifurcate . . . The hero dies in the third chapter, while in the fourth he is alive.' Like the fictional Ts'ui Pen, the real—or perhaps 'real'—Philip Roth has long been the creator of counterlives: Portnoy, Tarnopol, Kepesh, Zuckerman. He is accordingly well aware that his readers will approach his autobiography—his 'novelist's autobiography'—with a measure of suspicion. That he has called the book *The Facts* is no more than his way of upping the ante. Facts are slippery creatures, as we know, and Rothian facts are likely to be more slippery than most.

The Facts is, in fact, addressed not to us, the readers, but to the fictional Nathan Zuckerman, Roth's long-serving counterself. Apart from this, however, it begins factually enough: 'I will tell you that in the spring of 1987, at the height of a ten-year period of creativity, what was to have been minor surgery turned into a prolonged physical ordeal that led to an extreme depression that carried me right to the edge of emotional and mental dissolution.' After the crack-up, Roth began to 'render experience untransformed' so that he could 'retrieve my vitality, transform myself into *myself*'; or, perhaps, began to be reborn, like his characters, 'like you, Zuckerman, who are reborn in *The Counterlife* through your English wife, like your brother Henry, who seeks rebirth in Israel with his West Bank fundamentalists.' The book he gives us is much more than mere therapy, however. It's a vivid and often touching account of a writer's beginnings, which deserves a place beside Eudora Welty's recent, marvellously evocative book on the same theme.

Two passages are particularly striking. One is Roth's account of how, after the publication of *Goodbye, Columbus*, he was accused of being anti-Semitic, a self-hating Jew, and how, at a conference at Yeshiva University in New York, he 'realized that I was not just opposed but hated.' His responses to being so vilified have been—if I may be forgiven a personal note—very moving, even helpful, to this similarly beleaguered writer. I was able to recognize in myself the curious lethargy, the soporific torpor that overcomes Roth while he is under attack; to recognize, too, the stupid, humiliated rage that leads him to cry: 'I'll never write about Jews again!' And when the anger passes, and he understands that 'the most bruising public exchange of my life constituted not the end of my imagination's involvement with the Jews, let alone an excommunication, but the real beginning of my thralldom . . . This group whose embrace once had offered me so much security was itself fanatically insecure. My humiliation . . . was the luckiest break I could have had. I was branded'—then, too, he seems to speak directly, profoundly, not only to, but *for*, me.

The second passage is the one about his first, terrible marriage to Josie, or possibly 'Josie', who came close to destroying him, he tells us, and whose faking of a pregnancy to force him into wedlock he used unchanged in *My Life as a Man*. Josie is the one real monster in this book, the one 'character' for whom Roth feels the kind of anger that has motivated so much of his best work. So she is not only a monster, but the book's most unforgettable character.

It's true, though, that you begin to feel a little uneasy about Roth's philippic against his first wife, who is dead, after all, killed in a motor accident and unable to defend herself against his portrait of her. And were it not for Roth's last and best counterpunch, these doubts could have been substantial enough to undermine the book.

The stroke that saves it is Roth's decision to hand *The Facts* over to Nathan Zuckerman, whose reply to his author is

347

brilliant and savage. Roth has made himself and his family too nice, and as for Josie, she must have been 'both better and worse' than Roth allows: his true equal. Zuckerman, Roth's male other, recognizes in Josie his female counterpart. As for the book itself, 'Don't publish,' Zuckerman advises. The autobiography doesn't explain the most important things: the rage, and the work. Zuckerman and his English wife Maria need Roth to go on giving *them* life (even though they are filled with trepidation at what might lie in store for them); Roth's flirtation with 'real life' won't do.

As for the reader (this one, anyhow) he ends up voting for the Zuckerman version, but it's a close-run thing. As Maria says of Roth: 'The only person capable of commenting on his life is his imagination. Because the inhibition is just too tremendous in this form . . . He's not telling the truth.' *The Truth*, however, would probably have been less interesting than *The Facts*.

1989

SAUL BELLOW

Corde, the Chicagoan dean of journalism whose winter of discontent is the matter of *The Dean's December* by Saul Bellow, is in part the Dangling Man reincarnated. For much of the book he hangs about while various nooses tighten around his neck. (His name is surely no random choice.) Corde has accompanied his wife Minna, a distinguished astronomer and a defector, back to Bucharest to be present beside the deathbed of her mother Valeria. There isn't much he can do. 'Language was a problem.' Valeria, the fallen matriarch, is in the State hospital. Difficulties are being made to prevent her family from seeing her. Corde helps his wife and her aunt struggle with the system, but his efforts don't do much good. Most of the time he is left to his own devices, observing, thinking, worrying, remembering. And Romania, a precisely, almost lyrically described place of pollarded trees and informing concierges, comes to seem more like a projection of Corde's inner anguishes than a 'real' country; a grey, repressive Romania of the mind, in which the State sets 'the pain levels' for all its citizens.

Back in Chicago, a murder trial is taking place. Two blacks are accused of having killed one of Corde's students. Corde is bound up in the trial; he has had a hand in bringing the defendants to court, and is being attacked and vilified as a result. He has recently written a series of articles about Chicago. These pieces have made many powerful people angry, and embarrassed the college whose dean he is. Dangling in Romania, Corde awaits the result in the case, which is also, metaphorically, a case in which he is the accused.

This is an extraordinary book in that almost all its action takes place off-stage. 'Of course America is where the real action is,' says Corde's boyhood friend, Dewey Spangler, now a big-time Lippmanesque journalist whom Corde runs into in Bucharest. 'This is terrible news to have to tell humankind, but what else is there to say?' Corde's American life unfolds in the form of recollections, conversations, flashbacks, letters, rumours. Even in Romania, the matriarch Valeria must do her dying in the wings; the novel is only permitted to visit her a couple of times. This curious technique has a purpose. It clears the centre of the stage for Corde's inner monologue; and it is Corde's mind, agitated, relentlessly probing, analysing, thinking the world into being, that dominates the novel. Mere events become aspects of perception. It's impossible to overstate the energetic brilliance with which Bellow invests the world-according-to-Corde. This is an astoundingly well-written book.

Corde ranges over many different themes. And at first the selection seems almost arbitrary: astronomy (Minna), race, Chicago, communism, journalism, humanism, prison conditions, motherhood, even environmentalism, in the form of the scientist Peech who believes the world's ills are caused by the build-up of lead in the atmosphere—apocalypse caused by 'chronic lead insult'. But then you see how intricately Bellow has worked to shape these elements into an artistic whole. There are parallels, connections everywhere. Apparently 'lead insult' was also responsible for the fall of the Roman Empire, when lead was used to adulterate wines; and we are now in Romania, and lead is described as 'the Stalin of the metals' . . . And many more elegant correspondences are revealed: Minna's stars are the exalted opposites of the depths of the Chicago jails; Dewey Spangler's column about Corde, which costs him his job, is the echo of childhood letters which also got Corde into deep trouble; and the novel's many women, both American and Romanian, are connected and contrasted in endlessly subtle ways. *The Dean's December* seeks to be nothing less than a redescription, free from jargon, of received ideas and the whole accumulated detritus of the age, of Western civilization itself: the whole shooting-match, the works. It is a thrillingly ambitious book.

Never mind that it doesn't quite achieve its impossible aim. That its structure sometimes seems too ponderous and at others too shadowy. Never mind that Bellow's supreme gift, that of investing his fiction with the absolute authority of reality, poses its own problems: is the lead insult theory 'really' true? Haven't the dice been loaded too heavily against the novel's blacks? Should an allegory about the fall of the new Romes (Eastern and Western) be so magnificently disguised as naturalism?

This remains a pugnacious, feisty, quarrelsome, fierce book. It is a book to fight with, to be infuriated by; but it is also a book that will create in its readers the kind of passionate excitement and involvement that only real art can inspire. Like his dean, Bellow looks up to the stars with awe; but he knows the stars are not his job. His place, and his subject, is the earth.

1982

THOMAS PYNCHON

So, he's back, and the question that occurs to you on finishing *Vineland* is, what took him so long? Because this doesn't feel like a book written to break a block, it isn't congested or stop-start or stiff, matter of fact it's free-flowing and light and funny and maybe the most readily accessible piece of writing the old Invisible Man ever came up with. It is also not the book we thought Thomas Pynchon was writing. We heard he was doing something about Lewis and Clark? Mason and Dixon? A Japanese science fiction novel? And one spring in London a magazine announced the publication of a 900-page Pynchon megabook about the American Civil War, published in true Pynchonian style by a small press nobody ever heard of, and I was halfway to the door before I remembered what date it was, April the first, ho ho ho. What happened to those spectral books? Did they never exist? Are we about to get a great rush of Pynchon novels? The answer is blowin' in the wind.

Because one thing that has not changed about Mr P. is his love of mystification. The secrecy surrounding the publication of this book—his first novel since *Gravity's Rainbow* in 1973—has been, let's face it, ridiculous. I mean, as one of his characters might put it, *rilly*. So he wants a private life and no photographs and nobody to know his home address, I can dig it, I can relate to that (but, like, he should try it when it's compulsory instead of a free-choice option). But for his publishers to withhold copies and give critics maybe a *week* to deal with what took him almost two decades, now, that's truly weird, bad craziness, give it up.

Other things, too, have remained constant in the Pynchonian universe, where these are days of miracle and wonder, like *Doonesbury* written by Duke instead of Garry Trudeau, and the paranoia runs high, because behind the heavy scenes and bad trips and Karmic Adjustments move the shadowy invisible forces, the true Masters of the Universe, 'the unrelenting forces that leaned ever after . . . into Time's wind, impassive in pursuit, usually gaining, the faceless predators [who] had simply persisted, stone-humorless, beyond cause or effect, rejecting all attempts to bargain or accommodate, following through pools of night where nothing else moved wrongs forgotten by all but the direly possessed, continuing as a body to refuse to be bought off for any but the full price, which they had never named.'

That's what we're up against, folks, and what Mr Pynchon used to set against it in the old days was Entropy, seen as a slow, debauched, never-ending party, a perpetual coming-down, shapeless and meaningless and therefore unshaped and uncontrolled: freedom is chaos, he told us, but so is destruction, and that's the high-wire, walk it if you can. And now here we are in *Vineland*, and the entropy's still flowing, but there's something new to report, some faint possibility of redemption, some fleeting hints of happiness and grace; Thomas Pynchon, like Paul Simon's girl in New York City who calls herself the Human Trampoline, bouncing into Graceland.

It's 1984 in Vineland County, Northern California. Dates really matter in this book. Even the movies come with dates attached, e.g., *Return of the Jedi* (1983), *Friday the 13th* (1980) ('Everybody was Jason that year'), *Gidget Goes Hawaiian* (1961), *Godzilla, King of the Monsters* (1956): we're talking mass culture here, and mall culture, too, because this is a 1984 flowing with designer seltzer by Alaïa and Blass and Yves, and the malls have names like Noir Center (as in film noir) and the mall rats have names like Ché. And in this 1984 that Orwell could never have imagined the skies contain marauders who can remove people from commercial airlines in mid-air, and a research lab belonging to a 'shadowy world conglomerate' named Chipco can be stomped into Totality, flattened beneath a gigantic and inexplicable animal footprint, size 20,000 or thereabouts. This 1984 is also Ronald Reagan's re-election year, and that, for all the left-over hippies and sixties activists and survivors and casualties, could mean it's time for the 'last roundup'.

Listen closely now: Zoyd Wheeler, father of beautiful

teenage Prairie, whose mother Frenesi Gates went off with arch-baddie Brock Vond, Federal Prosecutor and psychopath, collects mental disability cheques from the State by jumping through plate-glass windows once a year. The novel begins with such a jump, and thereafter fragments into a myriad different narrative shards (but, at the end, the pieces all leap off the floor and fit miraculously together, as if a film were being run backwards). Prairie is obsessed with her vanished mother, and so is everyone else in the novel: so is Zoyd, so is Brock Vond who was her lover and who turned her from a radical film-maker, the child of a blacklist-and-Wobbly family, into an FBI sting specialist, turned her towards her own dark side. Frenesi, meanwhile, is out of sight, having been axed by Reaganomics from the slashed FBI budget, so that at the centre of this novel by the master of vanishing acts is a largely invisible woman, whom we learn through the eyes of others.

Now then: Vond appears to be after Prairie, maybe to use her against Frenesi, so Zoyd, as he dives for cover, sends her into hiding as well. Prairie's odyssey takes her closer and closer to Frenesi, by way of a band called Billy Barf and the Vomitones, whom she follows to a Mob wedding where she meets her mother's old friend, the Ninjette Darryl Louise (DL) Chastain, who was once obliged, by the Mob boss Ralph Wayvone, to try and assassinate Brock Vond by using, during the sexual act, the Ninja Death Touch known as the Vibrating Palm, which its victims never feel and which kills them twelve months later, while the killer is having lunch with the Police Chief—except that Vond, skilled in eluding Death ('He's the Road-runner,' says Wayvone, admiringly) manages to send along, in his place, the Japanese private eye Takeshi Fumimota, who gets the Vibrating Palm by mistake; and as if that weren't enough trouble for Takeshi, he's also being chased by the same malign forces as arranged for the Chipco stomping, which he investigated.

And, anyhow, through DL and Takeshi, Prairie gets to find the doors to her mother's past, on computer records and film archives and in the memory of Frenesi's old friends, and we reach the story's dark heart, namely the events that took place in the 1960s at Trasero County's College of the Surf, which renamed itself after the fashion of those loon-panted days the People's Republic of Rock 'n' Roll; and we hear, as Prairie hears it, how her mother betrayed the leader of this little revolution, who rejoiced in the name of Weed Atman, and who now, after death, still roams the forests of Northern California as a Thanatoid, a member of the undead, unable to find peace . . . and eventually Prairie's search for Frenesi, and Brock's search for Prairie and Frenesi which takes him, along with a huge strike force, to Vineland, comes to a climax complete with helicopters and Thanatoids and family reunions and an old woman and an old man who can remove your bones and leave the rest of you alive. You get the picture.

It either grabs you or it doesn't, I guess; it grabbed me. I laughed, many times, out loud, often at Pynchon's absurdly brilliant way with names (a manufacturer of microchip musical gimmickry is called Tokkata & Fuji, which to my mind is as funny as the German town in *Gravity's Rainbow* named Bad Karma); and at the little songs with which I'm happy to report he's still littering his texts, high points of this particular set being the Desi Arnaz-style croon, 'Es posible', and Billy Barf's 'three-note blues', 'I'm a Cop':

> *Fuck you, mister,*
> *Fuck your sister,*
> *Fuck your brother,*
> *Fuck your mother,*
> *Fuck your pop—*
> *Hey! I'm a cop!*

There is enough in *Vineland* to obsess the true, mainlining Pynchomane for a goodly time. One could consider, for example, the significance of the letter *V* in Pynchon's *œuvre*; his novel *V* was actually V-shaped, two narratives zeroing in on a point, and *Gravity's Rainbow*, being the flight path of a V-2 rocket, followed a deadly parabola which could also be described as an inverted V; and here's the letter again, *what does it mean*, with all the death-imagery in this novel, with its use of old Amerindian death-myths: are we being told that America, 1984, is in fact the land of the dead, V-land, the universe beyond the zero? And one could do a number of further riffs on the more allegorical of the names, e.g., Weed = marijuana + Atman = soul, and hey, 'Frenesi' turns out to be an anagram of Free + Sin, the two sides of her nature, light and dark, just as the hero of *Gravity's Rainbow*, Tyrone Slothrop, could be made to reveal his essence anagrammatically, turning into 'Sloth or Entropy'; sure, it's still working, that old anagrammar. 'Frenesi' more conventionally derives from the Old French *frenesie*, meaning frenzy or madness. Frenesi Gates: insanity's entrance, derangement's doorway.

But what is perhaps most interesting, finally, about Pynchon's novel is what is different about it. What is new here is the willingness with which Pynchon addresses, directly, the political development of the United States, and the slow (but not total) steamrollering of a radical tradition many generations and decades older than flower-power. There is a marvellously telling moment when Brock Vond's brainchild, his school for subversion in which lefties are re-educated and turned into tools of the State, is closed down because in Reagan's America the young think like that *to begin with*, they don't need re-education.

We have before us, at the end of the Greed Decade, that rarest of birds: a major political novel about what America has been doing to itself, to its children, all these many years. And as Thomas Pynchon turns his attention to the nightmares of the present rather than the past, his touch becomes lighter, funnier, more deadly. And most satisfying of all is that aforementioned hint of redemption, because this time entropy is not the only counterweight to power; community, it is suggested, might be another; and individuality; and family. These are the values the Nixon–Reagan era stole from the sixties and warped, aiming them back at America as weapons of control. They are values which *Vineland* seeks to recapture, by remembering what they meant before the dirt got thrown all over them, by recalling the beauty of Frenesi Gates before she turned.

Thomas Pynchon is no sentimentalist, however, and the balance between light and dark is expertly held throughout this novel, so that we remain uncertain until the final pages as to which will prevail, hippie heaven or Federal nemesis; and are left, at the last, with an image of such shockingly apt moral ambiguity that it would be quite wrong to reveal it here.

Vineland, Mr Pynchon's mythical piece of Northern California, is of course also 'Vinland', the country discovered by the Viking Leif Erikson long before Columbus, 'Vineland the Good'; that is to say, this crazed patch of California stands for America itself. And it is here, to Vineland, that one of America's great writers has, after long wanderings down his uncharted roads, come triumphantly home.

1990

KURT VONNEGUT

In Kurt Vonnegut's most famous novel, *Slaughterhouse 5*, the hero Billy Pilgrim ends up as an exhibit in a zoo on the planet Tralfamadore, where his couplings with a famous movie star are found mildly diverting. In *The Sirens of Titan*, the entire course of human history is subverted by a Tralfamadorean envoy whose spaceship has broken down on the moon. The Great Wall of China, the Pyramids, Stonehenge turn out to be his demands for spare parts. The envoy is carrying a message from Tralfamadore to another super-advanced species across the galaxy. This message is deemed important enough to justify manipulating thousands of years of human development.

The message reads: 'Hello.'

Vonnegut's readers have long been aware that the view from Tralfamadore is, to say the least, unflattering. And these days, Vonnegut's own attitude to *homo sapiens* is increasingly Tralfamadorean. Humankind, as readers of *Hocus Pocus* are frequently informed, is a pretty poor species, not nearly as bright as it thinks it is, and a lot more cruel. American humankind is probably even worse. Kurt Vonnegut's response is a sort of hip, cynical world-weariness, his tone halfway between jeremiad and shrug. He is the only important and original writer in the world whose entire *œuvre* can be summed up in three words: 'So it goes.'

In *Hocus Pocus*, Vonnegut's old weakness for so-it-goes catch-phrases has infected many of his characters, whose responses to life on the planet have shrunk alarmingly. One character faces everything in life, love, war and death by saying, 'I had to laugh like hell.' Another likes to end sentences by asking, 'So what, so what?' A black convict's defining phrase is harsher: 'See the Nigger fly the airplane.' And so on. The entire novel, its whole web of event and symbol, can be explained by two words, both place-names.

'America.' 'Vietnam.'

The narrator, Eugene Debs Hartke, named after an old American socialist politician, is a Vietnam veteran and the experience has damaged his soul, of course. Lest we miss this, one of his lovers suggests that he should tell any woman fool enough to fall in love with him, 'Welcome to Vietnam.' He is concerned to enumerate (1) the women he has slept with, and (2) the Vietnamese he has killed. These two numbers will turn out to be (you'll never guess) the same number.

So it goes.

Coming home from Vietnam is compared to an illicit visit to Bloomingdale's department store in New York City. The American presence in Vietnam is compared to the present-day Japanese 'invasion' of the American economy. Dollars are compared to Vietnamese corpses. These comparisons tell us nothing much about Vietnam, Bloomingdale's, the Japanese or money. They are supposed to tell us that human beings/Americans are beyond hope and tragedy, washed up, sunk in a kind of moral entropy. What they actually tell us, alas, is that Kurt Vonnegut is getting a little tired.

Eugene Debs Hartke teaches at a college for the educationally subnormal children of the economically super-affluent. What does this college symbolize?

'America.'

Across the lake is the Athena 'correctional facility', or nick, full of underprivileged black prisoners who escape, name themselves Freedom Fighters, and attack the college. What do the prisoners represent, and what is the allegorical meaning of their futile little break-out?

'Vietnam.' 'The Vietnam War.'

The convicts are only allowed to watch out-of-date television programmes. They can watch anything as long as it isn't relevant to their lives. (In this case, the convicts mean 'America'.) There is a computer game named GRIOT, a word for oral storyteller, which predicts human lives. Something is being said, have no doubt, about the Influence of Computers in America. And Tralfamadore is here, too, appearing in a story by an anonymous science-fiction writer, published in a girlie magazine. Once again, human history is being subverted, this time for the benefit of the planet's germs, which are more valuable to the aliens than the human race. It makes a person feel pretty darn small.

And so on.

The theme of this novel is damage, human damage, social damage, the awful damage of war, but it is itself damaged by a loss of the gaiety, the brilliant linguistic invention and intellectual sprightliness that used to be the upside of Vonnegut's deep pessimism. This is the writer who thought up *ice-nine*, the substance that froze all the water on earth in *Cat's Cradle*. This is the creator of Kilgore Trout, the science-fiction genius who, in *Hocus Pocus*, no longer merits a name, but who once told us unforgettable fables, such as the one in which God apologizes to the reader for starting an experiment that went wrong. The experiment was the Universe. The purpose of the experiment was to see how free will worked. So everything in the Universe is a machine, except for one being with free will. That being is the reader of the story. This is what God has to say to the reader: 'Sorry.'

That old hocus-pocus, language, just isn't working in this novel. To read it is to experience the sad pleasure of hearing a favourite voice trying to sing in its old, swooping, magical manner, occasionally reminding one of its old glories, but revealing, mostly, its decline. Only one long sequence—when Eugene Debs Hartke is fired from his teaching job because he has been uttering un-American thoughts, suggesting, for example, that 'the two principal currencies of the world were the Yen and fellatio', and thus allegedly undermining the confidence of his damaged students, who stand, don't forget, for America—has the authentic, sharp, funny Vonnegut touch. I wish there were more such scenes.

Many years ago, Kurt Vonnegut asked me if I was serious about writing. I said I was. He then said, if I remember correctly, that there was trouble ahead, that one day I would not have a book to write and I would still have to write a book.

It was a sad, and saddening, remark, because I don't think, though I may be wrong, that it was really about me.

PS: There's a little maths test at the end of *Hocus Pocus*, designed to establish whether or not the reader has been paying attention. By adding and subtracting various dates and figures scattered through the text, we arrive at the number of Hartke's lovers and victims.

If I have been paying attention properly, the number is 82. 'So what, so what?'

1990

GRACE PALEY

In the Art Foods Deli frequented by Grace Paley's character Faith, the sandwiches are named after local residents. 'Selena and Max are just divorced, but their sandwich will probably go on for another few years.' From another story, we learn that at the old people's home where Faith's redoubtable father Mr Darwin lives (the Children of Judea, Home for the Golden Ages, Coney Island Branch), the benches around the trees have been similarly named. 'That bench there, my favorite, is named Jerome (Jerry) Katzoff, six years old,' Mr Darwin says. 'It's a terrible thing to die young. Still, it saves a lot of time.'

The passing away of things is very much the theme of Grace Paley's collection *Later the Same Day*. Marriages like that of Selena and Max Retelof; old loves; the dream of Vicente who wanted to be a doctor and was persuaded to be an engineer; parents; old hopes. It is a book full of endings, endings faced with the firm, mild, rueful honesty that makes Grace Paley special. She writes as well of the death of a friend, Selena Retelof, whose ending is treated with a sort of passionate scrupulousness, as she does about the ridiculous immortality of Selena's sandwich. It is good to hear again the voice of this most sparing of writers (just three volumes of stories in a quarter-century), a voice as determined as ever to call things by their true names.

In *Later the Same Day*, Grace Paley has become, if anything, even more sparing, her stories more concentrated, purer. (She has described her working method as being one of continual revising and 'taking out the lies'.) There are a number of examples of the most technically demanding of all short fictions, the Very Very Short Story. The title pages of these stories consume as much paper as the texts. And yet these brief, eyeblink tales reveal fully formed worlds, full-blown tragedies of love, waste and death.

There is a fine, small parable of America in the story of

George, the man who thought he could improve the design of the pinball machine. And another, female immigrant (something very Russian hovers behind much of this work) is portrayed in all the unspoken anguish of one whose lover died young, in the VVSS with the roguishly Very Long Title, 'In This Country, But in Another Language, My Aunt Refuses to Marry the Men Everyone Wants Her To'.

Grace Paley has always been good at one-liners. There's a fine joke in the wonderful 'Dreamer in a Dead Language' about an old Jew trying to flee Germany in 1939. He points to country after country on the travel agent's globe and is told they're all full up. 'He pushes the globe away, disgusted. But he got hope. He says, So this one is used up, Herr Agent. Listen—you got another one?' But she is not to be put down as a merely wry, shoulder-shrugging, worldly-wise and world-weary lady. These stories, brief and extended, burn with a high-energy commitment to the great work of being alive.

They are stories full of the stories we all tell and live by, tall stories as well as short. They are stories whose characters can enter into dispute with the author, or at least her alter ego, most notably at the very end of the book, when the lesbian Cassie (in 'Listening') points out that Faith never tells *her* story. 'It's been women and men, women and men, fucking, fucking. Goddamnit, where is my woman and woman, woman-loving life in all this?' Faith, admitting her fault, asks for forgiveness, and receives a sharp answer. '"You are my friend, I know that, Faith, but I promise you, I won't forgive you," she said. "From now on, I'll watch you like a hawk. I do not forgive you."'

And they are stories in which the whole of a world, its children, its dead, its furniture, its snacks, is lovingly and unsentimentally named. Named, and not forgiven.

1985

TRAVELS WITH A GOLDEN ASS

There's a supernova exploding on the cover of *Time*.
NASA wants to put a man on Mars (no, don't mention
the 'Challenger' shuttle). The President is on TV,
apologizing, forgetting, having to correct himself the next
day. *Polyps for Reagan*, the graffiti say.

Representative Mario Biaggi of the Bronx and Meade H.
Esposito, once leader of Brooklyn's Democrats, are being
indicted for bribery, fraud and conspiracy. Bess Myerson,
1946's Miss America and New York's cultural affairs
commissioner, resigns after reports of serious misconduct.
The CIA has given the Contras ground plans, blueprints and
maps of key Nicaraguan installations, to help them with their
terrorist programme.

Up in his Prayer Tower in Tulsa, the evangelist Oral
Roberts threatens that God will 'recall' him unless his fans
cough up $8 million. (The fans come up with the cash.) In
New York, it's St Patrick's Day, so the entire city is dressed in
green and can be found throwing up all over Fifth Avenue.
California, of course, has its own religions. The Committee for
Self-Esteem has just held its first meeting. I thought Garry
Trudeau had made it up, but there it actually is, publicly
funded and everything, seeking to cure drug addiction, sex-
crimes and so forth by making people feel better about
themselves.

This is Rome near the end of its power, a famous New
York magazine editor tells me. Western civilization hasn't
long to go. Islam is coming, the Chinese, the darkness. We may
as well celebrate the brightness that we were. Improbable as
this sounds to an outsider, for whom the power of the United
States is the most glaring aspect of the place, many Americans
imagine themselves to be living in their twilight's last
gleaming.

It makes them act strangely. 'Now that I like you,' I am
informed by one Manhattan intellectual, 'I can tell you I

thought I wouldn't. I didn't think I could like a Muslim.' And it makes them touchy. 'Salman, as I grow older, I love this country more and more, and I don't like to hear it criticized.'

During my fortnight in the US (Pittsburgh, New York, San Francisco), I pass much time in the excellent company of a Moroccan writer of the second century AD, Lucius Apuleius, a colonial of the old Roman Empire, and I find that his portrait of that Roman world does indeed begin to look rather like contemporary America, but not quite in the way the editor meant.

The narrator of *The Golden Ass**, also named Lucius, is transformed by witchcraft into the tale's eponymous donkey, and his ass's-eye view of his age reveals a world of ubiquitous cynicism, great brutality, fearsome sorcery, religious cultism, banditry, murder. Friends betray friends, sisters betray sisters; corpses rise up and accuse their wives of poisoning them. There are omens and curses.

Eighteen centuries later, with a portentous supernova in the sky, cynicism seeps all the way down from the White House to a Chinese cabbie, who tells me of his hatred for communism and for poor countries, which adds up to Nicaragua. 'Always the same. Poor countries make trouble for the rest of us.' Three years out of Hong Kong, he's taken to abusing Manhattan's Puerto Ricans. Doesn't he feel that such bigotry sits uneasily in the mouth of a fellow-immigrant? 'Excuse me, but these people like to steal.' The morning paper carries a story about Chinese involvement in heroin smuggling, but he's unimpressed. 'Have a nice day.'

There have been several race killings of late, blacks murdered by whites sparking revenge-murders by blacks. Meanwhile, at the UN building, there's a demonstration protesting police violence against blacks in New York City. All this is familiar to the Ass.

For sorcery, one need look no further than the mumbo-jumbo of the Star Wars schemes; cultism and Jerry Falwell are everywhere; and as for banditry, Calero and his FDN, let's call

---

The Golden Ass by Apuleius, translated by Robert Graves, Penguin, 1950.

them the 'Contrabandits', are more dangerous than anything in Apuleius's book. Now that the so-called 'moderates', Cruz and Robelo, have left the Contra leadership, certain revisionist processes have begun. Conservative columnist William Safire demands that America support Calero; while, on radio, I hear Arturo Cruz described as the 'leftist wing' of the Contra. So we can do without him, the pinko.

Pittsburgh reveals a different American malaise. It's pleasant, spacious, 'America's most livable city', a place where the main university building is actually named the Cathedral of Learning. (Inside you find representative classrooms from around the world. The English Classroom boasts desks like church pews and stained-glass windows bearing coats of arms: City of Liverpool. Jane Austen. Charles Dickens. City of Bootle. That sort of thing.)

But there's another Pittsburgh, too. Mile upon mile of defunct steelworks bear witness to the collapse of a once-great industry. Unemployment is high. Pittsburgh's super-rich, the Carnegies and Mellons, long ago ceased to depend on steel; their fortunes float, now, on the oceans of pure finance. The poor weren't so lucky, and many, I hear, now earn a crust by servicing the mansions of the rich.

In San Francisco, twenty years after flower-power, the feeling of being in a plague city is difficult to avoid. The worst thing about AIDS, I'm told, is the speed at which it mutates. The most common symptoms used to be those of pneumonia, but already that's changing. New symptoms, new strains of the plague.

Susan Sontag recently published, in the *New Yorker*, a brilliant, moving short story, 'The Way We Live Now', about living with the illness. Neither the sick man, nor the illness, is named; the story is told by a crowd of voices, the voices of the patient's friends, of his entire world, voices taking on the story from one another, often in mid-sentence, creating an unforgettable vision of the disease as a crisis in all our lives. I have read nothing about AIDS that strikes deeper than Sontag's fiction. Perhaps, then, there is still a place, even in America, for art.

The picture of America emerging from these notes is, of course, in some sense 'unfair'. What you see depends on where you look. But the Apuleian America does exist, and I make no apology for looking at it.

The trouble is, what can a poor ass do? He observes, but cannot act. When donkey-Lucius sees a band of eunuch-priests assaulting a young labourer (and I can't resist drawing a parallel here with the US aggression against Nicaragua) he tries to shout, 'Help, help! Rape, rape! Arrest these he-whores!'

'But,' writes Apuleius, 'all that came out was "He-whore", "He-whore", in fine ringing tones that would have done credit to any ass alive.'

1985

THE DIVINE SUPERMARKET

Some years ago in South India I encountered the curious and unforgettable figure of Duane Gish, an American creationist scientist whose lectures were accompanied by a jolly slide show: when a slide of a chimpanzee came up, he'd say, 'Oops, that's my grandfather.' Gish gave me the model for the character of Eugene Dumsday in *The Satanic Verses*, and also got me interested in American fundamentalism, so when he cropped up on page 198 of *The Divine Supermarket*, it was like meeting an old friend. 'If you teach young people that everything started out as hydrogen gas, they will soon conclude that their ultimate destiny is a pile of dust,' burbled Duane. Malise Ruthven heard him out, came to a fastidiously disapproving conclusion ('The trouble with Dr Gish and his kind was not just that they didn't understand science: they appeared not to understand Christianity either'), climbed into his camper and drove away.

The Gish encounter exemplifies what's best and worst about this account of a voyage across religious America, a journey to all the New Zions and Rajneeshpurams and Appalachian snake churches that make up the metaphorical shopping mall in which the American soul, like the American body (Ruthven has quite a thing going against fat people), finds itself spoiled for choice. Ruthven has certainly covered a lot of ground, and unearthed all manner of bizarre creatures in the process. Apart from Gish, there are neo-Nazis at the Church of Jesus Christ–Aryan Nations, and a Christian counsellor on a radio phone-in show who is 'stumped for advice' when a caller complains that his wife is in fact his long lost sister, and the leftover sixties figure of Love Israel who first saw Jesus on an acid trip ('the God I saw was really nice'). But inclusiveness all too often results in superficiality. We never find out what makes Duane Gish tick; there's just time for him to make his pitch, be judged by Ruthven, and then it's off to the next place. Ruthven can be breathtakingly perfunctory: *half a page* on Malcolm X? At such times, *The Divine Supermarket* reads more like a tourist guide than a travel book: a kind of Fodor's Guide to God.

Readers new to the subject will surely be impressed by the inexhaustible vitality of religion in America: 68 new sects founded in the 1950s, and no less than 184 in the 1960s. And Ruthven is a pleasantly jaunty travelling companion, erudite enough to inform us that 'we owe the word *fundamentalism* indirectly to two Los Angeles businessmen, Lyman and Milton Stewart,' who financed the distribution of three million copies of the twelve volumes of religious discussion known as *The Fundamentals*. 'The word "fundamentalist" first appeared in 1919.' He also possesses the fine, sceptical intelligence of the scholar he is: 'Any form of learning is, at heart, inimical to fundamentalist certitudes,' he writes, while, at a Baptist rally, a preacher rails against the 'higher criticism' that is growing 'like a parasite in our universities'. And he's clear about how, for the majority of believers, a religious book (in this case, the Bible) means 'not a record of spiritual truth, or even of God's revelation to mankind, but a totem or shibboleth, a flag to be waved at the forces of modernity, hated because deeply feared.'

Such clarity is to be welcomed; and yet the disappointments mount and in the end outnumber the pleasures. The book doesn't seem to know what it is. In spite of its subtitle, there isn't much of a quest for the soul here. Saul Bellow once suggested that the very success of American materialism destroyed the possibility of a genuine spiritual life for the American people; no such meditations are to be found in Ruthven's book. Nor is he, as a travel writer, in the class of Chatwin or Theroux.

He often seems dominated by a timetable; because he has friends to meet in San Francisco, or because he wants to be home for Christmas, he hurries onward. He listens to innumerable official guides at various shrines, but there are few real characters in his book: when he spends an evening with a polygamist Mormon and his three wives, he tells us nothing at all about any of them. He misses out, too, on all the big names. At Rajneeshpuram he is too late for Ma Sheela and Rajneesh. At Jerry Falwell's headquarters he fails to meet Falwell, and in Bakker territory he meets neither Jim nor Tammy. Jimmy Swaggart is seen only on TV. There's no encounter with Billy Graham, and scarcely a mention of Louis Farrakhan.

Ruthven is well aware of the linear connections between religion and totalitarianism, but *The Divine Supermarket* doesn't really get to grips with the issue of power. No mention here of book burnings (Kurt Vonnegut's *Slaughterhouse 5* is one of the titles to be incinerated in recent years) or of the close connections between religion and the political power centres. Ruthven concludes that the proliferation of religious sects in America is the 'price of peace'. But when an American President believes (as Ronald Reagan claimed to believe) that Armageddon will take place in his lifetime, then religiosity in America begins to look more warlike than peaceful.

If all nations possess a National Delusion (the French have *la gloire*, Britain has its Greatness), then the great American delusion is that the New World is Utopia, what Melville called a nation 'predestinated at creation', a land in which New Jerusalems can and should be created. The most vivid and penetrating book yet written about this is Frances Fitzgerald's brilliant *Cities on a Hill*. Fitzgerald's portraits of the empires of Rajneesh and Falwell are everything that Ruthven's are not; they have depth, detail, characterization, time for reflection and a keen political edge. By comparison, Ruthven looks naïve. Describing the neo-Nazi Christians, he announces: 'In Britain . . . these people would have been silenced by the civil law, and rightly so. Freedom of speech stops short of incitement to murder.' Which makes one wonder where he's been for the last six months. One can only hope that his next book, *A Satanic Affair*, is more carefully considered. As it's being rushed out, however, one can't help fearing that Mr Ruthven may, once again, be travelling too fast.

1989

12

NAIPAUL AMONG THE BELIEVERS

'IN GOD WE TRUST'

IN GOOD FAITH

IS NOTHING SACRED?

ONE THOUSAND DAYS IN A BALLOON

NAIPAUL AMONG THE BELIEVERS

While watching the Iranian revolution on TV in Connecticut, V. S. Naipaul had the idea of journeying to four Muslim countries—Iran, Pakistan, Malaysia, Indonesia—to write about the new Islam being born there with varying intensities of labour pain.

Among the Believers is the result. And, because Naipaul's is a formidable talent, the book is studded with good things: the surrealist humour (wholly unintentional) with which a young Malaysian fundamentalist explains to Naipaul the solemn differences, in Islam, between mandatory, encourageable, non-encourageable, forbidden and discretionary coughing; the delicately drawn portraits of Behzad, the young communist adrift in the Iran of the mullahs, and of Shafi, who dreams of a Malaysia restored, through Islam, to the waste-free simplicities of village life—but a village life purged of its 'pagan', pre-Islamic aspects; the hypocrisy of Pakistan's arch-fundamentalist Maulana Maudoodi, lifelong opponent of Western materialism, who died in a Boston hospital to which he had gone 'to look for health . . . to reap where he had not wanted his people to sow'; and above all, a devastating portrait of Khomeini's hanging judge, Ayatollah Khalkhali, joking and boasting about the killing of the Shah's prime minister, Hoveyda.

But this is no ordinary travel book: it has theses to expound. The Islamic revival, Naipaul says, is a throwback to medieval times which seeks to create 'abstract men of the faith, men who would be nothing more than the rules.' Its 'act of renunciation' of the West is a fatal flaw, because it depends on 'the alien, necessary civilization going on'—Shafi's ideal village still needs a bus, a road, machinery; and in Indonesia, Naipaul is astonished to find a photocopier in a rural Islamic school. Finally, Naipaul sees communism and Islam as 'interchangeable revolutions', both springing from hate and rage: 'Behzad the communist spoke like Khomeini', and both wished to kill people. These are powerful indictments, and there is much truth in them.

The trouble is that it's a highly selective truth, a novelist's truth masquerading as objective reality. Take Iran: no hint in these pages that in the new Islam there is a good deal more than Khomeinism, or that the mullocracy's hold on the people is actually very fragile. Naipaul never mentions the Mujahideen-e-Khalq, whose leader Rajavi is committed to a 'multi-party democratic system of government'; but the Mujahideen are certainly 'believers'. And what of (or have we forgotten him already?) the Shah of Iran? Naipaul quotes just two criticisms of him: Ayatollah Shariatmadari says, 'The Shah was bad. He had forbidden polygamy and had thereby damaged women.' And the Bombay businessman who attacks the Shah ('He drained the country of billions . . . The people of Iran felt they had lost their country') is immediately discredited by the revelation that 'he was leaving Iran, after his twenty good years under the bad Shah, and going back to Bombay.' Are these really the only Muslims Naipaul could find to speak against the Shah? Did SAVAK get rid of all the rest?

Sins of omission . . . Naipaul is so anxious to prove the existence of an Islamic stranglehold on these countries that, in the Pakistan section, there is no discussion of the army at all. And yet the view that Pakistanis have never been a mullah-dominated people, that a military dictator is currently using Islamization as a means of shoring up his unpopular regime, surely deserves a little air time. In my experience of Pakistan, it is not difficult to find people who will talk openly in these terms. Naipaul actually finds one, a jeep-driver in Kaghan who tells him: 'These maulanas are using Islam as a tool . . . They want to destroy Pakistan.' This same jeep-driver has previously mentioned that it is now harder to get passports than it was under Mr Bhutto; and Naipaul, refusing to discuss the driver's attack on the theocracy, contents himself with a cheap gibe about the passports: 'Isn't it strange that the only freedom he wants is the freedom to leave the country?' . . . attacking the poor fellow for wanting something, a passport, that Naipaul himself takes for granted. The very thing, in fact, that has made Naipaul's journey possible.

Terrible things are being done today in the name of Islam; but simplification of the issues, when it involves omitting everything that can't easily be blistered by Naipaul's famous Olympian disgust, is no help. At one point, Naipaul tells his friend Shafi: 'I think that because you travelled to America with a fixed idea, you might have missed some things.' The criticism holds good for Naipaul's own journey in the opposite direction, and makes *Among the Believers*, for all its brilliance of observation and depiction, a rather superficial book.

1981

'IN GOD WE TRUST'

We stand at a moment in history in which, as we look around the planet, it appears that God—or, rather, formal religion—has begun once again to insist on occupying a central role in public life. There could scarcely be a more appropriate time to explore the subject of the relationships between politics and religions.

I am neither a trained theologian nor a professional in politics, so I can make no claim to any expertise. However, I have found myself, in my fiction, unable to avoid political issues; the distance between individuals and affairs of State is now so small that it no longer seems possible to write novels that ignore the public sphere. Sometimes one envies Jane Austen her fine disregard for the Napoleonic Wars. Today, with the television bringing visions of the world into every home, it seems somehow false to try and shut out the noise of gunfire, screams, weeping, to stop our ears against the inexorable ticking of the doomsday clock. As for religion, my work, much of which has been concerned with India and Pakistan, has made it essential for me to confront the issue of religious faith. Even the form of my writing was affected. If one is to attempt honestly to describe reality as it is experienced by religious people, for whom God is no symbol but an everyday fact, then the conventions of what is called realism are quite inadequate. The rationalism of that form comes to seem like a judgement upon, an invalidation of, the religious faith of the characters being described. A form must be created which allows the miraculous and the mundane to co-exist at the same level—as the same order of event. I found this to be essential even though I am not, myself, a religious man.

My relationship with formal religious belief has been somewhat chequered. I was brought up in an Indian Muslim household, but while both my parents were believers neither was insistent or doctrinaire. Two or three times a year, at the big Eid festivals, I would wake up to find new clothes at the foot of my bed, dress and go with my father to the great prayer-*maidan* outside the Friday Mosque in Bombay, and rise and fall with the multitude, mumbling my way through the uncomprehended Arabic much as Catholic children do—or used to do—with Latin. The rest of the year religion took a back seat. I had a Christian ayah (nanny), for whom at Christmas we would put up a tree and sing carols about baby Jesus without feeling in the least ill-at-ease. My friends were Hindus, Sikhs, Parsis, and none of this struck me as being particularly important.

God, Satan, Paradise and Hell all vanished one day in my fifteenth year, when I quite abruptly lost my faith. I recall it vividly. I was at school in England by then. The moment of awakening happened, in fact, during a Latin lesson, and afterwards, to prove my new-found atheism, I bought myself a rather tasteless ham sandwich, and so partook for the first time of the forbidden flesh of the swine. No thunderbolt arrived to strike me down. I remember feeling that my survival confirmed the correctness of my new position. I did slightly regret the loss of Paradise, though. The Islamic heaven, at least as I had come to conceive it, had seemed very appealing to my adolescent self. I expected to be provided, for my personal pleasure, with four beautiful female spirits, or *houris*, untouched by man or djinn. The joys of the perfumed garden; it seemed a shame to have to give them up.

From that day to this, I have thought of myself as a wholly secular person, and have been drawn towards the great traditions of secular radicalism—in politics, socialism; in the arts, modernism and its offspring—that have been the driving forces behind much of the history of the twentieth century. But perhaps I write, in part, to fill up that emptied God-chamber with other dreams. Because it is, after all, a room for dreaming in.

The dream is part of our very essence. Given the gift of self-consciousness, we can dream versions of ourselves, new selves for old. Waking as well as sleeping, our response to the world is essentially *imaginative*: that is, picture-making. We live in our pictures, our ideas. I mean this literally. We first construct pictures of the world and then we step inside the frames. We come to equate the picture with the world, so that, in certain circumstances, we will even go to war because we find someone else's picture less pleasing than our own. It is tempting to say that this behaviour conforms very well to the Hindu idea of *maya*, the veil of illusion that hangs before our limited human eyes and prevents us from seeing things as they truly are—so that we mistake the veil, *maya*, for reality. Dreaming is our gift; it may also be our tragic flaw.

Whichever it be, it is unquestionably our nature, and, perhaps, our explanation. And politics and religion, both in theory and in practice, are, I would suggest, manifestations of our dreaming selves. In political thought we seek to express our dreams of improvement, of betterment, of progress—our dreams, some may feel, of dreams. We seek to give life to these grand visions, and we assume that *we can do so*; that our dreams are attainable, that the world can be made what we wish if we wish it enough, that we are capable of *making history*. Thus most political discourse, because it places the human spirit in a position of power over events, can be seen as a dream of adequacy. An optimistic dream. The great universal religions, by contrast, ask us to accept our inferiority to a non-corporeal, omnipresent, omnipotent supreme being, who is both our creator and judge. The word 'Islam' means submission, and not only Islam but Christianity and Judaism, too, classically require of believers an act of submission to the will of God. That is, religion demands that God's will, not our small vanity, must prevail over history. To make it plain, we could say that religion places human beings beneath history. In this world we are not masters, but servants; so perhaps we can see religion, in this contrast, as a dream of our inadequacy, as a vision of our lessness.

Of course this is too simple, and so, contrariwise, as Tweedledee would say, let me counter-propose that the practice and experience of politics is very largely shaped by the hard reality of limitations—boundaries in space, time, resource, will and possibility. One cannot seriously propose the 'art of the possible' as a wholly optimistic enterprise; whereas religious systems offer, in place of the earthbound limitations and imperfections of political life, the transcendent joys of faith—eternity, immortality, everlasting bliss. So in this formulation our potential seems far smaller when seen through the lens of practical politics than when observed through the glass of transcendent faith. Now it is religion that seems like the good dream, and politics the nightmare.

We are entering a tricky, contradictory zone, full of paradoxes and blind alleys. Nevertheless, let me suggest that if political thought places us in an 'adult' relation to the historical process, whereas religion obliges us to be the 'children' of a wiser God, then religion, conversely, is also capable of speaking to and arousing our sense of the marvellous, in a manner to which political language can only occasionally aspire. And then there is the matter of disappointment. Any good advertising man will tell you that a product or service must never be oversold, because to claim too much for it increases the likelihood of consumer disappointment, of what they call a 'cognitive dissonance' between what you say and how the product performs. Consumer disappointment greatly reduces the likelihood of brand loyalty. In this respect religions have the great advantage of not having their most important promise tested until after the consumer is dead; whereas the promises of politicians, of political parties and movements and theorists, go wrong while we, in growing disillusion, watch. Even those ideas which have been, for a time, the most uplifting and galvanizing, end by inducing cognitive dissonances and damaging brand loyalty. It is a disillusioned age. So it is not surprising that some of us turn back towards belief-systems which at least have never made the mistake of promising us an earthly paradise.

It is immediately necessary to make some distinctions between the West and the East, because in certain important respects the starting-points are so different. A few years ago, I came across a rather brave and also slightly ludicrous attempt at enumerating the total number of gods at present extant in India, from the most minor tree- or water-sprite to Brahma and Allah themselves. The figure arrived at was, astoundingly, 330 million, that is, roughly one god for every two and a quarter human beings. The overwhelming fact about life in India is that this vast multitude of deities co-exists in everyday life with the doubly vast multitude of people. You bump into gods in the streets. You jostle past them, you step over their sleeping forms. They take your seat in the bus. What I mean is that these gods are no abstractions. They are as real to the faithful as their families and friends. (And, since the divine population is, we can presume, reasonably stable, whereas the humans have rapidly increased in number, we can see by projecting backwards that it is only relatively recently that the human population in India overtook the supernatural one . . .) The point is that the idea of large numbers of persons going *back* towards religion is an essentially Western one. In the East, relatively few people ever left their faiths. So when we speak of a religious 'revival', a revival of 'fundamentalism' or 'communalism', we are not speaking of a religious event, as we would be if we were describing an event in a Western country. We are, in fact, speaking of a political event that is almost always nationalist in its true character.

Christianity, which arose as a fusion of Jewish monotheism and Roman universalism, was radical in matters of the spirit—offering everyone, and not just the Chosen People, the chance of salvation; but, under the influence of St Paul, it took great care to avoid political confrontations. The *render unto Caesar* formula is, obviously, significant here. Thus from the earliest times we see in Christianity a willingness to separate Church and State, and admission that such a separation is possible and maybe even desirable. In the world of Islam, no such separation has ever occurred at the level of theory. Of all the great sacred texts the Qur'an is most concerned with the law, and Islam has always remained an overtly social, organizing, political creed which, again theoretically, has something to say about every aspect of an individual life.

It is, in a way, ironic that Pauline Christianity turned away from politics towards mysticism, for, as historians such as Hyam Maccoby have recently reminded us, crucifixion was at the time of Christ a penalty reserved *exclusively* for persons found guilty of acts of political—not theological—subversion. Christ died as a political revolutionary, but was largely de-politicized and wrapped in mysteries by Paul; Muhammad has never been 'withdrawn' from the public arena in this fashion. Thus the assumptions about the inter-penetration of political and religious affairs are very different in the two spheres.

But—and it's a big 'but', which brings me back to the point I alluded to about the connections of the present-day religious 'revivals' with nationalisms of various types—we cannot discuss religion in the modern world, even in such societies as India or the Ummah-Islam, as if it still operated in the world just as it did in the age before the rise of the nation-state. Then, as Benedict Anderson tells us in his book, *Imagined Communities: Reflections on the Origin and Spread of Nationalism*, Christendom and Islam were communities of this 'imagined' type, international groupings whose unity existed in the minds of the believers. And what enabled them to be imagined as unities was the existence of sacred languages through which the religions could be mediated to many different peoples speaking many different tongues. These languages, and the role of literate élites as the mediators of the languages to the largely illiterate masses (I am remembering my own mumbled parroting of Arabic prayers) provided the underpinning substructure of the great universal faiths. The decline in power of the sacred languages and their interpreters, and the parallel rise in the idea of the nation, changed the world's relationship to religious belief in the most fundamental way.

Anderson warns us against the idea that the imagined communities of nations simply grew out of the decaying bodies of the imagined communities of faith and the dynastic realms that supported them. Rather, he argues, quoting Erich Auerbach and Walter Benjamin, the crucial change was in our apprehension of time. Time, in the imagined community of Christendom, was held to be near its end; and also contained the idea of simultaneity—God's

381

eye could see all moments, past, present and future, so that the here and now was only part of the eternal. Benjamin calls this 'Messianic time'. Our modern concept of time, by contrast, is guided by ticking clocks. It moves forward. It is a 'homogeneous, empty time', in Benjamin's phrase. And, says Anderson, 'the idea of a sociological organism moving calendrically through homogeneous, empty time is a precise analogue of the idea of the nation.'

This is important stuff for a novelist, because what we are being told is that the idea of sequence, of narrative, of society as a story, is essential to the creation of nations. But writers insist, if they're any good, in having it both ways—to be both linear and Godlike, to express both the truths of simultaneity and those of linearity. John Berger has said that Man is two events: there is the event of his biology and the event of his consciousness. The first is linear, temporal. The second is simultaneous, multiform, protean.

I am suggesting that in the world since the idea of the nation-state began to be thought, the biological event of man has become dominant; that our sense of the world is now clock-ridden, so that we cannot—except briefly, in the act of creation or contemplation—regain the sense of Messianic time. When religion enters the political arena today, then, it does so as an event in linear time; that is, as a part of the world of the nation-state, and not a rejection of it.

Consider the so-called 'Islamic revival' or 'fundamentalist Islamic revival'. The sloganizing of the term 'Islam' by the West in recent years has been extensively examined by Edward Said in his book *Covering Islam*. What 'Islam' now means in the West is an idea that is not merely medieval, barbarous, repressive and hostile to Western civilization, but also united, unified, homogeneous, and therefore dangerous: an Islamic Peril to put beside the Red and Yellow ones. Not much has changed since the Crusades, except that now we are not even permitted a single, leavening image of a 'good Muslim' of the Saladin variety. We are back in the demonizing process which transformed the Prophet Muhammad, all those years ago, into the frightful and fiendish 'Mahound'.

Whereas—and, like Said, I must make clear that it is no part of my intention to excuse or apologize for the deeds of many 'Islamic' regimes—any examination of the facts will demonstrate the rifts, the lack of homogeneity and unity, characteristic of present-day Islam. The murky war between Iran and Iraq reveals, if it reveals nothing else, the primarily nationalistic character of the States involved. That both sides claimed the support of the Almighty is, of course, nothing new. In the English Civil War, both armies marched into battle singing hymns. Soldiers have always been encouraged to die by the idea that they have God on their side.

Khomeini's revolution was intensely nationalistic in character. The unity it forged between many widely disparate elements of Iranian society, from the high bourgeoisie to the oil-workers, was built upon the desire to depose a despot, to liberate a nation. Why did Khomeini, an exiled and archaic cleric, become the focus of this national effort? The answer must be sought in the torture chambers of the Shah, where the paid killers of the SAVAK forces broke all political opponents of the Shah's regime. But Pahlevi never dared to move as ruthlessly against the mosques, against the clergy, as he did against his secular enemies. As a result opposition gravitated to the theologians; there was a power vacuum, and Khomeini stepped into it with massive authority. That his revolution, when it triumphed, began at once to devour its makers does not invalidate the essentially nationalist impetus that lay behind it. And even today, after that auto-cannibalism, it must be admitted that the power of the glowering figure of Khomeini is not purely the product of his 'holiness', or of fear. He does, in a real sense, embody an idea of the Iranian nation. Perhaps he would have fallen by now if he did not.

I am reminded of a key phrase describing the Iranian revolution. It was coined by one of the revolution's main ideologues, Ali Shariati. He described what was happening as a 'revolt against history'. What a phrase! In these three unforgettable words, history is characterized as a colossal error, and the revolution sets out quite literally to turn back the clock. Time must be reversed. Can it be that Shariati wished to restore, in place of calendar-time, the old 'Messianic' time-sense of the imagined community of faith? I think not. Rhetoric, even when memorable, remains rhetoric. And in spite of all the pedantry, all the restoration of ancient laws, time in Iran has persisted in running forward. To believe otherwise would be to succumb to obscurantist illusions.

Tom Nairn has suggested that nationalism progresses in a two-faced, a Janus-headed manner; that, in plain terms, it always moves forward while claiming to look back, in a kind of progress-by-regression. This, or something like this, is to my mind a description of what is taking place in Iran. And there is one resonance of this Janus theory that I want to explore, because it is heard at the very beginning of Islam.

Arabia in the seventh century after Christ was undergoing a period of transition from the old nomadic culture to a new, urbanized, mercantile culture. What Maxime Rodinson calls the 'old tribal humanism' of the Bedouins was decaying under the pressure of the new, business-based ethics of a city like Mecca. Muhammad, an orphan himself at an early age, was in an excellent position to appreciate the way in which Meccan culture failed to care for the weak as dutifully as the nomads would have. And the ethic of the revelation he received when, at the age of forty, having married a wealthy older woman and made his fortune, he climbed Mount Hira and found there the Archangel Gabriel or Gibril ordering him to *recite* (the word *Al-Qur'an* means *the recitation*), has often been seen, at least in part, as a plea for a return to the code of the nomadic Bedouin. So we may say that the ideas of the Qur'an are in this sense backward-looking, nostalgic, against the current. But the people on whom Muhammad's words made the strongest initial impression were the poor, the people of the bazaar, the lower classes of Meccan society—precisely those people who knew that they would have been better off under the old nomadic system. Thus early Islam instantly acquired the character of a subversive, radical movement. When Khomeini speaks of a revolt against history, we can argue that he echoes, in his fashion, the Prophet himself; for Muhammad's revelation, too, was a revolt against his time.

Yet, plainly, history did move forward; nomadism did not once again become the Arab norm, nor, obviously was that truly Muhammad's aim. The birth of Islam was presided over by two gods: Allah, and also Janus.

Turning now to recent events in the Indian sub-continent, we find, once again, nationalistic and religious ideas inextricably intertwined. In independent India, the idea of secular nationalism has a particular importance. It would not be an exaggeration to say that the survival of the State may depend upon it. 'We have to build the noble mansion of free India,' Pandit Nehru said in his famous independence night speech, 'where all her children may dwell.' After the terrible communal killings of the Partition riots, it was plainer than ever that if India's remaining Muslims, Sikhs, Buddhists, Jains, Christians, Jews and Harijans (untouchables), as well as the Hindu majority, were to be able to live together in peace, the idea of a godless State must be elevated above all of the 330 million deities. The very idea that a Hindu *imperium* might ever take the place of the British Raj would—it was feared— provoke civil unrest on a scale that would dwarf the Partition troubles. It was, therefore, of great value and importance that the Congress Party under Nehru based its electoral appeal firmly on safeguarding the rights of minorities. It forged a unique electoral coalition between India's Muslims, Harijans and Brahmin Hindus—the only large, nationwide groupings— and for a long time seemed invincible as a result.

Now it can be argued forcefully that the idea of secularism in India has never been much more than a slogan; that the very fact of religious block voting proves this to be so; that the divisions between the communities have by no means been subsumed in a common 'Indian' or national identity; and that it is strange to speak of nationalism when the main impetus in present-day India comes from regionalist, even separatist political groups. And there is much truth in these criticisms. Still the union's survival is an answer of a sort, a rough and imperfect answer, but at least an indication that for many Indians the idea of the gigantic nation-state has taken root.

I am not trying to brush the criticisms aside. There is a crisis of nationalism in India. In the Punjab, in Bombay, in Assam, in Kashmir, communal violence has been breaking out once more; many Indian observers feel that this heightening of violence may not be a passing phenomenon. The point I want to make is that much of the present religious sectarianism, many of the centrifugal stresses in Indian society, can be traced to political, not religious, origins. And we will have to begin with the Emergency, and with Sanjay Gandhi. Because it was in the time of Sanjay that the Congress, and the government of Mrs Gandhi, abandoned its policy of representing the coalition of minorities, and began to transform itself into an overtly Hindu party. Not only Hindu, but Hindi: attempts to impose this language on the whole of India created much resentment, particularly in the South. Such actions invariably bring forth reactions; and the growth of communalist politics in India stemmed from this shift by the ruling party. From Hindu nationalism sprang separatism of all sorts; if Hindustan was really to be turned into the home of the Hindus, no wonder some Sikhs began to talk of a homeland. But nobody paid them much attention until, in the 1980s, Mrs Gandhi and Sanjay had actually helped to finance a firebrand Sikh politico-religious figure called Sant Jarnail Singh Bhindranwale; they were quite prepared, in the interest of a strong Central government, to foster communalism, and use Bhindranwale to split the vote of the regionalist Akali Dal Party. So, as we now know, Mrs Gandhi's murder was a part of a chain of events which she helped to forge. It is a tragic irony. But it cannot be understood in purely religious terms; more important, perhaps, is the struggle for power between the Centre and the States. And most tragic—with more profound implications even than the assassination—is the progressive alienation of minority groups which, like the Sikhs, have been in the main extremely loyal to the nation-state. In the aftermath of the revenge-killings of Sikhs that followed Mrs Gandhi's death, the idea of Khalistan, the separate Sikh State, ceased to seem like the pipe-dream of a few, and a little more like a safe haven to some of the many traumatized members of the Sikh community who had wanted nothing to do with Bhindranwale, who abhorred the assassination, but who had been held responsible for it by the Congress-led mobs.

Across the frontier in Pakistan, we find a very clear demonstration of the impracticability of trying to place religious beliefs at the centre of contemporary politics. Here, after all, is a State that was based on a faith; and the problems that have beset it ever since its birth are those of having been—as I've said elsewhere—*insufficiently imagined*. In other words, what Pakistan has been discovering, very painfully, is that no religion is any longer a sufficient basis for a society. The world has changed too much for that. As a result, pieces of the State have begun to break off; and the Zia dictatorship has done its best to break up what's left. We can perhaps best understand the tensions of modern Pakistan as the result of the resurgence of the old, suppressed nationalisms—Punjabi, Sindhi, Baloch—and the new, and inadequate, ideological unity. The Benazir Bhutto government has inherited a derelict State—a militarized, gangster-infested theocracy. Ms Bhutto must construct, at high speed and in unfavourable circumstances, nothing less than the institutions and processes of a modern nation-state. That is, history must be excavated from beneath the rubble of dogmatism and tyranny. Her best hope for success may lie in the realization of all Pakistan's citizens, Sindhis as well as Pathans, Punjabis as well as Balochis, that nothing is to be gained from Balkanization. The real possibility of such an outcome may be, strangely, what prevents it from happening. And if enlightened self-interest does guide Pakistanis to back away from that precipice, then the first constructive step will have been taken towards the making of a State with a real reason for being—let us say, a post-Islamic Pakistan.

From the powerful, wealthy, confident certainties of the nineteenth century, the West has arrived at a moment beyond consensus, a fractured time, in which doubt, anxiety, and a kind of rudderlessness dominate life. This loss of

certainty has been in many ways—for example, in the arts—
of great value. Just as an atom, when split, releases colossal
energy, so the old, rigid orthodoxies of colonial Europe
produced, by being broken, the unparalleled outburst of
newness and excitement that the modernist movement has
been. But such an event is, of course, ambiguous.

In the same period, the language of politics has become
more materialistic. Both on the right and the left, politicians
have learned to speak in the newspeak of economics. If an
airport is to be built in the midst of sleepy villages, the
distress of the locals is calculated, astoundingly, in cash
terms, and then balanced against other figures. The increasing
mechanization of society has created a mechanical politics;
one which no longer asks 'why' or 'whither' questions, but
only 'how'. As a result, the world of politics no longer
encompasses much of what real human beings actually care
about. It does not ask what kind of world we wish to live in; it
does not analyse the consequences of the choices that are
made for us; nor, but perhaps it never did, does it address
itself to the grievances and achings of the soul—of that other
event that we are, the one that perceives existence not as one-
thing-after-another, but as everything-at-once. Politics has
come to narrow the world down to things, and the idea, the
only idea, which is offered to make us accept this awful
limitation, is called progress. Progress: the dream of heaven
on earth.

But Western political systems, both of the liberal capitalist
and communist variety, have simply failed to deliver
progress. We now know the ever-expanding cake to be a
myth; the citizens of the West face futures of narrowing
horizons, diminishing prospects. One could say that the West
has lost the future; and without the future, the one validating
concept of its political systems is removed.

Poland's religious fervour, for example, seems deeply
nationalistic; those who mourn the death of a fallen priest
mourn his falling in a political struggle. We have a Pope
who is more politically involved than most—although
when his priests join forces with radical politics in South

America, he brings intense pressure on them to back off. And in the burning arenas of Northern Ireland and the Middle East, religious fervour cloaks equally fierce nationalist aspirations. We are near a millennium; once again, we have the idea of standing near the end of time. It is perhaps unsurprising that so many of us, awaking from the dream of politics, choose to fall into the dream of God. But that dream, today, is not a means of cancelling politics; it does not and cannot turn back the clock. The religious revivals of the world are continuations of the political process by other means.

At first glance the state of affairs in the United States of America does not seem to bear out the sort of ideas I've been propounding. In America, after all, the vision of the material, earthly paradise has not yet faded. The USA remains formidably wealthy and powerful, and it often appears that its political language still commands the belief of large numbers of its citizens. And yet, all over the land of the free, strange gods rule. Evangelists stalk the land and men and women walk forward for Christ. Such devout persons as John DeLorean are 'born again' into Christ. The followers of the Bhagwan Shree Rajneesh proliferate, and their livery, the colours of the sunset and the dawn, is everywhere to be seen. It is a time of Falwells and book-burnings. There was even a President who believed that the Apocalypse might very well come in his lifetime, and who had the button to prove it. In its way, the religious fundamentalism of the United States is as alarming as anything in the much feared world of Islam. How so? Where does it come from?

In the twenty-seven years since the killing of President Kennedy, there has been a good deal of disturbance in the American dream. The cult of individualism, of a man's (not so often a woman's) ability and right to pull himself up by his own bootstraps and wit, which lies at the heart of that dream, has produced more Oswalds, more Sirhans, more Mansons and Jim Joneses, than Lincolns, of late. The representative figure of American individualism is no longer that log-cabin-to-White-House President, but rather a lone man with a gun, seeking vengeance against a world that will not conform to his own sense of what has worth. It is Robert de Niro in *Taxi Driver*, or Charles Bronson in anything, or, in real life, the murderer Goetz who walked free after shooting down the man who asked him for a five-dollar bill on the subway. That is to say: the myth of the American hero has turned sour. The disorienting effects of such a transformation should not be underestimated.

In many other respects, too, it has been a bruising time to be an American. Fifteen years ago, Victor Charlie, the slope, the geek, inflicted on the US Army a humiliating defeat. Since then, America has lost further battles. Such loyal allies as Somoza in Nicaragua and the Shah of Iran have been overthrown. And let us not forget the taking of the hostages in Iran and the Lebanon.

The historian F. J. Turner's 'frontier thesis'—the idea that a country born with the urge to push a frontier westwards has needed, constantly, to find new frontiers, ever since it reached the Pacific—has long been a useful lens through which to view American history. The space race is only one subject which the thesis illuminates. In the last two decades many Americans have turned inwards in search of that new frontier. The enormous influences of psychiatry and psychotherapy can be adduced as evidence for this, as can the enormous body of literature about self-improvement.

When we examine the American self of this period, however, what do we find? We find that it has been the age of the great burn-out. Both radicals and conservatives—those who played with the drugs and great causes of the sixties and seventies on the one hand, and, say, the returning war veterans on the other—have entered a time of shock. It is interesting that so many writers in America today write very largely about this burn-out. Above all, in the spare, deliberately narrow-horizoned world of Raymond Carver, we sense a desire to turn away from the large canvas, from the great issues and events and the bold experiments that got America into such a mess, and to concentrate on minutiae, on the simplest things, on the first building blocks of life; to go back to basics, and try, by starting again, to salvage something: honesty, perhaps. Integrity. Truth.

I am arguing that in spite of America's continued affluence, the idea of 'progress', which is very close to a nation's sense of itself, has been badly damaged in America, too. And religion enters the story, once again, as a means of shoring up the crumbling patriotism of the American people—that is, as an aspect of the nationalist impulse, and not a replacement for it. Religion and patriotism have always gone hand in hand in a country in which schoolchildren are asked daily to perform an act of worship before the national flag. And in today's America, there is a new patriotism whose links with the religious revival are explicit. God is America's answer to its crisis of identity.

Myth, Roland Barthes tells us, is statistically on the right. If the left seeks always to de-mystify, then in a time when people need certainties, absolutes, it often fails to offer them what they ask for. The resulting crisis of liberalism is with us everywhere, and nowhere more than in the USA. History has done its best to shake America's certainty that it was *right*. America reacts by burying its head in the lap of God.

John Schlesinger's film *The Falcon and the Snowman* deals valuably with America's chosen blindness. It is the story of two young Americans, one a drug dealer, the other an employee in a high-security installation, who team up to sell secrets to the Russians, becoming what are called 'traitors'. The 'Falcon'—the one of the pair who has the access to the secrets—has a rather different view of treason. He decides to become a spy when he learns about CIA activities against Allende's Chilean government and the Whitlam government in Australia. To him, it is the CIA that is the traitor; it is the CIA which betrays the spirit of America. Memorably, he compares the activities of America as a superpower to those of predators (he owns a pet falcon, and knows a lot about the habits of such birds). If predators are not closely controlled, they swallow everything they can eat.

The 'traitors' also know that things have become so bad that not even a journalistic exposé can alter anything. Even

when Americans know what their government is doing—
even when they are told about Allende or Whitlam—they
choose not to care. America has chosen to be a State in which,
for example, it is possible for a President to denounce an
elected government (in Nicaragua) as a tyranny, while it is
conveniently forgotten that for the previous fifty years it was
America who supported the real, full-blooded Somoza
tyranny.

When the activities of a nation's representatives begin to
diverge so dramatically from its self-image as the guardian of
freedom and decency, then the country has to find ways of
turning away from the truth into cosy simplicities (God,
patriotism), in order not to see itself too plainly; in order not
to see that its picture of itself is in many ways a false one.

And if religion is the blindfold, so it is also the bedrock on
which, failing any other certainty, many Americans build
their sense that they are *right* to be, and do, as they are, and as
they do.

'In God We Trust': this sentiment is not from the walls of
any church, but on the currency of the United States: God and
Mammon, in the service of the world's most powerful nation,
united at last.

1985, 1990

In Good Faith

It has been a year since I last spoke in defence of my novel *The Satanic Verses*. I have remained silent, though silence is against my nature, because I felt that my voice was simply not loud enough to be heard above the clamour of the voices raised against me.

I hoped that others would speak for me, and many have done so eloquently, among them an admittedly small but growing number of Muslim readers, writers and scholars. Others, including bigots and racists, have tried to exploit my case (using my name to taunt Muslim and non-Muslim Asian children and adults, for example) in a manner I have found repulsive, defiling and humiliating.

At the centre of the storm stands a novel, a work of fiction, one that aspires to the condition of literature. It has often seemed to me that people on all sides of the argument have lost sight of this simple fact. *The Satanic Verses* has been described, and treated, as a work of bad history, as an anti-religious pamphlet, as the product of an international capitalist–Jewish conspiracy, as an act of murder ('he has murdered our hearts'), as the product of a person comparable to Hitler and Attila the Hun. It felt impossible, amid such a hubbub, to insist on the fictionality of fiction.

Let me be clear: I am not trying to say that *The Satanic Verses* is 'only a novel' and thus need not be taken seriously, even disputed with the utmost passion. I do not believe that novels are trivial matters. The ones I care most about are those which attempt radical reformulations of language, form and ideas, those that attempt to do what the word *novel* seems to insist upon: to see the world anew. I am well aware that this can be a hackle-raising, infuriating attempt.

What I have wished to say, however, is that the point of view from which I have, all my life, attempted this process of literary renewal is the result not of the self-hating, deracinated Uncle-Tomism of which some have accused me, but precisely of my determination to create a literary language and literary forms in which the experience of formerly colonized, still-disadvantaged peoples might find full expression. If *The Satanic Verses* is anything, it is a migrant's-eye view of the world. It is written from the very experience of uprooting, disjuncture and metamorphosis (slow or rapid, painful or pleasurable) that is the migrant condition, and from which, I believe, can be derived a metaphor for all humanity.

Standing at the centre of the novel is a group of characters most of whom are British Muslims, or not particularly religious persons of Muslim background, struggling with just the sort of great problems that have arisen to surround the book, problems of hybridization and ghettoization, of reconciling the old and the new. Those who oppose the novel most vociferously today are of the opinion that intermingling with a different culture will inevitably weaken and ruin their own. I am of the opposite opinion. *The Satanic Verses* celebrates hybridity, impurity, intermingling, the transformation that comes of new and unexpected combinations of human beings, cultures, ideas, politics, movies, songs. It rejoices in mongrelization and fears the absolutism of the Pure. *Mélange*, hotchpotch, a bit of this and a bit of that is *how newness enters the world*. It is the great possibility that mass migration gives the world, and I have tried to embrace it. *The Satanic Verses* is for change-by-fusion, change-by-conjoining. It is a love-song to our mongrel selves.

Throughout human history, the apostles of purity, those who have claimed to possess a total explanation, have wrought havoc among mere mixed-up human beings. Like many millions of people, I am a bastard child of history. Perhaps we all are, black and brown and white, leaking into one another, as a character of mine once said, *like flavours when you cook*.

The argument between purity and impurity, which is also the argument between Robespierre and Danton, the argument between the monk and the roaring boy, between primness and impropriety, between the stultifications of excessive respect and the scandals of impropriety, is an old one; I say, let it continue. Human beings understand themselves and shape their futures by arguing and challenging and questioning and saying the unsayable; not by bowing the knee, whether to gods or to men.

The Satanic Verses is, I profoundly hope, a work of radical dissent and questioning and reimagining. It is not, however, the book it has been made out to be, that book containing 'nothing but filth and insults and abuse' that has brought people out on to the streets across the world.

That book simply does not exist.

This is what I want to say to the great mass of ordinary, decent, fair-minded Muslims, of the sort I have known all my life, and who have provided much of the inspiration for my work: to be rejected and reviled by, so to speak, one's own characters is a shocking and painful experience for any writer. I recognize that many Muslims have felt shocked and pained, too. Perhaps a way forward might be found through the mutual recognition of that mutual pain. Let us attempt to believe in each other's good faith.

I am aware that this is asking a good deal. There has been too much name-calling. Muslims have been called savages and barbarians and worse. I, too, have received my share of invective. Yet I still believe—perhaps I must—that understanding remains possible, and can be achieved without the suppression of the principle of free speech.

What it requires is a moment of good will; a moment in which we may all accept that the other parties are acting, have acted, in good faith.

You see, it's my opinion that if we could only dispose of the 'insults and abuse' accusation, which prevents those who believe it from accepting that *The Satanic Verses* is a work of any serious intent or merit whatsoever, then we might be able, at the very least, to agree to differ about the book's real themes, about the relative value of the sacred and the profane, about the merits of purity and those of hotch-potch, and about how human beings really become whole: through the love of God or through the love of their fellow men and women.

And to dispose of the argument, we must return for a moment to the actually existing book, not the book described in the various pamphlets that have been circulated to the faithful, not the 'unreadable' text of legend, not two chapters dragged out of the whole; not a piece of blubber, but the whole wretched whale.

Let me say this first: I have never seen this controversy as a struggle between Western freedoms and Eastern unfreedom. The freedoms of the West are rightly vaunted, but many minorities—racial, sexual, political—just as rightly feel excluded from full possession of these liberties; while, in my lifelong experience of the East, from Turkey and Iran to India and Pakistan, I have found people to be every bit as passionate for freedom as any Czech, Romanian, German, Hungarian or Pole.

How is freedom gained? It is taken: never given. To be free, you must first assume your right to freedom. In writing *The Satanic Verses*, I wrote from the assumption that I was, and am, a free man.

What is freedom of expression? Without the freedom to offend, it ceases to exist. Without the freedom to challenge, even to satirize all orthodoxies, including religious orthodoxies, it ceases to exist. Language and the imagination cannot be imprisoned, or art will die, and with it, a little of what makes us human. *The Satanic Verses* is, in part, a secular man's reckoning with the religious spirit. It is by no means always hostile to faith. 'If we write in such a way as to pre-judge such belief as in some way deluded or false, then are we not guilty of élitism, of imposing our world-view on the masses?' asks one of its Indian characters. Yet the novel does contain doubts, uncertainties, even shocks that may well not be to the liking of the devout. Such methods have, however, long been a legitimate part even of Islamic literature.

What does the novel dissent from? Certainly not from people's right to faith, though I have none. It dissents most clearly from imposed orthodoxies *of all types*, from the view that the world is quite clearly This and not That. It dissents from the end of debate, of dispute, of dissent. Hindu communalist sectarianism, the kind of Sikh terrorism that blows up planes, the fatuousnesses of Christian creationism are dissented from as well as the narrower definitions of Islam. But such dissent is a long way from 'insults and abuse'. I do not believe that most of the Muslims I know would have any trouble with it.

What they have trouble with are statements like these: 'Rushdie calls the Prophet Muhammad a homosexual.' 'Rushdie says the Prophet Muhammad asked God for permission to fornicate with every woman in the world.' 'Rushdie says the Prophet's wives are whores.' 'Rushdie calls the Prophet by a devil's name.' 'Rushdie calls the Companions of the Prophet *scum and bums*.' 'Rushdie says that the whole Qur'an was the Devil's work.' And so forth.

It has been bewildering to watch the proliferation of such statements, and to watch them acquire the authority of truth by virtue of the power of repetition. It has been bewildering to learn that people, millions upon millions of people, have been willing to judge *The Satanic Verses* and its author, without reading it, without finding out what manner of man this fellow might be, on the basis of such allegations as these. It has been bewildering to learn that people *do not care about art*. Yet the only way I can explain matters, the only way I can try and replace the non-existent novel with the one I actually wrote, is to tell you a story.

The Satanic Verses is the story of two painfully divided selves. In the case of one, Saladin Chamcha, the division is secular and societal: he is torn, to put it plainly, between Bombay and London, between East and West. For the other, Gibreel Farishta, the division is spiritual, a rift in the soul. He has lost his faith and is strung out between his immense need to believe and his new inability to do so. The novel is 'about' their quest for wholeness.

Why 'Gibreel Farishta' (*Gabriel Angel*)? Not to 'insult and abuse' the 'real' Archangel Gabriel. Gibreel is a movie star, and movie stars hang above us in the darkness, larger than life, halfway to the divine. To give Gibreel an angel's name was to give him a secular equivalent of angelic half-divinity. When he loses his faith, however, this name becomes the source of all his torments.

Chamcha survives. He makes himself whole by returning to his roots and, more importantly, by facing up to, and learning to deal with, the great verities of love and death. Gibreel does not survive. He can neither return to the love of God, nor succeed in replacing it by earthly love. In the end he kills himself, unable to bear his torment any longer.

His greatest torments have come to him in the form of dreams. In these dreams he is cast in the role of his namesake, the Archangel, and witnesses and participates in the unfolding of various epic and tragic narratives dealing with the nature and consequences of revelation and belief. These dreams are not uniformly sceptical. In one, a non-believing landowner who has seen his entire village, and his own wife, drown in the Arabian Sea at the behest of a girl-seer who claimed the waters would open so that the pilgrims might undertake a journey to Mecca, experiences the truth of a miracle at the moment of his own death, when he opens his heart to God, and 'sees' the waters part. All the dreams do, however, dramatize the struggle between faith and doubt.

Gibreel's most painful dreams, the ones at the centre of the controversy, depict the birth and growth of a religion something like Islam, in a magical city of sand named Jahilia (that is 'ignorance', the name given by Arabs to the period before Islam). Almost all the alleged 'insults and abuse' are taken from these dream sequences.

The first thing to be said about these dreams is that they are *agonizingly painful to the dreamer*. They are a 'nocturnal retribution, a punishment' for his loss of faith. This man, desperate to regain belief, is haunted, possessed, by visions of doubt, visions of scepticism and questions and faith-shaking allegations that grow more and more extreme as they go on. He tries in vain to escape them, fighting against sleep; but then the visions cross over the boundary between his waking and sleeping self, they infect his daytimes: that is, they drive him mad. The dream-city is called 'Jahilia' not to 'insult and abuse' Mecca Sharif, but because the dreamer, Gibreel, has been plunged by his broken faith back into the condition the word describes. The first purpose of these sequences is not to vilify or 'disprove' Islam, but to portray a soul in crisis, to show how the loss of God can destroy a man's life.

See the 'offensive' chapters through this lens, and many things may seem clearer. The use of the so-called 'incident of the satanic verses', the quasi-historical tale of how Muhammad's revelation seemed briefly to flirt with the possibility of admitting three pagan and female deities into the pantheon, at the semi-divine, intercessory level of the archangels, and of how he then repudiated these verses as being satanically inspired—is, first of all, a key moment of doubt in dreams which persecute a dreamer by making vivid the doubts he loathes but can no longer escape.

The most extreme passage of doubting in the novel is when the character 'Salman the Persian'—named not to 'insult and abuse' Muhammad's companion Salman al-Farisi, but more as an ironic reference to the novel's author—voices his many scepticisms. It is quite true that the language here is forceful, satirical, and strong meat for some tastes, but it must be remembered that the waking Gibreel is a coarse-mouthed fellow, and it would be surprising if the dream-figures he conjures up did not sometimes speak as rough and even obscene a language as their dreamer. It must also be remembered that this sequence happens late in the dream, when the dreamer's mind is crumbling along with his certainties, and when his derangement, to which these violently expressed doubts contribute, is well advanced.

Let me not be disingenuous, however. The rejection of the three goddesses in the novel's dream-version of the 'satanic verses' story is also intended to make other points, for example about the religion's attitude to women. 'Shall He [God] have daughters while you have sons? That would be an unjust division,' read the verses still to be found in the Qur'an. I thought it was at least worth pointing out that one of the reasons for rejecting these goddesses was that *they were female*. The rejection has implications that are worth thinking about. I suggest that such highlighting is a proper function of literature.

Or again, when Salman the Persian, Gibreel's dream-figment, fulminates against the dream-religion's aim of providing 'rules for every damn thing', he is not only tormenting the dreamer, but asking the reader to think about the validity of religion's rules. To those participants in the controversy who have felt able to justify the most extreme Muslim threats towards me and others by saying that I have broken an Islamic rule, I would ask the following question: are all the rules laid down at a religion's origin immutable for ever? How about the penalties for prostitution (stoning to death) or thieving (mutilation)? How about the prohibition of homosexuality? How about the Islamic law of inheritance, which allows a widow to inherit only an eighth share, and which gives to sons twice as much as it does to daughters? What of the Islamic law of evidence, which makes a woman's testimony worth only half that of a man? Are these, too, to be given unquestioning respect: or may writers and intellectuals ask the awkward questions that are a part of their reason for being what they are?

Let no one suppose that such disputes about rules do not take place daily throughout the Muslim world. Muslim religious leaders may wish female children of Muslim households to be educated in segregated schools, but the girls, as they say every time anybody asks them, do not wish to go. (The Labour Party doesn't ask them, and plans to deliver them into the hands of the mullahs.) Likewise, Muslim divines may insist that women dress 'modestly', according to the Hijab code, covering more of their bodies than men because they possess what one Muslim recently and absurdly described on television as 'more adorable parts'; but the Muslim world is full of women who reject such strictures. Islam may teach that women should be confined to the home and to child-rearing, but Muslim women everywhere insist on leaving the home to work. If Muslim society questions its own rules daily—and make no mistake, Muslims are as accustomed to satire as anyone else—why must a novel be proscribed for doing the same?

But to return to the text. Certain supposed 'insults' need specific rebuttals. For example, the scene in which the Prophet's companions are called 'scum' and 'bums' is a depiction of the early persecution of the believers, and the insults quoted are clearly not mine but those hurled at the faithful by the ungodly. How, one wonders, could a book portray persecution without allowing the persecutors to be seen persecuting? (Or again: how could a book portray doubt without allowing the uncertain to articulate their uncertainties?)

As to the matter of the Prophet's wives: what happens in Gibreel's dreams is that the whores of a brothel *take the names* of the wives of the Prophet Mahound in order to arouse their customers. The 'real' wives are clearly stated to be 'living chastely' in their harem. But why introduce so shocking an image? For this reason: throughout the novel, I sought images that crystallized the opposition between the sacred and profane worlds. The harem and the brothel provide such an opposition. Both are places where women are sequestered, in the harem to keep them from all men except their husband and close family members, in the brothel for the use of strange males. Harem and brothel are antithetical worlds, and the presence in the harem of the Prophet, the receiver of a sacred text, is likewise contrasted with the presence in the brothel of the clapped-out poet, Baal, the creator of profane texts. The two struggling worlds, pure and impure, chaste and coarse, are juxtaposed by making them echoes of one another; and, finally, the pure eradicates the impure. Whores and writer ('I see no difference here,' remarks Mahound) are executed. Whether one finds this a happy or sad conclusion depends on one's point of view.

The purpose of the 'brothel sequence', then, was not to 'insult and abuse' the Prophet's wives, but to dramatize certain ideas about morality; and sexuality, too, because what happens in the brothel—called *Hijab* after the name for 'modest' dress as an ironic means of further highlighting the inverted echo between the two worlds—is that the men of 'Jahilia' are enabled to act out an ancient dream of power and possession, the dream of possessing the queen. That men should be so aroused by the great ladies' whorish counterfeits says something about *them*, not the great ladies, and about the extent to which sexual relations have to do with possession.

I must have known, my accusers say, that my use of the old devil-name 'Mahound', a medieval European demonization of 'Muhammad', would cause offence. In fact, this is an instance in which de-contextualization has created a complete reversal of meaning. A part of the relevant context is on page ninety-three of the novel. 'To turn insults into strengths, whigs, tories, Blacks all chose to wear with pride the names they were given in scorn; likewise, our mountain-climbing, prophet-motivated solitary is to be the medieval baby-frightener, the Devil's synonym: Mahound.' Central to the purposes of *The Satanic Verses* is the process of reclaiming language from one's opponents. (Elsewhere in the novel we find the poet Jumpy Joshi trying to reclaim Enoch Powell's notorious 'rivers of blood' simile. Humanity itself can be thought of as a river of blood, he argues; the river flows in our bodies, and we, as a collectivity, are a river of blood flowing down the ages. Why abandon so potent and evocative an image to the racists?) 'Trotsky' was Trotsky's jailer's name. By taking it for his own, he symbolically conquered his captor and set himself free. Something of the same spirit lay behind my use of the name 'Mahound'.

The attempt at reclamation goes even further than this. When Saladin Chamcha finds himself transformed into a goatish, horned and hoofy demon, in a bizarre sanatorium full of other monstrous beings, he's told that they are all, like him, aliens and migrants, demonized by the 'host culture's' attitude to them. 'They have the power of description, and we succumb to the pictures they construct.' If migrant groups are called devils by others, that does not really make them demonic. And if devils are not necessarily devilish, angels may not necessarily be angelic . . . From this premise, the novel's exploration of morality as internal and shifting (rather than external, divinely sanctioned, absolute) may be said to emerge.

The very title, *The Satanic Verses*, is an aspect of this attempt at reclamation. You call us devils? it seems to ask. Very well, then, here is the devil's version of the world, of 'your' world, the version written *from the experience* of those who have been demonized by virtue of their otherness. Just as the Asian kids in the novel wear toy devil-horns proudly, as an assertion of pride in identity, so the novel proudly wears its demonic title. The purpose is not to suggest that the Qur'an is written by the devil; it is to attempt the sort of act of affirmation that, in the United States, transformed the word *black* from the standard term of racist abuse into a 'beautiful' expression of cultural pride.

And so on. There are times when I feel that the original intentions of *The Satanic Verses* have been so thoroughly scrambled by events as to be lost for ever. There are times when I feel frustrated that the terms in which the novel is discussed seem to have been set exclusively by Muslim leaders (including those, like Sher Azam of the Bradford Council of Mosques, who can blithely say on television, 'Books are not my thing'). After all, the process of hybridization which is the novel's most crucial dynamic means that its ideas derive from many sources other than Islamic ones.

There is, for example, the pre-Christian belief, expressed in the Books of Amos and Deutero-Isaiah and quoted in *The Satanic Verses*, that God and the Devil were one and the same: 'It isn't until the Book of Chronicles, merely fourth century BC, that the word *Satan* is used to mean a being, and not only an attribute of God.' It should also be said that the two books that were most influential on the shape this novel took do not include the Qur'an. One was William Blake's *Marriage of Heaven and Hell*, the classic meditation on the interpenetration of good and evil; the other *The Master and Margarita* by Mikhail Bulgakov, the great Russian lyrical and comical novel in which the Devil descends upon Moscow and wreaks havoc upon the corrupt, materialist, decadent inhabitants and turns out, by the end, not to be such a bad chap after all.

The Master and Margarita and its author were persecuted by Soviet totalitarianism. It is extraordinary to find my novel's life echoing that of one of its greatest models.

Nor are these the only non-Muslim influences at work. I was born an Indian, and not only an Indian, but a Bombayite—Bombay, most cosmopolitan, most hybrid, most hotchpotch of Indian cities. My writing and thought have therefore been as deeply influenced by Hindu myths and attitudes as Muslim ones (and my movie star Gibreel is also a figure of inter-religious tolerance, playing Hindu gods without causing offence, in spite of his Muslim origins). Nor is the West absent from Bombay. I was already a mongrel self, history's bastard, before London aggravated the condition.

To be an Indian of my generation was also to be convinced of the vital importance of Jawaharlal Nehru's vision of a secular India. Secularism, for India, is not simply a point of view; it is a question of survival. If what Indians call 'communalism', sectarian religious politics, were to be allowed to take control of the polity, the results would be too horrifying to imagine. Many Indians fear that that moment may now be very near. I have fought against communal politics all my adult life. The Labour Party in Britain would do well to look at the consequences of Indian politicians' willingness to play the communalist card, and consider whether some Labour politicians' apparent willingness to do the same in Britain, for the same reason (votes), is entirely wise.

To be a Bombayite (and afterwards a Londoner) was also to fall in love with the metropolis. The city as reality and as a metaphor is at the heart of all my work. 'The modern city,' says a character in *The Satanic Verses*, 'is the *locus classicus* of incompatible realities.' Well, that turned out to be true. 'As long as they pass in the night, it's not so bad. But if they meet! It's uranium and plutonium, each makes the other decompose, boom.' It is hard to express how it feels to have attempted to portray an objective reality and then to have become its subject . . .

The point is this: Muslim culture has been very important to me, but it is not by any means the only shaping factor. I am a modern, and modern*ist*, urban man, accepting uncertainty as the only constant, change as the only sure thing. I believe in no god, and have done so since I was a young adolescent. I have spiritual needs, and my work has, I hope, a moral and spiritual dimension, but I am content to try and satisfy those needs without recourse to any idea of a Prime Mover or ultimate arbiter.

To put it as simply as possible: *I am not a Muslim*. It feels bizarre, and wholly inappropriate, to be described as some sort of heretic after having lived my life as a secular, pluralist, eclectic man. I am being enveloped in, and described by, a language that does not fit me. I do not accept the charge of blasphemy, because, as somebody says in *The Satanic Verses*, 'where there is no belief, there is no blasphemy.' I do not accept the charge of apostasy, because I have never in my adult life affirmed any belief, and what one has not affirmed one cannot be said to have apostasized from. The Islam I know states clearly that 'there can be no coercion in matters of religion'. The many Muslims I respect would be horrified by the idea that they belong to their faith *purely by virtue of birth*, and that any person so born who freely chose not to be a Muslim could therefore be put to death.

When I am described as an apostate Muslim, I feel as if I have been concealed behind a *false self*, as if a shadow has become substance while I have been relegated to the shadows. Sections of the non-Muslim British media have helped in the creation of other aspects of this false self, portraying me as egomaniacal, insolent, greedy, hypocritical and disloyal. It has been suggested that I prefer to be known by an Anglicization of my name ('Simon Rushton'). And, to perfect the double bind, this Salman Rushdie is also 'thin-skinned' and 'paranoid', so that any attempt by him to protest against falsifications will be seen as further proof of the reality of the false self, the golem.

The Muslim attack against me has been greatly assisted by the creation of this false self. 'Simon Rushton' has featured in several Muslim portrayals of my debased, deracinated personality. My 'greed' fits well into the conspiracy theory, that I sold my soul to the West and wrote a carefully planned attack on Islam in return for pots of money. 'Disloyalty' is useful in this context, too. Jorge Luis Borges, Graham Greene and other writers have written about their sense of an Other who goes about the world bearing their name. There are moments when I worry that my Other may succeed in obliterating me.

On 14 February 1989, within hours of the dread news from Iran, I received a telephone call from Keith Vaz, MP, during which he vehemently expressed his full support for me and my work, and his horror at the threat against my life. A few weeks later, this same gentleman was to be found addressing a demonstration full of men demanding my death, and of children festooned with murderous placards. By now Mr Vaz wanted my work banned, and threats against my life seemed not to trouble him any longer.

It has been that sort of year. Twelve months ago, the *Guardian*'s esteemed columnist, Hugo Young, teetered on the edge of racism when he told all British Muslims that if they didn't like the way things were in Britain, they could always leave ('if not Dagenham, why not Tehran?'); now this same Mr Young prefers to lay the blame for the controversy at my door. (I have, after all, fewer battalions at my disposal.) No doubt, Mr Young would now be relieved if I went back where I came from.

And, and, and. Lord Dacre thought it might be a good idea if I were beaten up in a dark alley. Rana Kabbani announced with perfect Stalinist fervour that writers should be 'accountable' to the community. Brian Clark (the author, ironically enough, of *Whose Life Is It Anyway?*), claiming to be on my side, wrote an execrable play which, mercifully, nobody has yet agreed to produce, entitled *Who Killed Salman Rushdie?*, and sent it along in case I needed something to read.

And Britain witnessed a brutalization of public debate that seemed hard to believe. Incitement to murder was tolerated on the nation's streets. (In Europe and the United States, swift government action prevented such incitement at a very early stage.) On TV shows, studio audiences were asked for a show of hands on the question of whether I should live or die. A man's murder (mine) became a legitimate subject for a national opinion poll. And slowly, slowly, a point of view grew up, and was given voice by mountebanks and bishops, fundamentalists and Mr John le Carré, which held that *I knew exactly what I was doing*. I must have known what would happen; therefore, did it on purpose, to profit by the notoriety that would result. This accusation is, today, in fairly wide circulation, and so I must defend myself against it, too.

I find myself wanting to ask questions: when Osip Mandelstam wrote his poem against Stalin, did he 'know what he was doing' and so deserve his death? When the students filled Tiananmen Square to ask for freedom, were they not also, and knowingly, asking for the murderous repression that resulted? When Terry Waite was taken hostage, hadn't he been 'asking for it'? I find myself thinking of Jodie Foster in her Oscar-winning role in *The Accused*. Even if I were to concede (and I do not concede it) that what I did in *The Satanic Verses* was the literary equivalent of flaunting oneself shamelessly before the eyes of aroused men, is that really a justification for being, so to speak, gang-banged? Is any provocation a justification for rape?

Threats of violence ought not to coerce us into believing the victims of intimidation to be responsible for the violence threatened. I am aware, however, that rhetoric is an insufficient response. Nor is it enough to point out that nothing on the scale of this controversy has, to my knowledge, ever happened in the history of literature. If I had told anyone before publication that such events would occur as a result of my book, I would instantly have proved the truth of the accusations of egomania . . .

It's true that some passages in *The Satanic Verses* have now acquired a prophetic quality that alarms even me. 'Your blasphemy, Salman, can't be forgiven . . . To set your words against the Word of God.' Et cetera. But to write a dream based around events that took place in the seventh century of the Christian era, and to create metaphors of the conflict between different sorts of 'author' and different types of 'text'—to say that literature and religion, like literature and politics, fight for the same territory—is very different from somehow knowing, in advance, that your dream is about to come true, that the metaphor is about to be made flesh, that the conflict your work seeks to explore is about to engulf it, and its publishers and booksellers; and you.

At least (small comfort) I wasn't wrong.

Books choose their authors; the act of creation is not entirely a rational and conscious one. But this, as honestly as I can set it down, is, in respect of the novel's treatment of religion, what 'I knew I was doing'.

I set out to explore, through the process of fiction, the nature of revelation and the power of faith. The mystical, revelatory experience is quite clearly a genuine one. This statement poses a problem to the non-believer: if we accept that the mystic, the prophet, is sincerely undergoing some sort of transcendent experience, but we cannot believe in a supernatural world, then *what is going on*? To answer this question, among others, I began work on the story of 'Mahound'. I was aware that the 'satanic verses' incident is much disputed by Muslim theologians; that the life of Muhammad has become the object of a kind of veneration that some would consider un-Islamic, since Muhammad himself always insisted that he was merely a messenger, an ordinary man; and that, therefore, great sensitivities were involved. I genuinely believed that my overt use of fabulation would make it clear to any reader that I was not attempting to falsify history, but to allow a fiction to take off from history. The use of dreams, fantasy, etc. was intended to say: the point is not whether this is 'really' supposed to be Muhammad, or whether the satanic verses incident 'really' happened; the point is to examine what such an incident might reveal about what revelation is, about the extent to which the mystic's conscious personality informs and interacts with the mystical event; the point is to try and understand the human event of revelation. The use of fiction was a way of creating the sort of distance from actuality that I felt would prevent offence from being taken. I was wrong.

Jahilia, to use once again the ancient Arab story-tellers' formula I used often in *The Satanic Verses*, both 'is and is not' Mecca. Many of the details of its social life are drawn from historical research; but it is also a dream of an Indian city (its concentric street-plan deliberately recalls New Delhi), and, as Gibreel spends time in England, it becomes a dream of London, too. Likewise, the religion of 'Submission' both is and is not Islam. Fiction uses facts as a starting-place and then spirals away to explore its real concerns, which are only tangentially historical. Not to see this, to treat fiction as if it were fact, is to make a serious mistake of categories. The case of *The Satanic Verses* may be one of the biggest category mistakes in literary history.

Here is more of what I knew: I knew that stories of Muhammad's doubts, uncertainties, errors, fondness for women abound in and around Muslim tradition. To me, they seemed to make him more vivid, more human, and therefore more interesting, even more worthy of admiration. The greatest human beings must struggle against themselves as well as the world. I never doubted Muhammad's greatness, nor, I believe, is the 'Mahound' of my novel belittled by being portrayed as human.

I knew that Islam is by no means homogeneous, or as absolutist as some of its champions make it out to be. Islam contains the doubts of Iqbal, Ghazali, Khayyám as well as the narrow certainties of Shabbir Akhtar of the Bradford Council of Mosques and Kalim Siddiqui, director of the pro-Iranian Muslim Institute. Islam contains ribaldry as well as solemnity, irreverence as well as absolutism. I knew much about Islam that I admired, and still admire, immensely; I also knew that Islam, like all the world's great religions, had seen terrible things done in its name.

The original incident on which the dream of the villagers who drown in the Arabian Sea is based is also a part of what I 'knew'. The story awed me, because of what it told me about the huge power of faith. I wrote this part of the novel to see if

I could understand, by getting inside their skins, people for whom devotion was as great as this.

He did it on purpose is one of the strangest accusations ever levelled at a writer. Of course I did it on purpose. The question is, and it is what I have tried to answer: what is the 'it' that I did?

What I did not do was conspire against Islam; or write— after years and years of anti-racist work and writing—a text of incitement to racial hatred; or anything of the sort. My golem, my false Other, may be capable of such deeds, but I am not.

Would I have written differently if I had known what would happen? Truthfully, I don't know. Would I change any of the text now? I would not. It's too late. As Friedrich Dürrenmatt wrote in *The Physicists*: 'What has once been thought cannot be unthought.'

The controversy over *The Satanic Verses* needs to be looked at as a political event, not purely a theological one. In India, where the trouble started, the Muslim fundamentalist MP Syed Shahabuddin used my novel as a stick with which to threaten the wobbling Rajiv Gandhi government. The demand for the book's banning was a power-play to demonstrate the strength of the Muslim vote, on which Congress has traditionally relied and which it could ill afford to lose. (In spite of the ban, Congress lost the Muslims and the election anyway. Put not your trust in Shahabuddins.)

In South Africa, the row over the book served the purpose of the regime by driving a wedge between the Muslim and non-Muslim members of the UDF. In Pakistan, it was a way for the fundamentalists to try and regain the political initiative after their trouncing in the general election. In Iran, too, the incident could only be properly understood when seen in the context of the country's internal political struggles. And in Britain, where secular and religious leaders had been vying for power in the community for over a decade, and where, for a long time, largely secular organizations such as the Indian Workers Association (IWA) had been in the ascendant, the 'affair' swung the balance of power back towards the mosques. Small wonder, then, that the various councils of mosques are reluctant to bring the protest to an end, even though many Muslims up and down the country find it embarrassing, even shameful, to be associated with such illiberalism and violence.

The responsibility for violence lies with those who perpetrate it. In the past twelve months, bookshop workers have been manhandled, spat upon, verbally abused, bookshop premises have been threatened and, on several occasions, actually fire-bombed. Publishing staff have had to face a campaign of hate mail, menacing phone calls, death threats and bomb scares. Demonstrations have, on occasion, turned violent, too. During the big march in London last summer, peaceful counter-demonstrations on behalf of humanism and secularism were knocked to the ground by marchers, and a counter-demo by the courageous (and largely Muslim) Women Against Fundamentalism group was threatened and abused.

There is no conceivable reason why such behaviour should be privileged because it is done in the name of an affronted religion. If we are to talk about 'insults', 'abuse', 'offence', then the campaign against *The Satanic Verses* has been, very often, as insulting, abusive and offensive as it's possible to be.

As a result, racist attitudes have hardened. I did not invent British racism, nor did *The Satanic Verses*. The Commission for Racial Equality (CRE), which now accuses me of harming race relations, knows that for years it lent out my video-taped anti-racist Channel 4 broadcast to all sorts of black and white groups and seminars. Readers of *The Satanic Verses* will not be able to help noticing its extremely strong anti-racist line. I have never given the least comfort or encouragement to racists; but the leaders of the campaign against me certainly have, by reinforcing the worst racist stereotypes of Muslims as repressive, anti-liberal, censoring zealots. If Norman Tebbit has taken up the old Powellite refrains and if his laments about the multi-cultural society find favour in the land, then a part of the responsibility at least must be laid at the door of those who burn, and would ban, books.

I am not the first writer to be persecuted by Islamic fundamentalism in the modern period; among the greatest names so victimized are the Iranian writer Ahmad Kasravi, stabbed to death by fanatics, and the Egyptian Nobel laureate Naguib Mahfouz, often threatened but still, happily, with us. I am not the first artist to be accused of blasphemy and apostasy; these are, in fact, probably the most common weapons with which fundamentalism has sought to shackle creativity in the modern age. It is sad, then, that so little attention has been paid to this crucial literary context; and that Western critics like John Berger, who once spoke messianically of the need for new ways of seeing, should now express their willingness to privilege one such way over another, to protect a religion boasting one billion believers from the solitary figure of a single writer brandishing an 'unreadable' book.

As for the British Muslim 'leaders', they cannot have it both ways. Sometimes they say I am entirely unimportant, and only the book matters; on other days they hold meetings at mosques across the nation and endorse the call for my killing. They say they hold to the laws of this country, but they also say that Islamic law has moral primacy for them. They say they do not wish to break British laws, but only a very few are willing openly to repudiate the threat against me. They should make their position clear; are they democratic citizens of a free society or are they not? Do they reject violence or do they not?

After a year, it is time for a little clarity.

To the Muslim community at large, in Britain and India and Pakistan and everywhere else, I would like to say: do not ask your writers to create *typical* or *representative* fictions. Such books are almost invariably dead books. The liveliness of literature lies in its exceptionality, in being the individual, idiosyncratic vision of one human being, in which, to our delight and great surprise, we may find our own image reflected. A book is a version of the world. If you do not like it, ignore it; or offer your own version in return.

And I would like to say this: life without God seems to

believers to be an idiocy, pointless, beneath contempt. It does not seem so to non-believers. To accept that the world, here, is all there is; to go through it, towards and into death, without the consolations of religion seems, well, at least as courageous and rigorous to us as the espousal of faith seems to you. Secularism and its work deserve your respect, not your contempt.

A great wave of freedom has been washing over the world. Those who resist—in China, in Romania—find themselves bathed in blood. I should like to ask Muslims—that great mass of ordinary, decent, fair-minded Muslims to whom I have imagined myself to be speaking for most of this piece—to choose to ride the wave; to renounce blood; not to let Muslim leaders make Muslims seem less tolerant than they are. *The Satanic Verses* is a serious work, written from a non-believer's point of view. Let believers accept that, and let it be.

In the meantime, I am asked, how do I feel? I feel grateful to the British government for defending me. I hope that such a defence would be made available to any citizen so threatened, but that doesn't lessen my gratitude. I needed it, and it was provided. (I'm still no Tory, but that's democracy.)

I feel grateful, too, to my protectors, who have done such a magnificent job, and who have become my friends.

I feel grateful to everyone who has offered me support. The one real gain for me in this bad time has been the discovery of being cared for by so many people. The only antidote to hatred is love.

Above all, I feel gratitude towards, solidarity with and pride in all the publishing people and bookstore workers around the world who have held the line against intimidation, and who will, I am sure, continue to do so as long as it remains necessary.

I feel as if I have been plunged, like Alice, into the world beyond the looking-glass, where nonsense is the only available sense. And I wonder if I'll ever be able to climb back through the mirror.

Do I feel regret? Of course I do: regret that such offence

has been taken against my work when it was not intended—when dispute was intended, and dissent, and even, at times, satire, and criticism of intolerance, and the like, but not the thing of which I'm most often accused, not 'filth', not 'insult', not 'abuse'. I regret that so many people who might have taken pleasure in finding their reality given pride of place in a novel will now not read it because of what they believe it to be, or will come to it with their minds already made up.

And I feel sad to be so grievously separated from my community, from India, from everyday life, from the world.

Please understand, however: I make no complaint. I am a writer. I do not accept my condition. I will strive to change it; but I inhabit it, I am trying to learn from it.

Our lives teach us who we are.

1990

IS NOTHING SACRED?

I grew up kissing books and bread.

In our house, whenever anyone dropped a book or let fall a chapati or a 'slice', which was our word for a triangle of buttered leavened bread, the fallen object was required not only to be picked up but also kissed, by way of apology for the act of clumsy disrespect. I was as careless and butter-fingered as any child and, accordingly, during my childhood years, I kissed a large number of 'slices' and also my fair share of books.

Devout households in India often contained, and still contain, persons in the habit of kissing holy books. But we kissed everything. We kissed dictionaries and atlases. We kissed Enid Blyton novels and Superman comics. If I'd ever dropped the telephone directory I'd probably have kissed that, too.

All this happened before I had ever kissed a girl. In fact it would almost be true, true enough for a fiction writer, anyhow, to say that once I started kissing girls, my activities with regard to bread and books lost some of their special excitement. But one never forgets one's first loves.

Bread and books: food for the body and food for the soul—what could be more worthy of our respect, and even love?

It has always been a shock to me to meet people for whom books simply do not matter, and people who are scornful of the act of reading, let alone writing. It is perhaps always astonishing to learn that your beloved is not as attractive to others as she is to you. My most beloved books have been fictions, and in the last twelve months I have been obliged to accept that for many millions of human beings, these books are entirely without attraction or value. We have been witnessing an attack upon a particular work of fiction that is also an attack upon the very ideas of the novel form, an attack of such bewildering ferocity that it has become necessary to restate what is most precious about the art of literature—to answer the attack, not by an attack, but by a declaration of love.

Love can lead to devotion, but the devotion of the lover is unlike that of the True Believer in that it is not militant. I may be surprised—even shocked—to find that you do not feel as I do about a given book or work of art or even person; I may very well attempt to change your mind; but I will finally accept that your tastes, your loves, are your business and not mine. The True Believer knows no such restraints. The True Believer knows that he is simply right, and you are wrong. He will seek to convert you, even by force, and if he cannot he will, at the very least, despise you for your unbelief.

Love need not be blind. Faith must, ultimately, be a leap in the dark.

The title of this lecture is a question usually asked, in tones of horror, when some personage or idea or value or place held dear by the questioner is treated to a dose of iconoclasm. White cricket balls for night cricket? Female priests? A Japanese takeover of Rolls-Royce cars? *Is nothing sacred?*

Until recently, however, it was a question to which I thought I knew the answer. The answer was No.

No, nothing is sacred in and of itself, I would have said. Ideas, texts, even people can be made sacred—the word is from the Latin *sacrare*, 'to set apart as holy'—but even though such entities, once their sacredness is established, seek to proclaim and to preserve their own absoluteness, their inviolability, the act of making sacred is in truth an event in history. It is the product of the many and complex pressures of the time in which the act occurs. And events in history must always be subject to questioning, deconstruction, even to declarations of their obsolescence. To respect the sacred is to be paralysed by it. The idea of the sacred is quite simply one of the most conservative notions in any culture, because it seeks to turn other ideas—Uncertainty, Progress, Change—into crimes.

To take only one such declaration of obsolescence: I would have described myself as living in the aftermath of the death of god. On the subject of the death of God, the

American novelist and critic William H. Gass had this to say, as recently as 1984:

> The death of god represents not only the realization that gods have never existed, but the contention that such a belief is no longer even irrationally possible: that neither reason nor the taste and temper of the times condone it. The belief lingers on, of course, but it does so like astrology or a faith in a flat earth.

I have some difficulty with the uncompromising bluntness of this obituary notice. It has always been clear to me that God is unlike human beings in that it can die, so to speak, in parts. In other parts, for example India, God continues to flourish, in literally thousands of forms. So that if I speak of living after this death, I am speaking in a limited, personal sense—my sense of God ceased to exist long ago, and as a result I was drawn towards the great creative possibilities offered by surrealism, modernism and their successors, those philosophies and aesthetics born of the realization that, as Karl Marx said, 'all that is solid melts into air.'

It did not seem to me, however, that my ungodliness, or rather my post-godliness, need necessarily bring me into conflict with belief. Indeed, one reason for my attempt to develop a form of fiction in which the miraculous might coexist with the mundane was precisely my acceptance that notions of the sacred and the profane both needed to be explored, as far as possible without pre-judgement, in any honest literary portrait of the way we are.

That is to say: the most secular of authors ought to be capable of presenting a sympathetic portrait of a devout believer. Or, to put it another way: I had never felt the need to totemize my lack of belief, and so make it something to go to war about.

Now, however, I find my entire world-picture under fire. And as I find myself obliged to defend the assumptions and processes of literature, which I had believed that all free men and women could take for granted, and for which all unfree men and women continue every day to struggle, so I am obliged to ask myself questions I admit to finding somewhat unnerving.

Do I, perhaps, find something sacred after all? Am I prepared to set aside as holy the idea of the absolute freedom of the imagination and alongside it my own notions of the World, the Text and the Good? Does this add up to what the apologists of religion have started calling 'secular fundamentalism'? And if so, must I accept that this 'secular fundamentalism' is as likely to lead to excesses, abuses and oppressions as the canons of religious faith?

A lecture in memory of Herbert Read is a highly appropriate occasion for such an exploration, and I am honoured to have been asked to deliver it. Herbert Read, one of the leading British advocates of the modernist and surrealist movements, was a distinguished representative of the cultural values closest to my heart. 'Art is never transfixed,' Read wrote. 'Change is the condition of art remaining art.' This principle is also mine. Art, too, is an event in history, subject to the historical process. But it is also *about* that process, and must constantly strive to find new forms to mirror an endlessly renewed world. No aesthetic can be a constant, except an aesthetic based on the idea of inconstancy, metamorphosis, or, to borrow a term from politics, 'perpetual revolution'.

The struggle between such ideas and the eternal, revealed truths of religion is dramatized this evening, as I hope I may be excused for pointing out, by my absence. I must apologize for this. I did, in fact, ask my admirable protectors how they would feel if I were to deliver my text in person. The answer was, more or less, 'What have we done to deserve this?' With regret, I took the point.

It is an agony and a frustration not be able to re-enter my old life, not even for such a moment. However, I should like to thank Harold Pinter, through his own mouth, for standing in my place.* Perhaps this event could be thought of as a form

---

Is Nothing Sacred? was the Herbert Read Memorial Lecture for 1990, delivered on the author's behalf by Harold Pinter at the Institute of Contemporary Arts, London, on 6 February 1990.

of secular revelation: a man receives a text by mysterious processes from Elsewhere—above? below? New Scotland Yard?—and brings it out before the people, and recites . . .

More than twenty years ago, I stood packed in at the back of this theatre, listening to a lecture by Arthur Koestler. He propounded the thesis that language, not territory, was the prime cause of aggression, because once language reached the level of sophistication at which it could express abstract concepts, it acquired the power of totemization; and once peoples had erected totems, they would go to war to defend them. (I ask pardon of Koestler's ghost. I am relying on an old memory, and that's an untrustworthy shoulder to lean on.)

In support of his theory, he told us about two tribes of monkeys living on, I think, one of the northern islands of Japan. The two tribes lived in close proximity in the woods near a certain stream, and subsisted, not unusually, on a diet of bananas. One of the tribes, however, had developed the curious habit of washing its bananas in the stream before eating them, while the other tribe continued to be non-banana-washers. And yet, said Koestler, the two tribes continued to live contentedly as neighbours, without quarrelling. And why was this? It was because their language was too primitive to permit them to totemize either the act of banana-washing or that of eating bananas unwashed. With a more sophisticated language at their disposal, both wet and dry bananas could have become the sacred objects at the heart of a religion, and then, look out!—Holy war.

A young man rose from the audience to ask Koestler a question. Perhaps the real reason why the two tribes did not fight, he suggested, was that there were enough bananas to go round. Koestler became extremely angry. He refused to answer such a piece of Marxist claptrap. And, in a way, he was right. Koestler and his questioner were speaking different languages, and their languages were in conflict. Their disagreement could even be seen as the proof of Koestler's point. If he, Koestler, were to be considered the banana-washer and his questioner the dry-banana man, then their command of a language more complex than the Japanese monkeys' had indeed resulted in totemizations. Now each of them had a totem to defend: the primacy of language versus the primacy of economics: and dialogue therefore became impossible. They were at war.

Between religion and literature, as between politics and literature, there is a linguistically based dispute. But it is not a dispute of simple opposites. Because whereas religion seeks to privilege one language above all others, one set of values above all others, one text above all others, the novel has always been *about* the way in which different languages, values and narratives quarrel, and about the shifting relations between them, which are relations of power. The novel does not seek to establish a privileged language, but it insists upon the freedom to portray and analyse the struggle between the different contestants for such privileges.

Carlos Fuentes has called the novel 'a privileged *arena*'. By this he does not mean that it is the kind of holy space which one must put off one's shoes to enter; it is not an arena to revere; it claims no special rights *except the right to be the stage upon which the great debates of society can be conducted.* 'The novel,' Fuentes writes, 'is born from the very fact that we do not understand one another, because unitary, orthodox language has broken down. Quixote and Sancho, the Shandy brothers, Mr and Mrs Karenin: their novels are the comedy (or the drama) of their misunderstandings. Impose a unitary language: you kill the novel, but you also kill the society.'

He then poses the question I have been asking myself throughout my life as a writer: *Can the religious mentality survive outside of religious dogma and hierarchy?* Which is to say: Can art be the third principle that mediates between the material and spiritual worlds; might it, by 'swallowing' both worlds, offer us something new—something that might even be called a secular definition of transcendence?

I believe it can. I believe it must. And I believe that, at its best, it does.

What I mean by transcendence is that flight of the human spirit outside the confines of its material, physical existence which all of us, secular or religious, experience on at least a few occasions. Birth is a moment of transcendence which we spend our lives trying to understand. The exaltation of the act of love, the experience of joy and very possibly the moment of death are other such moments. The soaring quality of transcendence, the sense of being more than oneself, of being in some way joined to the whole of life, is by its nature short-lived. Not even the visionary or mystical experience ever lasts very long. It is for art to capture that experience, to offer it to, in the case of literature, its readers; to be, for a secular, materialist culture, some sort of replacement for what the love of god offers in the world of faith.

It is important that we understand how profoundly we all feel the needs that religion, down the ages, has satisfied. I would suggest that these needs are of three types: firstly, the need to be given an articulation of our half-glimpsed knowledge of exaltation, of awe, of wonder; life is an awesome experience, and religion helps us understand why life so often makes us feel small, by telling us what we are *smaller than*; and, contrariwise, because we also have a sense of being special, of being *chosen*, religion helps us by telling us what we have been chosen by, and what for. Secondly, we need answers to the unanswerable: How did we get here? How did 'here' get here in the first place? Is this, this brief life, all there is? How can it be? What would be the point of that? And, thirdly, we need codes to live by, 'rules for every damn thing'. The idea of god is at once a repository for our awestruck wonderment at life and an answer to the great questions of existence, and a rule book, too. The soul needs all these explanations—not simply rational explanations, but explanations of the heart.

It is also important to understand how often the language of secular, rationalist materialism has failed to answer these needs. As we witness the death of communism in Central Europe, we cannot fail to observe the deep religious spirit with which so many of the makers of these revolutions are imbued, and we must concede that it is not only a particular political ideology that has failed, but the idea that men and women could ever define themselves in terms that exclude their spiritual needs.

It seems obvious, but relevant, to point out that in all the countries now moving towards freedom, art was repressed as viciously as was religion. That the Czech revolution began in the theatres and is led by a writer is proof that people's spiritual needs, more than their material needs, have driven the commissars from power.

What appears plain is that it will be a very long time before the peoples of Europe will accept any ideology that claims to have a complete, totalized explanation of the world. Religious faith, profound as it is, must surely remain a private matter. This rejection of totalized explanations is the modern condition. And this is where the novel, the form created to discuss the fragmentation of truth, comes in. The film director Luis Buñuel used to say: 'I would give my life for a man who is looking for the truth. But I would gladly kill a man who thinks he has found the truth.' (This is what we used to call a joke, before killing people for their ideas returned to the agenda.) The elevation of the quest for the Grail over the Grail itself, the acceptance that all that is solid *has* melted into air, that reality and morality are not givens but imperfect human constructs, is the point from which fiction begins. This is what J.-F. Lyotard called, in 1979, *La Condition Postmoderne*. The challenge of literature is to start from this point, and still find a way of fulfilling our unaltered spiritual requirements.

Moby Dick meets that challenge by offering us a dark, almost Manichean vision of a universe (the *Pequod*) in the grip of one demon, Ahab, and heading inexorably towards another; namely the Whale. The ocean always was our Other, manifesting itself to us in the form of beasts—the worm Ouroboros, Kraken, Leviathan. Herman Melville delves into these dark waters in order to offer us a very modern parable: Ahab, gripped by his possession, perishes; Ishmael, a man without strong feeling or powerful affiliations, survives. The self-interested modern man is the sole survivor; those who worship the Whale—for pursuit is a form of worship—perish by the Whale.

Joyce's wanderers, Beckett's tramps, Gogol's tricksters, Bulgakov's devils, Bellow's high-energy meditations on the stifling of the soul by the triumphs of materialism; these, and many more, are what we have instead of prophets and suffering saints. But while the novel answers our need for wonderment and understanding, it brings us harsh and unpalatable news as well.

It tells us there are no rules. It hands down no commandments. We have to make up our own rules as best we can, make them up as we go along.

And it tells us there are no answers; or, rather, it tells us that answers are easier to come by, and less reliable, than questions. If religion is an answer, if political ideology is an answer, then literature is an inquiry; great literature, by asking extraordinary questions, opens new doors in our minds.

Richard Rorty, in *Philosophy and the Mirror of Nature*, insists on the importance of historicity, of giving up the illusions of being in contact with Eternity. For him, the great error is what he calls 'foundationalism', which the theologian Don Cupitt, commenting on Rorty, calls 'the attempt, as old as (and even much older than) Plato, to give permanence and authority to our knowledge and values by purporting to found them in some unchanging cosmic realm, natural or noumenal, outside the flux of our human conversation.' It is better, Cupitt concludes, 'to be an adaptable pragmatist, a nomad.'

Michel Foucault, also a confirmed historicist, discusses the role of the author in challenging sacralized absolutes in his essay, 'What is an Author?' This essay argues, in part, that 'texts, books and discourses really began to have authors . . . to the extent that authors became subject to punishment, that is, to the extent that discourses could be transgressive.' This is an extraordinary, provocative idea, even if it is stated with Foucault's characteristic airiness and a complete absence of supporting evidence: *that authors were named only when it was necessary to find somebody to blame*. Foucault continues:

> In our culture (and doubtless in many others), discourse was not originally a product, a thing, a kind of goods; it was essentially an act—an act placed in the bipolar field of the sacred and the profane, the licit and the illicit, the religious and the blasphemous. Historically it was a gesture fraught with risks . . .

In our beginnings we find our essences. To understand a religion, look at its earliest moments. (It is regrettable that Islam, of all religions the easiest to study in this way, because of its birth during the age of recorded history, has set its face so resolutely against the idea that it, like all ideas, is an event inside history.) And to understand an artistic form, too, Foucault suggests, look at its origins. If he is right about the novel, then literature is, of all the arts, the one best suited to challenging absolutes of all kinds; and, because it is in its origin the schismatic Other of the sacred (and authorless) text, so it is also the art mostly likely to fill our god-shaped holes.

There are other reasons, too, for proposing the novel as the crucial art form of what I can no longer avoid calling the post-modern age. For one thing, literature is the art least subject to external control, because it is made in private. The act of making it requires only one person, one pen, one room, some paper. (Even the room is not absolutely essential.) Literature is the most low-technology of the art forms. It requires neither a stage nor a screen. It calls for no interpreters, no actors, producers, camera crews, costumiers, musicians. It does not even require the traditional apparatus of publishing, as the long-running success of samizdat literature demonstrates. The Foucault essay suggests that literature is as much at risk from the enveloping, smothering forces of the market economy, which reduces books to mere products. This danger is real, and I do not want to seem to be minimizing it. But the truth is that of all the forms, literature can still be the most free. The more money a piece of work costs, the easier it is to control it. Film, the most expensive of art forms, is also the least subversive. This is why, although Carlos Fuentes cites the work of film-makers like Buñuel, Bergman and Fellini as instances of successful secular revolts into the territory of the sacred, I continue to believe in the greater possibilities of the novel. Its singularity is its best protection.

Among the childhood books I devoured and kissed were large numbers of cheap comics of a most unliterary nature. The heroes of these comic books were, or so it seemed, almost always mutants or hybrids or freaks: as well as the Batman and the Spiderman there was Aquaman, who was half-fish, and of course Superman, who could easily be mistaken for a bird or a plane. In those days, the middle 1950s, the super-heroes were all, in their various ways, hawkish law-and-order conservatives, leaping to work in response to the Police Commissioner's Bat-Signal, banding together to form the Justice League of America, defending what Superman called 'truth, justice and the American way'. But in spite of this extreme emphasis on crime-busting, the lesson they taught children—or this child, at any rate—was the perhaps unintentionally radical truth that exceptionality was the greatest and most heroic of values; that those who were unlike the crowd were to be treasured the most lovingly; and that this exceptionality was a treasure so great and so easily misunderstood that it had to be concealed, in ordinary life, beneath what the comic books called a 'secret identity'. Superman could not have survived without 'mild-mannered' Clark Kent; 'millionaire socialite' Bruce Wayne made possible the nocturnal activities of the Batman.

Now it is obviously true that those other freakish, hybrid, mutant, exceptional beings—novelists—those creators of the most freakish, hybrid and metamorphic of forms, the novel, have frequently been obliged to hide behind secret identities, whether for reasons of gender or terror. But the most wonderful of the many wonderful truths about the novel form is that the greater the writer, the greater his or her exceptionality. The geniuses of the novel are those whose voices are fully and undisguisably their own, who, to borrow

William Gass's image, *sign every word they write*. What draws us to an author is his or her 'unlikeness', even if the apparatus of literary criticism then sets to work to demonstrate that he or she is really no more than an accumulation of influences. Unlikeness, the thing that makes it impossible for a writer to stand in any regimented line, is a quality novelists share with the Caped Crusaders of the comics, though they are only rarely capable of leaping tall buildings in a single stride.

What is more, the writer is there, in his work, in the reader's hands, utterly exposed, utterly defenceless, entirely without the benefit of an alter ego to hide behind. What is forged, in the secret act of reading, is a different kind of identity, as the reader and writer merge, through the medium of the text, to become a collective being that both writes as it reads and reads as it writes, and creates, jointly, that unique work, 'their' novel. This 'secret identity' of writer and reader is the novel form's greatest and most subversive gift.

And this, finally, is why I elevate the novel above other forms, why it has always been, and remains, my first love: not only is it the art involving least compromises, but it is also the only one that takes the 'privileged arena' of conflicting discourses *right inside our heads*. The interior space of our imagination is a theatre that can never be closed down; the images created there make up a movie that can never be destroyed.

In this last decade of the millennium, as the forces of religion are renewed in strength and as the all-pervasive power of materialism wraps its own weighty chains around the human spirit, where should the novel be looking? It seems clear that the renewal of the old, bipolar field of discourse, between the sacred and the profane, which Michel Foucault proposes, will be of central importance. It seems probable, too, that we may be heading towards a world in which there will be no real alternative to the liberal-capitalist social model (except, perhaps, the theocratic, foundationalist model of Islam). In this situation, liberal capitalism or democracy or the free world will require novelists' most rigorous attention, will require reimagining and questioning and doubting as never before. 'Our antagonist is our helper,' said Edmund Burke, and if democracy no longer has communism to help it clarify, by opposition, its own ideas, then perhaps it will have to have literature as an adversary instead.

I have made a large number of sweeping claims for literature during the course of this piece, and I am aware of a slightly messianic tone in much of what I've written. The reverencing of books and writers, by writers, is nothing particularly new, of course. 'Since the early 19th century,' writes Cupitt, 'imaginative writers have claimed—have indeed enjoyed—a guiding and representative role in our culture. Our preachers are novelists, poets, dramatists, film-makers and the like, purveyors of fiction, ambiguous people, deceivers. Yet we continue to think of ourselves as rational.'

But now I find myself backing away from the idea of sacralizing literature with which I flirted at the beginning of this text; I cannot bear the idea of the writer as secular prophet; I am remembering that one of the very greatest writers of the century, Samuel Beckett, believed that all art must inevitably end in failure. This is, clearly, no reason for surrender. 'Ever tried. Ever failed. Never mind. Try again. Fail better.'

Literature is an interim report from the consciousness of the artist, and so it can never be 'finished' or 'perfect'. Literature is made at the frontier between the self and the world, and in the act of creation that frontier softens, becomes permeable, allows the world to flow into the artist and the artist to flow into the world. Nothing so inexact, so easily and frequently misconceived, deserves the protection of being declared sacrosanct. We shall just have to get along without the shield of sacralization, and a good thing, too. We must not become what we oppose.

The only privilege literature deserves—and this privilege it requires in order to exist—is the privilege of being the arena of discourse, the place where the struggle of languages can be acted out.

Imagine this. You wake up one morning and find yourself in a large, rambling house. As you wander through it you realize it is so enormous that you will never know it all. In the house are people you know, family members, friends, lovers, colleagues; also many strangers. The house is full of activity: conflicts and seductions, celebrations and wakes. At some point you understand that there is no way out. You find that you can accept this. The house is not what you'd have chosen, it's in fairly bad condition, the corridors are often full of bullies, but it will have to do. Then one day you enter an unimportant-looking little room. The room is empty, but there are voices in it, voices that seem to be whispering just to you. You recognize some of the voices, others are completely unknown to you. The voices are talking about the house, about everyone in it, about everything that is happening and has happened and should happen. Some of them speak exclusively in obscenities. Some are bitchy. Some are loving. Some are funny. Some are sad. The most interesting voices are all these things at once. You begin to go to the room more and more often. Slowly you learn that most of the people in the house use such rooms sometimes. Yet the rooms are all discreetly positioned and unimportant-looking.

Now imagine that you wake up one morning and you are still in the large house, but all the voice-rooms have disappeared. It is as if they have been wiped out. Now there is nowhere in the whole house where you can go to hear voices talking about everything in every possible way. There is nowhere to go for the voices that can be funny one minute and sad the next, that can sound raucous and melodic in the course of the same sentence. Now you remember: there is no way out of this house. Now this fact begins to seem unbearable. You look into the eyes of the people in the corridors—family, lovers, friends, colleagues, strangers, bullies, priests. You see the same thing in everybody's eyes. *How do we get out of here?* It becomes clear that the house is a prison. People begin to scream, and pound the walls. Men arrive with guns. The house begins to shake. You do not wake up. You are already awake.

Literature is the one place in any society where, within the secrecy of our own heads, we can hear *voices talking about everything in every possible way*. The reason for ensuring that that privileged arena is preserved is not that writers want the absolute freedom to say and do whatever they please. It is that we, all of us, readers and writers and citizens and generals and godmen, need that little, unimportant-looking room. We do not need to call it sacred, but we do need to remember that it is necessary.

'Everybody knows,' wrote Saul Bellow in *The Adventures of Augie March*, 'there is no fineness or accuracy of suppression. If you hold down one thing, you hold down the adjoining.'

Wherever in the world the little room of literature has been closed, sooner or later the walls have come tumbling down.

1990

ONE THOUSAND DAYS IN A BALLOON

A hot-air balloon drifts slowly over a bottomless chasm, carrying several passengers. A leak develops; the balloon starts losing height. The pit, a dark yawn, comes closer. Good grief! The wounded balloon can bear just one passenger to safety; the many must be sacrificed to save the one! But who should live, who should die? And who could make such a choice?

In point of fact, debating societies everywhere regularly make such choices without qualms, for of course what I've described is the given situation of that evergreen favourite, the Balloon Debate, in which, as the speakers argue over the relative merits and demerits of the well-known figures they have placed in disaster's mouth, the assembled company blithely accepts the faintly unpleasant idea that a human being's right to life is increased or diminished by his or her virtues or vices—that we may be born equal but thereafter our lives weigh differently in the scales.

It's only make-believe, after all. And while it may not be very nice, it does reflect how people actually think.

I have now spent over a thousand days in just such a balloon; but, alas, this isn't a game. For most of these thousand days, my fellow-travellers included the Western hostages in the Lebanon, and the British businessmen imprisoned in Iran and Iraq, Roger Cooper and Ian Richter. And I had to accept, and did accept, that for most of my countrymen and countrywomen, my plight counted for less than the others'. In any choice between us, I'd have been the first to be pitched out of the basket and into the abyss. 'Our lives teach us who we are,' I wrote at the end of my essay 'In Good Faith'. Some of the lessons have been harsh, and difficult to learn.

Trapped inside a metaphor, I've often felt the need to redescribe it, to change the terms. This isn't so much a balloon, I've wanted to say, as a bubble, within which I'm simultaneously exposed and sealed off. The bubble floats above and through the world, depriving me of reality, reducing me to an abstraction. For many people, I've ceased to be a human being. I've become an issue, a bother, an 'affair'. Bullet-proof bubbles, like this one, are reality-proof, too. Those who travel in them, like those who wear Tolkien's rings of invisibility, become wraith-like if they're not careful. They get lost. In this phantom space a man may become the bubble that encases him, and then one day—pop!—he's gone forever.

It's ridiculous—isn't it?—to have to say, But I *am* a human being, unjustly accused, unjustly embubbled. Or is it I who am being ridiculous, as I call out from my bubble, *I'm still trapped in here, folks; somebody, please, get me out*?

Out there where you are, in the rich and powerful and lucky West, has it really been so long since religions persecuted people, burning them as heretics, drowning them as witches, that you can't recognize religious persecution when you see it?. . . The original metaphor has reasserted itself. I'm back in the balloon, asking for the right to live.

What is my single life worth? Despair whispers in my ear: 'Not a lot.' But I refuse to give in to despair.

I refuse to give in to despair because I've been shown love as well as hatred. I know that many people do care, and are appalled by the crazy, upside-down logic of the post-*fatwa* world, in which a single novelist can be accused of having savaged or 'mugged' a whole community, becoming its tormentor (instead of its tarred and feathered victim) and the scapegoat for all its discontents. Many people do ask, for example: When a white pop-star-turned-Islamic-fanatic speaks approvingly about killing an Indian immigrant, how does the Indian immigrant end up being called the racist?

Or, again: What minority is smaller and weaker than a minority of one?

I refuse to give in to despair even though, for a thousand days and more, I've been put through a degree course in worthlessness, my own personal and specific worthlessness. My first teachers were the mobs marching down distant boulevards, baying for my blood, and finding, soon enough, their echoes on English streets. I could not understand the force that makes parents hang murderous slogans around their children's necks. I have learned to understand it. It burns books and effigies and thinks itself holy. But at first, as I watched the marchers, I felt them trampling on my heart.

Once again, however, I have been saved by instances of fair-mindedness, of goodness. Every time I learn that a reader somewhere has been touched by *The Satanic Verses*, moved and entertained and stimulated by it, it arouses deep feelings in me. And there are more and more such readers nowadays, my post-bag tells me, readers (including Muslims) who are willing to give my burned, spurned child a fair hearing at long last. Milan Kundera writes to say that he finds great tenderness towards Muslim culture in the book, and I'm stupidly grateful. A Muslim writes to say that in spite of the book's 'shock tactics' its ideas about the birth of Islam are very positive; at once, I find myself wishing upon a star that her co-religionists may somehow, impossibly, come to agree with her.

Sometimes I think that, one day, Muslims will be ashamed of what Muslims did in these times, will find the 'Rushdie affair' as improbable as the West now finds martyr-burning. One day they may agree that—as the European Enlightenment demonstrated—freedom of thought is precisely freedom from religious control, freedom from accusations of blasphemy. Maybe they'll agree, too, that the row over *The Satanic Verses* was at bottom an argument about who should have power over the grand narrative, the Story of Islam, and that that power must belong equally to everyone. That even if my novel were incompetent, its attempt to retell the Story would still be important. That if I've failed, others must succeed, because those who do not have power over the story that dominates their lives, power to retell it, rethink it, deconstruct it, joke about it, and change it as times change, truly are powerless, because they cannot think new thoughts.

One day. Maybe. But not today.

Today, my education in worthlessness continues, and

what Saul Bellow would call my 'reality instructors' include: the media pundit who suggests that a manly death would be better for me than hiding like a rat; the letter-writer who points out that of course the trouble is that I *look* like the Devil, and wonders if I have hairy shanks and cloven hooves; the 'moderate' Muslim who writes to say that Muslims find it 'revolting' when I speak about the Iranian death threats (it's not the *fatwa* that's revolting, you understand, but my mention of it); the rather more immoderate Muslim who tells me to 'shut up', explaining that if a fly is caught in a spider's web, it should not attract the attention of the spider. I ask the reader to imagine how it might feel to be intellectually and emotionally bludgeoned, from a thousand different directions, every day for a thousand days and more.

Back in the balloon, something longed-for and heartening has happened. On this occasion, *mirabile dictu*, the many have not been sacrificed, but saved. That is to say, my companions, the Western hostages and the jailed businessmen, have by good fortune and the efforts of others managed to descend safely to earth, and have been reunited with their families and friends, with their own, free lives. I rejoice for them, and admire their courage, their resilience. And now I'm alone in the balloon.

Surely I'll be safe now? Surely, now, the balloon will drop safely towards some nearby haven, and I, too, will be reunited with my life? Surely it's my turn now?

But the balloon is over the chasm again; and it's still sinking. I realize that it's carrying a great deal of valuable freight. Trading relations, armaments deals, the balance of power in the Gulf—these and other matters of great moment are weighing down the balloon. I hear voices suggesting that if I stay aboard, this precious cargo will be endangered. The national interest is being redefined; am I being redefined out of it? Am I to be jettisoned, after all?

When Britain renewed relations with Iran at the United Nations in 1990, the senior British official in charge of the negotiations assured me in unambiguous language that something very substantial had been achieved on my behalf. The Iranians, laughing merrily, had secretly agreed to forget the *fatwa*. (The diplomat telling me the story put great stress on this cheery Iranian laughter.) They would 'neither encourage nor allow' their citizens, surrogates, or proxies to act against me. Oh, how I wanted to believe that! But in the year-and-a-bit that followed, we saw the *fatwa* restated in Iran, the bounty money doubled, the book's Italian translator severely wounded, its Japanese translator stabbed to death; there was news of an attempt to find and kill me by contract killers working directly for the Iranian government through its European embassies. Another such contract was successfully carried out in Paris, the victim being the harmless and aged ex-Prime Minister of Iran, Shapour Bakhtiar.

It seems reasonable to deduce that the secret deal made at the United Nations hasn't worked. Dismayingly, however, the talk as I write is all of improving relations with Iran still further, while the 'Rushdie case' is described as a side-issue.

Is this a balloon I'm in, or the dustbin of history?

Let me be clear: *there is nothing I can do to break this impasse.* The *fatwa* was politically motivated to begin with, it remains a breach of international law, and it can only be solved at the political level. To effect the release of the Western hostages in the Lebanon, great levers were moved; great forces were brought into play; for Mr Richter, seventy million pounds in frozen Iraqi assets were 'thawed'. What, then, is a novelist under terrorist attack worth?

Despair murmurs, once again: 'Not a plugged nickel.'

But I refuse to give in to despair.

You may ask why I'm so sure there's nothing I can do to help myself out of this jam.

At the end of 1990, dispirited and demoralized, feeling abandoned, even then, in consequence of the British Government's decision to patch things up with Iran, and with my marriage at an end, I faced my deepest grief, my unquenchable sorrow at having been torn away from, cast out of, the cultures and societies from which I'd always drawn my strength and inspiration—that is, the broad community of

British Asians, and the broader community of Indian Muslims. I determined to make my peace with Islam, even at the cost of my pride. Those who were surprised and displeased by what I did perhaps failed to see that I was not some deracinated Uncle Tom Wog. To these people it was apparently incomprehensible that I should seek to make peace between the warring halves of the world, which were also the warring halves of my soul—and that I should seek to do so in a spirit of humility, instead of the arrogance so often attributed to me.

In 'In Good Faith' I wrote: 'Perhaps a way forward might be found through the mutual recognition of [our] mutual pain,' but even moderate Muslims had trouble with this notion: what pain, they asked, could I possibly have suffered? *What was I talking about?* As a result, the really important conversations I had in this period were with myself.

I said: Salman, you must send a message loud enough to be heard all over the world. You must make ordinary Muslims see that you aren't their enemy, and make the West understand a little more of the complexity of Muslim culture. It was my hope that Westerners might say, well, if he's the one in danger, and yet he's willing to acknowledge the importance of his Muslim roots, then perhaps we ought to start thinking a little less stereotypically ourselves. (No such luck, though. The message you send isn't always the one that's received.)

And I said to myself: Admit it, Salman, the Story of Islam has a deeper meaning for you than any of the other grand narratives. Of course you're no mystic, mister, and when you wrote *I am not a Muslim* that's what you meant. No supernaturalism, no literalist orthodoxies, no formal rules for you. But Islam doesn't have to mean blind faith. It can mean what it always meant in your family, a culture, a civilization, as open-minded as your grandfather was, as delightedly disputatious as your father was, as intellectual and philosophical as you like. Don't let the zealots make *Muslim* a terrifying word, I urged myself; remember when it meant *family* and *light*.

I reminded myself that I had always argued that it was

necessary to develop the nascent concept of the 'secular Muslim', who, like the secular Jews, affirmed his membership of the culture while being separate from the theology. I had recently read the contemporary Muslim philosopher Fouad Zakariya's *Laïcité ou Islamisme*, and been encouraged by Zakariya's attempt to modernize Islamic thought. But, Salman, I told myself, you can't argue from outside the debating chamber. You've got to cross the threshold, go inside the room, and *then* fight for your humanized, historicized, secularized way of being a Muslim. I recalled my near-namesake, the twelfth-century philosopher Ibn Rushd (Averroës), who argued that (to quote the great Arab historian Albert Hourani), 'not all the words of the Qu'ran should be taken literally. When the literal meaning of Qu'ranic verses appeared to contradict the truths to which philosophers arrived by the exercise of reason, those verses needed to be interpreted metaphorically.' But Ibn Rushd was a snob. Having propounded an idea far in advance of its time he qualified it by saying that such sophistication was only suitable for the élite; literalism would do for the masses. Salman, I asked myself, is it time to pick up Ibn Rushd's banner and carry it forward; to say, nowadays such ideas are fit for everybody, for the beggar as well as the prince?

It was with such things in mind—and with my thoughts in a state of some confusion and torment—that I spoke the Muslim creed before witnesses. But my fantasy of joining the fight for the modernization of Muslim thought, for freedom from the shackles of the Thought Police, was stillborn. It never really had a chance. Too many people had spent too long demonizing or totemizing me to listen seriously to what I had to say. In the West, some 'friends' turned against me, calling me by yet another set of insulting names. Now I was spineless, pathetic, debased; I had betrayed myself, my Cause; above all, I had betrayed *them*.

I also found myself up against the granite, heartless certainties of Actually Existing Islam, by which I mean the political and priestly power structure that presently dominates and stifles Muslim societies. Actually Existing Islam has failed to create a free society anywhere on Earth, and it wasn't about to let me, of all people, argue in favour of one. Suddenly I was (metaphorically) among people whose social attitudes I'd fought all my life—for example, their attitudes about women (one Islamicist boasted to me that his wife would cut his toe-nails while he made telephone calls, and suggested I found such a spouse) or about gays (one of the Imams I met in December 1990 was on TV soon afterwards, denouncing Muslim gays as sick creatures who brought shame on their families and who ought to seek medical and psychiatric help). Had I truly fallen in among such people? *That was not what I meant at all.*

Facing the utter intransigence, the philistine scorn of so much of Actually Existing Islam, I reluctantly concluded that there was no way for me to help bring into being the Muslim culture I'd dreamed of, the progressive, irreverent, sceptical, argumentative, playful and *unafraid* culture which is what I've always understood as *freedom*. Not me, not in this lifetime, no chance. Actually Existing Islam, which has all but deified its Prophet, a man who always fought passionately against such deification; which has supplanted a priest-free religion by a priest-ridden one; which makes literalism a weapon and redescriptions a crime, will never let the likes of me in.

Ibn Rushd's ideas were silenced in their time. And throughout the Muslim world today, progressive ideas are in retreat. Actually Existing Islam reigns supreme, and just as the recently destroyed 'Actually Existing Socialism' of the Soviet terror-state was horrifically unlike the utopia of peace and equality of which democratic socialists have dreamed, so also is Actually Existing Islam a force to which I have never given in, to which I cannot submit.

There is a point beyond which conciliation looks like capitulation. I do not believe I passed that point, but others have thought otherwise.

I have never disowned my book, nor regretted writing it. I said I was sorry to have offended people, because I had not set out to do so, and so I am. I explained that writers do not agree with every word spoken by every character they create—a truism in the world of books, but a continuing mystery to *The Satanic Verses'* opponents. I have always said that this novel has been traduced. Indeed, the chief benefit of my meeting with the six Islamic scholars on Christmas Eve 1990 was that they agreed that the novel had no insulting motives. 'In Islam, it is a man's intention that counts,' I was told. 'Now we will launch a world-wide campaign on your behalf to explain that there has been a great mistake.' All this with much smiling and friendliness and handshaking. It was in this context that I agreed to suspend—not cancel—a paperback edition, to create what I called a space for reconciliation.

Alas, I overestimated these men. Within days, all but one of them had broken their promises, and recommenced to vilify me and my work as if we had not shaken hands. I felt (most probably I had been) a great fool. The suspension of the paperback began at once to look like a surrender. In the aftermath of the attacks on my translators, it looks even more craven. It has now been more than three years since *The Satanic Verses* was published; that's a long, long 'space for reconciliation'. Long enough. I accept that I was wrong to have given way on this point. *The Satanic Verses* must be freely available and easily affordable, if only because if it is not read and studied, then these years will have no meaning. Those who forget the past are condemned to repeat it.

'Our lives teach us who we are.' I have learned the hard way that when you permit anyone else's description of reality to supplant your own—and such descriptions have been raining down on me, from security advisers, governments, journalists, Archbishops, friends, enemies, mullahs—then you might as well be dead. Obviously, a rigid, blinkered, absolutist world-view is the easiest to keep hold of; whereas the fluid, uncertain, metamorphic picture I've always carried about is rather more vulnerable. Yet I must cling with all my might to that chameleon, that chimera, that shape-shifter, my own soul; must hold on to its mischievous, iconoclastic, out-of-step clown-instincts, no matter how great the storm. And if that plunges me into contradiction and paradox, so be it; I've lived in that messy ocean all my life. I've fished in it for my art. This turbulent sea was the sea outside my bedroom window in Bombay. It is the sea by which I was born, and which I carry within me wherever I go.

'Free speech is a non-starter,' says one of my Islamic extremist opponents. No, sir, it is not. Free speech is the whole thing, the whole ball game. Free speech is life itself.

That's the end of my speech from this ailing balloon. Now it's time to answer the question. What is my single life worth?

Is it worth more or less than the fat contracts and political treaties that are in here with me? Is it worth more or less than good relations with a country which, in April 1991, gave 800 women seventy-four lashes each for not wearing a veil; in which the eighty-year-old writer Mariam Firouz is still in jail, and has been tortured; and whose Foreign Minister says, in response to criticism of his country's lamentable human rights record, 'International monitoring of the human rights situation in Iran should not continue indefinitely . . . Iran could not tolerate such monitoring for long'?

You must decide what you think a friend is worth to his friends, what you think a son is worth to his mother, or a father to his son. You must decide what a man's conscience and heart and soul are worth. You must decide what you think a writer is worth, what value you place on a maker of stories, and an arguer with the world.

Ladies and gentlemen, the balloon is sinking into the abyss.

1991

OTHER BOOKS BY SALMAN RUSHDIE

Grimus
Midnight's Children
Shame
The Jaguar Smile
The Satanic Verses
Haroun and the Sea of Stories